California
Real Estate Principles

Third Edition

Prentice Hall Series in California Real Estate

Dennis J. McKenzie, Editor

CALIFORNIA REAL ESTATE FINANCE, 4th EDITION
Robert J. Bond, Alfred Gavello, Dennis J. McKenzie, and Carden Young

CALIFORNIA REAL ESTATE PRINCIPLES, 3rd EDITION
Dennis J. McKenzie, Lowell Anderson, Frank Battino, Cecilia Hopkins

THE ESSENTIALS OF REAL ESTATE ECONOMICS, 2nd EDITION
Dennis J. McKenzie and Richard M. Betts

BASIC REAL ESTATE APPRAISAL, 2nd EDITION
Richard M. Betts and Silas Ely

LEGAL ASPECTS OF CALIFORNIA REAL ESTATE, 2nd EDITION
Louis B. Hansotte

UPDATED

CALIFORNIA REAL ESTATE PRINCIPLES

THIRD EDITION

Dennis J. McKenzie, Realtor®
McKenzie Real Estate Seminars

Lowell Anderson, Professor
Cerritos College

Frank Battino, Realtor
Merritt College

Cecilia A. Hopkins, Ph.D.
College of San Mateo

PRENTICE HALL, Englewood Cliffs, New Jersey 07632

Updated 1991.

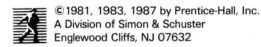 ©1981, 1983, 1987 by Prentice-Hall, Inc.
A Division of Simon & Schuster
Englewood Cliffs, NJ 07632

Printed in the United States of America

10 9 8 7 6 5 4 3

ISBN 0-13-115635-7

Prentice-Hall International (UK) Limited, *London*
Prentice-Hall of Australia Pty. Limited, *Sydney*
Prentice-Hall Canada Inc., *Toronto*
Prentice-Hall Hispanoamericana, S.A., *Mexico*
Prentice-Hall of India Private Limited, *New Delhi*
Prentice-Hall of Japan, Inc., *Tokyo*
Simon & Schuster Asia Pte. Ltd., *Signapore*
Editora Prentice-Hall do Brasil, Ltda., *Rio de Janeiro*

PREFACE

This book is an outgrowth of years of teaching real estate principles at California community colleges. The material is current and designed to maintain student interest. This new edition incorporates all of the latest real estate changes.

It is impossible to acknowledge all the assistance we have received from students, colleagues, and friends. We hope we have successfully communicated the insights that they have given to us. Particular thanks go to the many other real estate instructors who have participated at instructor and coordinator workshops sponsored by the California Department of Real Estate, the Community College Chancellor's Office, and the California Association of Real Estate Teachers.

Special recognition is given to Carden Young, instructor at American River College, Sacramento City College, and real estate lecturer for University of Southern California; to Hugh Stanton, instructor and coordinator of real estate at Ohlone College; to Marjorie Reed, coordinator of real estate, San Diego Community Colleges; to William Reid, instructor of real estate; and to Si Ely, real estate instructor, Santa Monica City College. They all reviewed the manuscript and submitted many helpful suggestions for which we are most grateful. The manuscript was edited by Barbara Wrede and assembled and typed by Frankie Jimboy. Many illustrations were provided by Allison McKenzie. We also thank the staff at John Wiley & Sons, Inc., for helping us through the publishing maze.

Dennis J. McKenzie
Lowell Anderson
Frank Battino
Cecilia A. Hopkins

CONTENTS

Chapter 1
Introduction to Real Estate

Preview

California property ownership has had an interesting and romantic history. In this chapter, the historical, legal, civic, and economic importance of real estate will be stressed. This chapter will also highlight the characteristics and differences between real and personal property and their effect on today's real estate market. At the conclusion of the chapter you will be able to:

1. *Trace the history of real estate property ownership in California.*

2. *List the four-part definition of real property.*

3. *Explain the term "bundle of rights," and list each of those rights.*

4. *List the five legal tests of a fixture and explain their meaning.*

1.1 PRESENT AND HISTORICAL IMPORTANCE OF REAL ESTATE

Real estate touches the lives of more people than any other single commodity. Real property provides two-thirds of all the national wealth and contributes to a substantial amount of commerce in the United States.

Impressive Statistics

Of almost 2.5 billion acres of land in the United States, nearly 100 million acres are in California. According to the U.S. Bureau of Census, the population in California is presently over 28.5 million, with a projected increase of 10 million by the year 2000.

These statistics are important only if they help people to become aware of the significance of real estate in their lives.

Historical Importance of Real Estate

California has perhaps the most interesting and romantic history of any state in the Union. The historical story of California can be told in terms of the use and occupancy of its land.

The earliest inhabitants of California were the native American Indians. Although they led a nomadic existence, they were still governed by tribal rights to the land they occupied, including hunting, fishing, and gathering rights. The American Indians respected and cherished the land, because they recognized that their survival was based upon products derived from the land.

Spanish Rule

In 1513, a Spanish explorer by the name of Balboa first sighted the Pacific Ocean and claimed it for the king of Spain. Many other Spanish explorers followed in the ensuing years. The years 1542 to 1822 were known as the period of exploration, discovery, and colonization.

The Spanish colonizers established forts called *presidios* in selected areas along the California coast to protect against invaders. Communities and agricultural villages known as *pueblos* appeared throughout the land to supply food for colonizers. During this period, the land was under Spanish domination. All land was held in the name of the king of Spain and private activities were governed by the law of Spain. Spain did not recognize the ownership rights of native American Indians.

During Spanish occupation of California, missionaries strived to spread Christianity among the natives by establishing a string of 21 missions ranging from San Diego to Sonoma, north of San Francisco.

Mexican Rule in California

In 1822, Mexico, then a territory of Spain, established her independence and, in the process, took over the territory of California. During the Mexican reign, the colonization of the territory of California continued to expand. Large Mexican land grants, called *ranchos,* were created and given to private citizens. Much of this rancho land was converted to agricultural use.

Under Mexican rule, colonization was encouraged, and land grants made extensive private ownership a reality for the first time in California history.

American Rule in California

American settlers coming from the east were confronted by Mexican authorities, and these tensions led to the Mexican-American War in 1846. In 1848, the Treaty of Guadalupe Hidalgo ended the war with Mexico, and California became a territory of the United States.

California achieved full statehood September 9, 1850, and from that time on, the population rapidly increased, augmented by the gold rush in the Sacramento valley. The new California legislature adopted a land ownership recording system, which recognized and protected some of the early Mexican land grants.

1.2 PROPERTY RIGHTS

As you launch into your study of real estate, it is important to differentiate between real estate in a physical sense, such as land and buildings, and real property in the legal sense, that of property rights.

The law defines property as "that which is the subject of ownership." It explains ownership as essentially, "the right of one or more persons to possess and to use the thing which is owned, to the exclusion of others."

Technically, then, in the legal sense, the word "property" does not refer exclusively to the thing owned. In fact, real estate law is concerned with the rights and the interests that the owner has in the thing he or she owns.

What kind of rights does an individual have as an owner of real property? The law designates these rights, which accompany ownership, as the *"bundle of rights."*

Bundle of rights

The right to own property.

The right to possess property.

The right to use property.

The right to enjoy property.

The right to encumber property or borrow money on property.

The right to dispose of property.

The right to exclude those who do not share ownership of the property from all of the above mentioned rights.

Although owners of real estate have a "bundle of rights," they have certain responsibilities to other persons regarding the use they can make of their property. Their rights are not absolute, or unlimited. Ownership rights are subject to government control to promote public health, safety, and welfare. Zoning, building codes, and antidiscrimination laws are all examples of government control of property rights. These restrictions to the rights of a real property owner come under the designation of the police power of the government.

1.3 REAL PROPERTY VERSUS PERSONAL PROPERTY

To better understand regulations relating to the acquisition and transfer of real property, we need to distinguish between real and personal property.

The law states that anything that is not real property is personal property. Likewise, any property that is not personal property is real property. To fully understand this concept, we need to understand what we mean by "real property."

Real property consists of: (1) *land*, (2) *that which is affixed to the land*, (3) *that which is appurtenant or incidental to the land, and* (4) *that which is immovable by law.*

Land

Land is the *solid material of the earth such as soil, rock, or other substances.* It can be composed of mountains, valleys, swamps, or any other kind of terrain. The technical definition of land includes:

1. Surface of the land.

2. Airspace above the land.

3. Materials and substances beneath the surface to the center of the earth.

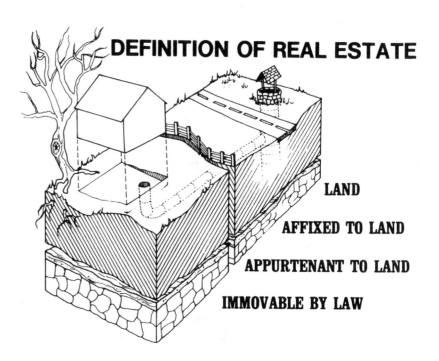

DEFINITION OF REAL ESTATE

LAND

AFFIXED TO LAND

APPURTENANT TO LAND

IMMOVABLE BY LAW

SURFACE OF THE LAND   The surface of the land is defined as the space on the surface of the earth, upon which we live. This includes lateral support—support from adjoining land, and subjacent support—support from underlying strata.

AIRSPACE   Airspace is more difficult to define. Modern theories, based on air travel, generally agree that an owner of real property owns a reasonable amount of airspace above the land, with the remainder being public highway. Moreover, landowners have the right to prevent a use of airspace which would interfere with their use of the land. However, the issue of what constitutes a "reasonable amount" is currently determined by the courts on a case-by-case basis whenever a lawsuit arises between disputing parties.

MINERALS IN THE GROUND   Solid minerals contained in the land—such as coal, iron ore, or gold—are real property until they are taken from the ground, at which time they become personal property. A landowner who deeds the land to another, conveys the minerals contained in the land, unless the mineral rights have already been sold to some other party.

When mineral rights have been reserved by the former owner, or conveyed to another person, the owner of the mineral rights has an implied easement to enter upon the surface of the property to extract the minerals.

Oil and gas are a special class of minerals and, because of their ambulatory nature, are not considered capable of ownership until reduced to possession. However, the right to drill for oil and gas rests with the surface landowner or the owner of the mineral rights, if they belong to someone other than the surface landowner.

WATER RIGHTS A working knowledge of the water rights of a property owner should include an understanding of the following issues:

1. Underground water rights.

2. Right of Appropriation.

3. Riparian water rights.

Underground Water Underground, or percolating, water is water which is not confined to a well, a defined channel, or a water bed. In California, the landowner has no ownership of specific underground water, nor absolute ownership of waters running across or bordering property, such as a lake or a stream. Under the *"Doctrine of Correlative User"* the landowner may take, in common with other owners, only his or her share of underground (percolating) waters for beneficial use.

Right of Appropriation The right of appropriation is that right given to the state to give permission to a nonriparian owner to take water from a river or lake.

Riparian Rights Owners of land which borders cn a lake or water course enjoy certain benefits regarding use of the water, under a concept known as *riparian rights*. While they have no absolute ownership of the waters, each owner has a personal right, along with other landowners, to the use of such waters in a "reasonable manner." Basically each owner has a right to an equal amount of water in proportion to the amount of land owned, and in light of the needs of all interested parties.

Affixed to the Land The second component of the definition of real property is *"that which is affixed to the land,"* or anything regarded as a permanent part of the land. This includes:

1. Things permanently resting on the land, such as buildings.

2. Things permanently attached to a building, such as fixtures.

3. Things attached to the land by roots, such as trees.

Trees, shrubs, and vines that are the natural products of nature are generally considered part of the land to which they are attached by roots. In other words, they continue to be considered to be real property until they are severed or gathered, at which time they become personal property. On the other hand, farm products such as growing crops which are the result of annual labor are considered to be goods and are governed by laws of personal property. Growing vegetable crops are sometimes referred to as *emblements.*

Appurtenant to the Land

The third component of the definition of real property is *that which is appurtenant, or incidental to the land.* That which is appurtenant to the land is anything which, by right, is used by the land for its benefit and "goes with the land." Examples might be:

1. Easements—such as the rights of way over adjoining lands, or even passages for light, air, or heat from or across the land of another. (Easements will be discussed in detail in a subsequent chapter.)

2. Stock in a mutual water company is another example of an appurtenance. A mutual water company is a nonprofit company organized by or for water users in a specific district to develop and furnish water to its stockholders at reasonable rates. Usually each share is considered to be appurtenant to a specific piece of real property and cannot be sold separately. In other words, the stock is considered real property and transfers with the property.

Immovable by Law

Real property is also defined as any property that is *immovable by law.* When, by law, an item of personal property is required to stay with the land, that item becomes real property.

Personal Property

As was indicated previously, anything that is not real property is personal property.

Personal property is movable, while real property is considered to be immovable. Other names for personal property are *chattels* or *choses.* Examples of personal property include stocks, money, contracts, furniture, automobiles, mortgages, and so on.

Other distinctions that might be made between real and personal property are:

1. Contracts involving the sale of real property must be in writing and signed by the person whose title is being transferred. In the sale of personal property, the transaction need not be in writing if the price is less than five hundred dollars.

2. Personal property when sold is usually transferred by using a bill of sale. Real property is transferred by delivery of a written instrument called a deed.

The Status of Property Can Change

Real property can become personal property, and personal property can become real property. For example, trees growing in a forest are considered real property. The trees are cut and transported to the planing mill, where they are made into boards, thus becoming personal property. The boards are used in the construction of a building, changing them back to real property. The building eventually outlives its usefulness and is torn down. The salvaged lumber becomes personal property once again.

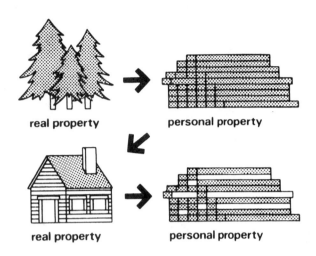

real property   personal property

real property   personal property

1.4 FIXTURES

Fixtures are items of personal property that are attached to the land in such a manner as to be considered part of the land itself. Depending upon the specific circumstances, certain items of personal property may or may not become so integrated with the land that it is considered to be part of the real property and, consequently, belongs to the current owner of the real estate. The concept of fixtures can become a touchy question when land is bought or sold, or when a tenant makes improvements on the property. If a legal dispute arises, the court must make a decision as to whether the property in question is a fixture and must remain with the real property, or whether the item is still personal property and can be removed and taken by the seller, or the tenant.

Tests of a Fixture

To help determine whether an item is a fixture and consequently real property, or is not a fixture and consequently personal property, the courts have established "five tests of a fixture," which include *method of attachment, adaptability, relationship of parties, intention of parties, and agreement between parties.*

1. The courts are concerned with the method by which the property is incorporated into or attached to the land and its consequent degree of permanence. In other words, is it nailed, cemented, welded, or bolted down? Or is it simply leaning against the building or hanging on the wall?

2. The courts are concerned with the adaptability to ordinary use of the attached personal property. In other words, is the item in question customized, or can it easily be used in some other building? Wall-to-wall carpeting would be considered a fixture, because it had been cut to a particular size and shaped room, and the carpet is attached to a tack strip which is nailed to the floor. Customized draperies may also become fixtures.

3. The courts are concerned with the relationship between the person who adds the article, and the party with whom he or she may be transacting business. In other words, is the dispute between a landlord and a tenant, a buyer and a seller, or a borrower and a lender?

   In a dispute between a landlord and a tenant, the courts today tend to favor the tenant; between a buyer and a seller, the courts tend to favor the buyer; between a borrower and a lender, the courts will lean toward the lender.

4. The intention of the person attaching the personal property to the land is very important. Intention is indicated by action or agreement of the parties, whether it be expressed or merely implied. If intention can be proved, the courts will consider this the most important test.

5. The courts will also look to the existence of any agreements between the parties regarding the item in question. In other words, has a right to the property been established by those parties concerned by the signing of an agreement, such as mentioning the item in the listing or purchase contract?

Take Proper Precautions

Many times problems arise between buyers and sellers regarding fixtures. Therefore, it behooves people to clearly spell out, in the purchase contract, the intentions of the seller and the buyer regarding the items of personal property or fixtures to be included in the sales price.

The purchase contract should state if the carpets, stove, or any other questionable item is included as a part of the sales price or if the seller reserves the right to remove these items after the sale.

Exception to the Fixture Rule

For every good rule, there is often an exception. In the case of fixtures, there are certain items that remain personal property after they have been affixed to real property. Articles of personal property, which a business tenant has attached to real property because of their necessity to the trade or business, are called *trade fixtures*. Examples are shelving, counters, or cash registers. These trade fixtures are viewed as the personal property of the business tenant and the tenant has the right to remove these items. However, a residential tenant in a house or apartment might install room dividers or different light fixtures. These fixtures may or may not be viewed as the personal property of the tenant. As noted above, the courts do tend to favor the tenant. In many cases, these fixtures may be removed by the tenant, provided the premises are not damaged in the process of removal. However, the right to remove is not absolute; it depends upon the circumstances in each and every case.

SUMMARY   California's colorful history is closely tied to the concept of land ownership. A study of the early inhabitants of the state gives a better understanding of the foundation upon which real estate laws and regulations have been built.

Ownership of real property includes certain property rights called the "bundle of rights." The bundle includes the right to own, possess, use, enjoy, encumber, dispose of, and exclude.

Real property is defined as (1) land; (2) that which is appurtenant to the land, such as easements or stock in a mutual water company; (3) that which is affixed to the land, known as fixtures; and (4) that which is immovable by law.

The status of property can change. Real property can become personal property and personal property can be changed to real property.

In determining the status of real versus personal property, the courts have developed five tests to determine whether or not an item is a fixture. These tests are *M*ethod of attachment, *A*daptability, *R*elationship of the parties, *I*ntention of the parties to the transaction, and the existence of and *A*greement between the parties involved (the *MARIA* memory tool).

Important Terms and Concepts

Appurtenant	Real property
Bundle of rights	Riparian rights
Correlative user	Tests of a fixture
Fixture	Treaty of Guadalupe Hidalgo
Personal property	

REVIEWING YOUR UNDERSTANDING

1. Which group of explorers and colonizers set up presidios and pueblos in the early days of California?
   (a) Mexicans
   (b) Americans
   (c) Spanish
   (d) Indians

2. Which of the following is *not* considered to be one of the "bundle of rights?"
   (a) The right to own property
   (b) The right to pay taxes
   (c) The right to enjoy
   (d) The right to encumber

3. The definition of land includes all but one of the following:
   (a) Airspace above the land
   (b) Hills and valleys
   (c) Rocks and soil
   (d) Oil deposits beneath the surface

4. The rights afforded an owner of land bordering on a water course, to use that water in a reasonable manner, are called:
   (a) Appropriation rights
   (b) Water rights
   (c) Riparian rights
   (d) Subjacent privileges

5. Wall-to-wall carpeting in a single-family dwelling is usually considered to be:
   (a) A fixture
   (b) A chattel
   (c) Removable
   (d) Separate property

6. Which of the following is appurtenant to the land and goes with the land?
   (a) Stock in a mutual water company
   (b) Trade fixtures
   (c) An easement
   (d) Both (a) and (c)

7. In a dispute between a buyer and seller, the courts would tend to favor the:
   (a) Seller
   (b) Buyer
   (c) The one with the most money
   (d) Neither party

8. In what year was California granted statehood?
   (a) 1821
   (b) 1846
   (c) 1848
   (d) 1850

9. The main feature of personal property is:
   (a) Title is transferred by a deed
   (b) Its immobility
   (c) Its value is less than real property
   (d) None of these

10. Which two terms do not belong together?
    (a) Bundle of rights—use and enjoyment
    (b) Real estate—land
    (c) Correlative user—water rights
    (d) Personal property—easement

Chapter 2
Part I: Legal Description, Method of Acquiring Title, and Deeds

Preview

In Part I of this chapter, you will study land descriptions, stressing the lot, block, and tract; metes and bounds; and U.S. Government survey methods for describing land.

You will also explore five ways of acquiring title to real estate, including an explanation of deeds used in California. At the conclusion of Part I you will be able to:

1. *List the three major methods used to legally describe land.*

2. *Find a parcel of land using each of the three location methods; be able to calculate acreage.*

3. *Outline five ways of acquiring title to real estate.*

4. *Discuss the difference between a grant deed, quitclaim deed, and warranty deed.*

5. *Briefly describe the purpose of the California recording system.*

2.1 LAND DESCRIPTIONS

Three reasons the description of real property is essential are:

1. To specifically identify and locate areas of real property ownership.

2. To satisfy buyers who are interested in the precise dimensions and area of their property.

3. To minimize land description disputes between neighbors by establishing set boundary lines.

In addition to these three reasons, the law requires that every parcel of land sold, mortgaged, or leased must be properly described or identified. Legal descriptions are usually based upon the field notes of a civil engineer or a surveyor. When dealing with property, such descriptions can usually be obtained from title insurance policies, deeds, deeds of trust, or mortgages.

Modern surveyors establish exact directions and distances by means of transits and measuring tapes. Aerial photography is also used in modern mapping.

Early Methods Used

Today's survey methods are a far cry from the methods used in early California. One early method of land measurement employed two men on horseback. Each would drag an end of a cord or rawhide strip called a *thong,* which was about 100 *varas* in length. (A vara is about 33 inches.) One rider would remain stationary while the other rode past. When the length of the thong was reached, this would be repeated by the other rider until one of them arrived at the end of the property. The number of thong lengths passed would then be counted and the dimensions of the property would be determined.

In another early method, the circumference of a wagon wheel was measured. A leather strip was tied to a spoke and then, by rolling the wheel on the ground, the revolutions of the wheel could be counted and the distance recorded.

Present-Day Land Descriptions

There are three major methods used today to legally describe and locate land. They are:

1. Lot, block and tract system.

2. Metes and bounds system.

3. U.S. government survey, commonly called the U.S. section and township system.

Lot, Block and Tract System

The California Subdivision Map Act requires that all new subdivisions be either mapped or platted. A map of each subdivision is recorded in the recorder's office of the county in which the land is located.

When a large parcel of land is divided into small parcels, it is called subdividing. At that time, a subdivision map is filed in the county recorder's office; it is assigned a tract name and/or number. Once subdivision maps are recorded, legal descriptions are created by making reference to a particular lot in the block in that tract in which the property is located.

Example. "All of lot 4 in Block A of Tract number 2025 in the city of Bellflower, Los Angeles County, California. As per map recorded in Book 76 page 83 of maps in the office of the recorder of said county."

Tract 2025

1	6	1	6
2	7	2	7
3 A	8	3 B	8
4	9	4	9
5	10	5	10

This type of identification is commonly found in urban areas of California, where extensive subdividing has taken place.

Metes and Bounds System

The metes and bounds system of land location is used most often when the property in question is not covered by a recorded subdivision map, or when the property is so irregular in shape that it is impractical to describe under the section and township system.

Metes refers to the measurement of length, such as inches, feet, yards, rods, meters, and miles. *Bounds* refers to the use of boundaries, both natural and artificial, such as rivers, roads, fences, boulders, creeks, iron pipes, etc. So metes and bounds means to *measure the boundaries.* This system is one of the oldest used methods and is often found in land descriptions in both rural and urban areas.

A common term in this system is *bench mark,* which is a mark on a fixed or enduring object, often used as an elevation point by a surveyor.

Another term is *angular lines.* Many surveys using metes and bounds description are based on angles and directions from a given north-south line, which is obtained with a compass. Angles are a deflection from this north-south line. Deflections will be to the east or west of the north-south line.

There are 360° in a circle and 180° in a half-circle. Each degree is divided into 60 minutes and each minute divided into 60 seconds. The bearing of a course is described by measuring easterly or westerly from the north and south lines.

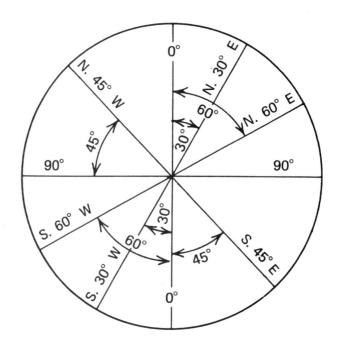

Although the metes and bounds land description is one of the oldest forms, it is also one of the most complicated. The system ranges from just simple distances between given land marks to surveyor readings, based on angles found in the arc of a circle.

In using the metes and bounds method, three important points must be stressed:

1. You must start at a given point of beginning.

2. You must follow, in detail, the boundaries of the land in courses and distances from one point to another.

3. You must always return to the point of beginning, thus enclosing the boundary lines.

Example. Here is a legal description using the metes and bounds method.

"Beginning at a point on the southerly line of Harbor Ave., 200 ft. westerly of the southwest corner of the intersection of Harbor Ave. and 8th St.; running thence due south 300 ft. to the northerly line of Cribbage St.; thence westerly along the northerly line of Cribbage St., 200 ft.; thence northerly and parallel to the first course, 300 ft. to the southerly line of Harbor Ave., thence easterly along the southerly line of Harbor Ave., 200 ft. to the point of beginning."

One major weakness in using a metes and bounds system is that markers or points of beginning often disappear or have been moved or replaced. In later years this makes it difficult to find the exact corners of a parcel.

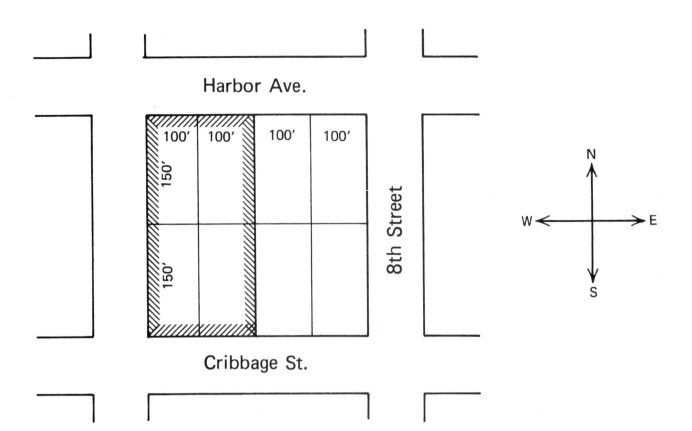

U.S. Government Section and Township System

The U.S. Government section and township method of survey is used primarily to describe agricultural or rural land. The system originated in the early 1880s with a survey of public lands made by the U.S. Surveyor General.

The U.S. Government survey system establishes monuments as points of beginning. The monuments are intersected by two imaginary lines, one running east and west called a *base line,* and another running north and south called the *meridian line.*

Due to its peculiar shape, the State of California requires *three* of these principal base lines and meridians. They are:

1. *Humboldt Base Line and Meridian,* which is the point of beginning for describing land in the northwestern part of California. The actual point of beginning is on Mt. Pierce, just south of Eureka, California.

2. *Mt. Diablo Base Line and Meridian,* which is the point of beginning for describing land in the central part of California. The actual point of beginning is on Mt. Diablo near Walnut Creek, California.

3. *San Bernardino Base Line and Meridian,* which is used to describe land in southern California. The actual point of beginning is the

CALIFORNIA BASE LINES & MERIDIANS

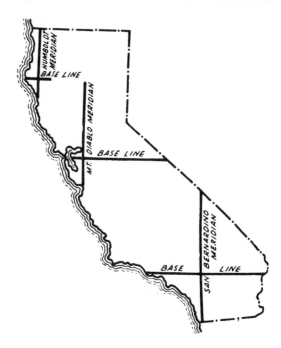

intersection of Base Line Street and Meridian Avenue in the City of San Bernardino, California.

Range lines run parallel to the principal meridians at six-mile intervals. *Township lines* run parallel to the principal base lines at six-mile intervals. The resulting grid of squares containing approximately 36 square miles each are called *townships.*

In order to identify each of these townships, a numbering system utilizing an assignment of two location numbers has been devised. The identity of each township is determined by its position north or south of the base line, and east or west of the meridian line. A legal description might be, for example:

"Township 2 North, Range 3 East, San Bernardino Base Line and Meridian. (T2N, R3E, SBBL & M) (The X indicates the township.) (See illustration on top of next page.)

Sections in a Township

Townships are in turn divided into *sections.* Each township contains 36 squares or sections, each one mile square. These sections are uniformly numbered from 1 to 36 with Section 1 located in the northeast corner of the township.

Not only is each section one mile square, but each contains 640

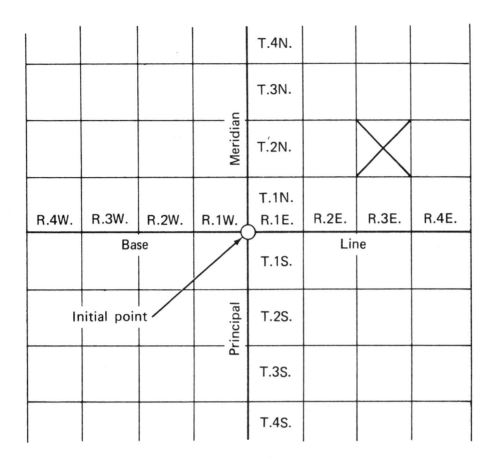

acres. Each section can be divided into smaller parcels of land, such as:

A quarter of a section = 160 acres

A quarter of a ¼ section = 40 acres

A quarter of a ¼ of a ¼ section = 10 acres

The division can be smaller and smaller until the size of the parcel is identified. The division need not be in quarters; it may also be in halves. (See illustration on top of following page.)

PITFALL	Due to the earth's curvature, some sections in townships are distorted and may not contain a full 640 acres; thus computing acreage under the U.S. Government system will give approximate figures. An accurate measure of actual acreage is best left to licensed engineers or surveyors.

TOWNSHIP

6	5	4	3	2	1
7	8	9	10	11	12
18	17	16	15	14	13
19	20	21	22	23	24
30	29	28	27	26	25
31	32	33	34	35	36

MAP OF A SECTION

The following additional measurements will help in computing land measurements:

One mile = 5280 feet or 320 rods

One rod = 16½ feet

One acre = 43,560 square feet

One square acre = 208.71 feet × 208.71 feet

Commercial acre = standard acre less land needed for streets, sidewalks, curbs

2.2 METHODS OF ACQUIRING TITLE

Now that you know the difference between real and personal property, and you know the three main ways of legally describing real property, let's discuss how a person goes about acquiring title to real property.

According to the Civil Code, the five ways of acquiring property are by *will, succession, accession, occupancy, and transfer.*

Acquiring Property by Will

A *will* is a legal instrument by which a person disposes of his or her property, upon their death. California law recognizes three types of wills: (1) a witnessed will, (2) a holographic will, and (3) a nuncupative will.

A *witnessed will* is a formal typewritten document signed by the individual who is making it, wherein he or she declares in the presence of at least two witnesses that it is his or her will. Then two witnesses in turn sign the will. It is recommended that this document be prepared by an attorney.

A *holographic will* is a document written, dated, and signed in its entirety in the handwriting of the maker. It requires no witnesses.

The *nuncupative will* is rarely used, and when it is, it can only be used to dispose of personal property. It is sometimes called an "oral will" since it requires no writing, but can only be used under certain conditions and in actual contemplation of immediate death. The property to be transferred can only be personal property and has a limit of $1,000. The entire transaction must be put in writing within 30 days by someone who witnessed the oral declaration.

Special Terms   Transferring property by will involves a number of special terms that you need to understand.

Testator. Male person who makes a will.

Testatrix. Female person who makes a will.

Executor. Male person named in the will by the maker to handle the estate at death.

Executrix. Female person named in the will by the maker to handle the estate of the deceased.

Administrator. Male person appointed by the court to handle the estate, when no will is left.

Administratrix. Female person appointed by the court to handle the estate when no will is left.

Devise. A gift of real property by will.

Devisee. Person receiving real property by will.

Bequest, legacy. A gift of personal property by will.

Legatee. Person receiving personal property by will.

Codicil. A change in a will.

Intestate. A situation where a person dies without leaving a will. He or she is said to have died intestate.

Testate. A situation where a person dies leaving a will.

Probate   Legal title to property being acquired by will is subject to the control of the probate court. The purpose of a probate hearing is to identify the creditors of the deceased and pay off these creditors. Then if any property remains, the probate court determines who are the rightful heirs and distributes the remaining property.

The law requires that upon the death of the owner, all property is subject to the temporary possession of an *executor (trix)* or an *administrator (trix)*.

Probate action is taken in a superior court and the estate property may be sold during the probate period for the benefit of the heirs or to cover court costs. In a probate real estate sale, certain standards must be met and certain actions taken. The initial offer in a probate real estate sale must be for at least 90 percent of the inheritance tax appraisal. The court is petitioned to confirm the sale, and at the hearing the court may accept additional bids. The first additional bid must be at least 10 percent of the first $10,000 of the original bid and 5 percent of any excess. Subsequent bids may be for less. The court confirms the final sale and sets the broker's commissions, if a broker is involved. Probate fees paid to executors, administrators and attorneys are set by the courts and vary depending upon the size and complexity of the estate. It should be noted that certain types of property holdings need not be probated. This will be discussed in Part II of this chapter.

Acquiring Property by Succession

When a deceased person leaves no will, the law provides for the disposition of their property. The State of Califonia dictates who will get the property under the law of *intestate succession,* with succession meaning the handing down of property to another person.

When a person dies intestate, the property of the deceased is divided into two categories: separate property and community property. The laws of intestate succession are different for each of these categories. When a person dies and leaves separate property, this means that the surviving spouse did not have an interest in said property. If a person leaves community property this means a surviving spouse has a one-half interest in the property.

When *separate property* is involved, the following disposition of property is made:

1. When a deceased person leaves a spouse and one child, the separate property is divided one-half to the spouse, and the child receives the other half.

2. When a deceased person leaves a spouse and two or more children, the spouse receives one-third and the children equally divide the other two-thirds.

3. There are other divisions made by the courts in the event that a person dies leaving no spouse or children. The usual rule is the property goes to the next of kin, such as parents, brothers, sisters, and so on.

If a person dies intestate and leaves *community property,* the deceased person's interest always passes to the surviving spouse, not to the children.

KEY POINT On matters of wills and estates, *always* consult an experienced attorney! Do-it-yourself estate planning is not recommended!

Acquiring Property by Accession

You may acquire title to property that is added to your existing real estate. This process is called *accession.*

Examples include: (1) accretion, (2) avulsion, (3) addition of fixtures, and (4) improvements made in error.

ACCRETION

The gradual accumulation of soil on property bordering a stream, river, or an ocean shore line is called *accretion.* The soil thus deposited is referred to as *alluvion,* or *alluvion deposits.* The gradual wearing away of land by the action of water, wind, or glacial ice is known as *erosion;* while *reliction* is the action wherein the water, sea or river recedes permanently below the usual water line. When this takes place, the owner of the property that borders on the sea or river may acquire title to the newly exposed land.

AVULSION

Avulsion occurs when a river or stream, by sudden violence, carries away a part of the bank and bears it to the opposite bank or to another part of the same bank. The owner of the part carried away may reclaim it within one year after the avulsion. However, the owner must reclaim the title by applying some act of ownership, such as cultivation of the soil within one year; if not, then the land belongs to the property owner to whom the land is now attached.

ADDITION OF FIXTURES

Addition occurs when a person affixes personal property to the land of another without an agreement permitting removal. The thing so affixed may then become the property of the landowner.

IMPROVEMENTS MADE IN ERROR

An *improvement made in error* occurs when a person, in good faith, affixes improvements to the land of another, erroneously believing that he or she has a right to do so. In some cases these erroneous improvements may pass to the landowner. But in most cases the person who made the improvements in error is permitted to remove the improvements and if need be pay damages to the owner of the land on which the improvements were made.

Acquiring Property by Occupancy

Real property or the use of real property can be gained through (1) abandonment and (2) adverse possession.

ABANDONMENT

A party who holds a leasehold interest (the tenant) in a piece of property may abandon his or her interest or any improvements made thereon. If this should occur, the landlord may reacquire possession and full control of the premises. In other words, when a tenant leaves before the lease expires, the landlord may reacquire the use of the property at that time, and in some cases not be obligated to refund rental payments or return any improvements made on the property.

There are technical rules regarding the landlord's right to re-rent the property. If a tenant abandons the premises and leaves personal property, the landlord may after due notification dispose of such personal property.

ADVERSE POSSESSION

Adverse possession is a method of acquiring physical possession of property by a person who is not the actual owner. This physical possession may develop into legal title if the following five conditions are met:

1. There must be actual occupation *open* and *notorious.* This means that the claim of possession must not be kept a secret. In other words, if the present owner inspects the property, possession or use by another person should be apparent. You do not actually have to reside on the property, but must show your intentions of holding and possessing the land, through some type of improvement to the land. For example: If the property were farmland, the cultivation of crops, the grazing of cattle, or the fencing of the property might constitute possession.

2. There must be occupancy *hostile* to the true owner's title. This means, without permission or rental payment of any kind to the owner. Permission to use the property defeats the hostile use, and thus title by adverse possession.

3. There must be a *claim of right* or *color of title.* Under claim of right, the claimant enters as an intruder and remains; under color of title, claimants base their right on some court decree or upon a defective written instrument.

4. There must be *continuous* and *uninterrupted* possession for a period of five years.

5. There must be the *payment of all real property taxes* levied and assessed for a period of *five consecutive years.* The fact that the true owner is also paying the taxes does not necessarily defeat the rights of the adverse possessor, as long as the possessor also pays the taxes.

Adverse possession is not common in California because of the five requirements listed above. It is not possible to obtain title by adverse possession to public lands, nor against an incompetent private landowner.

Acquiring Property by Transfer

Without question, the most common method of acquiring property is by transfer. Where property is conveyed from one person to another by act of parties or by law, it can be said to be acquired by transfer. There are five basic types of transfers: (1) private grant, (2) public grant, (3) gift, (4) public dedication, and (5) court action (or involuntary transfer).

PRIVATE GRANT

Private grant occurs when an owner voluntarily conveys his or her ownership rights to another. The basic instrument used in this transaction is a deed. (Deeds will be discussed in detail later.)

PUBLIC GRANT

When a governmental agency deeds property to an individual or institution, it is called a public grant.

In the early years of our country's history, public grants were made through laws enacted by Congress.

The Preemption Act of 1862 allowed persons living on federal land, who were known as squatters, to acquire 160 acres of land at a cost of approximately $1.25 per acre.

The Homestead Act of 1862 allowed vast stretches of public land to be homesteaded. The heads of families or persons over 21 years of age could obtain 160 acres. They had to file a declaration of homestead with the county recorder or at a land office and had to agree to occupy and improve the land. After residing on it for five years, they received a document from the government called a *patent,* which conveyed ownership to the homesteader.

Other public grants were made by the government for railroads, educational institutions, national parks, cities, and towns.

GIFT

A property owner may voluntarily transfer property to a private person without giving or receiving any considerations or remuneration. In case of real property, the transaction normally would be evidenced by a gift deed. Depending upon the value of the gift, there may or may not be a gift tax liability.

PUBLIC DEDICATION

A property owner may also give land to a public body for a particular use such as a street, a park, bridges, schools, playgrounds, and so on. This act is called public dedication. The dedication is valid only if the public body accepts the property.

COURT ACTION (INVOLUNTARY TRANSFER)

There are a variety of situations in which a court of law may be called upon to establish legal title. The most common of these involuntary transfers are: partition action, foreclosure action, bankruptcy, escheat, and eminent domain.

Partition action
Foreclosure action
Bankruptcy
Escheat
Eminent domain

Partition action is a court action wherein the co-owners of property may sue other co-owners for severance of their respective interests. If the property cannot be physically divided, the court can order a sale, and divide the proceeds among the former owners.

Foreclosure action takes place when a person holding a delinquent lien on property institutes proceedings requesting the sale of property. In California, delinquent real estate loans are foreclosed using a process called a "trustee's sale" which is discussed in Chapter 7.

Bankruptcy can be either voluntary or involuntary. When an individual cannot meet credit obligations, he or she may voluntarily file bankruptcy or may be adjudged bankrupt by the courts. Title to real property is vested in a court-appointed trustee, who sells the property to pay the claims of creditors. Under certain circumstances a family home can be protected against forced sale by the bankruptcy court.

Escheat is the legal process whereby ownership of real property reverts to the state, for lack of heirs or want of legal ownership.

The probate courts will do all in their power to locate possible heirs. After escheat proceedings are instituted, the title is held in trust by the state for seven years. If at the end of that time no heirs have come forth, the title will transfer to the state with all rights of ownership. Every year millions of dollars worth of property escheats to the State of California due to the lack of heirs.

Eminent domain is the power of the state to take land from private ownership by due process of law.

Use of eminent domain is often referred to as "condemnation proceedings." These proceedings may be instituted by all levels of government and by public utilities or railroads.

Two things are legally required to use the power of eminent domain:

1. The property must be taken for a public use.

2. The owner must be paid just compensation. Most courts have ruled that the "fair market value" is the proper basis for determining just compensation.

2.3 INSTRUMENTS USED IN THE TRANSFER OF REAL PROPERTY

Under English common law, no written document was needed to transfer title to real property. Rather, a twig, a stone, or a handful of dirt passing from one owner to the next owner in the presence of witnesses was symbolic of the transfer of property. Other methods of transfer were simply a statement made before witnesses in sight of the land, followed by entry upon the land by the new owner. Today under California law, the transfer of ownership of real property may be done by a single written instrument known as a *deed.*

A deed is a written document by which (when properly executed, delivered, and accepted) title to real property is transferred from one person called a *grantor,* to another person called a *grantee.* The grantor is the person who gives title and a grantee is the person who receives title. In a real estate sale, the grantor is the seller, and the grantee is the buyer.

Throughout this book we will use words to designate the parties in an agreement that end in the letters *or* and *ee*—such as:

Trustor and trustee

Lessor and lessee

Vendor and vendee

Optionor and optionee

To understand these terms, remember this rule:

> The *or* ending denotes the *giver* and
> the *ee* ending indicates the *receiver.*

Example.   A lessor (owner) gives a lease to the lessee (tenant).

Essentials of a Valid Deed

A valid deed must contain certain essential elements:

1. *Deed must be in writing.* Legal instruments required to be in writing come under the *Statute of Frauds.* According to this statute, when the title to real property is to be voluntarily conveyed, it must be accomplished by an instrument in writing, usually a deed.

2. *Parties must be correctly described.* In order for a deed to be valid, the parties must be properly described. This means that the grantor (seller) and the grantee (buyer) must be certain and absolute.

Example.   A deed from "A" to "B" *or* "C" is not absolute. The word "or" creates the problem. A deed from "A" to "B" *and* "C" is absolute. The word "and" makes it certain.

Since there are so many individuals with like or similar names, it is also important that the parties to a deed be indentified as clearly as possible in order to avoid any later confusion as to true identity.

If possible, the full legal name should be used and the legal status of the individual should be shown. Remember, the full name includes middle name or initial, if any, and the legal status should refer to the relationship between parties such as husband and wife.

3. *Grantor must be competent to convey and capable of receiving title.* Everyone is competent to convey except:
   a. *minors*—persons under the age of 18 years, unless the minor is classified as emancipated, in which case a minor can legally contract for real estate
   b. *incompetents*—a person of unsound mind, judicially declared incompetent
   c. *convicts*—persons imprisoned for life or under a death penalty

Question: Can an infant take title to real property?

Answer: Yes, an infant can receive title by gift or inheritance but cannot convey title without a guardian or other court approval.

Question: Can a person take title under an assumed name?

Answer: Yes, but upon resale it may be difficult to prove identity for a notary public.

4. *Description of the property must be clear.* The property in the deed must be properly described. This means any description which definitely identifies the property so that it can be located with certainty, meets the test of the law. In most cases, the legal description is either a lot, block, and tract; a metes and bounds; or a U.S. Government survey description.

5. *There must be a granting clause.* A granting clause means that the deed must contain words indicating the intention of the owner to convey the property. The exact words are not specified; however, the words, "I hereby grant," "I hereby convey," or "I hereby transfer" will satisfy the requirements of a granting clause.

6. *Deed must contain the signature of the grantor.* To be valid, a deed must be signed by all grantors named in the deed. If there is more than one owner, all must sign. For instance, both husband and wife must sign deeds to convey community property.

   Under certain guidelines, state law allows a grantor's name to be signed by an "attorney in fact," acting under a valid power of attorney.

   California permits a person who is unable to sign his or her name to sign by mark, as long as a witness is present. The witness then signs the deed according to the manner prescribed by law.

Delivery of the Deed Is Required

A deed is not effective unless it is delivered and accepted. This does not mean a mere turning over of the physical possession of the document. The grantor must have a clear and honest intention to pass title immediately, before there is a legal delivery.

1. *Evidence of delivery.* The best evidence is actually handing the deed to the grantee. However, manual delivery is not necessary, as a deed may be delivered to a third party for the benefit of the grantee—for example, depositing the deed in escrow. Again, manual delivery does not in itself constitute delivery, the proof lies in the *intent* of the grantor to pass title. If and when the deed is recorded, recording of the deed presumes valid delivery.

2. *Time of delivery.* To be effective, a deed must be delivered to the grantee during the grantor's lifetime. It cannot be used to take the place of a will.

   A deed that is delivered to a grantee with the condition that it is not to take effect until the death of the grantor is not valid since the intent to pass title would not occur during the lifetime of the grantor.

3. *Date of delivery.* A deed is presumed to be delivered as of its date of writing or execution. If no date exists, its date is presumed to be the date of delivery. The lack of a date does not invalidate the deed.

4. *Conditional delivery.* Delivery of a deed must be absolute. It cannot be delivered to a grantee subject to conditions. For example, to avoid ultimate probate proceedings with regard to his property, "A" gives a deed to "B" telling "B" that he is not to record until "A" dies. This is a conditional delivery and is not valid.

Acceptance

The deed must be accepted by the grantee and this acceptance must be voluntary and unconditional. It is usually accomplished by certain words, acts, or conduct on the grantee's part which lead to the presumption of voluntary acceptance.

Acknowledgement

A deed is a real estate document that need not be recorded to be valid. However, if the grantee wishes to record the deed, it must first be acknowledged.

An *acknowledgement* is a formal declaration before a duly authorized officer (usually a notary public) by the person who signed a document, stating the signature is voluntarily given and that he or she is the person whose signature appears on the document.

Nonessentials in a Deed

Many of the items listed above are essentials for a deed to be valid. Here are some items that are not required, but are commonly found in a deed.

A deed does not have to contain, but commonly has: (1) an acknowledgement, (2) a date, and (3) a recording number issued by the county.

However, it must be remembered that a deed is *void* or *invalid* if the:

1. Grantor is incompetent.

2. Deed is signed in blank.

3. Deed is never delivered.

4. Deed is a forgery.

5. Grantee does not exist (fictitious or deceased).

6. Deed is altered in escrow.

TYPES OF DEEDS

Grant Deed   In California, the grant deed is the most commonly used instrument for transferring title to real estate. A grant deed carries two "implied warranties" (these are not expressed in the document).
The implied warranties are:

1. That the grantor has not already conveyed title to any other person.

2. That the estate being conveyed is free from encumbrances made by the grantor or any other person claiming under the grantor, other than those disclosed to the grantee.

The grant may include easements and building restrictions. A grant deed also conveys any *after acquired title*. After acquired title means that if after the grantor deeds the property to the grantee, the grantor should acquire an additional interest, that interest automatically passes to the grantee.

Quitclaim Deed   This type of deed provides the grantee with the least protection of any deed. A quitclaim deed carries no implied warranties. In this type of deed, the grantor merely relinquishes any right or claim he or she has

Humboldt Land Title Company

NAME John R. Buyer and Mary M.
ADDRESS Buyer
CITY & 1739 Elm Street
STATE Somewhere, CA 95501

——————— SPACE ABOVE THIS LINE FOR RECORDER'S USE ———————

DOCUMENTARY TRANSFER TAX $ 86.90 COMPUTED ON FULL VALUE OF PROPERTY CONVEYED. __X__ , OR COMPUTED ON
FULL VALUE LESS LIENS AND ENCUMBRANCES REMAINING AT TIME OF SALE _____ Humboldt Land

Susan Escrow Officer Title Company
SIGNATURE OF DECLARANT OR AGENT DETERMINING TAX. FIRM NAME

HUMBOLDT
Land TITLE Co.

Grant Deed

A.P. No. 671-243-29

ORDER NO. 123456   THIS FORM FURNISHED BY HUMBOLDT LAND TITLE COMPANY

FOR A VALUABLE CONSIDERATION, receipt of which is hereby acknowledged.

RALPH J. SELLER and ALICE R. SELLER, husband and wife

hereby GRANT(S) to

JOHN R. BUYER and MARY M. BUYER, husband and wife,
as community property

the following described property in the City of Somewhere
County of Acme , State of California: described as

Lot 7, Block B of Tract Number 1291, recorded
on April 22, 1973 in Map Book 75, Page 97, in
the County Recorder's Office, Acme County,
California

Assessor's Parcel No. 671-243-29

Dated January 3, 1990

Ralph J. Seller
Ralph J. Seller
Alice R. Seller
Alice R. Seller

STATE OF CALIFORNIA
COUNTY OF Acme } SS.

On January 3, 1990) before me, the under
signed, a Notary Public in and for said County and State, personally
appeared Ralph J. Seller and
Alice R. Seller, husband and
wife

————————————————, known to me
to be the person S whose name S are subscribed to the within
instrument and acknowledged that they executed the same.

Jane B. Notary
Signature of Notary

FOR NOTARY SEAL OR STAMP

NOTARY PUBLIC
COUNTY, CALIFORNIA
My commission expires Oct. 25, 19__

in the property. If the grantor has absolute ownership, then that is what is conveyed. If the grantor has no claim or right, this type of deed transfers what the grantor has—nothing!

In other words, it merely says, "Such as I have is yours."

The quitclaim deed is usually used to remove some matters of title from the record, such as the removal of an easement or recorded restriction.

Sheriff's Deed

The court may order an owner's property sold after rendering a judgment for a money debt against the property owner. The successful bidder at this type of sale receives a sheriff's deed which contains no warranties.

Gift Deed

A person who wishes to make a gift of real property to another individual may convey that property by gift deed. The consideration given in a gift deed is usually "love and affection." A gift deed is considered valid unless it is being used to defraud creditors, in which case the creditors may void the deed.

Tax Deed

A deed issued by the tax collector after the sale of land which previously reverted to the state because of nonpayment of property taxes. The tax sale procedure will be presented in Chapter 13.

Warranty Deed

This type of deed is seldom used in California. Under a warranty deed, the grantor is legally responsible for the condition of the title; therefore, sellers in California are reluctant to sign warranty deeds. Instead, sellers sign grant deeds and leave the legal responsibility for the condition of the title to title insurance companies.

Trust Deed (or Deed of Trust)

A trust deed conveys "bare legal title" (but no possession) of property to a third party called a trustee. This deed differs from others in that the title is held by the trustee as security for a loan (lien) until such a time as the loan is paid off or until the borrower defaults on his or her payments. Trust deeds are financing instruments and they will be explained in Chapter 7.

Deed of Reconveyance

This deed is executed by the trustee to the borrower (trustor). When a beneficiary (the lender) notifies the trustee that the trustor has repaid a loan, the trustee reconveys the title back to the trustor using a deed of reconveyance. This instrument will also be discussed in Chapter 7.

2.4 THE RECORDING SYSTEM

The recording of a deed and many other title instruments, while not required by law, protects the new owner's rights. Under the Spanish and Mexican governments there were no recording laws in California. Shortly after California became a state, the legislature adopted a recording system by which evidence of title or interest in real property could be collected and held for public view at a convenient and safe place. This safe public place is the county recorder's office.

To be accepted for recording by a county recorder the deed must have:

1. Acknowledgement (be notarized).

2. Name and address to which future tax statements can be mailed.

3. Basis for computing the transfer tax.

4. Names of all parties involved in the transaction.

5. Adequate legal description.

Once a document is recorded, it is said that the world has *constructive notice* of the contents of the document.

The recording system also shows sequential transfers of property from the original owner to the present owner. This successive list of owners is called a *chain of title.*

Recorded documents are filed in books called grantor-grantee indexes. Most counties have reduced their title records to microfilm or microfiche for easy handling and storage.

There is a general rule which says *"The First to Record Is the First in Right."*

Example. "A" deeds to "B", who does not record. If "A" then deeds to "C" who does record, under the general rule, "C" would probably get the property because "C" recorded first.

However, there are two exceptions to this rule:

1. If the party who recorded first has knowledge of a prior unrecorded interest, the recording of a deed will not defeat the unrecorded deed.

2. If the first party failed to record, but took possession of the property, the possession by an unrecorded owner can defeat a later recorded deed.

Example. "A" deeds to "B" who does not record, but "B" takes physical possession of the property. "A" then deeds to "C" who does not make a physical inspection of the property. "C" then records the deed. Who will probably win? Answer: "B", because physical possession gives notice to all parties, including "C", that "B" has a prior interest in the property.

Moral: Always physically inspect a property before you purchase. Do not rely upon the public records only!

SUMMARY   There are three major types of land description: lot, block, and tract; metes and bounds; and U.S. Government survey system.

Five ways of acquiring title to property are: by will, succession, accession, occupancy, and transfer.

To be valid a deed must contain certain essential elements and the deed must have proper delivery and acceptance.

Major types of deeds are: grant deed, quitclaim deed, warranty deed, sheriff's deed, and gift deed. The most common is the grant deed, and it contains two implied warranties.

California has adopted a recording system designed to protect the rights of property owners and lien holders.

Important Terms and Concepts

Accession	Grantor
Accretion	Holographic will
Administrator (trix)	Intestate
Adverse possession	Lot, block, and tract
Alluvion	Metes and bounds
Avulsion	Nuncupative will
Codicil	Probate
Eminent domain	Quitclaim deed
Escheat	Succession
Executor (trix)	Testator (trix)
Grant deed	U.S. Government survey system
Grantee	Warranty deed
	Witnessed will

REVIEWING YOUR UNDERSTANDING

1. Ms. Jones was killed in an automobile accident. When the courts were called upon to distribute her property, they found she had died intestate. This would mean that she had died:
   (a) Leaving no property
   (b) Leaving no heirs
   (c) In debt
   (d) Without a will

2. If a married man with two children died without leaving a will, separate property purchased by him before he married and maintained as separate property during the marriage would be distributed as follows:
   (a) One half to the children
   (b) One half to the widow
   (c) All to the widow
   (d) One third to the widow and two thirds to the children

3. How many acres are there in a parcel of property which includes

the following: the NW ¼ of the SW ¼; and the E ½ of the NW ¼; and the NE ¼ of the SW ¼ of Section 5?
(a) 320 acres
(b) 160 acres
(c) 40 acres
(d) None of the above

4. The state urgently needs a piece of property to complete a project for public use. The owner did not wish to sell. Which method could be used to acquire the property?
(a) Dedication
(b) Escheat
(c) Police power
(d) Eminent domain

5. The term escheat is a legal term meaning:
(a) That a fraud has been committed
(b) That an agent's license has been revoked
(c) That property under mortgage can be conveyed
(d) None of the above

6. The water flowing down a river gradually builds up the land along the bank by leaving deposits of soil; this action is called:
(a) Accretion
(b) Reliction
(c) Avulsion
(d) Erosion

7. Which of the following statements concerning wills is *not* correct?
(a) A nuncupative will is considered to be an oral will.
(b) A holographic will can be signed by an "X" if it is witnessed.
(c) An administratrix is appointed by a probate court.
(d) A person who receives real property by will is known as a devisee.

8. Deeds are used to transfer property. Which deed contains no implied or expressed warranties?
(a) Warranty deed
(b) Grant deed
(c) Quitclaim deed
(d) None of the above

9. The executrix of an estate is:
(a) Selected by the heirs
(b) Appointed by the superior court
(c) Named in the testator's will
(d) Named by the decedent's attorney

10. To be valid, a deed must:
(a) Contain a legal description of the property
(b) Be signed by a competent grantee
(c) Both (a) and (b) are necessary
(d) Neither (a) nor (b) are necessary

Part II: Estates and Methods of Holding Title

Preview

Chapter Two, Part II discusses freehold and less-than-freehold estates.

In addition various methods of holding title, including joint tenancy, tenancy in common, community property, and tenancy in partnership will be presented, stressing the characteristics, advantages, and disadvantages of each. When you have completed Part II of this chapter you will be able to:

1. *Explain the difference between freehold and less-than-freehold estates.*

2. *Describe the key differences in taking title to property as joint tenants as opposed to tenants in common.*

3. *Explain the difference between community property and separate property.*

2.5 ESTATES

An estate is an interest in property. If the estate is in real property, you have a real estate interest. Estates fall into two major classifications: freehold estates and less-than-freehold estates.

Freehold Estates

A freehold estate represents one's interest as an *owner* of real property. Freehold estates can be subdivided into fee estates and life estates. (See illustration on top of page 36.)

1. *Fee estates* or *fee simple estates* can be:
    (a) *fee simple absolute* which the owner holds without any qualifications or limitations via private deed restrictions. This is the highest form of interest an individual can have in land.
    (b) *fee simple qualified* (defeasible) which the owner holds subject to special conditions or limitations or private deed restrictions that limit the use of the property.

Example. A parcel of land may carry a restriction that prohibits the sale of alcoholic beverages on the premises. If the owner fails to adhere to the restriction, the owner may be liable in a lawsuit for damages or in extreme cases the title may revert back to the grantor or creator of the restriction.

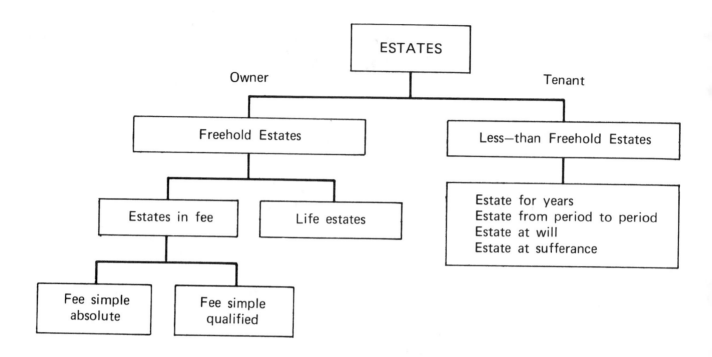

2. *Life estates* are created by deed or will for the life of one or more designated human beings. The life tenant has all the rights of possession, or income, during the life of the designated person(s).

If the person granting the life estate designates that the title is to go to some other person upon the death of the life estate holder, the person so designated is said to have an *estate in remainder.*

Example. In Figure 2-1, A deeds a life estate to B for the life of B. When B dies, the property passes to C. B holds the life estate, C holds the estate in remainder.

If the property is to be returned to the person who gave the life estate or to the heirs, that person is said to have an *estate in reversion.*

Example. In Figure 2-2, A deeds a life estate to B for B's life, with the provision that when B dies, the title reverts back to A. B holds a life estate; A holds the estate in reversion.

Another possibility is a *grant reserving* a *life estate.* Among life estates this is probably the most common.

Example. In Figure 2-3, A deeds title to B, but A reserves or keeps a life estate for the rest of A's life. Upon death of A possession and use passes to B.

Less-than-Freehold Estates

Less-than-freehold estates are interests held by *tenants* who rent or lease property. They are also called lessees, or leaseholders, and will be discussed in detail in Chapter 11, "Landlord and Tenant Relations."

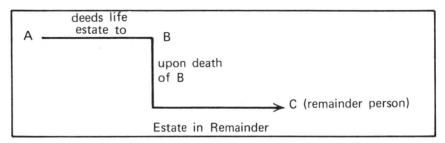

Figure 2-1

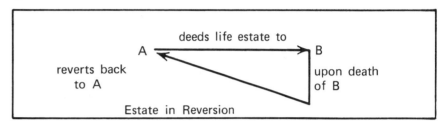

Figure 2-2

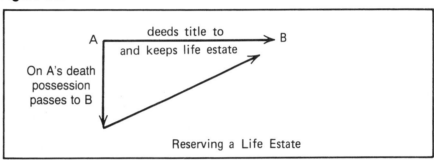

Figure 2-3

2.6 METHODS OF HOLDING TITLE

When persons acquire ownership of real property, they must decide how to hold title. Title may be held separately, or concurrently with someone else where two or more persons have ownership rights.

Ownership in Severalty

When a person receives real property individually and holds it solely in his or her own name, it is technically known as *ownership in severalty.* In other words, he or she alone enjoys the benefits of the property, including the rights expressed in the "bundle of rights" and is subject to any encumbrances on the property.

A person can hold title in severalty under any one of the following titles, depending upon the owner's legal status:

A single man	A married man
A single woman	A married woman
An unmarried man	A widower
An unmarried woman	A widow

If a person wishes to indicate separate property ownership, they can add the words "sole and separate property" to any of the above.

A corporation can hold title in severalty such as "Acme Company, a California Corporation."

Concurrent Ownership

Concurrent ownership is when two or more people hold title together. There are numerous types of concurrent ownership, but for our purposes the most important are: joint tenancy, tenancy in common, community property, and tenancy in partnership.

JOINT TENANCY

Joint tenancy exists when two or more persons are joint and equal owners of the same undivided interest in real property. In order to create a valid joint tenancy, four unities must exist:

1. *Unity of time.* This means that the owners must have acquired their interest at the same time.
2. *Unity of title.* This means that all owners must come into title on the same document. Consider this example: A and B are joint tenants. B sells her interest to C. A and C are tenants in common because they each took title on a different document at a different time.
3. *Unity of interest.* This means that all owners must have equal shares or interest in the property. For example, two owners each have one-half interest; four owners, each with one-quarter interest.
4. *Unity of possession.* This means that all owners must have equal rights of possession.

If any of these unities are missing, the joint tenancy is invalid, and the rules of tenancy in common will apply.

IMPORTANT CHARACTERISTICS

The most important characteristic of joint tenancy is the *right of survivorship*. This means that if one tenant dies, the surviving tenants acquire the deceased's interest without a court action.

Example.

1. A and B take title to property as joint tenants. B dies; A becomes the sole owner because of the right of survivorship.

2. A, B, and C take title to a property as joint tenants. C dies and her interest automatically passes to the survivors A and B. A and B are still joint tenants between each other, each owning a one-half interest in the property.

OTHER CHARACTERISTICS OF JOINT TENANCY

In addition to the unities of time, title, interest, and possession and the right of survivorship, joint tenancy has these characteristics:

1. You cannot will your interest in joint tenancy property.

2. All joint tenants must have equal shares.

3. Interest in the property is undivided. In other words, each owner can use every square foot, and he or she cannot say, "this is my half, and this is yours."

4. No probate procedure is required to distribute the interest upon the death of one of the owners. The interest goes to the surviving co-owners. However, there is some paperwork required to shift the remaining interest to the surviving joint tenant. But this paperwork is minor in comparison to a complete probate.

5. A joint tenant may sell or convey his or her interest without approval of the other tenant(s). This action may break the joint tenancy and create a tenancy in common.

   Example. A and B are joint tenants. B sells her interest to C. A and C are now tenants in common. Why? Because B selling to C violated the unities of time and title.

6. A corporation is not allowed to hold title as a joint tenant.

7. A surviving tenant acquires the interest of the deceased joint tenant, free from the debts created individually by the deceased joint tenant.

TENANCY IN COMMON   When two or more persons are owners of an undivided interest in property, they can hold title as *tenants in common*. Tenancy in common has these characteristics:

1. There is no right of survivorship, meaning that upon the death of a tenant in common, his or her interest passes to the heirs, *not the surviving co-tenants*. This requires a probate proceeding.

2. Each owner *may* hold an unequal interest—that is, he or she may own unequal shares.

   Example. A, B, C, and D hold title as tenants in common. These owners might share their interest as follows:

   A might own one-quarter interest

   B might own one-eighth interest

   C might own one-eighth interest

   D might own one-half interest

3. Each co-tenant may sell, convey, or encumber his or her interest without the consent of the co-tenants.

4. Each owner may will his or her interest to his or her heirs and upon death, the heirs take their place among the owners as tenants in common.

5. Each owner has equal rights of possession and must pay his or her share of the expenses, such as property taxes.

While living, any tenant in common may sell their share and the new owner becomes a tenant in common with the other owner or owners.

Example.   A and B are tenants in common, A dies and his interest passes to his heir, X. X and B will be tenants in common.

OR

A, B, and C are tenants in common. If C sells her interest to D, A, B, and D become tenants in common.

WHAT IF?

To test your understanding, answer the following questions:

1. A and B are joint tenants. If B dies, who gets what?

2. A and B are joint tenants. If B sells to C, what is the relationship between A and C?

3. A and B are tenants in common. If B dies, who gets what?

4. A and B and C are joint tenants. C sells his interest to D. What is the relationship between A and B and D?

Answers

1. B's interest passes to A who now holds title in severalty.

2. A and C are tenants in common.

3. A and the heirs of C are tenants in common.

4. A and B are joint tenants to each other and tenants in common with D.

TENANCY IN PARTNERSHIP

Tenancy in partnership exists when two or more persons, as partners, pool their interest, assets, and efforts in a business venture with each to share in the profits or the losses.

Tenancy in partnership has the following characteristics:

1. Each partner has an equal right with other partners to possession of specific partnership property for partnership purposes. Unless the other partners agree, however, one partner has no right of possession for any other purpose.

2. A partner's right in specific partnership property is not assignable

except in connection with the assignment of rights of all the partners in the same property.

3. A partner's right in specific partnership property is not subject to attachment or execution, except on a claim against the partnership.

4. There is a form of survivorship pertaining to this method of holding title.

Example. A and B own property, as partners. A dies, B receives title in trust until the disposition of the property. In other words, the title rests in the survivor *only* long enough to carry on the business *only* for the purpose of winding up the partnership affairs.

COMMUNITY PROPERTY

Community property ownership is another kind of ownership held by more than one person, but in this case it can only be held by a husband and wife. Community property is defined as all property acquired during a valid marriage.

California is a community property state. This means that property acquired by husband and wife after marriage is presumed to be community property. However, there are a few exceptions:

1. All property owned by husband or wife before marriage can remain *separate property* after marriage so long as the property is not commingled with community property causing it to lose its separate property identity.

2. All property acquired by either spouse during marriage by gift or inheritance remains separate property, so long as it is not commingled with community property.

3. All income and profits from separate property as well as any property acquired from the proceeds of separate property remains separate property as long as said income and profits are not commingled.

In effect, a husband and wife are general partners, each owning one-half of the community property. Each spouse has equal management and control of the community property. Neither spouse may convey or encumber real estate held as community property unless the other spouse also signs the contracts or documents involved.

Each spouse has the right to dispose of his or her half of the community property by will to whomever they wish. But if either spouse dies intestate, the surviving spouse receives all of the property. Death of one spouse involves a probate, but the probate process for community property has been streamlined and is not as long as a regular probate.

| **LEE MARVIN CASE** | In the Marvin *vs.* Marvin case, the California courts have held that unmarried persons who cohabitate may create property rights and obligations.
All the implications of this precedent-setting case will need further testing in the courts. It appears that couples who cohabitate in an unmarried state might need to discuss this situation with an attorney. They may find it advisable to reduce to contract form an agreement on how to handle previously owned property and property accumulated during cohabitation, in the event they should separate at a later date. |

SUMMARY

Freehold estates consist of *fee estates* and *life estates,* representing the rights of an *owner* of real property. Fee estates may be either *fee simple absolute* with no restrictions, or *fee simple qualified* with some limitations and restrictions. Life estates are granted for the life of one or more persons and may be a remainder type or a reversion type of life estate.

Ownership in severalty is when title is held in sole ownership. Concurrent ownership is when title is held by two or more persons. Common examples of concurrent ownership are joint tenancy, tenancy in in common, tenancy in partnership, and community property.

In California, property acquired by husband and wife during marriage is considered to be community property. Property acquired by either spouse before marriage or by inheritance or gift during marriage is treated as separate property unless it is commingled with the community property. Methods of holding title have important tax consequences that should be discussed with an attorney.

Important Terms and Concepts

Community property	Joint tenancy
Estate in remainder	Less-than-freehold estate
Estate in reversion	Life estate
Fee estate	Ownership in severalty
Fee simple absolute	Right of survivorship
Fee simple qualified	Separate property
Four unities of joint tenancy	Tenancy in common
Freehold estate	Tenancy in partnership

1. Which of the following statements is false?
   (a) The right of survivorship is present in a tenancy in common.
   (b) A life estate tenant is responsible for payment of the property tax.
   (c) A leasehold estate is a less-than-freehold estate.
   (d) Unity of possession is present in both joint tenancy and tenancy in common ownerships.

2. Which of the following terms do not belong together?
   (a) Joint tenancy—probate hearing
   (b) Tenancy in common—equal interest
   (c) Tenancy in common—severalty estate
   (d) All of the above do not belong together

3. Which of the following is considered to be a less-than-freehold estate?
   (a) Fee simple absolute
   (b) Life estate
   (c) Leasehold estate
   (d) Fee simple defeasible

4. The single most important characteristic of joint tenancy is:
   (a) Equal rights of use
   (b) Equal interest
   (c) Right of survivorship
   (d) Right to encumber

5. It is impossible for a corporation to hold title as a:
   (a) Trustee
   (b) Joint tenant
   (c) Tenants in common
   (d) California corporation

6. Which of the following is *not* one of the four unities of joint tenancy?
   (a) Time
   (b) Interest
   (c) Security
   (d) Title

7. A deeds a life estate to B; upon B's death, title is to pass to C. This is an example of a:
   (a) Perpetual estate
   (b) Less-than-freehold estate
   (c) Remainder estate
   (d) Fee simple estate

8. The term fee simple defeasible is best described in which statement?
   (a) Owner holds a title without limitations.
   (b) Owner holds a less-than-freehold estate.
   (c) Owner holds title subject to deed restrictions.
   (d) Owner holds an estate in remainder.

9. Smith and Jones are joint tenants; Jones sells his half of the property to Brown. Brown will take title with Smith as:
   (a) Joint tenants
   (b) Tenants in common
   (c) Ownership in severalty
   (d) Separate property

10. Community property is defined as property acquired by husband and wife:
    (a) Before marriage
    (b) After marriage
    (c) By either party, by gift or inheritance
    (d) Before or after marriage

Chapter 3
Encumbrances, Liens, and Homesteads

Preview In this chapter you will study money and non-money type encumbrances. The discussion of non-money encumbrances will center around easements, encroachments, and private and public restrictions.

Money encumbrances are defined as *liens*. The liens discussed will include mechanics' liens, tax liens, special assessment liens, attachments, and judgment liens.

In addition, the California homestead law will be presented whereby homeowners may protect their homes against a forced sale by certain types of creditors. At the conclusion of this chapter you will be able to:

1. *Define encumbrance, lien, easement, and encroachment.*

2. *Explain the difference between private deed restrictions and public restrictions.*

3. *Describe the key characteristics of mechanics' liens, tax liens, and judgment liens.*

4. *Discuss the details of the California homestead law.*

3.1. ENCUMBRANCES In real estate an *encumbrance* is anything that affects the title. In other words, any right or interest in the property possessed by someone else other than the owner is an encumbrance. Encumbrances affect the value of the owner's title. In short, an encumbrance is anything that burdens the title with legal obligations.

Encumbrances fall into two basic categories: non-money encumbrances and money encumbrances.

Non-Money Encumbrances Encumbrances that affect the physical condition of the property such as easements, public and private restrictions, and encroachments are called non-money encumbrances.

Easements An *easement* is a right to enter or use another person's property or a portion thereof within certain limitations without paying any rent or being considered a trespasser.

In California, the most common type of easement is a right of way, also called an easement for ingress (entering) and egress (exit) from the property.

Two important terms used in connection with this type of right of way are *dominant tenement* and *servient tenement.* The property that benefits from the easement (Property B in Figure 3-1) is described as the "dominant tenement." The property subject to the easement or upon which the easement is imposed (Property A in Figure 3-1) is described as the "servient tenement."

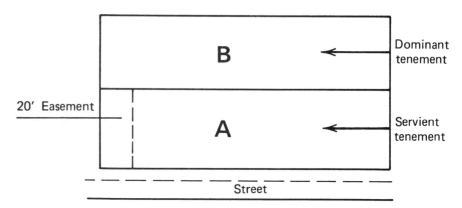

Figure 3-1

A right of way easement is usually designated as *nonexclusive,* meaning that when it is created it doesn't prevent the owner from using the land and that part covered by the easement.

In addition to the right to pass over another's property, other examples of easements include: rights to take water, wood, minerals, and other things; conducting sports upon the land; the right of receiving air, light, or heat from over, or discharging the same upon or over the land; or the right of using a wall as a party wall.

When an easement is attached to a dominant tenement, it is considered to be appurtenant or belonging to the land. Under the definition of real property is it considered part of real property and passes automatically as part of property in the event of a transfer. These easements are called *easement appurtenant.*

Some easements do not have a dominant tenement. They are known as *easement in gross.*

When a utility company wishes to erect poles or string wires over private lands, they obtain an easement in gross. Easements in gross do not benefit a parcel of land, but rather allow someone to pass over the land for a personal use, not to reach an adjoining parcel of land; therefore there is no dominant landowner.

Creation of Easements   Easements can be created in a number of ways. The most common are by: (1) deed, (2) necessity, (3) dedication, (4) condemnation, and (5) prescription.

BY DEED   Easements are not created orally. Rather, they are set forth in writing in the form of a written grant (such as a deed or contract). An easement must comply with the usual requirements of a deed, and be signed by the owner of the property (servient tenement) over which the easement lies. Examples: A grants an easement to B to cross A's property or A deeds title to B, but reserves an easement over B's property for A's use.

BY NECESSITY OR BY IMPLICATION   When a purchaser of a piece of property finds that he or she has no access to the street without passing over the property of another, the property is considered "landlocked." In this situation, the landlocked owner can appeal to the courts and ask for an easement over the portion of land, if any, the seller of the landlocked parcel may own. If the seller of the landlocked parcel does not have an adjoining parcel to cross over, the buyer of the landlocked parcel may be permanently landlocked. Also an easement can be implied. For example, A deeds a portion of land to B but fails to mention an easement. However there is an existing road. B has an implied right to use the road over A's property.

BY DEDICATION   An owner may voluntarily dedicate a portion of land for public access. Examples might include streets, access to the beach, and footpaths.

BY CONDEMNATION   Quite often an easement is created through condemnation. This means that government, as well as utility companies and railroads, may acquire an easement through condemnation proceedings known as eminent domain. The easement must be acquired for public use and the owner reimbursed for the value lost to the property.

BY PRESCRIPTION   An easement by prescription means that a person acquires an easement by use. In order to obtain an easement by prescription, a person must comply with four basic requirements:

1. A person must openly and notoriously use the land of another.

2. The easement use must be continuous and uninterrupted for five years.

3. The easement use must be hostile to the true owner's wishes, meaning without the owner's permission.

4. There must be a claim of right or color of title. This means the easement user must feel that he or she has some right to cross the land of another, or have a document that falsely purports to give the easement user an easement right.

Termination of an Easement

Easements may be terminated in several ways:

1. The most common method is by express release. The dominant tenement usually issues a quitclaim deed to the servient tenement owner, and that extinguishes the easement.

2. Another way easements can be terminated is by a court proceeding called a quiet title action.

3. When the same person becomes the owner of the dominant tenement and the servient tenement, the easement is terminated by merger of title.

4. The filing of a formal abandonment will terminate an easement.

5. A prescription easement may be terminated automatically by nonuse for a period of five years. However, termination by nonuse only applies to prescriptive easements, *not deeded* easements.

Other Types of Non-Money Encumbrances

In addition to easements, other examples of non-money type encumbrances are private deed restrictions, public restrictions, and encroachments.

PRIVATE DEED RESTRICTIONS

An owner of property may place in a deed certain restrictions or limits on the use of the property being sold. The restrictions will limit the use of the property to not only the new owner, but all subsequent owners.

These restrictions are often referred to as C,C, and R's, meaning covenants, conditions, and restrictions.

A *covenant* is a promise on the part of the individual accepting it to do or not to do certain things. If a grantee (buyer) violates a covenant, he or she has broken a promise and the grantor (seller) may institute court proceedings. The grantor may sue for dollar damages, or get an injunction against the grantee prohibiting continuation of the violation of restriction.

A *condition* is a restriction that places a limitation on the grantee's (buyer's) ownership. However, the main difference between a covenant and a condition is the degree of punishment if a violation occurs. If a condition is violated, it may give the grantor the right to demand the forfeiture of the grantee's title to the property.

Some restrictions are legal and some are not. A classic example of restrictions that are unethical, illegal, and unenforceable are those relating to racial discrimination.

Any discrimination based on race, color, creed, religion, national origin, sex, marital status, or physical handicap are prohibited by state and/or federal law. A detailed discussion of fair housing laws is contained in Chapter 12.

PUBLIC RESTRICTIONS   When the government imposes restrictions on property, they are called public restrictions.

Government using a provision called *police power* has the right to impose restrictions on the use of private property in order to protect the health, safety, morals, and welfare of its citizens.

Police power includes such public restrictions as:

1. Zoning regulations that dictate what type of land use may exist in given geographical areas.

2. Building codes that mandate rules and regulations governing quality construction.

3. Health codes to protect and regulate the public's quality of water and the effectiveness of sanitation systems.

ENCROACHMENTS   Another type of physical encumbrance is an encroachment. An *encroachment* is the wrongful construction of a building or improvement on or over the land of another.

Examples of possible encroachments are shown in Figure 3-2.

According to the Statute of Limitations, the party whose land is encroached upon has only three years in which to bring action for the removal of any such encroachment. If the owner allows the time limitation to run out, the owner runs the risk that the encroachment on the property may become permanent. However, some encroachments are above the ground, such as a neighbor's tree limb extending into your airspace. Above the ground encroachments have no statute of limitation and an action for removal can be brought at any time.

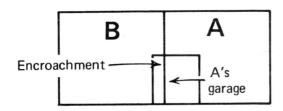

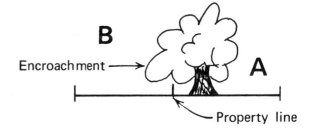

Figure 3-2

3.2 LIENS A *lien* is a money-encumbrance. It is a type of encumbrance where a specific property is held as security for the payment of a money debt.

Liens can be classified as voluntary, involuntary, general, or specific.

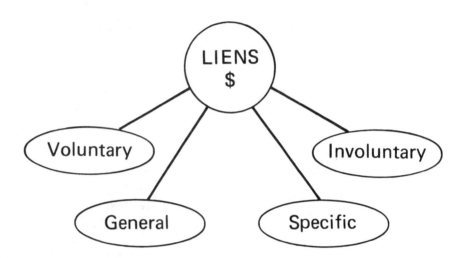

Voluntary Lien A *voluntary lien* is a lien which is freely accepted by the property owner. An example of voluntary liens would be a mortgage or a deed of trust, which an owner signs when obtaining a real estate loan. (Deeds of trust and mortgages will be discussed in detail in Chapter 7.)

Involuntary Lien *Involuntary liens* are liens which are imposed by law and which the owner does not freely accept. Examples of involuntary liens include mechanic's liens, tax liens, attachments, and judgment liens.

General Lien A lien which applies to all the property of an owner, unless exempt by law is a *general lien.* Examples of general liens include income tax and judgment liens.

Specific Lien A lien against a particular single piece of property is a *specific lien.* Examples of specific liens include mortgages, trust deeds, property taxes, and mechanic's liens.

Types of Liens
MECHANICS' LIENS Before discussing the details of this type of lien, we need to know what is meant by a "mechanic." A mechanic is anyone hired to do work that improves real property. In short, a *mechanic* is anyone who performs labor, bestows services, or furnishes material or equipment on a construction project. This will include: contractor, subcontractor, carpenters, plumbers, painters, plasterers, laborers, material and equipment suppliers, architects, and landscape gardeners as well as

those workers involved in demolition and removal of old buildings and grading and filling of land.

The California state constitution allows any qualified mechanic who does not receive payment to file a lien against the specific property upon which work was done.

The mechanic's lien must be based on a valid contract, written or verbal, between the claimant and the owner, or owner's general contractor. The mechanic's lien law is based on the theory that improvements contribute additional value to the land; therefore, the property's owner should be held responsible for wages and materials.

The key provisions of the mechanic's lien law are illustrated below.

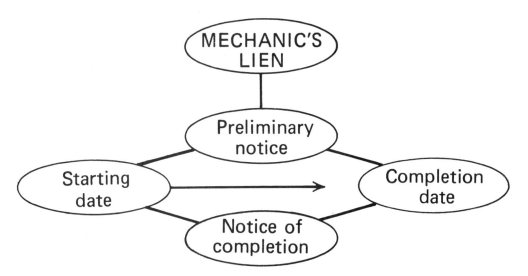

Preliminary Notice   The law requires that every mechanic or material supplier must give written notice to the owner, general contractor, and the construction lender, if there is one, of their right to file a lien against the property, if they are not paid. This notice should be served within *20 days* of the first furnishing of labor, services, equipment or material to the jobsite.

Failure to give the preliminary notice within 20 days does not preclude the right to give a preliminary notice at a later time, but the mechanic's claim rights may be subordinated to other claims.

Starting Date   In order to create a valid mechanic's lien claim, the law requires that the lien must be recorded within a specified period of time after completion of the project. The law has determined the following situations to be equivalent to completion:

1. Owner occupies the property and work stops.

2. Owner accepts the work as being completed; files a document called a *notice of completion.*

3. Work on the project ceases for a continuous 60-day period.

4. Work ceases for a continuous period of 30 days or more and owner files a *notice of cessation.*

Notice of Completion

A *notice of completion,* if filed by the owner, must show the date of the completion, name and address of the owner, the nature of the interest or estate of the owner, a description of the property, and the name of the contractor if any.

To be valid, a notice of completion must be recorded within *10 days* after the completion of the project.

Statutory Time Period

There are two situations that establish time periods for filing liens.

1. If the owner files a notice of completion, the original contractor has *60 days* in which to file a lien, all others have *30 days.*

2. If no notice of completion is filed or if the notice is invalid, all parties, including the contractors and subcontractors have *90 days* to file their liens.

Termination of a Mechanic's Lien

1. A mechanic's lien is terminated when the debt has been paid, either by voluntary action or by forced foreclosure sale.

2. A mechanic's lien is automatically terminated if the mechanic fails to institute a court foreclosure within 90 days after filing the mechanic's lien. In other words, once a mechanic's lien is recorded, a mechanic has only 90 days to bring foreclosure action. If mechanics wait more than 90 days, they lose their rights to foreclosure upon the property. They still can personally sue the owner for the amount owed but cannot foreclose the mechanics' lien and force the sale of the home.

Notice of Nonresponsibility

If a tenant orders work on a property without the landlord's approval, can the landlord be held responsible for any unpaid work? The answer is *yes.* However, a landlord can protect himself against mechanic's liens due to work ordered by a tenant if the landlord files a *notice of nonresponsibility.*

This must be done within ten days of the date of discovery of the work being done. It is accomplished by recording a copy of a notice of nonresponsibility in the county recorder's office and posting a notice on the property. This gives the workers notice that the owner will not be financially responsible for the work project and therefore the workers must look to the tenant for payment.

Priority of Claim

When a mechanic's lien is placed against a given piece of property, its priority over a construction loan will be determined by the beginning date of the project. The law states that even though a mechanic's lien is recorded after a construction loan is recorded, the mechanic's lien is given priority if any work had been done or materials furnished prior to recording the construction loan.

Ordinarily when loans are made for construction, the title insurance company will inspect the property to make sure no work has been done or materials delivered before allowing the lender to advance construction funds.

If there are multiple mechanics' liens against a property, they all share on a parity with each other. This means that the first mechanic to record a lien *does not* have a superior right over the second mechanic's lien and so on. If there are multiple mechanics' liens and the property is sold for lien payments, each mechanic receives a share of the proceeds based on their prorata share of the work.

Summary of Mechanics' Liens Dates

1. Preliminary notice should be given within *20 days* of beginning of work.

2. If the owner files a *notice of completion* within *ten days* of completion of the project:
   a. original contractors have *60 days* to file
   b. all others have *30 days* to file

3. If the owner *does not* file a notice of completion or if the notice is invalid, all mechanic's have *90 days* to file from the day work was finished.

4. Once a valid mechanic's lien is filed, the mechanic must bring a court foreclosure action within *90 days* to enforce the lien.

5. A notice of nonresponsibility must be filed by the landlord within *10 days* of the discovery of work ordered by a tenant.

TAX LIENS

The purpose of taxation is to provide money to cover government expenses. A tax lien arises when a person does not pay taxes when due and their property is encumbered to ensure payment.

Tax liens may include:

1. Unpaid real property taxes.

2. Unpaid federal income taxes.

3. Unpaid state inheritance taxes.

4. Unpaid gift taxes.

Taxes and their consequence are covered in detail in Chapter 13. The point to stress here is that government has the power to levy taxes. If the taxpayer refuses to pay the levy, the government has the right to place a lien against the taxpayer's property and foreclose upon the property for back taxes.

SPECIAL ASSESSMENT

Special assessments are levied against all property owners in a district. The basic purpose is to defray the cost of specific local improvements, such as streets, sewers, schools, and so on. Even though assessments are usually paid with property taxes, they differ in that property taxes are a general tax levied to pay general government expenses, while assessments are for a single purpose. If a person refuses to pay their assessment, government and/or bondholders can foreclose upon the assessee's property. Special assessments will be discussed later in Chapter 13.

ATTACHMENTS AND JUDGMENTS

An *attachment* is a legal process whereby property, personal or real, is seized pending the outcome of a court action. A *judgment* is a decision of the court as a result of a lawsuit. A judgment is the final determination of the rights of the parties involved in a court proceeding.

The purpose of the attachment is to have the property of the defendant available to satisfy a judgment in favor of the plaintiff. In some cases it may take several months before the case is tried and a judgment is issued. In that time an unscrupulous defendant might secretly sell or give away his or her property making it impossible to satisfy the judgment.

Under an attachment, the seizure and holding of the property is merely symbolic. The defendant may still keep the property, but a notice is posted on the property and the attachment is recorded. The attachment remains a lien upon all real property attached, three days from date of levy. However, so much property is exempt from attachment, such as personal residence, most of the debtor's wages, and so on, that the use of an attachment has declined in recent years. Instead of seeking an attachment, many creditors go directly for a judgment.

A judgment (court decision) does not automatically create a lien on real property. In order for a judgment to become a lien, an abstract of the judgment (summary of the judgment) must be recorded with the county recorder. It then becomes a general lien on all real property located in the county in which the abstract is recorded.

The judgment lien normally runs for ten years and any real property acquired during the ten-year period automatically becomes encumbered by the judgment lien. The abstract of judgment may be recorded in any number of California counties. If a creditor wishes to tie up anything a debtor might own in California, the creditor can record the abstract of judgment in all 58 counties. Abstracts of judgments from California courts cannot normally be recorded in other states. It takes a separate court proceeding in each state.

WRIT OF EXECUTION

In order to collect a judgment the creditor will request a *writ of execution.* The court will then order the sheriff to seize and sell the property to satisfy the judgment. A public auction is then held and the property is sold to the highest bidder.

In the event that the judgment is paid before the sale, the judgment creditor issues to the judgment debtor a *satisfaction of judgment.* When this notice is recorded, the judgment is released and lien lifted from the property.

3.3 HOMESTEAD LAW   The California homestead law is designed to protect a homeowner's equity in a personal residence from forced sale by certain types of creditors. The term homestead means personal dwelling and should not be confused with the federal homestead laws of early American history, whereby the government gave away land to encourage settlement.

Requirements   There are certain essentials that must be observed in the filing of a homestead exemption. If these rules are not followed, the homestead is void.

1. A homestead must be recorded to be valid. A homestead declaration must be recorded in the recorder's office showing that the claimant is a head of family, if such is the case, or when the declaration is made by the wife, that the husband has not made such declaration and that she, therefore, makes it for their joint benefit. In addition to a husband or wife, the state liberally interprets a "head of family" to be just about any relative living in the home.

2. The homestead statement must declare that the claimant is residing on the premises and claims this as a homestead.

3. The homestead statement must include a description of the premises. The dwelling house may be a single- or multiple-family dwelling, a condominium, a stock cooperative, a community apartment project, a mobile home, or a yacht. Any owner-occupied residential property can be used, but the owner may only have one homestead exemption at a time.

Protection Afforded   When the declaration of a homestead is properly completed and recorded, the head of the household is entitled to an exemption protection of $75,000 (person 65 or over, $100,000)*, while any other person may have an exemption of $50,000. These exemption figures do not reflect the actual value of the property. The homestead exemption is intended to protect the *equity* the owner has in the property.

When the courts rule that a home has too much equity and therefore is to be sold to satisfy the debts of the homeowner, the owner retains the exemption portion and the creditor is awarded the difference.

Example.
Homestead Property A

	$100,000	home
	− 90,000	loan
	$ 10,000	equity

This home *cannot be sold* by judgment creditors as the equity is within the homestead exemption.

Homestead Property B

	$50,000	home
	-0-	loan
	$50,000	equity

*Certain low income homeowners 55 years or over also have $100,000 maximum. These homestead amounts became effective 1/1/91.

This home *can be sold* by judgment creditors as the equity exceeds the homestead exemption. However, the homeowner (debtor) is allowed to keep the amount of the exemption and the creditor only gets the excess.

$50,000	Equity
−45,000	exemption to head of family homeowner
$ 5,000	excess to creditor

The proceeds from any forced sale will be allocated in the following order:

1. To the discharge of all prior liens and encumbrances, if any.

2. To the homestead claim, the amount of the exemption.

3. To the satisfaction of the execution.

4. To the homestead claimant if there is a balance.

The Six-Month Rule

In the event that the owner voluntarily wishes to sell to move to another home or if the owner is forced to sell the home to satisfy an execution and the homeowner's equity is converted to cash, the homestead law applies what is known as the *six-month rule.*

The owner has six months in which to invest this equity money in a new home. The homeowner may then file a homestead on the new home and thereby continue to protect the equity against creditors.

> Remember, the law states that a party cannot have more than one homestead at the same time, and a homestead can only be placed on owner occupied residential property.

Homesteads Protection

Homesteads protect against forced sale of the family home due to bankruptcy and execution of judgments as long as the homestead is properly filed and the equity in the home does not exceed the homestead exemption.

Homesteads do not protect against forced sale of the family home due to mortgage or trust deed foreclosures and mechanic's liens. Even if the homestead is recorded *before* the trust·deed and mechanic's lien, a homestead *never defeats* a trust deed or mechanic's lien.

Termination of Homestead

A homestead may be terminated in either of two ways:

1. The owner may sell the home which automatically terminates a homestead. On the other hand, the homestead will not be terminated if the owner merely moves out and rents the home. The rule is that a property must be owner-occupied at the time of filing the homestead. An owner can later move and rent the property and still have a valid homestead.

2. The homeowner who has filed a declaration of homestead can terminate a homestead by filing a notice of abandonment. If one spouse dies, the homestead stays in force for the surviving spouse. A dissolution of marriage will not terminate a homestead if one spouse remains in possession of the title. However, if death or divorce results in only one occupant, the exemption will be reduced from $75,000 to $50,000 unless the person is 65 years or older, or 55 years and low income. Then the exemption remains $100,000.

SUMMARY

Encumbrances are burdens on title which can be either physical or money encumbrances. Physical (non-money) encumbrances include easements, private and public restrictions, and encroachments. Money encumbrances are called liens and they include mechanic's liens, tax liens, judgment liens, mortgages, and deeds of trust.

An easement is the right to use another's land, with the most common easement being a right of way for ingress and egress. Easements are created by deed, implication, necessity, dedication, condemnation, and prescription. They may be removed by deed, court action, merger of title, filing an abandonment, or nonuse for five years in the case of prescriptive easements.

Private restrictions placed in a deed are known as C,C, and R's, which stand for covenants, conditions, and restrictions. Public restrictions such as zoning, building codes, health regulations, and so on, are imposed by governments.

An encroachment is the wrongful extension of a building or improvement on or over the land of another. There are statutory time periods in which an owner must sue to force removal.

Liens (money encumbrances) may be voluntary or involuntary and may be general or specific. Mechanic's liens are involuntary liens that may be placed upon a property by anyone who performs labor or provides a service on a construction project, in order to guarantee that they are paid for their services. Starting dates and completion dates are extremely important, and the law specifies the exact time limits involved in carrying out a mechanics' lien right.

Judgments are considered general liens and may attach all property owned by the debtor in the county in which the abstract of judgment is filed. An abstract of judgment creates a lien for ten years on real estate located within the county where the judgment is recorded.

The homestead exemption law provides a limited amount of protection in the event a judgment is obtained against a homeowner. If properly completed and recorded, the head of a household is entitled to a $75,000 exemption (person 65 or over, $100,000), while a person under 65 years receives $50,000. A homestead can only be declared on owner-occupied residential property and only one homestead can be held at a time. Homesteads can be terminated by selling the property or filing a declaration of abandonment.

Important Terms and Concepts

Attachment

Covenants, conditions, and restrictions

Dominant tenement

Easement appurtenant

Encroachment

Encumbrance

Homestead

Judgment

Lien

Mechanic's lien

Notice of completion

Notice of nonresponsibility

Servient tenement

Writ of execution

REVIEWING YOUR UNDERSTANDING

1. An easement on a parcel of land may be removed from the records by one of the following:
   (a) Reconveyance deed
   (b) An unlawful detainer action
   (c) Recording a quitclaim deed executed by the user of the easement
   (d) A lis pendens action

2. Materials were delivered to a building site for the construction of a commercial building. In order to be sure of collection for the cost of the material the supplier should file a:
   (a) Homestead declaration
   (b) Preliminary notice
   (c) Surety bond
   (d) A subordination lien

3. The terms ingress and egress have reference to:
   (a) Utilities
   (b) Streams
   (c) Encroachments
   (d) Easements

4. An easement is defined as:
   (a) A general lien on real property
   (b) An encumbrance on real property
   (c) An equitable restriction on real property
   (d) A specific lien on real property

5. A homestead can be declared invalid in all of the following ways except:
   (a) By renting property
   (b) By making untrue statements in the declaration
   (c) Selling the property
   (d) Filing an abandonment of homestead

6. When a property owner discovers that a neighbor has built a fence on a portion of his or her property, how long does the property owner have to bring an action against the neighbor?
(a) Six months
(b) Two years
(c) Three years
(d) Indefinitely

7. A mechanic's lien can be filed and recorded for the benefit of:
(a) Painters
(b) Subcontractors
(c) Material suppliers
(d) All of these

8. Which of the following documents does not have to be recorded to be valid?
(a) Mechanic's lien
(b) Deed
(c) Homestead declaration
(d) None of the above needs be recorded to be valid

9. One way of acquiring an easement is by prescription. Which of the following would *not* be one of the requirements for the creation of this type of easement?
(a) Pay property taxes for five years
(b) Hostile to the true owner's wishes
(c) Open and notorious use
(d) Under some right of claim or color of title

10. When a plaintiff takes a case to court and a judgment is rendered against the defendant, in order to create a lien on the defendant's property, the instrument that is recorded would be:
(a) A writ of attachment
(b) An abstract of judgment
(c) A writ of execution
(d) A lis pendens action

Chapter 4
Real Estate Agency

Preview   Agency is an important concept in real estate. This chapter defines agency, discusses the creation of agencies, and analyzes the duties and responsibilities of real estate agents. When you have completed this chapter you will be able to:

1. *Define agency and then list the three ways in which agencies are created.*
2. *Discuss the fiduciary relationship that exists between a principal and a real estate agent.*
3. *List and give examples of several real estate agency violations.*
4. *Describe the agency differences between salespersons and brokers.*
5. *Explain how agents are regulated by government and professional trade associations.*
6. *List and give examples of six ways in which real estate agencies are terminated.*

4.1 AGENCY   The California Civil Code defines agency as "the representation of another person called a principal, by an agent, in dealings with third persons." An agent, therefore, is empowered to represent a principal in negotiating with a third party for the principal's benefit.

Agencies are not required by law. However, due to the complexity of business and for convenience, principals frequently prefer to have experts represent them in transactions. Examples of agents are travel agents, insurance agents, and real estate agents.

There are two broad categories of agency. The first category is called *general agency* and the second is called *special agency.* A general agent is one who has broad powers to act on behalf of the principal. A special agent has limited or well-defined powers, perhaps confined to a single transaction. Most real estate agencies are special in nature, with powers normally limited to the sale of a specific property.

REAL ESTATE AGENCY

Principal — Seller — Appoints → Agent — Real Estate Broker — To find → Third Party — Buyer

Employer-Employee and Independent Contractor Distinctions

A real estate agency differs from an employer-employee pact. It also differs from an independent contractor relationship.

An employer-employee relationship exists when an individual is hired by another to perform certain services under the strict supervision of the employer. The degree of direction over the individual hired is important in determining whether that individual is an employee or an independent contractor.

For example, assume that Jones hired Brown to perform office work. Jones requires that Brown work from 9:00 A.M. to 5:00 P.M. Monday through Friday. Jones carefully supervises the method in which Brown performs work duties. Further, Jones provides fringe benefits and deducts money from Brown's paycheck each week for income taxes and social security. Under these circumstances Brown is clearly an employee, and an employer-employee relationship exists.

An independent contractor relationship exists when an individual is hired to accomplish results with little or no supervision required. Assume that Jones hires West to perform janitorial services for an office. Jones pays West a fixed amount of money per month and does not supervise West. West is free to clean the office at a self-determined pace and at his or her own time schedule, provided it is after business hours. Further, Jones does not provide fringe benefits and does not take deductions for social security or income taxes. West, under these circumstances, is an independent contractor and not an employee.

A real estate agency differs from both an employer-employee relationship and an independent contractor relationship. Whereas an employee works for an employer, and is under the control of the employer for all work activities, a real estate agent's activities are not under the complete control of a principal. For example, most sellers do not tell a real estate broker when to open the real estate office, when to take a lunch hour, or when to return home!

A real estate agency is also different from an independent contractor relationship in that the agent is not free to do anything to achieve a sale. An agent must respect the lawful instructions of the principal. For example, a seller engages a real estate agent to find a buyer under certain *terms* and *conditions* which the agents must do to receive a commission.

Creation of Real Estate Agencies

Agencies are created in three ways: by *agreement,* by *ratification,* or by *estoppel.*

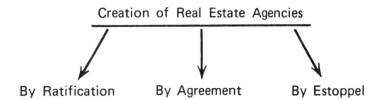

Creation of Real Estate Agencies

By Ratification   By Agreement   By Estoppel

Special Test Note

Sometimes agency test questions ask the difference between an *actual* agent and an *ostensible* agent. An actual agent is appointed by a principal orally or in writing; an ostensible agent is appointed via a principal's actions rather than words.

By far, the greatest number of real estate agencies are created by agreement. The principal (usually the seller) orally, in writing, or by their mutual actions, appoints a real estate agent. The authorization to sell (listing agreement) is the document most frequently used to appoint real estate agents. The authorization to sell specifies the powers delegated to the agent, the terms and conditions of the proposed sale of the property, and the circumstances under which a brokerage commission is earned, as well as the brokerage amount. As outlined in Chapter 5, there are different types of listing agreements and each has different powers of agency.

The second method of creating an agency is by ratification. Under this concept no agency is currently in existence; however, a series of events then occur which creates an agency relationship. In other words, an unauthorized agent performs a service on your behalf of which you were unaware. Upon learning of the service which turns out to be beneficial, you accept the responsibility for the agent's act. As an example, assume that Smith, a real estate broker, approaches Johnson with an offer from a buyer to buy Johnson's store when Johnson had not previously considered selling the store. Johnson likes the price and terms and decides that it would be advantageous to sell the property. By accepting the offer and agreeing to pay a commission, Johnson has created an agency with broker Smith. In essence, Johnson ratified broker Smith's unauthorized actions by accepting the buyer's offer.

The third method of creating an agency is by estoppel. Estoppel is the situation where an individual knowingly allows another person to purport to be his or her agent when in fact an agent has not been appointed. If an innocent third party is later damaged because of this action, the owner may not be able to deny that an agency exists. An example would be an owner who allows a real estate broker to pretend that the broker is the owner's agent. The broker solicits a buyer, who relying upon the broker's statements, borrows money to purchase the owner's property. If the owner refuses to sell stating that "the broker is not my agent" the owner may be   stopped or prevented from denying that an agency existed.

Fiduciary Relationship

When a real estate agent is appointed by the principal (seller) to represent the seller in negotiations with a buyer, a *fiduciary relation-*

ship is established. This relationship is one of trust and loyalty and obligates the agent to act in the principal's best interest. It is probably the agent's most important duty. An agent cannot act in a manner which is detrimental to this fiduciary relationship. The agent cannot (1) profit from the agency without the consent of the principal, (2) must obey all lawful instructions of the principal, and (3) may not discriminate in the rental or sale of real property. Virtually all real estate agencies exist between the seller (principal) and the agent. Therefore, an agent is bound to do the very best for the seller which includes trying to get the best price and terms for the property.

Aside from price and terms, however, the agent owes a degree of allegiance to the buyer. The agent must be honest and truthful and disclose any known defects in the property. Above all else, an agent must not misrepresent the property to a prospective buyer.

Although rarely done, a buyer may appoint a real agent and pay a fee to that agent to find property for the buyer. Under these circumstances the agent is bound to reveal this fact to the seller.

A real estate agent may represent and collect a fee from both the buyer and seller in a transaction. This is called *dual agency* or *divided agency.* However, the agent must disclose this fact to each of the principals before collecting said fees. (See *Dual Agency* box on the left.)

A real estate agent may assign some of his or her duties to other agents. This occurs when the real estate agent cooperates with other agents, called *subagents,* in attempting to seek purchasers for the property. The approval of the principal is required if subagents are also to work on the property. The same fiduciary relationship exists between subagents and principal as exists between the real estate agent and the principal. Subagents are required to try to get the best price and terms for the seller even if they are from another brokerage office and they have secured a buyer independently. Likewise, subagents must be honest and truthful and not misrepresent the property to buyers.

4.2 SOME AGENCY VIOLATIONS

There are several hundred thousand real estate licensees in California. The percentage of these licensees who violate agency laws is very small. Of those who are disciplined, most have committed violations unintentionally or through ignorance. Through education, examination, and on-the-job training, real estate licensees learn their duties and responsibilities and therefore reduce the possibility of agency violations. The following, from the Department of Real Estate *Reference Book,* are examples of types of agency violations. The appropriate sections of the Real Estate Law are cited as a reference.

Misrepresentation. Section 10176(a). Many complaints received by the real estate commissioner allege misrepresentation on the part of

Multi-State Sale

Problem: A California broker wants to sell a property in another state where the California agent is not licensed.

Solution: The California broker cooperates with a licensed broker in that particular state. Both parties may then share the commission.

the broker or salesperson. This includes not only what was said but also the failure of a broker or salesperson to disclose a material fact about the property. Can a real estate agent withhold information about a defect in the property? No, failure to disclose is a type of misrepresentation!

False promise. Section 10176(b). A false promise and a misrepresentation are not the same thing. A misrepresentation is a false statement of fact. A false promise is a false statement about what the promisor is going to do in the future. To prove false promise, the injured party must show that the promise was impossible of performance and that the person making the promise knew it to be impossible. An example might be, "Buy this home and it will double in value in six weeks!"

Continued misrepresentation. Section 10176(c). This section gives the commissioner the right to discipline a licensee for "a continued and flagrant course of misrepresentation or making a false promise through real estate agents or salespersons."

Divided agency. Section 10176(d). This section requires a licensee to inform all principals if the licensee is acting as agent for more than one party in a transaction. An example is the licensee who receives a selling commission from the owner of a piece of property and, at the same time, receives an additional fee from the buyer without the knowledge of both.

Commingling. Section 10176(e). Commingling takes place when a broker has mixed the funds of principals with the broker's own moneys. To prevent commingling, most real estate brokers establish a trust fund account at a bank and the funds of a principal are deposited into this account. *Conversion* is not the same thing as commingling. Conversion is misappropriating and using the client's money. This is a crime that carries a jail sentence.

Definite termination date. Section 10176(f). This section of the law requires a specified termination date for all exclusive contracts between a real estate agent and a principal relating to transactions for which a real estate license is required. What is a definite termination date has been the subject of a number of lawsuits. Generally, it can be said that if a definite date is specified in the contract or if a definite period of time is indicated, the requirement is satisfied. However, where it cannot be determined from the exclusive listing contract when the listing is to expire, then the real estate agent may be in violation of the law.

Secret profit. Section 10176(g). Secret profit cases usually arise when the broker, who already has a higher offer from another buyer, makes a low offer, usually through a "dummy" purchaser. The difference is the secret profit. Many attorneys contend that an agent is guilty of secret profit if the real estate agent derives any profit other than the agreed commission without disclosing the nature of the profits to the principal.

Listing—option. Section 10176(h). This section requires a licensee who has used a form which is both an option and a listing to inform the principal of the amount of profit the licensee will make and to obtain the written consent of the principal approving the amount of such profit, before the licensee may exercise the option. This section does not apply where a licensee is using an option only.

The reason for this requirement in the law is that a licensee, acting as an agent, occupies a highly confidential position of a fiduciary nature. The law imposes upon an agent the responsibility to do nothing which will act to the detriment of the principal, and to keep the principal informed of any fact of which the principal should be aware. This section is provided to prevent unauthorized profits by requiring the broker to give the principal full information.

Other possible violations include dishonest dealing, obtaining license by fraud, false advertising, conviction of crime, negligence, misuse of trade name, inducement of panic selling, plus many others.

Recovery Fund

The State of California has a unique program whereby the public can recover money when there are uncollectable court judgments obtained against a real estate licensee on the basis of fraud, misrepresentation, deceit, or conversion of trust funds in a transaction. Called the Recovery Fund, this program is financed using a portion of real estate licensing fees. The maximum amount of money a person may receive from the fund is currently limited (1988) to $20,000 per individual claim, up to a $100,000 maximum for multiple claims against any one real estate licensee.

Responsibilities of Principals to Agents and Buyers

Agency is a two-way street. As real estate agents have responsibilities to principals, so also do principals owe certain responsibilities to agents. A principal should advise the real estate agent of any defects of the property so that the agent may disclose the defects to a prospective buyer. Similarly, a seller should not withhold pertinent information from the agent nor should the seller distort facts about the property. See Chapter 5, Seller Disclosure Statement Requirements.

Sellers usually enter into a contract (listing agreement) to have an agent sell their property. Those contracts should be honored and commissions should be paid when the property is sold. Sellers should not deal directly with prospective purchasers to evade the payment of a commission.

> *Note:* For a discussion on trust funds and the agent's responsibility for handling a client's money, see Appendix C, Chapter 15.

"AS IS SALE"

This brings up the concept of an "as is sale." While an "as is" sale is legal, laws and regulations require that the buyer must be fully informed as to the condition of the property including any known defects before the buyer becomes bound by a purchase contract. If the buyer is fully informed and still wishes to proceed with the sale, then an "as is" transaction is permissible. "Caveat emptor" the old Latin phrase meaning "let the buyer beware" is no longer a defense in court in real estate transaction. If a seller withholds material facts about the property, such as structural defects known to the seller, the seller can be sued by the buyer.

PIECE OF THE PIE

Commission

"I want a real estate license so I will be able to get a share of the commission when I buy and sell my own properties."

There are people who do not wish to become real estate agents to serve the public, but want a license to deal for their own account.

Is this a good idea? The answer is not clear-cut—it depends!

When a licensee buys and sells real estate as a principal, regulations require the licensee to disclose to the opposite party that they have a real estate license. Sometimes sellers and/or buyers refuse to deal with licensees as principals for fear that the licensee will take advantage of them.

In some cases the seller will allow the licensee-buyer a portion of the commission. However, there have been cases where the seller absolutely refused to allow the listing broker to share the commission with a buyer-licensee. Also, a person who speculates in real estate as a licensee may have some income tax problems that would not occur if the investor was unlicensed and used the services of a real estate agent.

4.3 REGULATIONS OF BROKERS AND SALESPERSONS

Real Estate Broker Versus Salesperson

While both brokers and salespersons are licensed by the state of California Department of Real Estate, a salesperson's license is valid only when under the employ of a real estate broker. It is through this employment with an agent (the broker) that a salesperson becomes an agent. Therefore, only a real estate broker can contract directly with a principal. A real estate salesperson must use the broker's name when signing a listing agreement with a seller. (Requirements to become a real estate agent are discussed in detail in Chapter 15.)

Considered an employee of the broker by the state, a real estate salesperson is usually in an independent contractor status with the broker for other purposes such as income tax, social security, and so on. The broker has strict responsibilities to supervise the activities of real estate salespersons. For example, a broker must date and initial listing and purchase contracts procured by the salesperson within five business days. In other matters, however, the broker usually treats the salesperson as an independent contractor and does not require the salesperson to be at work at certain hours, or so on. The salesperson is responsible for final results, not the method used to attain the results.

By law, real estate salespersons are required to have a written employment contract with their broker. Commission details between the broker and salesperson should also be in writing. A real estate salesperson can receive compensation only from his or her broker. When escrow is closed the escrow company sends the entire commission to the employing broker who in turn writes separate checks to the salesperson for his or her share.

Violation of agency law by a real estate salesperson may subject the salesperson to disciplinary action and may also be a cause for disciplinary action against the employing broker who by law is responsible for certain of the salesperson's acts.

Regulation of Real Estate Agents

Real estate agents are regulated by government and professional trade associations. The California real estate commissioner, using the employees of the California Department of Real Estate, is empowered to enforce the real estate law and to issue regulations which are enforced in the same manner as law.

(See Chapter 15, page 281 for details regarding Real Estate Commissioner's regulation of licensees.)

Commissioner's Code of Ethics

The California Real Estate Commissioner has established, by regulations, a Code of Ethics that applies to all real estate licensees. The Code of Ethics lists examples of unethical behavior by real estate licensees and requires that licensees refrain from such behavior. In addition, the Code of Ethics outlines positive steps real estate licensees can undertake to improve the public's image of a real estate agent. The commissioner's Code of Ethics can be found in Appendix B, Chapter 15.

Filing Complaints

If a person wishes to file a complaint about a real estate agent, the procedure is to send a written complaint to the real estate commissioner. The commissioner then assigns the complaint to a deputy for investigation. Statements about the incident are taken from witnesses and the licensee. In addition the real estate agent's records and accounts may be audited. An informal conference may be called to allow the investigating deputy to determine the seriousness of the complaint. If a violation of the law has occurred, a formal hearing is called and the agent's license may be suspended or revoked. Every year the commissioner receives several thousand complaints about real estate licensees, but after an investigation, a majority are dismissed as not being in violation of real estate law or regulations.

Trade Associations

There are several national, state, and local professional real estate trade associations, such as the National Association of Realtors and the National Association of Real Estate Brokers.

The role of trade associations is presented in detail in Chapter 15.

BROKER - SALESPERSON CONTRACT

(INDEPENDENT CONTRACTOR)

CALIFORNIA ASSOCIATION OF REALTORS® STANDARD FORM

THIS AGREEMENT, made this ___First___ day of ___January___ , 19_9-_ , by and between

___Samuel L. Broker_____ hereinafter referred to as Broker and_____

___Amy W. Salesperson_____ hereinafter referred to as Salesperson,

WITNESSETH:

WHEREAS, Broker is duly licensed as a real estate broker by the State of California, and

WHEREAS, Broker maintains an office, properly equipped with furnishings and other equipment necessary and incidental to the proper operation of business, and staffed suitably to serving the public as a real estate broker, and

WHEREAS, Salesperson is now engaged in business as a real estate licensee, duly licensed by the State of California.

NOW, THEREFORE, in consideration of the premises and the mutual agreements herein contained, it is understood and agreed as follows:

1. Broker agrees, at Salesperson's request, to make available to Salesperson all current listings in the office, except such as Broker may choose to place in the exclusive possession of some other Salesperson. In addition, at Salesperson's discretion and at Salesperson's request Broker may, from time to time, supply Salesperson with prospective listings; Salesperson shall have absolute discretion in deciding upon whether to handle and the method of handling any such leads suggested by Broker. Nothing herein shall be construed to require that Salesperson accept or service any particular listing or prospective listing offered by Broker; nor shall Broker have any right or authority to direct that Salesperson see or service particular parties, or restrict Salesperson's activities to particular areas. Broker shall have no right, except to the extent required by law, to direct or limit Salesperson's activities as to hours, leads, open houses, opportunity or floor time, production, prospects, reports, sales, sales meeting, schedule, services, inventory, time off, training, vacation, or other similar activities.

At Salesperson's request and at Salesperson's sole discretion Broker agrees to furnish such advice, information and full cooperation as Salesperson shall desire. Broker agrees that thereby Broker obtains no authority or right to direct or control Salesperson's actions except as specifically required by law (including Business and Professions Code Section 10177 (h)) and that Salesperson assumes and retains discretion for methods, techniques and procedures in soliciting and obtaining listings and sales, rentals, or leases of listed property.

2. Broker agrees to provide Salesperson with use, equally with other Salespersons, of all of the facilities of the office now operated by Broker in connection with the subject matter of this contract, which office is now maintained at ___507 Main Street,_____ ___Somewhere, California 95500_____ .

3. Until termination hereof, Salesperson agrees to work diligently and with Salesperson's best efforts to sell, lease or rent any and all real estate listed with Broker, to solicit additional listings and customers, and otherwise promote the business of serving the public in real estate transactions to the end that each of the parties hereto may derive the greatest profit possible, provided that nothing herein shall be construed to require that Salesperson handle or solicit particular listings, or to authorize Broker to direct or require that Salesperson to do so. Salesperson assumes and agrees to perform no other activities in association with Broker, except to solicit and obtain listings and sales, rentals, or leases of property for the parties' mutual benefit, and to do so in accordance with law and with the ethical and professional standards as required in paragraph 4 below.

4. Salesperson agrees to commit no act of a type for which the Real Estate Commissioner of the State of California is authorized by Section 10176 of the California Business & Professions Code to suspend or to revoke license.

5. Broker's usual and customary commissions from time to time in effect, shall be charged to the parties for whom services are performed except that Broker may agree in writing to other rates with such parties.

Broker will advise all Salespersons associated with Broker of any special commission rates made with respect to listings as provided in this paragraph.

When Salesperson shall have performed any work hereunder whereby any commission shall be earned and when such commission shall have been collected, Salesperson shall be entitled to a share of such commission as determined by the current commission schedule set forth in Broker's written policy, except as may otherwise be agreed in writing by Broker and Salesperson before completion of any particular transaction.

6. In the event that two or more Salespeople participate in such work, Salesperson's share of the commission shall be divided between the participating Salespersons according to agreement between them or by arbitration.

7. In compliance with Section 10138 of the California Business and Professions Code, all commissions will be received by Broker; Salesperson's share of such commissions, however, shall be payable to Salesperson immediately upon collection or as soon thereafter as practicable.

8. In no event shall Broker be personally liable to Salesperson for Salesperson's share of commissions not collected, nor shall Salesperson be entitled to any advance or payment from Broker upon future commissions, Salesperson's only remuneration being Salesperson's share of the commission paid by the party or parties for whom the service was performed. Nor shall Salesperson be personally liable to Broker for any commission not collected.

9. Broker shall not be liable to Salesperson for any expenses incurred by Salesperson or for any of his acts except as specifically required by law, nor shall Salesperson be liable to Broker for office help or expense. Salesperson shall have no authority to bind Broker by any promise or representation unless specifically authorized in writing in a particular transaction. Expenses which must by reason of some necessity be paid from the commissions, or are incurred in the collection of, or in the attempt to collect the commission, shall be paid by the parties in the same proportion as provided for herein in the division of commissions.

Salesperson agrees to provide and pay for all necessary professional licenses and dues. Broker shall not be liable to reimburse Salesperson therefor.

In the event Broker elects to advance sums with which to pay for the account of Salesperson professional fees or other items, Salesperson will repay the same to Broker on demand and Broker may deduct such advances from commissions otherwise payable to Salesperson.

10. This agreement does not constitute a hiring by either party. It is the parties' intention that so far as shall be in conformity with law the Salesperson be an independent contractor and not Broker's employee, and in conformity therewith that Salesperson retain sole and absolute discretion and judgment in the manner and means of carrying out Salesperson's selling and soliciting activities. Therefore, the parties hereto are and shall remain independent contractors bound by the provisions hereof. Salesperson is under the control of Broker as to the result of Salesperson's work only and not as to the means by which such result is accomplished. This agreement shall not be construed as a partnership and Broker shall not be liable for any obligation incurred by Salesperson.

11. In accordance with law, Salesperson agrees that any and all listings of property, and all employment in connection with the real estate business shall be taken in the name of Broker. Such listings shall be filed with Broker within twenty-four hours after receipt of same by Salesperson.

Salesperson shall receive a commission in accordance with the current commission schedule set forth in the Broker's written policy based upon commissions actually collected from each firm listing solicited and obtained by Salesperson. In consideration therefore Salesperson agrees to and does hereby contribute all right and title to such listings to the Broker for the benefit and use of Broker. Salesperson and all other Salespeople associated with Broker to whom Broker may give the listing. Salesperson shall have the rights provided in paragraph 13 hereof with respect to listings procured by Salesperson prior to termination.

12. On completion of work in process, this agreement may be terminated by Salesperson at any time. Except for cause, this agreement may not be terminated by Broker except on 30 days' prior written notice to Salesperson. On the occurrence of any of the following causes, Broker may terminate this agreement:

(a) Election of Broker to sell its entire business, or to cease doing business at the office specified in paragraph 2;
(b) Any breach of this agreement by Salesperson;
(c) Cessation of Salesperson to be licensed;
(d) Failure of Salesperson to comply with any applicable law, or regulation of the Real Estate Commissioner;
(e) The filing by or against Salesperson of any petition under any law for the relief of debtors; and
(f) Conviction of Salesperson of any crime, other than minor traffic offenses.

13. When this agreement has been terminated, Salesperson's regular proportionate share of commission on any sales Salesperson has made that are not closed, shall, upon the closing of such sales, be paid to Salesperson, if collected by Broker, and except in cases of termination for cause Salesperson shall also be entitled to receive the portion of the commissions, received by Broker after termination, allocable to the listing (but not the sale) as set forth in Broker's current commissions schedule, on any listings procured by Salesperson during Salesperson's association with Broker, subject, however, to deductions as provided in paragraph 14.

14. In the event Salesperson leaves and has transactions pending that require further work normally rendered by Salesperson, Broker shall make arrangements with another Salesperson in the organization to perform the required work, and the Salesperson assigned shall be compensated for completing the details of pending transactions and such compensation shall be deducted from the terminated Salesperson's share of the commission.

15. Arbitration—In the event of disagreement or dispute between Salesperson in the office or between Broker and Salesperson arising out of or connected with this agreement which cannot be adjusted by and between the parties involved, the disputed disagreement shall be submitted to the Real Estate Board of which Broker is a member for arbitration pursuant to the provisions of its Bylaws, said provisions being hereby incorporated by reference, and if the Bylaws of such Board include no provision for arbitration, then arbitration shall be pursuant to the rules of the American Arbitration Association, which rules are by this reference incorporated herein.

16. Salesperson shall not after the termination of this contract use to Salesperson's own advantage, or the advantage of any other person or corporation, any information gained for or from the files or business of Broker.

17. Salesperson agrees to indemnify Broker and hold Broker harmless from all claims, demands and liabilities, including costs and attorney's fees. to which Broker is subjected by reason of any action by Salesperson taken or omitted pursuant to this agreement.

18. All notices hereunder shall be in writing. Notices may be delivered personally, or by mail, postage prepaid, to the respective addresses noted below. Either party may designate a new address for purposes of this agreement by notice to the other party. Notices mailed shall be deemed received as of 5:00 P.M. of the second business day following the date of mailing.

WITNESS the signatures of the parties hereto the day and year first above written. In duplicate.

WITNESS Joseph Helper

WITNESS Peter Goodsell

BROKER Samuel L. Broker
507 Main Street, Somewhere,CA.
ADDRESS

SALESPERSON as INDEPENDENT CONTRACTOR
Amy W. Salesperson
444 Peer Road, Somewhere, CA.
ADDRESS

The point to stress here is that real estate trade associations have membership rules and codes of ethics to monitor the activities of members. This indirectly works as a form of self-regulation. Members who violate the real estate trade association rules of conduct can be suspended from membership and in the process lose many benefits.

4.4 TERMINATION OF AGENCY

There are six basic ways to terminate a real estate agency.

1. Termination by *completion of the agency* agreement. The agent fulfills his or her responsibilities by securing a buyer who is ready, willing, and able to buy the property on the exact terms of the listing or on other terms agreeable to the seller. When this occurs, the agent is eligible for the commission and is normally paid at close of escrow.

2. Termination by *expiration of time.* If an agent fails to find a ready, willing, and able buyer by the termination date of the listing, the agency is terminated. Most listings contain a clause, however, that provides for the agent to give the seller a list of prospects to whom the agent has shown the property during the term of the listing. If any of these prospects buys the property directly from the seller during the designated protection period after the listing expires, then the agent is entitled to a commission. Additional details will be presented in the next chapter.

3. Termination by *death of the principal or death of the agent.* An agency is automatically terminated if either the principal or agent dies during the term of the listing. One exception is if the principal dies after a purchase agreement is signed, the agent is entitled to the commission. The sale is usually binding on the heirs of the decedent.

4. Termination by *destruction of the property.* If a major catastrophe such as an earthquake or fire occurs causing damage to the property, the agency is terminated.

5. Termination by *mutual consent.* The principals and the agent can mutually agree to terminate the agency.

6. Termination by *unilateral action* of the agent or the principal. Either party may terminate the agency unilaterally. However, the party that cancels the agency may be liabile for damages. If a principal cancels the agency, the agent is usually entitled to the full commission or at a minimum, to reimbursement for expenses and time spent.

SUMMARY

Agency is the representation of a principal by an agent in dealings with third persons. An agent is therefore empowered to represent a principal in making contracts with a third party for the principal's benefit. A real estate agency occurs when a seller appoints a real estate broker to find a buyer. There are two broad categories of agency: general agency and special agency. Real estate agents are usually special agents.

A real estate agency differs from both an employer-employee relationship and an independent contractor relationship. Whereas an employee only works for the employer, a real estate agent acts for a principal in addition to working for the principal. A real estate agent is liable for his or her acts as well as final results whereas an independent contractor is only responsible for final results.

Agencies are created in three ways: by agreement, ratification, or estoppel. Most real estate agencies are created by written agreement. A fiduciary relationship is established when a real estate agent is appointed by the principal. This relationship is one of trust and loyalty and obligates the real estate agent to act in the principal's best interest. The agent, nonetheless, owes the buyer disclosure of all known defects. A real estate agent must be honest and truthful and must not misrepresent the sale.

Agency violations may include misrepresentation, false promise, divided agency, commingling, definite termination date, and secret profit.

A principal should advise a real estate agent of any known defects to the property. A seller should not withhold information from the real estate agent or buyer. A seller can be held liable for distortion of facts about the property.

A real estate broker can contract directly with a principal, whereas a salesperson cannot. It is only through the real estate salesperson's association with a broker that the salesperson becomes an agent. Salespersons must have a written employment contract with a broker and can receive compensation only from the employing broker.

Real estate agents are regulated by the California Department of Real Estate and by professional trade associations, if they are members of those organizations.

Agencies are terminated by completion of the agency agreement, by expiration of time, by death of the principal or agent, by destruction of the property, by mutual consent, and by unilateral termination by the agent or the principal.

Important Terms and Concepts		
	Agent	Independent contractor
	Commingling	Misrepresentation
	Commissioner's Code of Ethics	Principal
	Divided agency	Recovery fund
	False promise	Secret profit
	Fiduciary	Special agency
	General agency	

1. A real estate agency exists between:
   (a) Seller and buyer
   (b) Broker and principal
   (c) Borrower and lender
   (d) Landlord and tenant

2. A fiduciary relationship is best described as:
   (a) Ethics and loyalty
   (b) Ethics and trust
   (c) Trust and confidence
   (d) Loyalty and trust

3. A real estate salesperson is:
   (a) A direct agent
   (b) An agent by virtue of his or her association with a broker
   (c) An employee of the seller
   (d) An employee of the buyer

4. A subagent owes a chief responsibility to the:
   (a) Buyer
   (b) Listing agent
   (c) Employing broker
   (d) None of the above

5. Which of the following is *not* a method of creating an agency?
   (a) Ratification
   (b) Agreement
   (c) Estoppel
   (d) Doctrine of realty determination

6. Which of the following is *not* a method of terminating an agency?
   (a) Estoppel
   (b) Mutual consent
   (c) Completion of agency
   (d) Expiration of time

7. Of which must a principal advise an agent?
   (a) Termite infestation discovered earlier
   (b) Leaky roof
   (c) An inoperative fireplace
   (d) All of the above

8. Which of the following is *not* a true statement?
   (a) Both salespersons and brokers are required to be licensed.
   (b) A broker is a direct agent.
   (c) A salesperson can earn money from two different brokers.
   (d) All of the above are true statements.

9. An agent owes the buyer:
   (a) The duty to see that the property is sold at the lowest possible price

(b) Disclosure of known defects
(c) A fiduciary relationship
(d) All of the above

10. The real estate commissioner:
   (a) Enforces the real estate law
   (b) Issues regulations which have the force of law
   (c) Heads the Department of Real Estate
   (d) All of the above

Chapter 5
Real Estate Contracts

Preview
This chapter presents the legal requirements for an enforceable contract. The chapter includes a definition of a contract, outlines the essential elements of a valid contract, and then discusses how contracts are terminated. Two important real estate contracts, the authorization to sell (listing agreement) and purchase agreement (deposit receipt) are discussed in detail. When you have completed this chapter, you will be able to:

1. *Define contracts and list the legal requirements for an enforceable contract.*

2. *Describe how contracts are terminated or discharged.*

3. *List seven provisions that should be part of a real estate contract.*

4. *Explain the purpose of an authorization to sell (listing agreement) and then discuss the various types of listing agreements.*

5. *Discuss the purpose of an option contract.*

6. *Discuss the purpose of a purchase agreement (deposit receipt) and then explain the meaning of each clause that appears in a typical purchase agreement.*

5.1 LEGAL REQUIREMENTS FOR ENFORCEABLE CONTRACTS

A *contract* is generally defined as an agreement between two or more persons consisting of a promise or mutual promises to either perform or not to perform certain acts. If the contract is executed under proper conditions, the law will enforce the contract and recognize the performance of the parties as a duty.

A *unilateral* contract may be created by only one party extending a promise without a reciprocal promise by another party. An example is a reward. If you lost your wallet and offered $50 for its return, this would be a unilateral contract since you are the only person making an offer. However, most real estate contracts are *bilateral* in nature, in which a promise is made for another promise. An example is a listing agreement where an agent promises to use diligence to secure a purchaser if the owner promises among other things to sell the property under the terms outlined.

A contract may be created by expression or by implication. An *expressed contract* is one wherein the parties have agreed to perform an act or acts either orally or under a written agreement. An *implied contract* is one wherein the parties have not formally agreed either orally or through a written agreement to perform an act. Instead, they agree to perform by their actions rather than by words.

As an example, if you reached agreement with a contractor to build a fence around your home under specific conditions, you have created an expressed contract. On the other hand, assume that you had talked to the contractor about the fence but that your discussions had been inconclusive with no promises made. The next day the contractor appears on your property with a load of materials and begins building the fence. If you do not stop the contractor and the fence is built, an implied contract may be established.

A contract can also be labeled as an *executed* contract or an *executory* contract. In an executed contract all parties have performed and fulfilled their obligations. An executory contract means that some act of the contract remains to be completed by one or more of the parties.

Legal Effects of Contracts

Once a contract is created, what are the prospects that the agreement will stand up in court in the event of a dispute? Four important legal terms are presented below.

1. *Valid.* A valid contract is a binding and enforceable contract. You can sue on it and it is, naturally, the best type of contract that you can have.

2. *Void.* An agreement which the courts will not consider a contract—no legal effect. An example would be a contract by a minor (someone under 18 years old) to purchase a home. A minor may acquire real property through will or by a gift. However, a minor may not buy or sell real property except through a court appointed person

acting on his or her behalf. An exception is a new category of minor—an emancipated minor. Examples of emancipated minors are those minors who are serving in the military service or whose parents have been relieved of responsibility for their minors' actions. Emancipated minors can legally contract for real property.

3. *Voidable.* A contract where one of the parties (the injured party) has the option of proceeding with the contract or calling it off.

4. *Unenforceable.* A contract which, although valid, cannot be sued upon. An example would be an oral agreement for the sale of real property by an agent for a commission.

Essential Elements of a Real Estate Contract   The essential elements for an enforceable real estate contract are: (1) parties capable of contracting, (2) mutual consent, (3) lawful object, (4) a sufficient consideration, and according to the Statute of Frauds, (5) must be in writing.

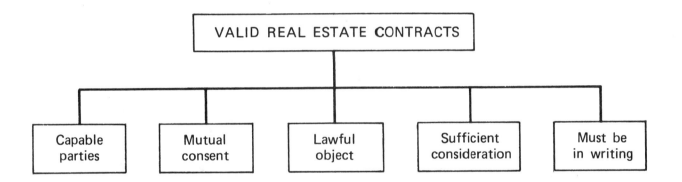

PARTIES CAPABLE OF CONTRACTING   For a contract to be valid, there must be at least two or more parties with the capacity to contract. As a general rule anyone is capable of contracting. However, there are some exceptions. A minor is incapable of contracting for real property unless the minor is emancipated. Persons who are declared incompetent by the courts cannot contract. Like minors, however, incompetents may acquire title to real property by gift or by will. Certain classifications of convicts are considered incapable of contracting. On the other hand, foreigners may hold and sell real property although there are certain federal restrictions. Partnerships and corporations are regarded as artificial beings, and may also hold and dispose of real property.

MUTUAL CONSENT   The parties to the contract must mutually agree to be bound to the terms of the contract. This is exemplified by an offer by one party and an acceptance by the other. The offer must be definite and certain in its terms. A typical example is where a buyer makes an offer to purchase real estate under certain terms and conditions, and the seller accepts the offer and the acceptance is communicated to the buyer. The offer and acceptance constitute mutual consent.

LAWFUL OBJECT

A contract must have a lawful object. An object is what is required to be done or not to be done. A contract is void if there is a single object and that one object is unlawful or impossible to perform. If there are many lawful objects in the contract and one or more unlawful objects, usually only the lawful objects will be valid, and the other objects will be void. A contract for a gambling debt in California, or a contract to commit a crime would not be a lawful object. Therefore the contracts would not be valid.

SUFFICIENT CONSIDERATION

Consideration is a benefit conferred or agreed to be conferred on the person making the promise or on any other person, or a detriment suffered or agreed to be suffered. It can be the return of a promise for another promise. The consideration must have some value. In many cases the consideration is money, but it need not be. It must be something of value in exchange for something of value and is termed a "valuable" consideration. For example, love and affection is a "good" consideration on a gift deed.

THE STATUTE OF FRAUDS

According to the Statute of Frauds, found in the California Civil Code, a real estate contract must be in writing to be enforceable in the courts. Similarly, any change from the original contract must also be in writing and dated and initialed by the parties involved. The purpose of the law is to prevent perjury, forgery, and dishonest conduct on the part of unscrupulous people in proving the existence and terms of certain important types of contracts. Practically speaking, a written understanding of the terms agreed on often eliminates ambiguities and misunderstandings at a later date.

The California Civil Code requires that the following contracts be in writing.

1. An agreement that by its terms is not to be performed within a year from the making thereof.

2. A special promise to answer for the debt, default, or miscarriage of another, except in the cases provided for in Section 2794.

3. An agreement made on consideration of marriage other than a mutual promise to marry.

4. An agreement for the leasing for a longer period than one year, or for the sale of real property, or of an interest therein.

5. An agreement authorizing or employing an agent, broker, or any other person, to purchase or sell real estate, or to lease real estate

for a period longer than one year, or to procure, introduce, or find a purchaser or seller of real estate or a lessee or lessor of real estate where such lease is for a period longer than one year, for compensation or a commission.

6. An agreement that by its terms is not to be performed during the lifetime of the promisor, or an agreement to devise or to bequeath any property, or to make any provision for any reason by will.

7. An agreement by a purchaser of real property to pay an indebtedness secured by a mortgage or deed of trust on the property purchased, unless assumption of said indebtedness by the purchaser is specifically provided for in the conveyance of such property.

Any contract that does not comply with the above is not void but is unenforceable.

Discharge of Contracts

Contracts can be discharged in a number of ways. *Full performance* is the normal situation, wherein the parties accomplish what they set out to do in the contract. At the other extreme is a *breach* of the contract which means that one of the parties did not fulfill their part of the agreement. In the case of a breach the injured party has a number of legal remedies available.

Two of the more common remedies are to (1) sue for damages or to (2) sue for specific performance.

When you sue for damages you are attempting to receive monetary compensation for the damage since the other party will not complete the contract. When you sue for specific performance you are asking the court to compel the other party to perform according to the contract.

Statute of Limitations

In order to bring a lawsuit, you must institute the lawsuit within the legally prescribed time period. If you fail to initiate the lawsuit within the prescribed period of the Statute of Limitations, you may have no remedy in the courts and your rights to sue are said to have "outlawed." Examples of limitation periods are:

1. Three years for removal of encroachments.

2. Five years for recovery of title to property.

3. Four years to sue for foreclosure under a mortgage.

Other methods of contract discharge are by:

1. Part performance.

2. Substantial performance.

3. Impossibility of performance.

4. Agreement between the parties.

5. Release.

6. Operation of law.

7. Acceptance of a breach of contract.

Provisions in Contracts

The following provisions should be part of a real estate contract:

1. The date of the agreement.

2. The names and addresses of the parties to the contract.

3. A description of the property.

4. The consideration.

5. Reference to the creation of new mortgages or deeds of trust, if any, and the terms thereof; also the terms and conditions of existing mortgages, if any.

6. Any other provisions that may be required or requested by either of the parties.

7. The date and place of closing the contract.

Real Estate Licensees Should Not Practice Law

It must be stressed that a real estate agent is not licensed to practice law. Therefore a real estate agent should not create a contract from a blank sheet of paper. Current practice only allows a real estate agent to fill in blanks on a preprinted real estate form.

Another point—on some occasions a discrepancy occurs between a preprinted clause in a contract and a handwritten clause. The usual rule is that the handwritten clause supercedes the preprinted clause.

5.2 AUTHORIZATION TO SELL

Commonly referred to as the *listing agreement,* the authorization to sell is one of the most common contracts found in a real estate transaction. An authorization to sell is the formal contract wherein the owner of the property (the seller) agrees to sell the property under certain stipulated conditions. The listing agreement creates an employment contract between a real estate broker and the seller.

As noted in the previous chapter, the authorization to sell also establishes an agency relationship between the broker and the principal. This agency is referred to as a fiduciary relationship.

An authorization to sell is a bilateral contract in that there is an exchange of promises. The seller promises to sell at a stipulated price and to pay the broker a commission upon delivery of a ready, willing, and able buyer. The broker promises to use diligence in attempting to procure a purchaser. The seller may make additional promises regarding the terms. Thus there is a reciprocity of promises and a bilateral contract.

Different Types of Authorizations to Sell

There are essentially four different types of authorization to sell: open listing, exclusive agency listing, exclusive authorization and right-to-sell listing, and net listing.

OPEN LISTING

The open listing is one which can be given simultaneously to more than one agent. Only one commission is payable and that is payable to the agent who first procures an offer acceptable to the seller. Even the owner may sell the property to his or her own prospective buyer, without paying a commission to any agent. For the above reasons, most agents are generally reluctant to spend their time on this type of listing arrangement.

EXCLUSIVE AGENCY LISTING

In an exclusive agency listing one broker is named in the contract. The named broker may cooperate with other brokers and agree to share his or her commission with them if they bring in a buyer. The seller reserves the right to sell the property him- or herself to prospects he or she finds without paying a commission. An exclusive agency listing must have a definite termination date.

EXCLUSIVE AUTHORIZATION AND RIGHT-TO-SELL LISTING

The exclusive authorization and right-to-sell listing is the most common form of listing used in the real estate business. The broker is entitled to a commission no matter who sells the property including the owner during a specific time period. Since the broker can expect compensation assuming the listing is reasonably salable, the broker is willing to spend considerable time attempting to procure a purchaser. The broker is also more likely to spend money to advertise and promote the property.

The listing broker may cooperate with other brokers who then become subagents of the seller and agree to split the commission. An exclusive authorization and right-to-sell listing, like the exclusive agency listing, must contain a definite termination date.

NET LISTING

Under a net listing, the seller stipulates a set sum of money which is to be received by the seller regardless of the sales price. An example would be the case wherein the seller of a small home stipulated that he or she needed to net $20,000 after paying off the first deed of trust of $125,000, pest control work, escrow, and other miscellaneous fees totaling $2,000. Assuming the broker sold the property for $155,000 the broker would be entitled to a brokerage fee of $8,000.

	Costs	
$155,000 sales price	$125,000 first deed of trust	
−147,000 costs	2,000 pest control, escrow, misc.	
$ 8,000 brokerage	20,000 net to seller	
	$147,000 total costs	

Under the provisions of real estate law, the broker must notify the seller of the amount of commission the broker is earning before the seller agrees to sign the purchase contract with the buyer. Failure to disclose this fact may result in revocation or suspension of the agent's license. A net listing may be taken on an open, exclusive agency, or exclusive authorization and right-to-sell form.

MULTIPLE LISTING SERVICE

The multiple listing service (MLS) is a listing service usually operated by brokers of a real estate board. Listings are placed on the MLS and that information is then disseminated to all the members of the MLS. The seller gets significantly greater market exposure through this type of service, since most MLS systems have hundreds or even thousands of members. Through this kind of mass exposure, the seller has a good chance of receiving the best price and terms.

Virtually any type of listing can be placed on the MLS but because of practical considerations, the exclusive authorization and right-to-sell listing is predominantly used. Under the terms of MLS, the listing broker controls the listing and agrees to split the commission in some manner with the cooperating agents.

5.3 PURCHASE AGREEMENT AND DISCLOSURE RULE

The purchase agreement, often referred to as the *deposit receipt,* is a contract between the buyer and the seller for the purchase of real property. It is also a receipt for the buyer's deposit for the performance of the contract. Additionally, it spells out the payment of the brokerage commission to be paid by the seller.

The Offer

The prospective buyer stipulates the price and terms of the offer, and the offer is then put on the purchase agreement form. By regulations, all offers must be presented to the seller. If the seller accepts the offer, communication of acceptance must be delivered back to the buyer. At that time there is a binding contract since offer, acceptance, and notification of the acceptance have occurred. At any time prior to receiving communication, that the seller has accepted the offer, the buyer can withdraw the offer and not be liable on the contract. Copies of the offer and the completed agreement with acceptance must be left with each of the parties.

Rejection of the Offer

If the terms of the offer are unrealistic, the seller may reject the offer outright. The legal affect of this is that no contract exists since there has been no acceptance. The buyer, however, may make another offer.

Counter Offers

If the seller feels that the offer is basically a good one, but that there should be a change in price or terms, the seller may make a counteroffer to the buyer.

A *counteroffer* is in effect merely an offer made by the seller to the buyer. As such, the legal requirements for withdrawal or acceptance and communication of acceptance exist in reverse order. If the buyer accepts the changes, that fact must be indicated in writing and communication of acceptance of the counteroffer must be delivered back to the seller. At any point prior to the communication of acceptance of the counteroffer, the seller may withdraw the counteroffer.

Transfer Disclosure Statement (effective 1/87)

Sellers of residential 1–4 units must furnish buyers with a completed disclosure statement. This disclosure statement details various facts about the property—needed repairs, condition of appliances, improvements added with or without building permits, and so on.

The details noted are based upon an inspection conducted by the real estate agents involved in the sale and upon statements made by the sellers. This statement must be provided even if the transaction is an "as is sale." The responsibility for providing this disclosure rests with the real estate agents. If no agents are involved, the seller must provide the statement. The disclosure statement must be signed by the sellers and all real estate agents involved in the transaction.

Ideally, the disclosure statement should be given to the buyers *before* they sign the purchase contract. If the disclosure statement is given after the purchase contract is signed, the buyer has a three day right to cancel the sale (see Page 361 for a sample form.)

Options

An *option* is a contract between the owner of a property *(the optionor)* and a potential purchaser *(a optionee)*. Under an option, the optionor gives to the optionee the right to purchase real estate under a set of terms and conditions, within a designated time period. To be binding the optionee must pay consideration to the optionor.

Here is the key point—*the optionee is not required to exercise the option* (purchase the property). The optionee has the choice of buying or not buying. If the optionee decides to buy, the owner must sell under the terms of the option. If the optionee decides not to buy, the optionor keeps the option fee.

Many times a combination of lease and option are used, whereas a person leases the property for a certain time and then has the option to purchase the property when the lease expires.

Record Keeping

A real estate broker is required to keep for three years copies of all listings, deposit receipts, cancelled checks, trust funds and any other documents in connection with any transaction for which a real estate broker license is required.

5.4 SAMPLE CONTRACTS

Pages 85-90 are samples of contracts typically used in a simple real estate sale. The forms are published by the California Association of Realtors. All forms reprinted with permission, but indorsement not implied.

The forms are:
1. Exclusive Authorization and Right to Sell

2. Disclosure Regarding Real Estate Agency Relationship

3. Real Estate Purchase Contract and Receipt for Deposit

CALIFORNIA ASSOCIATION OF REALTORS

EXCLUSIVE AUTHORIZATION AND RIGHT TO SELL
MULTIPLE LISTING AUTHORIZATION
THIS IS INTENDED TO BE A LEGALLY BINDING AGREEMENT — READ IT CAREFULLY.
CALIFORNIA ASSOCIATION OF REALTORS® (CAR) STANDARD FORM

1. **EXCLUSIVE RIGHT TO SELL:** I hereby employ and grant _____
hereinafter called "Broker," the exclusive and irrevocable right commencing on _____, 19_____, and expiring at
midnight on _____, 19_____, to sell or exchange the real property situated in the City of _____,
County of _____, California described as follows: _____
_____

2. **TERMS OF SALE:** The purchase price shall be _____
_____ ($_____), to be paid as follows _____
_____

   The following items of personal property are included in the above stated price: _____
_____

3. **MULTIPLE LISTING SERVICE (MLS):** Broker is a Participant of _____
ASSOCIATION/BOARD OF REALTORS® Multiple Listing Service (MLS) and this listing information will be provided to the MLS to be published and disseminated
to its Participants in accordance with its Rules and Regulations. Broker is authorized to cooperate with other real estate brokers, to appoint subagents and to
report the sale, its price, terms and financing for the publication, dissemination, information and use by authorized Association/Board members, MLS Participants
and Subscribers.

4. **TITLE INSURANCE:** Evidence of title shall be a California Land Title Association policy of title insurance in the amount of the selling price.

**Notice: The amount or rate of real estate commissions is not fixed by law. They are set by each Broker individually and may be negotiable between the
Seller and Broker.**

5. **COMPENSATION TO BROKER:** I hereby agree to compensate Broker, irrespective of agency relationship(s), as follows:

   (a) _____ percent of the selling price, or $_____, if the property is sold during the term hereof, or any extension thereof, by Broker
   or through any other person, or by me on the terms herein set forth, or any other price and terms I may accept, or _____ percent of the price shown in 2,
   or $_____, if said property is withdrawn from sale, transferred, conveyed, leased, or rented without the consent of Broker, or made
   unmarketable by my voluntary act during the term hereof or any extension thereof.

   (b) The compensation provided for in subparagraph (a) above if property is sold, conveyed or otherwise transferred within _____ calendar days after the
   termination of this authority or any extension thereof to anyone with whom Broker has had negotiations prior to final termination, provided I have received
   notice in writing, including the names of the prospective purchasers, before or upon termination of this agreement or any extension hereof. However, I shall
   not be obligated to pay the compensation provided for in subparagraph (a) if a valid listing agreement is entered into during the term of said protection period
   with another licensed real estate broker and a sale, lease or exchange of the property is made during the term of said valid listing agreement.

   (c) I authorize Broker to cooperate with other brokers, to appoint subagents, and to divide with other brokers such compensation in any manner acceptable to brokers.

   (d) In the event of an exchange, permission is hereby given Broker to represent all parties and collect compensation or commissions from them, provided there
   is full disclosure to all principals of such agency. Broker is authorized to divide with other brokers such compensation or commissions in any manner acceptable
   to brokers.

   (e) Seller shall execute and deliver an escrow instruction irrevocably assigning Broker's compensation in an amount equal to the compensation provided in
   subparagraph (a) (above) from the Seller's proceeds.

6. **DEPOSIT:** Broker is authorized to accept and hold on Seller's behalf a deposit to be applied toward purchase price.

7. **HOME PROTECTION PLAN:** Seller is informed that home protection plans are available. Such plans may provide additional protection and benefit to a Seller
and Buyer. Cost and coverage may vary.

*8. **KEYBOX:** I authorize Broker to install a KEYBOX: (Initial) YES (____/____)   NO (____/____)
Refer to reverse side for important keybox information.

9. **SIGN:** Authorization to install a FOR SALE/SOLD sign on the property: (Initial) YES (____/____)   NO (____/____)

10. **PEST CONTROL:** Seller shall furnish a current Structural Pest Control Report of the main building
and all structures of the property, except _____.   (Initial) YES (____/____)   NO (____/____)

11. **DISCLOSURE:** Unless exempt, Seller shall provide a Real Estate Transfer Disclosure Statement concerning the condition of the property. I agree to save and
hold Broker harmless from all claims, disputes, litigation, and/or judgments arising from any incorrect information supplied by me, or from any material fact known
by me which I fail to disclose.   (Initial) (____/____)

*12. **TAX WITHHOLDING:** Seller agrees to perform any act reasonably necessary to carry out the provisions of FIRPTA (Internal Revenue Code §1445) and California
Revenue and Taxation Code §§18805 and 26131, and regulations promulgated thereunder. Refer to the reverse side for withholding provisions and exemptions.

13. **EQUAL HOUSING OPPORTUNITY:** This property is offered in compliance with federal, state, and local anti-discrimination laws.

*14. **ARBITRATION OF DISPUTES: Any dispute or claim in law or equity arising out of this contract or any resulting transaction shall be decided by
neutral binding arbitration in accordance with the rules of the American Arbitration Association, and not by court action except as provided by
California law for judicial review of arbitration proceedings. Judgment upon the award rendered by the arbitrator(s) may be entered in any court
having jurisdiction thereof. The parties shall have the right to discovery in accordance with Code of Civil Procedure §1283.05. The following matters
are excluded from arbitration hereunder: (a) a judicial or non-judicial foreclosure or other action or proceeding to enforce a deed of trust, mortgage,
or real property sales contract as defined in Civil Code §2985, (b) an unlawful detainer action, (c) the filing or enforcement of a mechanic's lien,
(d) any matter which is within the jurisdiction of a probate court, or (e) an action for bodily injury or wrongful death, or for latent or patent defects
to which Code of Civil Procedure §337.1 or §337.15 applies. The filing of a judicial action to enable the recording of a notice of pending action,
for order of attachment, receivership, injunction, or other provisional remedies, shall not constitute a waiver of the right to arbitrate under this
provision.**

**"NOTICE: BY INITIALLING IN THE SPACE BELOW YOU ARE AGREEING TO HAVE ANY DISPUTE ARISING OUT OF THE MATTERS INCLUDED IN
THE 'ARBITRATION OF DISPUTES' PROVISION DECIDED BY NEUTRAL ARBITRATION AS PROVIDED BY CALIFORNIA LAW AND YOU ARE GIVING
UP ANY RIGHTS YOU MIGHT POSSESS TO HAVE THE DISPUTE LITIGATED IN A COURT OR JURY TRIAL. BY INITIALLING IN THE SPACE BELOW
YOU ARE GIVING UP YOUR JUDICIAL RIGHTS TO DISCOVERY AND APPEAL, UNLESS THOSE RIGHTS ARE SPECIFICALLY INCLUDED IN THE
'ARBITRATION OF DISPUTES' PROVISION. IF YOU REFUSE TO SUBMIT TO ARBITRATION AFTER AGREEING TO THIS PROVISION, YOU MAY BE
COMPELLED TO ARBITRATE UNDER THE AUTHORITY OF THE CALIFORNIA CODE OF CIVIL PROCEDURE. YOUR AGREEMENT TO THIS ARBITRATION
PROVISION IS VOLUNTARY."**

**"WE HAVE READ AND UNDERSTAND THE FOREGOING AND AGREE TO SUBMIT DISPUTES ARISING OUT OF THE MATTERS INCLUDED IN THE
'ARBITRATION OF DISPUTES' PROVISION TO NEUTRAL ARBITRATION."**

(Initial) BROKER (_____) SELLER (____/____)

15. **ATTORNEY'S FEES:** In any action, proceeding or arbitration arising out of this agreement, the prevailing party shall be entitled to reasonable attorney's fees and costs.

16. **ADDITIONAL TERMS:** _____

17. **ENTIRE AGREEMENT:** I, the Seller, warrant that I am the owner of the property or have the authority to execute this agreement. The Seller and Broker further
intend that this agreement constitutes the complete and exclusive statement of its terms and that no extrinsic evidence whatsoever may be introduced in any
judicial or arbitration proceeding, if any, involving this agreement.

I acknowledge that I have read and understand this agreement, including the information on the reverse side, and have received a copy.

Date _____, 19 _____   _____, California

Seller _____   Address _____

Seller _____   City _____ State _____ Zip _____

In consideration of the above, Broker agrees to use diligence in procuring a purchaser.   Phone _____

Real Estate Broker _____   By _____

Address _____   City _____ Date _____

THIS STANDARDIZED DOCUMENT FOR USE IN SIMPLE TRANSACTIONS HAS BEEN APPROVED BY THE CALIFORNIA ASSOCIATION OF REALTORS® IN FORM ONLY. NO REPRESENTATION IS MADE
AS TO THE APPROVAL OF THE FORM OF ANY SUPPLEMENTS NOT CURRENTLY PUBLISHED BY THE CALIFORNIA ASSOCIATION OF REALTORS® OR THE LEGAL VALIDITY OR ADEQUACY OF ANY
PROVISION IN ANY SPECIFIC TRANSACTION. IT SHOULD NOT BE USED IN COMPLEX TRANSACTIONS OR WITH EXTENSIVE RIDERS OR ADDITIONS.

A REAL ESTATE BROKER IS THE PERSON QUALIFIED TO ADVISE ON REAL ESTATE TRANSACTIONS. IF YOU DESIRE LEGAL OR TAX ADVICE, CONSULT AN APPROPRIATE PROFESSIONAL.

This form is available for use by the entire real estate industry. The use of this form is not intended to identify the user as a REALTOR®. REALTOR® is a registered collective membership mark which may be used
only by real estate licensees who are members of the NATIONAL ASSOCIATION OF REALTORS® and who subscribe to its Code of Ethics.

* REFER TO REVERSE SIDE FOR ADDITIONAL INFORMATION.
Copyright © 1988, CALIFORNIA ASSOCIATION OF REALTORS®
525 South Virgil Avenue, Los Angeles, California 90020
Revised 3/89

FORM A-14

┌─ OFFICE USE ONLY ─┐
Reviewed by Broker or Designee _____
Date _____

EQUAL HOUSING OPPORTUNITY
SF-Oct-89

DISCLOSURE REGARDING
REAL ESTATE AGENCY RELATIONSHIPS
(As required by the Civil Code)
CALIFORNIA ASSOCIATION OF REALTORS® (CAR) STANDARD FORM

When you enter into a discussion with a real estate agent regarding a real estate transaction, you should from the outset understand what type of agency relationship or representation you wish to have with the agent in the transaction.

SELLER'S AGENT

A Seller's agent under a listing agreement with Seller acts as the agent for the Seller only. A Seller's agent or a subagent of that agent has the following affirmative obligations:
To the Seller:
   (a) A Fiduciary duty of utmost care, integrity, honesty, and loyalty in dealings with the Seller.
To the Buyer & the Seller:
   (a) Diligent exercise of reasonable skill and care in performance of the agent's duties.
   (b) A duty of honest and fair dealing and good faith.
   (c) A duty to disclose all facts known to the agent materially affecting the value or desirability of property that are not known to, or within the diligent attention and observation of, the parties.

An agent is not obligated to reveal to either party any confidential information obtained from the other party which does not involve the affirmative duties set forth above.

BUYER'S AGENT

A selling agent can, with a Buyer's consent, agree to act as agent for the Buyer only. In these situations, the agent is not the Seller's agent, even if by agreement the agent may receive compensation for services rendered, either in full or in part from the Seller. An agent acting only for a Buyer has the following affirmative obligations:
To the Buyer:
   (a) A fiduciary duty of utmost care, integrity, honesty, and loyalty in dealings with the Buyer.
To the Buyer & Seller:
   (a) Diligent exercise of reasonable skill and care in performance of the agent's duties.
   (b) A duty of honest and fair dealing and good faith.
   (c) A duty to disclose all facts known to the agent materially affecting the value or desirability of the property that are not known to, or within the diligent attention and observation of, the parties.

An agent is not obligated to reveal to either party any confidential information obtained from the other party which does not involve the affirmative duties set forth above.

AGENT REPRESENTING BOTH SELLER & BUYER

A real estate agent, either acting directly or through one or more associate licensees, can legally be the agent of both the Seller and the Buyer in a transaction, but only with the knowledge and consent of both the Seller and the Buyer.

In a dual agency situation, the agent has the following affirmative obligations to both the Seller and the Buyer:
   (a) A fiduciary duty of utmost care, integrity, honesty and loyalty in the dealings with either Seller or the Buyer.
   (b) Other duties to the Seller and the Buyer as stated above in their respective sections.

In representing both Seller and Buyer, the agent may not, without the express permission of the respective party, disclose to the other party that the Seller will accept a price less than the listing price or that the Buyer will pay a price greater than the price offered.

The above duties of the agent in a real estate transaction do not relieve a Seller or a Buyer from the responsibility to protect their own interests. You should carefully read all agreements to assure that they adequately express your understanding of the transaction. A real estate agent is a person qualified to advise about real estate. If legal or tax advice is desired, consult a competent professional.

Throughout your real property transaction you may receive more than one disclosure form, depending upon the number of agents assisting in the transaction. The law requires each agent with whom you have more than a casual relationship to present you with this disclosure form. You should read its contents each time it is presented to you, considering the relationship between you and the real estate agent in your specific transaction.

This disclosure form includes the provisions of article 2.5 (commencing with Section 2373) of Chapter 2 of Title 9 of Part 4 of Division 3 of the Civil Code set forth on the reverse hereof. Read it carefully.

I/WE ACKNOWLEDGE RECEIPT OF A COPY OF THIS DISCLOSURE.

BUYER/SELLER_____ Date_____ TIME_____ AM/PM

BUYER/SELLER_____ Date_____ TIME_____ AM/PM

AGENT _____ By _____ Date_____
     (Please Print)   (Associate Licensee or Broker-Signature)

CONFIRMATION
REAL ESTATE AGENCY RELATIONSHIPS

Subject Property Address_____.

The following agency relationship(s) is/are hereby confirmed for this transaction:

LISTING AGENT: _____   **SELLING AGENT:** _____
is the agent of (check one):   (if not the same as Listing Agent)
   ☐ the Seller exclusively; or   is the agent of (check one):
   ☐ both the Buyer and Seller   ☐ the Buyer exclusively; or
                                          ☐ the Seller exclusively; or
                                          ☐ both the Buyer and Seller

I/WE ACKNOWLEDGE RECEIPT OF A COPY OF THIS CONFIRMATION.

Seller_____ Date_____   Buyer _____ Date_____

Seller_____ Date_____   Buyer _____ Date_____

Listing Agent_____ By _____ Date_____
         (Please Print)   (Associate Licensee or Broker-Signature)

Selling Agent_____ By _____ Date_____
         (Please Print)   (Associate Licensee or Broker-Signature)

     A REAL ESTATE BROKER IS QUALIFIED TO ADVISE ON REAL ESTATE. IF YOU DESIRE LEGAL ADVICE, CONSULT YOUR ATTORNEY.

This form is available for use by the entire real estate industry. The use of this form is not intended to identify the user as a REALTOR®. REALTOR® is a registered collective membership mark which may be used only by real estate licensees who are members of the NATIONAL ASSOCIATION OF REALTORS® and who subscribe to its Code of Ethics.

FORM AD-11/AC-6
(combined)

┌─── OFFICE USE ONLY ───┐
Reviewed by Broker or Designee _____
Date _____

EQUAL HOUSING
OPPORTUNITY
SF-Sep-89

REAL ESTATE PURCHASE CONTRACT AND RECEIPT FOR DEPOSIT
THIS IS MORE THAN A RECEIPT FOR MONEY. IT IS INTENDED TO BE A LEGALLY BINDING CONTRACT. READ IT CAREFULLY.
CALIFORNIA ASSOCIATION OF REALTORS® (CAR) STANDARD FORM

_____ , California, _____ , 19 _____

Received from _____

herein called Buyer, the sum of _____ Dollars $_____

evidenced by ☐ cash, ☐ cashier's check, ☐ personal check or ☐ _____ , payable to _____

_____ , to be held uncashed until acceptance of this offer as deposit on account of purchase price of

_____ Dollars $_____

for the purchase of property, situated in _____ , County of _____ California,

described as follows: _____

1. **FINANCING:** The obtaining of Buyer's financing is a contingency of this agreement.

    A. DEPOSIT upon acceptance, to be deposited into _____ $ _____

    B. INCREASED DEPOSIT within _____ days of acceptance to be deposited into _____ $ _____

    C. BALANCE OF DOWN PAYMENT to be deposited into _____ on or before _____ $ _____

    D. Buyer to apply, qualify for and obtain a NEW FIRST LOAN in the amount of _____ $ _____

        payable monthly at approximately $_____ including interest at origination not to exceed _____%,

        ☐ fixed rate, ☐ other _____ all due _____ years from date of origination. Loan fee not to

        exceed _____ . Seller agrees to pay a maximum of _____ FHA/VA discount points.

        Additional terms _____

        _____

    E. Buyer ☐ to assume, ☐ to take title subject to an EXISTING FIRST LOAN with an approximate balance of .... $ _____

        in favor of _____ payable monthly at $_____ including interest at _____% ☐ fixed rate,

        ☐ other _____ . Fees not to exceed _____ .

        Disposition of impound account _____

        Additional terms _____

    F. Buyer to execute a NOTE SECURED BY a ☐ first, ☐ second, ☐ third DEED OF TRUST in the amount of .... $ _____

        IN FAVOR OF SELLER payable monthly at $_____ ☐ or more, including interest at _____% all due

        _____ years from date of origination, ☐ or upon sale or transfer of subject property. A late charge of _____

        _____ shall be due on any installment not paid within _____ days of the due date.

        ☐ Deed of Trust to contain a request for notice of default or sale for the benefit of Seller. Buyer ☐ will, ☐ will not execute a request

        for notice of delinquency. Additional terms _____

        _____

    G. Buyer ☐ to assume, ☐ to take title subject to an EXISTING SECOND LOAN with an approximate balance of .... $ _____

        in favor of _____ payable monthly at $_____ including interest at _____%

        ☐ fixed rate, ☐ other _____ . Buyer fees not to exceed _____ .

        Additional terms _____

    H. Buyer to apply, qualify for and obtain a NEW SECOND LOAN in the amount of .... $ _____

        payable monthly at approximately $_____ including interest at origination not to exceed _____% ☐ fixed rate,

        ☐ other _____ , all due _____ years from date of origination.

        Buyer's loan fee not to exceed _____ . Additional terms _____

    I. In the event Buyer assumes or takes title subject to an existing loan, Seller shall provide Buyer with copies of applicable notes and Deeds

        of Trust. A loan may contain a number of features which affect the loan, such as interest rate changes, monthly payment changes, balloon

        payments, etc. Buyer shall be allowed _____ calendar days after receipt of such copies to notify Seller in writing of disapproval.

        FAILURE TO NOTIFY SELLER IN WRITING SHALL CONCLUSIVELY BE CONSIDERED APPROVAL. Buyer's approval shall not be

        unreasonably withheld. Difference in existing loan balances shall be adjusted in ☐ Cash, ☐ Other _____

        _____

    J. Buyer agrees to act diligently and in good faith to obtain all applicable financing. _____

        _____

        _____

    K. ADDITIONAL FINANCING TERMS: _____

        _____

        _____

        _____

    L. TOTAL PURCHASE PRICE .... $ _____

2. **OCCUPANCY:** Buyer ☐ does, ☐ does not intend to occupy subject property as Buyer's primary residence.

3. **SUPPLEMENTS:** The ATTACHED supplements are incorporated herein:

        ☐ Interim Occupancy Agreement (CAR FORM IOA-11)   ☐ _____

        ☐ Residential Lease Agreement after Sale (CAR FORM RLAS-11)   ☐ _____

        ☐ VA and FHA Amendments (CAR FORM VA/FHA-11)   ☐ _____

4. **ESCROW:** Buyer and Seller shall deliver signed instructions to _____ the escrow holder, within _____ calendar days

    of acceptance of the offer which shall provide for closing within _____ calendar days of acceptance. Escrow fees to be paid as follows: _____

    _____

    _____

Buyer and Seller acknowledge receipt of copy of this page, which constitutes Page 1 of _____ Pages.

Buyer's Initials (_____) (_____)   Seller's Initials (_____) (_____)

THIS STANDARDIZED DOCUMENT FOR USE IN SIMPLE TRANSACTIONS HAS BEEN APPROVED BY THE CALIFORNIA ASSOCIATION OF REALTORS® IN FORM ONLY. NO REPRESENTATION IS MADE AS TO THE APPROVAL OF THE FORM OF ANY SUPPLEMENTS NOT CURRENTLY PUBLISHED BY THE CALIFORNIA ASSOCIATION OF REALTORS® OR THE LEGAL VALIDITY OR ADEQUACY OF ANY PROVISION IN ANY SPECIFIC TRANSACTION. IT SHOULD NOT BE USED IN COMPLEX TRANSACTIONS OR WITH EXTENSIVE RIDERS OR ADDITIONS.

A REAL ESTATE BROKER IS THE PERSON QUALIFIED TO ADVISE ON REAL ESTATE TRANSACTIONS. IF YOU DESIRE LEGAL OR TAX ADVICE, CONSULT AN APPROPRIATE PROFESSIONAL.

Copyright © 1989, CALIFORNIA ASSOCIATION OF REALTORS®
525 South Virgil Avenue, Los Angeles, California 90020
REVISED 2/89

BROKER'S COPY

┌─── OFFICE USE ONLY ───┐
Reviewed by Broker or Designee _____
Date _____

M-MB-Aug-89

Subject Property Address: _____

5. TITLE: Title is to be free of liens, encumbrances, easements, restrictions, rights and conditions of record or known to Seller, other than the following: (a) Current property taxes, (b) covenants, conditions, restrictions, and public utility easements of record, if any, provided the same do not adversely affect the continued use of the property for the purposes for which it is presently being used, unless reasonably disapproved by Buyer in writing within _____ calendar days of receipt of a current preliminary report furnished at _____ expense, and (c) _____
_____
Seller shall furnish Buyer at _____ expense a California Land Title Association policy issued by _____
_____. Company, showing title vested in Buyer subject only to the above. If Seller is unwilling or unable to eliminate any title matter disapproved by Buyer as above, Buyer may terminate this agreement. If Seller fails to deliver title as above, Buyer may terminate this agreement; in either case, the deposit shall be returned to Buyer.

6. VESTING: Unless otherwise designated in the escrow instructions of Buyer, title shall vest as follows: _____
_____

(The manner of taking title may have significant legal and tax consequences. Therefore, give this matter serious consideration.)

7. PRORATIONS: Property taxes, payments on bonds and assessments assumed by Buyer, interest, rents, association dues, premiums on insurance acceptable to Buyer, and _____ shall be paid current and prorated as of ☐ the day of recordation of the deed; or ☐ _____. Bonds or assessments now a lien shall be ☐ paid current by Seller, payments not yet due to be assumed by Buyer; or ☐ paid in full by Seller, including payments not yet due; or ☐ _____. County Transfer tax shall be paid by _____. The _____ transfer tax or transfer fee shall be paid by _____. **PROPERTY WILL BE REASSESSED UPON CHANGE OF OWNERSHIP. THIS WILL AFFECT THE TAXES TO BE PAID.** A Supplemental tax bill will be issued, which shall be paid as follows: (a) for periods after close of escrow, by Buyer (or by final acquiring party if part of an exchange), and (b) for periods prior to close of escrow, by Seller. TAX BILLS ISSUED AFTER CLOSE OF ESCROW SHALL BE HANDLED DIRECTLY BETWEEN BUYER AND SELLER.

8. POSSESSION: Possession and occupancy shall be delivered to Buyer, ☐ on close of escrow, or ☐ not later than _____ days after close of escrow, or ☐ _____.

9. KEYS: Seller shall, when possession is available to Buyer, provide keys and/or means to operate all property locks, and alarms, if any.

10. PERSONAL PROPERTY: The following items of personal property, free of liens and without warranty of condition, are included: _____
_____
_____

11. FIXTURES: All permanently installed fixtures and fittings that are attached to the property or for which special openings have been made are included in the purchase price, including electrical, light, plumbing and heating fixtures, built-in appliances, screens, awnings, shutters, all window coverings, attached floor coverings, TV antennas, air cooler or conditioner, garage door openers and controls, attached fireplace equipment, mailbox, trees and shrubs, and _____ except _____

12. SMOKE DETECTOR(S): State law requires that residences be equipped with an operable smoke detector(s). Local law may have additional requirements. Seller shall deliver to Buyer a written statement of compliance in accordance with applicable state and local law prior to close of escrow.

13. TRANSFER DISCLOSURE: Unless exempt, Transferor (Seller), shall comply with Civil Code §§1102 et seq., by providing Transferee (Buyer) with a Real Estate Transfer Disclosure Statement: (a) ☐ Buyer has received and read a Real Estate Transfer Disclosure Statement; or (b) ☐ Seller shall provide Buyer with a Real Estate Transfer Disclosure Statement within _____ calendar days of acceptance of the offer after which Buyer shall have three (3) days after delivery to Buyer, in person, or five (5) days after delivery by deposit in the mail, to terminate this agreement by delivery of a written notice of termination to Seller or Seller's Agent.

14. TAX WITHHOLDING: Under the Foreign Investment in Real Property Tax Act (FIRPTA), IRC §1445, *every* Buyer of U.S. real property *must*, unless an exemption applies, deduct and withhold from Seller's proceeds 10% of the gross sales price. Under California Revenue and Taxation Code §§18805 and 26131, the Buyer must deduct and withhold an additional one-third of the amount required to be withheld under federal law. The primary FIRPTA exemptions are: No withholding is required if (a) Seller provides Buyer with an affidavit under penalty of perjury, that Seller is not a "foreign person," or (b) Seller provides Buyer with a "qualifying statement" issued by the Internal Revenue Service, or (c) Buyer purchases real property for use as a residence and the purchase price is $300,000 or less and Buyer or a member of Buyer's family has definite plans to reside at the property for at least 50% of the number of days it is in use during each of the first two twelve-month periods after transfer. Seller and Buyer agree to execute and deliver as directed any instrument, affidavit, or statement reasonably necessary to carry out those statutes and regulations promulgated thereunder.

15. MULTIPLE LISTING SERVICE: If Broker is a Participant of an Association/Board multiple listing service ("MLS"), the Broker is authorized to report the sale, its price, terms, and financing for the publication, dissemination, information, and use of the authorized Association/Board members, MLS Participants and Subscribers.

16. ADDITIONAL TERMS AND CONDITIONS:
ONLY THE FOLLOWING PARAGRAPHS 'A' THROUGH 'K' *WHEN INITIALLED BY BOTH BUYER AND SELLER* ARE INCORPORATED IN THIS AGREEMENT.
Buyer's Initials   Seller's Initials
_____/_____   _____/_____   **A. PHYSICAL AND GEOLOGICAL INSPECTION:** Buyer shall have the right, at Buyer's expense, to select a licensed contractor and/or other qualified professional(s), to make "Inspections" (including tests, surveys, other studies, inspections, and investigations) of the subject property, including but not limited to structural, plumbing, sewer/septic system, well, heating, electrical, built-in appliances, roof, soils, foundation, mechanical systems, pool, pool heater, pool filter, air conditioner, if any, possible environmental hazards such as asbestos, formaldehyde, radon gas and other substances/products, and geologic conditions. Buyer shall keep the subject property free and clear of any liens, indemnify and hold Seller harmless from all liability, claims, demands, damages, or costs, and repair all damages to the property arising from the "Inspections." All claimed defects concerning the condition of the property that adversely affect the continued use of the property for the purposes for which it is presently being used (☐ or as _____) shall be in writing, supported by written reports, if any, and delivered to Seller within _____ calendar days FOR "INSPECTIONS" OTHER THAN GEOLOGICAL, and/or within _____ calendar days FOR GEOLOGICAL "INSPECTIONS," **of acceptance of the offer.** Buyer shall furnish Seller copies, at no cost, of all reports concerning the property obtained by Buyer. When such reports disclose conditions or information unsatisfactory to the Buyer, which the Seller is unwilling or unable to correct, Buyer may cancel this agreement. Seller shall make the premises available for all Inspections. BUYER'S FAILURE TO NOTIFY SELLER IN WRITING SHALL CONCLUSIVELY BE CONSIDERED APPROVAL.

Buyer's Initials   Seller's Initials
_____/_____   _____/_____   **B. CONDITION OF PROPERTY:** Seller warrants, through the date possession is made available to Buyer: (1) property and improvements, including landscaping, grounds and pool/spa, if any, shall be maintained in the same condition as upon the date of acceptance of the offer, and (2) the roof is free of all known leaks, and (3) built-in appliances, and water, sewer/septic, plumbing, heating, electrical, air conditioning, pool/spa systems, if any, are operative, and (4) Seller shall replace all broken and/or cracked glass; (5) _____
_____

Buyer's Initials   Seller's Initials
_____/_____   _____/_____   **C. SELLER REPRESENTATION:** Seller warrants that Seller has no knowledge of any notice of violations of City, County, State, Federal, Building, Zoning, Fire, Health Codes or ordinances, or other governmental regulation filed or issued against the property. This warranty shall be effective until the date of close of escrow.

Buyer and Seller acknowledge receipt of copy of this page, which constitutes Page 2 of _____ Pages.
Buyer's Initials (_____) (_____)   Seller's Initials (_____) (_____)

┌─────────────────────────────────┐
│ ──── OFFICE USE ONLY ────   │
│ Reviewed by Broker or Designee __ │
│ Date _____   │
└─────────────────────────────────┘

BROKER'S COPY

M-MB-Jun-89

REAL ESTATE PURCHASE CONTRACT AND RECEIPT FOR DEPOSIT (DL-14 PAGE 2 OF 4)

☐ Subject Property Address _____

Buyer's Initials   Seller's Initials

_____ / _____   _____ / _____   **D. PEST CONTROL:** (1) Within _____ calendar days of acceptance of the offer, Seller shall furnish Buyer at the expense of ☐ Buyer, ☐ Seller, a current written report of an inspection by _____ , a licensed Structural Pest Control Operator, of the main building, ☐ detached garage(s) or carport(s), if any, and ☐ the following other structures on the property:
_____

(2) If requested by either Buyer or Seller, the report shall separately identify each recommendation for corrective measures as follows:
"Section 1": Infestation or infection which is evident.
"Section 2": Conditions that are present which are deemed likely to lead to infestation or infection.

(3) If no infestation or infection by wood destroying pests or organisms is found, the report shall include a written Certification as provided in Business and Professions Code § 8519(a) that on the date of inspection "no evidence of active infestation or infection was found."

(4) All work recommended to correct conditions described in "Section 1" shall be at the expense of ☐ Buyer, ☐ Seller.

(5) All work recommended to correct conditions described in "Section 2," if requested by Buyer, shall be at the expense of ☐ Buyer, ☐ Seller.

(6) The repairs shall be performed with good workmanship and materials of comparable quality and shall include repairs of leaking showers, replacement of tiles and other materials removed for repairs. It is understood that exact restoration of appearance or cosmetic items following all such repairs is not included.

(7) Funds for work agreed to be performed after close of escrow, shall be held in escrow and disbursed upon receipt of a written Certification as provided in Business and Professions Code § 8519(b) that the inspected property "is now free of evidence of active infestation or infection."

(8) Work to be performed at Seller's expense may be performed by Seller or through others, provided that (a) all required permits and final inspections are obtained, and (b) upon completion of repairs a written Certification is issued by a licensed Structural Pest Control Operator showing that the inspected property "is now free of evidence of active infestation or infection."

(9) If inspection of inaccessible areas is recommended by the report, Buyer has the option to accept and approve the report, or within _____ calendar days from receipt of the report to request in writing further inspection be made. BUYER'S FAILURE TO NOTIFY SELLER IN WRITING OF SUCH REQUEST SHALL CONCLUSIVELY BE CONSIDERED APPROVAL OF THE REPORT. If further inspection recommends "Section 1" and/or "Section 2" corrective measures, such work shall be at the expense of the party designated in subparagraph (4) and/or (5), respectively. If no infestation or infection is found, the cost of inspection, entry and closing of the inaccessible areas shall be at the expense of the Buyer.

(10) Other _____
_____

Buyer's Initials   Seller's Initials

_____ / _____   _____ / _____   **E. FLOOD HAZARD AREA DISCLOSURE:** Buyer is informed that subject property is situated in a "Special Flood Hazard Area" as set forth on a Federal Emergency Management Agency (FEMA) "Flood Insurance Rate Map" (FIRM), or "Flood Hazard Boundary Map" (FHBM). The law provides that, as a condition of obtaining financing on most structures located in a "Special Flood Hazard Area," lenders require flood insurance where the property or its attachments are security for a loan.

The extent of coverage and the cost may vary. For further information consult the lender or insurance carrier. No representation or recommendation is made by the Seller and the Broker(s) in this transaction as to the legal effect or economic consequences of the National Flood Insurance Program and related legislation.

Buyer's Initials   Seller's Initials

_____ / _____   _____ / _____   **F. SPECIAL STUDIES ZONE DISCLOSURE:** Buyer is informed that subject property is situated in a Special Studies Zone as designated under §§ 2621-2625, inclusive, of the California Public Resources Code; and, as such, the construction or development on this property of any structure for human occupancy may be subject to the findings of a geologic report prepared by a geologist registered in the State of California, unless such a report is waived by the City or County under the terms of that act.

Buyer is allowed _____ calendar days from acceptance of the offer to make further inquiries at appropriate governmental agencies concerning the use of the subject property under the terms of the Special Studies Zone Act and local building, zoning, fire, health, and safety codes. When such inquiries disclose conditions or information unsatisfactory to the Buyer, which the Seller is unwilling or unable to correct, Buyer may cancel this agreement. BUYER'S FAILURE TO NOTIFY SELLER IN WRITING SHALL CONCLUSIVELY BE CONSIDERED APPROVAL.

Buyer's Initials   Seller's Initials

_____ / _____   _____ / _____   **G. ENERGY CONSERVATION RETROFIT:** If local ordinance requires that the property be brought in compliance with minimum energy Conservation Standards as a condition of sale or transfer, ☐ Buyer, ☐ Seller shall comply with and pay for these requirements. Where permitted by law, Seller may, if obligated hereunder, satisfy the obligation by authorizing escrow to credit Buyer with sufficient funds to cover the cost of such retrofit.

Buyer's Initials   Seller's Initials

_____ / _____   _____ / _____   **H. HOME PROTECTION PLAN:** Buyer and Seller have been informed that Home Protection Plans are available. Such plans may provide additional protection and benefit to a Seller or Buyer. The CALIFORNIA ASSOCIATION OF REALTORS® and the Broker(s) in this transaction do not endorse or approve any particular company or program:

a) ☐ A Buyer's coverage Home Protection Plan to be issued by _____
Company, at a cost not to exceed $_____ , to be paid by ☐ Buyer, ☐ Seller; or

b) ☐ Buyer and Seller elect not to purchase a Home Protection Plan.

Buyer's Initials   Seller's Initials

_____ / _____   _____ / _____   **I. CONDOMINIUM/P.U.D.:** The subject of this transaction is a condominium/planned unit development (P.U.D.) designated as unit _____ and _____ parking space(s) and an undivided interest in community areas, and _____
_____ . The current monthly assessment charge by the homeowner's association or other governing body(s) is $_____ . As soon as practicable, Seller shall provide Buyer with copies of covenants, conditions and restrictions, articles of incorporation, by-laws, current rules and regulations, most current financial statements, and any other documents as required by law. Seller shall disclose in writing any known pending special assessment, claims, or litigation to Buyer. Buyer shall be allowed _____ calendar days from receipt to review these documents. If such documents disclose conditions or information unsatisfactory to Buyer, Buyer may cancel this agreement. BUYER'S FAILURE TO NOTIFY SELLER IN WRITING SHALL CONCLUSIVELY BE CONSIDERED APPROVAL.

Buyer's Initials   Seller's Initials

_____ / _____   _____ / _____   **J. LIQUIDATED DAMAGES: If Buyer fails to complete said purchase as herein provided by reason of any default of Buyer, Seller shall be released from obligation to sell the property to Buyer and may proceed against Buyer upon any claim or remedy which he/she may have in law or equity; provided, however, that by initialling this paragraph Buyer and Seller agree that Seller shall retain the deposit as liquidated damages. If the described property is a dwelling with no more than four units, one of which the Buyer intends to occupy as his/her residence, Seller shall retain as liquidated damages the deposit actually paid, or an amount therefrom, not more than 3% of the purchase price and promptly return any excess to Buyer. Buyer and Seller agree to execute a similar liquidated damages provision, such as CALIFORNIA ASSOCIATION OF REALTORS® Receipt for Increased Deposit (RID-11), for any increased deposits. (Funds deposited in trust accounts or in escrow are not released automatically in the event of a dispute. Release of funds requires written agreement of the parties, judicial decision or arbitration.)**

Buyer and Seller acknowledge receipt of copy of this page, which constitutes Page 3 of _____ Pages.

Buyer's Initials (_____) (_____)   Seller's Initials (_____) (_____)

┌─────────────────────────────────┐
│   OFFICE USE ONLY   │
│ Reviewed by Broker or Designee _____ │
│ Date _____   │
└─────────────────────────────────┘

EQUAL HOUSING OPPORTUNITY

M-MB-Aug-89

BROKER'S COPY

Subject Property Address _____

K. ARBITRATION OF DISPUTES: Any dispute or claim in law or equity arising out of this contract or any resulting transaction shall be decided by neutral binding arbitration in accordance with the rules of the American Arbitration Association, and not by court action except as provided by California law for judicial review of arbitration proceedings. Judgment upon the award rendered by the arbitrator(s) may be entered in any court having jurisdiction thereof. The parties shall have the right to discovery in accordance with Code of Civil Procedure § 1283.05. The following matters are excluded from arbitration hereunder: (a) a judicial or non-judicial foreclosure or other action or proceeding to enforce a deed of trust, mortgage, or real property sales contract as defined in Civil Code § 2985, (b) an unlawful detainer action, (c) the filing or enforcement of a mechanic's lien, (d) any matter which is within the jurisdiction of a probate court, or (e) an action for bodily injury or wrongful death, or for latent or patent defects to which Code of Civil Procedure § 337.1 or § 337.15 applies. The filing of a judicial action to enable the recording of a notice of pending action, for order of attachment, receivership, injunction, or other provisional remedies, shall not constitute a waiver of the right to arbitrate under this provision.

Any dispute or claim by or against broker(s) and/or associate licensee(s) participating in this transaction shall be submitted to arbitration consistent with the provision above only if the broker(s) and/or associate licensee(s) making the claim or against whom the claim is made shall have agreed to submit it to arbitration consistent with this provision.

"NOTICE: BY INITIALLING IN THE SPACE BELOW YOU ARE AGREEING TO HAVE ANY DISPUTE ARISING OUT OF THE MATTERS INCLUDED IN THE 'ARBITRATION OF DISPUTES' PROVISION DECIDED BY NEUTRAL ARBITRATION AS PROVIDED BY CALIFORNIA LAW AND YOU ARE GIVING UP ANY RIGHTS YOU MIGHT POSSESS TO HAVE THE DISPUTE LITIGATED IN A COURT OR JURY TRIAL. BY INITIALLING IN THE SPACE BELOW YOU ARE GIVING UP YOUR JUDICIAL RIGHTS TO DISCOVERY AND APPEAL, UNLESS THOSE RIGHTS ARE SPECIFICALLY INCLUDED IN THE 'ARBITRATION OF DISPUTES' PROVISION. IF YOU REFUSE TO SUBMIT TO ARBITRATION AFTER AGREEING TO THIS PROVISION, YOU MAY BE COMPELLED TO ARBITRATE UNDER THE AUTHORITY OF THE CALIFORNIA CODE OF CIVIL PROCEDURE. YOUR AGREEMENT TO THIS ARBITRATION PROVISION IS VOLUNTARY."

"WE HAVE READ AND UNDERSTAND THE FOREGOING AND AGREE TO SUBMIT DISPUTES ARISING OUT OF THE MATTERS INCLUDED IN THE 'ARBITRATION OF DISPUTES' PROVISION TO NEUTRAL ARBITRATION."

Buyer's Initials   Seller's Initials
_____ / _____   _____ / _____

17. **OTHER TERMS AND CONDITIONS:** _____
_____
_____
_____
_____

18. **ATTORNEY'S FEES:** In any action, proceeding or arbitration arising out of this agreement, the prevailing party shall be entitled to reasonable attorney's fees and costs. .

19. **ENTIRE CONTRACT:** Time is of the essence. All prior agreements between the parties are incorporated in this agreement which constitutes the entire contract. Its terms are intended by the parties as a final expression of their agreement with respect to such terms as are included herein and may not be contradicted by evidence of any prior agreement or contemporaneous oral agreement. The parties further intend that this agreement constitutes the complete and exclusive statement of its terms and that no extrinsic evidence whatsoever may be introduced in any judicial or arbitration proceeding, if any, involving this agreement.

20. **CAPTIONS:** The captions in this agreement are for convenience of reference only and are not intended as part of this agreement.

21. **AGENCY CONFIRMATION:** The following agency relationship(s) are hereby confirmed for this transaction:
   LISTING AGENT: _____ is the agent of (check one):
                        (Print Firm Name)
   ☐ the Seller exclusively; or ☐ both the Buyer and Seller

   SELLING AGENT: _____ (if not the same as Listing Agent) is the agent of (check one):
                        (Print Firm Name)
   ☐ the Buyer exclusively; or ☐ the Seller exclusively; or ☐ both the Buyer and Seller.

22. **AMENDMENTS:** This agreement may not be amended, modified, altered or changed in any respect whatsoever except by a further agreement in writing executed by Buyer and Seller.

23. **OFFER:** This constitutes an offer to purchase the described property. Unless acceptance is signed by Seller and a signed copy delivered in person, by mail, or facsimile, and received by Buyer at the address below, or by _____ who is authorized to receive it, on behalf of Buyer, within _____ calendar days of the date hereof, this offer shall be deemed revoked and the deposit shall be returned. Buyer has read and acknowledges receipt of a copy of this offer. This agreement and any supplement, addendum or modification relating hereto, including any photocopy or facsimile thereof, may be executed in two or more counterparts, all of which shall constitute one and the same writing.

REAL ESTATE BROKER _____   BUYER _____
By _____   BUYER _____
Address _____   Address _____
_____   _____
Telephone _____   Telephone _____

ACCEPTANCE

The undersigned Seller accepts and agrees to sell the property on the above terms and conditions and agrees to the above confirmation of agency relationships (☐ subject to attached counter offer).

Seller agrees to pay to Broker(s) _____

compensation for services as follows: _____

Payable: (a) On recordation of the deed or other evidence of title, or (b) if completion of sale is prevented by default of Seller, upon Seller's default, or (c) if completion of sale is prevented by default of Buyer, only if and when Seller collects damages from Buyer, by suit or otherwise, and then in an amount not less than one-half of the damages recovered, but not to exceed the above fee, after first deducting title and escrow expenses and the expenses of collection, if any. Seller shall execute and deliver an escrow instruction irrevocably assigning the compensation for service in an amount equal to the compensation agreed to above. In any action, proceeding, or arbitration between Broker(s) and Seller arising out of this agreement, the prevailing party shall be entitled to reasonable attorney's fees and costs. The undersigned has read and acknowledges receipt of a copy of this agreement and authorizes Broker(s) to deliver a signed copy to Buyer.

Date _____ Telephone _____   SELLER _____
Address _____
_____   SELLER _____

Real Estate Broker(s) agree to the foregoing.
Broker _____ By _____ Date _____
Broker _____ By _____ Date _____

This form is available for use by the entire real estate industry. The use of this form is not intended to identify the user as a REALTOR®. REALTOR® is a registered collective membership mark which may be used only by real estate licensees who are members of the NATIONAL ASSOCIATION OF REALTORS® and who subscribe to its Code of Ethics.

_____ OFFICE USE ONLY _____
Reviewed by Broker or Designee _____
Date _____

Page 4 of _____ Pages.

BROKER'S COPY

M-MB-Aug-89

SUMMARY   A contract is an agreement between parties wherein each exchanges a promise or promises to either perform or not to perform certain acts. A unilateral contract is one wherein there is a promise made by only one party. A bilateral contract is one wherein each of the parties exchanges promises. Contracts may be created by expression or implication. Contracts can be valid, void, voidable, and unenforceable.

There are certain essential elements of a real estate contract. They are parties capable of contracting, mutual consent, a lawful object, sufficient consideration, and according to the Statute of Frauds, the contract must be in writing. An executed contract is one which has been completed or fulfilled. An executory contract is one that remains to be fulfilled.

Full performance discharges or terminates a contract. Contracts can also be terminated by expiration of time, mutual consent, plus other technical means. A breach of contract means that one of the parties did not fulfill his or her part of the agreement. The two most common remedies for a breach are to sue for damages or to sue for specific performance. The Statute of Limitations prescribes the time period within which a lawsuit must be filed. Beyond the prescribed period, a person's rights are said to have outlawed.

A real estate contract should contain the date of the agreement, names and addresses of the parties, a description of the property, the consideration, mortgage terms, the date and place of closing the contract, and any other provisions required or requested by the parties.

A listing agreement is the contract between the principal, usually the seller, and the real estate broker. Types of listings include open, exclusive agency, exclusive authorization and right-to-sell, and net listing. Multiple listing service is an organization whereby member brokers agree to pool listings and share information and commissions.

The purchase agreement and receipt for deposit is the contract between the buyer and seller. To be binding there are certain requirements that must be met. Common real estate forms were provided in this chapter, with an explanation of the various clauses contained in each form.

Important Terms and Concepts

Bilateral contract

Counteroffer

Deposit receipt

Exclusive agency listing

Exclusive authorization and right-to-sell listing

Executed

Executory

Expressed contract

Implied contract

Mutual consent

Multiple listing service

Net listing

Open listing

Options

Statute of Frauds

Statute of Limitations

Unenforceable

Unilateral contract

Valid

Void

Voidable

REVIEWING YOUR UNDERSTANDING

1. Which of the following would *not* be covered by the Statute of Frauds?
   (a) The payment of an agent's commission
   (b) A two year lease
   (c) An agreement not to be performed within the lifetime of the promissor
   (d) A six-month tenancy

2. Which of the following are considered essential elements of a contract?
   (a) Consent of the parties
   (b) A lawful object
   (c) Consideration
   (d) All of the above

3. Contracts may be discharged by:
   (a) Impossibility of performance
   (b) Agreement of the parties
   (c) Choices (a) and (b) are both correct
   (d) None of the above

4. The most common form of listing found in California is:
   (a) Open listing
   (b) Exclusive authorization and right-to-sell listing
   (c) Net listing
   (d) Exclusive agency listing

5. Which of the following listings must have a definite termination date by law?
   (a) Net listing
   (b) Exclusive agency
   (c) Exclusive authorization and right-to-sell
   (d) Choices (b) and (c) are both correct

6. Of the following listings, which stipulates that the agent may earn anything over the seller's stipulated amount after giving the seller proper disclosure?
   (a) Net listing
   (b) Exclusive agency
   (c) Exclusive authorization and right-to-sell
   (d) Open listing

7. A listing is a (an):
   (a) Unilateral contract
   (b) Bilateral contract
   (c) Choices (a) and (b) are both correct
   (d) None of the above

8. A deposit receipt:
   (a) Is a receipt for the deposit
   (b) Is a real estate contract when properly executed
   (c) Reaffirms the brokerage commission
   (d) All of the above are correct

9. Which of the following statements is true if, during the escrow period, a fire destroys the home being sold?
   (a) Buyer must complete the purchase.
   (b) Buyer need not complete the purchase but seller retains the deposit.
   (c) Buyer need not complete the purchase and is entitled to his deposit back.
   (d) None of the above.

10. After signing a deposit receipt, the seller later decides not to sell. The buyer may:
    (a) Simply cancel the agreement and is entitled to the return of any deposit
    (b) Sue for specific performance
    (c) (a) and (b) above are both correct
    (d) None of the above are correct

Chapter 6
Practical Real Estate Mathematics

Preview   This chapter will help you to understand the fundamentals of mathematics as they apply to real estate.

Basic concepts of addition, subtraction, multiplication, division, fractions, and decimals, will be briefly reviewed to set a solid foundation for more complicated computations. At the conclusion of this chapter, you will be able to:

1. *Solve problems related to investment, discounting notes, appraisal, commissions, interest and loans, cost and selling price, square footage and area calculations, prorations and documentary transfer taxes.*

2. *Use amortization and other tables to simplify real estate mathematical computations.*

6.1 REVIEW OF FUNDAMENTALS   The practical application of real estate mathematics often creates apprehension in some people. The use of calculators and the development of helpful tables can do much to alleviate these fears. An understanding of the simple formulas presented in this lesson will help students gain confidence in their ability to solve everyday real estate mathematical problems.

Much of the difficulty some people have with mathematics comes from a lack of knowledge or forgetfulness of some of the basic rules of mathematics, particularly with regard to percentages, decimals, and fractions.

Decimals   Before we attempt to solve various real estate mathematical problems, we need to review the concept of decimals.

A decimal is the period that sets apart the whole number from the fractional part of the number. The position of the decimal in a number will determine the value of the number.

All numbers to the right of the decimal are less than one. The first position to the right of the decimal is the "tenth" position; the second is the "hundredth"; the third is the "thousandth"; the fourth is the "ten thousandth"; the fifth is the "hundred thousandth"; and so on.

TABLE 6-1

Percentage	Decimal	Fraction
4½%	0.045	45/1000
6⅔%	0.0667	1/15
10%	0.10	1/10
12½%	0.125	1/8
16⅔%	0.1667	1/6
25%	0.25	1/4
33⅓%	0.333	1/3
50%	0.50	1/2
66⅔%	0.6667	2/3
75%	0.75	3/4
100%	1.00	1/1

To the left of the decimal are the whole numbers. The first position is known as the "units" position; the second is the "tens"; the third is the "hundreds"; the fourth is the "thousands"; the fifth is the "ten thousands"; the sixth is the "hundred thousands"; and so on.

Table 6-1 may help to clarify the relationships among percentages, decimals, and fractions.

Converting Percentages to Decimals

To remove the percentage sign, simply move the decimal two places to the left to form a usable decimal number (see Table 6-2).

TABLE 6-2

8%	converts to	.08
25%	converts to	.25
9.5%	converts to	.095
105%	converts to	1.05

Many times an answer will appear as a decimal and you may wish to convert the answer to an answer with a percentage sign (%). To do this simply reverse the procedure (see Table 6-3).

TABLE 6-3

.08	converts to	8%
.25	converts to	25%
.095	converts to	9.5%
1.05	converts to	105%

| **Addition of Decimal Numbers** | When adding numbers with decimals, place figures in a vertical column and make sure each decimal is in a direct vertical line. |

Example.

```
  126.06
    5.715
  400.8
  532.575
```

Subtraction of Decimal Numbers

The same procedure is used to subtract one decimal number from another.

Example.

```
  $18,450.60
 −    425.20
  $18,025.40
```

Multiplication of Decimal Numbers

Multiply the two numbers in the normal fashion and then mark off the total number of decimal places in the answer that there are in the two numbers being multiplied.

Example.

```
    7.064    (multiplicand)
 ×  37.6     (multiplier)
  265.6064   (product)
```

Division of Decimal Numbers

In a division problem which contains a decimal in the divisor, it is necessary to remove that decimal before preceding with the problem. Mentally move the decimal in the dividend the same number of places shown in the divisor. Add zeros to the dividend if the dividend has fewer digits than are needed to carry out the division process. The decimal point in the quotient (answer) will appear directly above the imaginary decimal in the dividend.

Example.

```
                    6000.
(divisor) .045 /270.000
                270
                000    (quotient)
```

When no decimal appears in the divisor, the decimal in the quotient will appear directly above the decimal in the dividend.

Example.

```
        3.02
  24/72.48
     72
        48
        48
```

6.2 VARIABLES Most real estate problems involve three variables—two known and one unknown. It is the student's responsibility to find the unknown variable. The three variables are termed *Paid, Made,* and *Rate* (%). The relationship among these variables is shown in Figure 6-1.

These basic formulas evolve from the illustration:

$$Made = Paid \times Rate$$

$$Paid = Made \div Rate$$

$$Rate = Made \div Paid$$

In any problem involving these formulas, one quantity will be unknown and you must determine from the given information whether you must multiply or divide the others to compute the third variable.

To assist in this process Table 6-4 equates various real estate terms with the three terms shown in Figure 6-1.

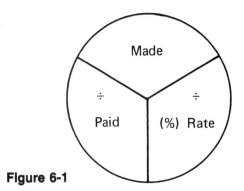

Figure 6-1

TABLE 6-4

Amount Made	Amount Paid	Rate (%)
1. Income investment, of yield	Amount of investment	Percentage return
2. Sales commission	Selling price	Rate of commission
3. Documentary transfer tax	Taxable equity	Transfer tax rate
4. Monthly rent	Investment amount	Rate of return
5. Annual net income	Property value	Capitalization rate
6. Interest	Principal	Rate × time
7. Discount amount	Loan balance	Rate of discount
8. Area of property	Length	Width

If the terms in the problem relate to those in Table 6-4, substitute the amounts in the problem into any one of the three formulas previously given, depending on what is to be determined.

Investment Problems   To find the amount of money to be invested when the income and rate of return are known:

$$\text{Amount of investment (paid)} = \frac{\text{Income (made)}}{\text{Rate (\% of return)}}$$

To find the rate (%) of return when the income and the amount invested are known:

$$\text{Rate (\%)} = \frac{\text{Income (made)}}{\text{Amount invested (paid)}}$$

To find the income when the amount invested and the rate (%) are known:

$$\text{Income (made)} = \text{Amount invested (paid)} \times \text{Rate (\%)}$$

Sample investment problems using the preceding formulas follow.

Caution: When you are given monthly figures, always convert them to annual figures (for example, $80 per month $\times$ 12 = $960 per year).

PROBLEM 1   If an investor wants to earn $50 per month from a savings account and the account pays 5 percent simple interest, how much must be put in the account?

The given variables are:

Income = $600 per year ($50 $\times$ 12 months)
Rate of return = 5%

The unknown variable is the amount of investment. By substituting in the formula, we obtain

$$\text{Amount} = \frac{\$600}{5\% \text{ or } .05} \qquad .05\overline{)600.00} \quad 12,000.$$

Amount of investment = $12,000.00

PROBLEM 2   An investor bought a parcel of property for $45,000. Assuming the property was later listed at $60,000, and sold for that amount. What is the rate (%) of profit the investor made on this sale?

The given variables are:

Paid = $45,000
Made = $15,000   ($60,000 − $45,000)

The unknown variable is the rate of profit. By substituting in the formula we obtain

$$\frac{.33}{\$45000 \overline{\smash{\big)}\,15000.00}} \quad \text{or 33\%}$$
$$\underline{13500\ 0}$$
$$1500\ 00$$
$$\underline{1350\ 00}$$

Discounting Notes
PROBLEM 3

A $5,000 note to a private lender is to be paid off in twelve months. The borrower is to pay the $5,000 plus 8 percent interest on the due date. An investor purchases the note today at a discount rate of 10 percent. What is the investor's rate of return on the amount invested?

The first step is to determine the amount made.

Paid × Rate = Made

By subsituting in the formula, we obtain

$5000 × .08 = $400 (interest to the lender on due date)
$5000 × .10 = $500 (discount allowed investor)
        Made = $900
         Paid = $5000 less 10% or $4500

The given variables are:

Made = $900
Paid = $4500

The unknown variable is the rate (%).

Made ÷ Paid = Rate

Substitution results in:

$$\frac{.20}{\$4500 \overline{\smash{\big)}\,900.00}}$$
$$\underline{900\ 0}$$
$$0$$

Rate or percentage of profit = .20 or 20%

Appraisal Problems

In appraisal problems, use the formula:

Paid × Rate (%) = Made

Value of property × Capitalization rate = Net income or net loss

Value = Made ÷ Rate (capitalization rate)

Capitalization rate = Made ÷ Paid (value of property)

Income or loss = Paid × Capitalization rate

PROBLEM 4

A triplex nets an income of $500 per month per apartment unit. A prospective investor is interested in purchasing the property and he or she demands an investment rate (capitalization rate) of 9 percent. What should the investor pay for the triplex?

$500 per unit × 3 units = $1,500 income per month

$1,500 × 12 months = $18,000 annual income

The given variables are:

Made = $18,000
Rate = 9%

The unknown variable is the paid. Substitution in the formula, results in

$$
\begin{array}{r}
200000. \\
.09\overline{)18000.00} \\
18 \\
\hline
0000\ 00
\end{array}
$$

The amount to be invested (purchase price) = $200,000.

PROBLEM 5 An investor pays $400,000 for a six-unit apartment house which has an income of $550 rent per month per unit with total expenses of $3,600 per year. What capitalization rate (%) will the investor make on the investment?

Gross income = 12 months × 550 = $6600 × 6 units = $39,600
                                    Less expenses   3,600
                                    Net made $36,000

By substituting in the formula:

$$
\begin{array}{r}
.09 \\
400,000\overline{)36000.00} \\
36000 \\
\hline
00
\end{array}
$$

The capitalization rate = 9%.

Commission Problems In commission problems:

Paid figure refers to the selling price.

Rate is the commission rate.

Made is the amount of commission.

PROBLEM 6 A real estate salesperson found a buyer for a $70,000 condo. The seller agreed to pay 6 percent commission on the sale to the broker. The broker pays the salesperson 40 percent of the commission. What is the salesperson's commission?

The unknown variable is the made. Substitution in the formula results in:

Paid = $70,000 (selling price)
Rate = 40% of 6%

Made (commission) = Paid (selling price) × Rate

$70,000	$4,200
× .06	× .40
$ 4,200 Total commission	$1,680 Salesperson's commission

The amount of the salesperson's share of the commission = $1,680.

PROBLEM 7 A real estate office listed a plot of ground for $75,000 with an agreed commission of 10 percent. The broker presents an offer of 10 percent less than the listed price, which the seller agreed to accept, if the broker will reduce the amount of commission by 25 percent. If the agreement is satisfactory, what is the amount of commission?

The missing variable is the made.

Paid = $75,000 less 10% or $7,500 = $67,500
Rate = 10% less 25% = 7½% or (.075)

Substitution in the formula results in:

Made (commission) = Paid (selling price) × Rate

$75,000	.100	$67,500
−7,500	−.025	× .075
$67,500	.075	$ 5,062.50

The amount of commission = $5,062.50

There are a variety of commission splits in actual practice.

A broker could take a listing and make the sale, and receive the entire commission. Possibly, one or more salespersons in a broker's office could be involved; if so, the salespeople would divide the commission with the broker.

A listing may be taken by Broker A and be placed in multiple listing. If the sale was made by Broker B, he or she would split the commission with Broker A's office. One of Broker B's salespersons may make the sale. If so, the salesperson would split the office's share of the commission with Broker B.

Commission splits between multiple listing brokers vary, with 50/50 being the most common. In some cases this split could be 40 percent to the listing broker's office and 60 percent to the selling broker's office.

When the listing and the sale are in-house, the splits might be:

20% to the listing salesperson

40% to the salesperson making the sale

40% to the broker

OR

35% to the listing salesperson

35% to the salesperson making the sale

30% to the broker

The amount of the commission split depends on the individual broker's commission schedule. An example of a possible commission split between real estate brokers and salespersons might be: If $70,000 is the sales price, 6% × $70,000 = $4,200, the total amount of commission. Commission is paid by the seller as follows:

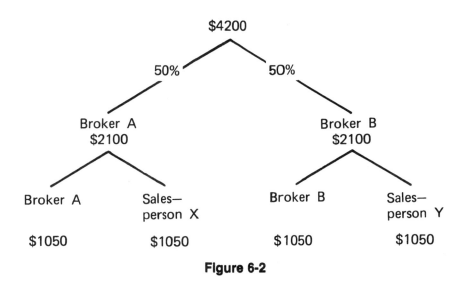

Figure 6-2

Interest and Loan Problems

Interest is a rental amount or charge for the use of money. It is determined by the rate of interest charged, and the amount to be borrowed. When borrowing money, the borrower is obligated to pay back the amount borrowed as well as the interest on the amount borrowed, per agreed upon terms between the borrower and the lender.

> *Note:* In working with interest problems, it is very important to convert monthly figures to annual figures.

To solve interest problems, you will use these terms and formula.

Interest is the charge for the use of money expressed as dollars.

Principal is the amount of money borrowed.

Rate is the percentage of interest charged on the principal.

Time represents the interval between payments on principal and/or interest. In the formula it is expressed as years or a fraction of a year.

$$\text{Interest} = \text{Principal} \times \text{Rate} \times \text{Time} \quad (I = P \times R \times T)$$

By applying this formula to our standard made, paid, rate formula, the *paid* figure refers to the amount of the loan or the principal, *rate* (%) is the rate of interest multiplied by the years or fraction of a year, and *made* is the amount of interest expressed in money. The following formulas are therefore derived:

$$\frac{\text{Amount}}{\text{of loan}} = \frac{\text{Amount of interest}}{\text{Rate of interest} \times \text{time}} \qquad \text{or } P = \frac{I}{R \times T}$$

$$\frac{\text{Rate of}}{\text{interest}} = \frac{\text{Amount of interest}}{\text{Amount of loan} \times \text{time}} \qquad \text{or } R = \frac{I}{P \times T}$$

$$\frac{\text{Amount of}}{\text{interest}} = \frac{\text{Amount of}}{\text{loan}} \times \frac{\text{Rate of}}{\text{interest}} \times \text{Time} \quad \text{or } I = P \times R \times T$$

PROBLEM 8   If you borrowed $8,000 for one year and paid $640 interest what rate of interest did you pay?

The known variables are:

Paid = $8,000
Made = $640 × 1 year = $640 per year

Substitution results in:

Rate = Made ÷ Paid   or $\dfrac{I}{P \times T}$

$$\begin{array}{r} .08 \\ \hline \$8000\,\overline{)640.00} \\ \underline{640\ 00} \end{array} \qquad \text{or} \qquad \frac{640}{8000 \times 1}$$

PROBLEM 9   If one month's interest is $45.00 on a seven-year straight note (interest only note) and the note calls for interest at 9 percent per year, what is the amount of the loan?

The known variables are:

Rate = 9%
Made = $45 × 12 months = $540 interest per year

Substitution in the formula results in:

Paid = Made ÷ Rate

$$\begin{array}{r} 6000. \\ \hline .09\,\overline{)540.00} \\ 54 \\ \underline{\hphantom{0}} \\ 0\ 00 \end{array}$$

Proof: $6,000   Principal
          × .09   Rate
        $540.00   Interest paid for year

Cost and Selling Price Problems

In dealing with cost problems you are given a selling price and are asked to calculate the profit, or the cost before a fixed profit.

The first step is to consider the cost figure as 100 percent. Next, add the profit percent to the 100 percent and then divide the total percentage into the selling price.

PROBLEM 10

A sold a piece of real property for $60,000, which allowed her to make a 20 percent profit. What did she pay for the property?

Substitution in the formula results in:

Cost = Selling price ÷ (Profit % + 100%)

$$\text{Cost} = 1.20\overline{)60,000.00} \quad \begin{array}{c} 50,000. \\ \end{array}$$
$$\begin{array}{c} 60\ 0 \\ \hline 00\ 00 \end{array}$$

She paid $50,000 for the property.

PROBLEM 11

Another problem arises when the seller receives a given net amount and you are asked to establish the selling price or amount of the loan.

For instance, you offer your urban lot for sale asking for a certain net amount. A broker who found a buyer gave you a check for $37,600. He had already deducted a 6 percent commission. What did the lot sell for?

The formula used to solve this problem is:

$$\text{Selling price} = \frac{\text{Net amount received}}{100\% - \text{Commission rate}}$$

Substitution in this formula results in:

Selling price = $37,600 ÷ (100% − 6%) or 94%

$$\text{Selling price} = .94\overline{)37,600.00} \quad \begin{array}{c} 40,000. \\ \end{array}$$
$$\begin{array}{c} 376 \\ \hline 00\ 00 \end{array}$$

6.3 SQUARE FOOTAGE AND AREA CALCULATIONS

Problems related to square footage are simple. The technique is used when you desire to know the amount of square feet in a property. When you have determined the square footage, you can then refer to an index on residential property to determine the cost per square foot or obtain estimates per square foot from local contractors. The cost per square foot multiplied by the square footage gives an estimate of value of a building or a vacant lot.

The basic formula for determining the area of a piece of property is:

$$Area = Length \times Width$$

In Figure 6-3 we substitute these terms in our basic symbol.

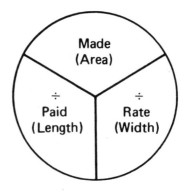

The following formulas can be used:

Area = Length × Width
Length = Area ÷ Width
Width = Area ÷ Length

PROBLEM 12 What would be the depth or length of a piece of vacant land containing six acres, with a width or front footage of 400 feet on the county road? (Remember there are 43,560 square feet in an acre.)
Convert the piece of property into square feet by multiplying 43,560 by 6 = 261,360 square feet.

Substitution in the formula results in:

Length = Area ÷ Width

Length = 261,360 ÷ 400 = 653.4 feet

Proof: 400 feet × 653.4 feet = 261,360 square feet

If the piece of property you are measuring is irregular in shape, try to make rectangles and triangles of the area given. (The area of a triangle = altitude × base ÷ 2.)
An example of this type of computation is given in Problem 13.

PROBLEM 13 Use the following diagrams and (a) compute the square footage of the lot. (b) Then find the total cost of the garage and house. The garage is valued at $30 per square foot. The house is priced at $75 per square foot.

Insert dotted lines in the diagram in order to form a rectangle A and a triangle B.

1. Compute the area in rectangle A as follows: 110 × 100 = 11,000 square feet.

2. Compute the area of the triangle B as follows: 40 × 100 ÷ 2 = 2,000 square feet.

Thus the size of the lot is:

11,000 + 2,000 = 13,000 square feet

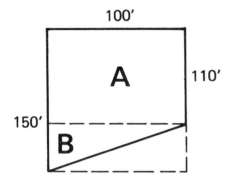

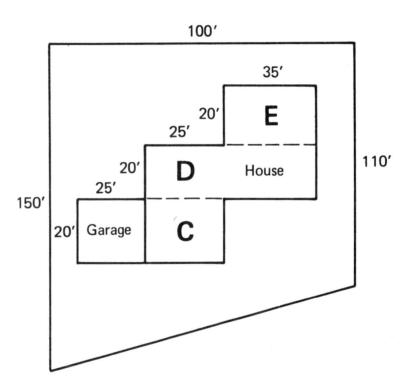

To figure the area in the house:

1. Place dotted lines as indicated in the diagram, thus forming three rectangles C, D, E, in the house.

2. Compute the area of each rectangle as follows:

Rectangle C = 25 × 20 = 500 square feet
Rectangle D = 60 × 20 = 1,200 square feet
Rectangle E = 20 × 35 = 700 square feet
        Total = 2,400 square feet in house

3. Compute the area of the garage as follows:
20 × 25 = 500 square feet

4. Compute the costs as follows:

$$2,400 \text{ square feet} \times \$75 \text{ per square foot} = \$180,000$$
$$500 \text{ square feet} \times \$30 \text{ per square foot} = \underline{\$\ 15,000}$$
$$\text{Total} = \$195,000$$

ANSWERS
(a) 13,000 square feet in the lot
(b) $195,000 for the total improvements

6.4 PRORATION

Ownership of real property entails certain expenses. Some of these expenses are paid in advance, others in arrears. They may be paid for by the owner prior to the sale of the property, or the buyer assumes the payments that have not been made by the owner at close of escrow.

It is only fair that expenses paid in advance should be credited to the seller, and the buyer debited; and by the same token, expenses not paid by the seller, up to the close of escrow should be debited to the seller and credited to the buyer.

Proration is the act of making an equitable distribution of these expenses in escrow at the close of the sale.

There are actually four basic steps in proration:

1. Determine the number of days to be prorated.

2. Tabulate the cost per day.

3. Multiply the number of days by the cost per day.

4. Determine whether the amount should be a credit or a debit to the seller or to the buyer.

Remember: In determining prorations assume that there are 30 days in a month and 360 days in the year.

Expenses that are subject to proration are real property taxes, interest on loans assumed, hazard insurance, and prepaid rents, if the property is income producing.

PROBLEM 14
Ms. A sells her home on September 1, 1990, upon which she has an existing loan of $40,000. The interest on the loan is 9 percent. Buyer B assumes A's loan with interest paid to August 15, 1990. The buyer also assumes an existing three-year hazard insurance policy for $180 per year, paid by A until October 15, 1991. Ms. A also neglected to

pay her property taxes of $900 for the year. What is the interest proration and who is credited or debited? What is the insurance proration and who is credited or debited? What is the tax proration?

Figure the proration on the interest:

Step 1. August 15 to September 1 = 15 days

Step 2. $40,000 × 9% ÷ 360 = $10 per day

Step 3. 15 days × $10 per day = $150 interest

Step 4. credit the buyer and debit the seller

Figure the proration on the insurance policy:

Step 1. September 1, 1990 through October 15, 1991 = 405 days

Step 2. $180 ÷ 360 = $.50 per day

Step 3. 405 days × $.50 = $202.50

Step 4. credit the seller and debit the buyer

Figure the tax proration as follows:

Step 1. July 1 to September 1 = 60 days

Step 2. $900 ÷ 360 = $2.50

Step 3. 60 days × $2.50 = $150

Step 4. debit the seller and credit the buyer

Note: A general rule to use in proration is as follows: When expenses are paid *beyond escrow,* credit the seller and debit the buyer.

When expenses are paid *short of escrow,* debit the seller and credit the buyer.

6.5 DOCUMENTARY TRANSFER TAX

A state law permits the county recorder to apply a documentary transfer tax, when real property is transferred. The amount of the tax is placed on the deed and is computed based on the following schedule:

1. $1.10 for $1,000 of value transferred, or $.55 for every $500 or fraction thereof.

2. When the terms of the sale are all cash, the documentary transfer tax is paid on the entire sales price. A new loan by the buyer is treated the same as an all cash sale.

3. When the buyer assumes the seller's existing loan, the amount of the loan on property is exempt and is subtracted from the total selling price and the tax is only computed on the equity amount. The transfer tax can be paid by either the buyer or seller, but custom usually has the seller pay the tax.

PROBLEM 15   Seller A sells her home for $210,000. The buyer obtains new financing for the sales price. How much documentary transfer tax must be paid on the property?

$$\frac{\$210,000}{1,000} = 210 \times \$1.10 = \$231$$

PROBLEM 16   Seller A sells his condo for $87,500, but in this case the buyer *assumes* the seller's existing $50,000 loan. What is the documentary transfer tax?

$87,500	Sales price
− 50,000	Existing loan assumed
$37,500	Equity transferred

$$\frac{\$37,500}{1,000} = 37.5 \times \$1.10 = \$41.25 \text{ Documentary transfer tax}$$

6.6 USE OF TABLES   In order to facilitate mathematical computations, shortcut tables have been devised.

Interest Computation   We previously discussed the method of arriving at the amount of interest to be paid using formula $I = P \times R \times T$. Computations, remember, are based on a 30-day month and 360-day year.

Let's explore an example using both the conventional method and the use of an interest table (see Table 6-5).

PROBLEM 17   What is the interest on a $6,500 loan for one year, three months, and 20 days at 9 percent interest?

CONVENTIONAL METHOD

$P \times R \times T = I$

Principal is $6,500
Rate is 9%
Time is 470 days (1 year + 3 months + 20 days)
Thus:

$$\$6,500 \times .09 \times 1.3056 \left(\frac{470}{360}\right) = \begin{array}{l} \$763.75 \quad \text{(approximate)} \\ \$763.78 \quad \text{(actual)} \end{array}$$

1 year and 3 months = 15 months

Under the 9% column, the 30-day factor = 7.5000

15 months × 7.5000 = 112.50 + the 20-day factor of 5.00 = 117.50

$117.50 × 6.5 (number of thousand) = $763.75

Amortization Tables

Amortization tables are used to facilitate the compilation of figures dealing with monthly payments for various amounts of loans at various interest rates and terms. A typical table showing various rates of interest and terms is shown in Table 6-6 on bottom of page 112.

A typical table shows along one axis a list of various loan terms expressed in years and the other axis contains various amounts of interest. At the intersection of any two axes in the table itself is found the monthly payment to pay off $1,000 in dollars and cents for various interest rates.

PROBLEM 18

A $60,000 loan for 30 years at 10 percent interest will have what monthly payment?

In solving this problem by using the amortization table, use the following procedure:

Go to the 10% interest column, and follow it down to the 30-year line. There you will find the factor 8.78. This means $8.78 per month will pay off $1,000 in 30 years. Our loan amount is $60,000, therefore,

$$\frac{\$60,000}{\$1,000} = 60$$

Thus 60 × $8.78 = $526.80 per month will pay off a $60,000 loan at 10% in 30 years.

TABLE 6-5 Interest Table Figured on $1,000
360 Days to the Year

Days	5%	6%	7%	8%	9%	10%
1	0.1389	0.1667	0.1944	0.2222	0.2500	0.2778
2	0.2778	0.3333	0.3889	0.4444	0.5000	0.5556
3	0.4167	0.5000	0.5833	0.6666	0.7500	0.8334
4	0.5556	0.6667	0.7778	0.8888	1.0000	1.1112
5	0.6944	0.8333	0.9722	1.1111	1.2500	1.3890
6	0.8333	1.0000	1.1667	1.3333	1.5000	1.6668
7	0.9722	1.1667	1.3611	1.5555	1.7500	1.9446
8	1.1111	1.3333	1.5556	1.7777	2.0000	2.2224
9	1.2500	1.5000	1.7500	2.0000	2.2500	2.5002
10	1.3889	1.6667	1.9444	2.2222	2.5000	2.7780
11	1.5278	1.8333	2.1389	2.4444	2.7500	3.0558
12	1.6667	2.0000	2.3333	2.6666	3.0000	3.3336
13	1.8056	2.1667	2.5278	2.8888	3.2500	3.6114
14	1.9444	2.3333	2.7222	3.1111	3.5000	3.8892
15	2.0833	2.5000	2.9167	3.3333	3.7500	4.1670
16	2.2222	2.6667	3.1111	3.5555	4.0000	4.4448
17	2.3611	2.8333	3.3055	3.7777	4.2500	4.7226
18	2.5000	3.0000	3.5000	4.0000	4.5000	5.0004
19	2.6389	3.1667	3.6944	4.2222	4.7500	5.2782
20	2.7778	3.3333	3.8889	4.4444	5.0000	5.5560
21	2.9167	3.5000	4.0833	4.6666	5.2500	5.8338
22	3.0556	3.6667	4.2778	4.8888	5.5000	6.1116
23	3.1944	3.8333	4.4722	5.1111	5.7500	6.3894
24	3.2222	4.0000	4.6667	5.3333	6.0000	6.6672
25	3.4722	4.1667	4.8611	5.5555	6.2500	6.9450
26	3.6111	4.3333	5.0555	5.7777	6.5000	7.2228
27	3.7500	4.5000	5.2500	6.0000	6.7500	7.5006
28	3.8889	4.6667	5.4444	6.2222	7.0000	7.7784
29	4.0278	4.8333	5.6389	6.4444	7.2500	8.0562
30	4.1667	5.0000	5.8333	6.6666	7.5000	8.3340

31st day

TABLE 6-6 Table of Monthly Payments to Amortize $1,000 Loan

Term of Years	9%	10%	11%	12%	12½%	13%	13½%	14%	14½%	15%
10	12.67	13.22	13.78	14.35	14.64	14.93	15.23	15.53	15.83	16.13
15	10.15	10.75	11.37	12.00	12.33	12.65	12.99	13.32	13.66	14.00
20	9.00	9.66	10.32	11.01	11.36	11.72	12.08	12.44	12.80	13.17
25	8.40	9.09	9.80	10.53	10.90	11.28	11.66	12.04	12.43	12.81
30	8.05	8.78	9.52	10.29	10.67	11.06	11.85	11.85	12.25	12.64
35	7.84	8.60	9.37	10.16	10.55	10.95	11.36	11.76	12.17	12.57

PROBLEM 19   If an individual made payments of $1,234.60 per month including 12 percent on a fully amortized thirty-year loan, what was the original amount of the loan?

At the intersection where the 30-year line intersects with the 12% interest line is $10.29 or a $1,000 loan.

$1,234.60 ÷ 10.29 = 120 × 1,000 = $120,000 loan (approximate)

PROBLEM 20   If you borrowed $48,000 using a fully amortized home equity loan, and were to make payments of $559.68, including 13 1/2 percent interest, how many years would it take to pay off the loan?

Reduce $559.68 to the amount of each payment per $1,000 as follows:

$559.68 ÷ 48 = $11.66

Using the 13½% interest column, locate the amount $11.66. This amount falls on the 25-year loan term line.

PROBLEM 21   If an individual borrowed $76,000 using a fully amortized loan and paid at $782.04 per month including interest, for a period of 30 years, what would the rate of interest be?

Divide $782.04 by 76 to determine the amount of each payment per $1,000:

$782.04 ÷ 76 = $10.29

Using the table, the intersection of the 30-year line and the $10.29 = 12% interest rate.

SUMMARY   In this chapter we have laid the foundation for real estate mathematics by discussing the basic computations using decimals and fractions in adding, subtracting, multiplying, and dividing.

In most real estate transactions there are three variables—two of these will be given and you will be asked to solve for the third: Three formulas can be used to solve many real estate problems.

Made = Paid × Rate (%)
Rate = Made ÷ Paid
Paid = Made ÷ Rate

In this chapter problems related to investments, discounting notes, appraisal, commissions, interest and loans, cost and selling price problems, and square footage and area problems were presented. Prorations and the documentary transfer taxes were computed.

As an aid to rapid calculation, interest tables, amortization tables, and financial pocket calculators can reduce the time needed to determine a correct answer.

Important Terms and Concepts

Amortization table

Capitalization rate

Commission split

Decimals

Documentary transfer tax

Interest = Principal × Rate × Time

Principal

Proration

REVIEWING YOUR UNDERSTANDING

1. An investor purchased a four-unit apartment. Each unit rented for $600 per month, with a vacancy factor of 5 percent and operating expenses of $8,000 annually. To realize a capitalization rate of 10 percent, how much should the investor have paid for the property?
   (a) $127,500
   (b) $105,000
   (c) $179,300
   (d) $193,600

2. Mrs. B sold her condo for $63,000. This was 20 percent more than her commission to the broker, and other selling costs. How much was her profit?
   (a) $12,600
   (b) $10,500
   (c) $15,250
   (d) $5,250

3. Mr. A decides to place part of his earnings in a savings account. He hopes to earn $150 monthly at 6 percent interest. To realize this, how much must he deposit?
   (a) $15,000
   (b) $9,000
   (c) $25,000
   (d) $30,000

4. Ms. Jones purchased a lot for $70,000; she assumed an existing loan for $40,000. The seller agrees to pay the documentary transfer tax. What is the tax?
   (a) $77.00

(b) $33.00
(c) $45.00
(d) None of the above is correct

5. Mr. and Mrs. Smith paid their annual property taxes of $720. They sold their home on April 1. On the settlement sheet, what entry would be made?
   (a) Debit the seller $180
   (b) Credit the seller $240
   (c) Credit the buyer $180
   (d) Credit the seller $180

6. Mr. Brown sold his rural cabin for $60,000. He purchased it one year ago for $40,000. What percentage profit did he realize on the sale?
   (a) 66⅔ percent
   (b) 50 percent
   (c) 33⅓ percent
   (d) 48 percent

7. Broker B received a listing at a 6 percent commission. If her commission amounted to $6,300, what was the listing price?
   (a) $26,800
   (b) $110,000
   (c) $105,000
   (d) $10,500

8. If you were to borrow $42,000 and make fully amortized payments for 15 years including 9 percent interest, using the amortizaton table, what would be your monthly payments?
   (a) $426.30
   (b) $10.15
   (c) $375.20
   (d) None of the above

9. If you owned a four-acre parcel of land and wished to divide it into eight equal lots each 400 feet deep, what would be the width of each lot?
   (a) 55.40 feet
   (b) 54.45 feet
   (c) 435.6 feet
   (d) 45.54 feet

10. A payment of $840 per month principal and interest is made on a $66,000 loan which includes interest at 13 percent. How much of the payment is principal the first month?
    (a) $715
    (b) $100
    (c) $95
    (d) None of the above

Chapter 7
Introduction to Real Estate Finance

Preview   This chapter stresses the legal aspects of real estate finance. When you have completed this chapter you will be able to:

1. *Describe two types of promissory notes and then explain adjustable rate loans.*

2. *Explain deeds of trust (trust deeds), installment sales contracts, and describe the foreclosure process (trustee's sale).*

3. *Define acceleration, alienation, and prepayment penalty clauses.*

4. *Outline the principles of the Real Property Loan Law and truth-in-lending regulations.*

7.1 REAL ESTATE FINANCING INSTRUMENTS   Access to money and credit is the key factor in most real estate transactions. Real estate is expensive and few people ever accumulate enough savings to pay all cash for property. Therefore, the completion of a real estate sale hinges upon the buyer's ability to obtain financing. Even people who have sufficient funds rarely pay cash for real estate. Income tax deductions and an investment concept called *leverage* (see this chapter's appendix) favor purchasing real estate with borrowed funds. Thus, whether by necessity or by choice, financing is essential for most real estate transactions.

Real Estate Financing Process

Real estate financing usually involves five phases: (1) application, (2) analysis, (3) processing, (4) closing, and (5) servicing.

The lending process begins by having the prospective borrower complete a lender's loan application form. A loan application form requests information about the borrower's financial status, such as level and consistency of income, personal assets, existing debts, and current expenses. The loan application form also asks for data concerning the property, including its location, its age, and the size of the lot and any existing improvements.

REAL ESTATE FINANCING PROCESS

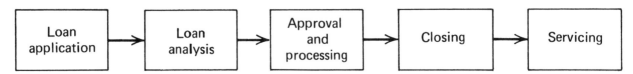

Once the application is completed, the lender reviews the form and uses it as a screening device to determine if the prospective borrower and the subject property appear to meet the lender's requirements. If it becomes obvious that the borrower or the property are unacceptable for a loan, the lender informs the applicant. If it appears that both the borrower and the property might be acceptable, the analysis phase begins.

Analysis involves an in-depth appraisal of the property and a professionally compiled credit report on the prospective borrower. After the appraisal and credit report are completed, and assuming that both are favorable, the lender then presents the terms and cost of financing to the borrower. The borrower may accept, reject, or attempt to negotiate the financing terms with the lender. Assuming that an agreement is reached, the processing phase begins.

Processing involves drawing up loan papers, preparing disclosure forms regarding loan fees, and issuing instructions for the escrow and title insurance company. Each lender establishes its own processing pattern in view of its special in-house needs.

Once the loan package has been processed, the closing phase begins. Closing the loan involves signing all loan papers and then, in conjunction with the other terms of the sale, transferring the property. In Southern California, many times the lender handles the entire escrow. In much of Northern California, after the loan papers have been signed, they are usually forwarded to the escrow department of a title insurance company which closes the sale.

After the title has been transferred and the escrow is closed, the loan servicing phase begins. Loan servicing refers to the record-keeping process once the loan has been placed. Many lenders do their own servicing, while others pay independent mortgage companies to handle the paperwork. The goal of loan servicing is to see that the lender makes the expected yield on the loan by promptly collecting and processing the loan payments with minimum cost.

Promissory Notes   When money is borrowed to purchase real estate, the borrower agrees to repay the loan by signing a *promissory note,* which outlines the terms of repayment and sets the due date. The promissory note is legal evidence that a debt is owed. The two types of promissory notes in general use are the *straight note* and the *installment note.*

The straight note is frequently referred to as an "interest only" note. Under a straight note the borrower agrees to pay the interest, usually monthly, and to pay the entire principal in a lump sum on the due date. For example, if you borrow $50,000 for 30 years at a 12 percent interest rate using a straight note, the monthly payments would be $500 per month. The $500 payments cover just the monthly interest. Thus, 30 years hence, on the due date, you must pay back the entire $50,000 principal. In other words, the payments were only large enough to cover the monthly interest and did not reduce the $50,000 principal. (Proof: $50,000 × 12% = $6,000 ÷ 12 months = $500 per month.)

The second and by far the most common type of real estate promissory note is the installment note. *An installment note requires payments that include both principal and interest.* If you borrow $50,000 for 30 years at 12 percent interest payable at $514.31 per month including both principal and interest, you will find that at the end of 30 years the entire debt is liquidated. Each monthly payment of $514.31 includes not only the monthly interest due, but also reduces a portion of the $50,000 principal. By the time the due date arrives 30 years hence, the entire principal has been paid back. *An installment loan that includes principal and interest of equal installment payments that liquidate the debt is called a fully amortized loan.* Under such an amortized loan there is no large *balloon payment* on the due date of the loan.

One variation of the installment note is to have monthly payments that are large enough to pay the monthly interest and reduce some of the principal, but the monthly principal portion is not sufficient to entirely liquidate the debt by the due date. Thus, on the due date the remaining unpaid principal must be paid in a lump sum, often referred to as a *balloon payment.* (Any payment more than double the normal amount is called a balloon payment.) Fifty thousand dollars for 30 years at 12 percent interest payable at $510.00 per month would require a balloon payment of $15,050.36 on the due date. Why? Because the $510.00 per month was enough to cover the monthly interest ($500.00), but it was not enough to cover the monthly interest and all of the monthly principal (that would have taken $514.31 per month). Thus the difference over the 30-year life of the loan comes to $15,050.36, which must be paid on the due date in the form of a

DO NOT DESTROY THIS NOTE - WHEN PAID, SURRENDER TO TRUSTEE FOR RECONVEYANCE

Note Secured by Deed of Trust

Installment Note — Interest Included — Contains Acceleration Clause

$ 75,000.00 Somewhere, California, April 22, 19 8-

In installments as herein stated, for value received, I promise to pay to First Acme Bank, or order,

at 123 Main Street, Somewhere, California 95500

the sum of Seventy Five Thousand and No/100 DOLLARS,

with interest from April 22, 199- on unpaid principal at the rate of Eleven (11%) per cent per annum; principal and interest payable in installments of Seven Hundred Fourteen and 24/100 ($714.24) Dollars or more on the First day of each and every month, beginning on the First day of June 19 9-

and continuing until said principal and interest have been paid.

Each payment shall be credited first on interest then due and the remainder on principal; and interest shall thereupon cease upon the principal so credited. Should default be made in payment of any installment when due the whole sum of principal and interest shall become immediately due at the option of the holder of this note. Principal and interest payable in lawful money of the United States. If action be instituted on this note I promise to pay such sum as the Court may fix as attorney's fees. This note is secured by a Deed of Trust to HUMBOLDT LAND TITLE COMPANY, a California corporation.

All sums secured hereby may be declared due and payable at the option of the payee herein upon the sale, conveyance, alienation, lease, succession, assignment or other transfer of the property described in the Deed of Trust given to secure payment of the indebtedness referred to herein.

John J. Borrower

John J. Borrower

Alice M. Borrower

Alice M. Borrower

Figure 7-1

Courtesy of Humboldt Land Title Company.

balloon payment. Loan payments and balloon payments can be calculated using financial tables or financial calculators. Figure 7-1 is an example of a fully amortized installment note.

Adjustable Rate Loan

Some real estate lenders will allow a borrower to choose either a fixed interest rate or an adjustable rate loan. The *fixed interest rate* is the traditional real estate loan where the interest rate does not change over the life of the loan. Under the *adjustable rate* plan, the rate may move up or down. Therefore, your monthly payment may decrease or increase over the life of the loan.

HOW DOES IT WORK? Adjustable rate loans, also called adjustable rate mortgages (ARMs), have the following characteristics:

1. They are usually offered at a lower initial interest rate than traditional fixed interest rate loans.

2. Once the initial interest rate is established, the rate is tied to some neutral index which is beyond the control of the lender or the borrower.

3. The index is usually a government index. The cost-of-money index of the 11th District of the Federal Home Loan Bank in San Francisco is frequently used. Some adjustable rate loans are tied to certain U.S. Treasury notes and commercial prime rates.

4. Although not required, most lenders place a cap on how high the rate can climb. A typical cap is 5%; therefore if the initial interest rate is 10%, the maximum it can rise to is 15%.

5. The adjustment period can vary, with some lenders adjusting the rate at either six-month, one-year, or three-year intervals.

6. The maximum increase or decrease per year is established in the lender's contract, with a maximum change of 2% per adjustment period being typical.

7. If the interest rate increases because of a change in the index, in some cases the borrower has the option of: (a) increasing the monthly payment so the term of the loan remains the same, or (b) maintaining the same monthly payment and increasing the term of the loan. Usually, the maximum term a 30-year loan may be extended is 40 years. Once a 40-year term is reached, any increase in interest rate must increase the monthly payment. If the interest rate drops below the initial rate, the borrower can continue the existing payments (which will shorten the term) or decrease the monthly payments.

8. The borrower must be notified at least 30 days prior to a change in rate. After the notification, the borrower has 90 days to pay off the loan without a prepayment penalty.

9. Adjustable rate mortgages are usually assumable in that they usually do not have alienation (due on sale) clauses.

10. Some ARMs may be negative amortized loans. This means the payments may not cover the annual interest. The unpaid interest is added to the principal, making the loan larger. This can cause some unknown problems in later years.

Other Alternative Types of Real Estate Loans

Other experimental types of loans include names like FLIP (flexible payment mortgage), GPM (graduated payment mortgage), and SAM (shared appreciation mortgage), plus many other loans called "alphabet soup" financing. The details of these alternative loan types can be found in a textbook on real estate finance, such as *California Real Estate Finance,* Fourth ed., by Robert J. Bond, Alfred Gavello, Dennis J. McKenzie, and Carden Young (New York: John Wiley & Sons, Inc., 1990)

PURPOSE OF ADJUSTABLE RATE AND OTHER ALTERNATIVE LOANS

Alternative real estate loans have been recommended by financial experts and real estate economists for many years. Here are some of the reasons.

Institutional lenders have a constant problem with cycles of tight and loose money. This unsteady flow of funds is disruptive to their operations and the housing industry. When money is tight, it flows out of saving institutions because depositors can obtain higher yields elsewhere.

Advocates of alternative loans say that this problem can be reduced by using adjustable rate mortgages. If money gets tight and interest rates rise, the savings institutions should be allowed to increase the rate they pay their depositors in order to prevent an outflow of savings. However, in order to pay higher interest on savings accounts, lenders must receive a higher interest rate on their existing loans. With an adjustable rate mortgage, lenders could increase interest rates on their existing loans when they increase the savings rate.

Another problem facing lending institutions deals with old, low, fixed interest rate loans currently on the lender's books. If the current cost of money exceeds the interest rates on these older loans, the institutions are losing money on these loans. That means that the interest rate on new loans must be increased to compensate for the loss on these old loans. In effect, new borrowers are subsidizing the old borrowers. If all the borrowers were on an adjustable rate, this subsidizing process would not be as severe.

Those who are opposed to alternative loans argue that lenders are merely shifting the risk of rising interest rates to the borrower.

Adjustable rate mortgages are not new. They have been used for many years in Canada and in some European countries. In California, the Cal-Vet loan program has been using adjustable rates since the program was started over 50 years ago.

Deeds of Trust

To give added assurance that a borrower will pay the loan lenders require collateral or security for the loan. To give something as security for a loan without giving up possession is called *hypothecation*. A real estate lender's most logical security is real property owned or about

DEED OF TRUST

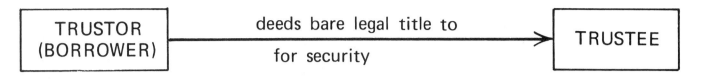

TRUSTOR (BORROWER) → deeds bare legal title to for security → TRUSTEE

When debt is paid:

DEED OF RECONVEYANCE

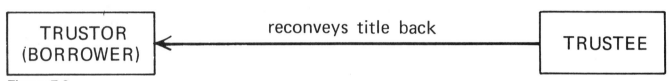

TRUSTOR (BORROWER) ← reconveys title back ← TRUSTEE

Figure 7-2

to be acquired by the borrower. To secure an interest in the borrower's real property, lenders in California use a deed of trust (also called a trust deed).

A deed of trust is a three-party instrument consisting of a borrower *(trustor)*, a lender *(beneficiary)*, and a neutral third party *(trustee)*. Under a deed of trust (trust deed) the trustor deeds legal title to the trustee who keeps the title as security until the promissory note is repaid. Once the debt is repaid, the beneficiary (lender) orders the trustee to reconvey the title back to the trustor (borrower). If the trustor should default on the loan, the beneficiary can order the trustee to hold a trustee's sale and sell the property to obtain the cash needed to pay the loan. Figure 7-2 illustrates how title is passed between a trustor and trustee in a deed of trust and a deed of reconveyance.

In other states, frequently a mortgage is used to secure a real estate loan instead of a deed of trust. But in California mortgages are rare—most lenders insist on deeds of trust instead. Why? Because in most cases deeds of trust favor the lender over the borrower. If the borrower should default under a deed of trust, the lender can order the trustee to sell the property without a court proceeding, and it can be accomplished in approximately four months. Once the sale takes place, the borrower loses all rights to redeem the property.

Foreclosure under a mortgage usually requires a court proceeding and can take up to one year. After the foreclosure takes place, the borrower has a one-year right of redemption. In short, most California real estate lenders prefer to use deeds of trust rather than mortgages as security instruments because foreclosure is quicker and cheaper with a deed of trust. Figure 7-3 is an example of a standard form deed of trust.

Special Clauses

In addition to repayment terms, many real estate financing instruments contain special clauses or loan conditions that the borrower and lender agree to honor. Three common clauses that appear in promissory notes and deeds of trust are:

1. *Acceleration clause.* A clause that gives the lender the right to call all sums immediately due and payable upon the happening of certain events, such as nonpayment of monthly obligations, nonpayment of real property taxes, or willful destruction of the subject property.

2. *Alienation (due on sale) clause.* A specific type of acceleration clause that gives the lender the right to call the loan due and payable if the borrower conveys legal title to a new owner. After a period of controversy, the issue is now settled. Effective October 15, 1985, all due on sales clauses became enforceable. (See this chapter's Appendix for history.)

3. *Prepayment penalty clause.* A clause that allows a lender to charge the borrower a penalty if the loan is paid before the scheduled due date. A typical prepayment penalty is six-month's interest on the amount prepaid which exceeds 20 percent of the original principal amount of the loan. Example: $100,000 original loan at 10 percent interest. Assume that two years later the loan balance is $98,000. If the borrower pays the loan off, the penalty may be as follows:

$100,000   Original loan amount × 20% = $20,000

$ 98,000	Existing loan balance
− 20,000	Allowed to be paid without penalty
$ 78,000	Subject to prepayment penalty
× .10%	Interest rate
$ 7,800	One-year's interest

$2\overline{)7,800}$ = $3,900 six-month's interest as prepayment penalty

However, penalties do vary with the lender. Some loans have no prepayment charge. Or, in other cases, a lender may waive the penalty. For example, a lender may waive the prepayment penalty if the seller has the new buyer finance the purchase with the same lender. California regulations prohibit lenders from charging a prepayment penalty on owner-occupied home loans, if the loan has been on the lender's books for more than five years. This law affects home loans made after 1975. There is no prepayment penalty on FHA-insured or VA-guaranteed home loans.

RECORDED AT THE REQUEST OF:

Humboldt Land Title Company

AFTER RECORDING MAIL TO:

First Acme Bank

123 Main Street

Somewhere, CA. 95500

HUMBOLDT *Land* **TITLE** *Co*

Short Form Deed of Trust
WITH RENT ASSIGNMENT

313 – 75 HUM ORDER NO. 998877DM

This DEED OF TRUST, dated __April 22, 199-__ , between

JOHN J. BORROWER AND ALICE M. BORROWER __, herein called TRUSTOR,

whose address is __789 Elm Street__, Somewhere, California 95500 (Zip)
(Number and Street), (City) (State)

Humboldt Land Title Company , a California corporation, herein called TRUSTEE, and

FIRST ACME BANK, a California corporation __, herein called BENEFICIARY,

WITNESSETH: That Trustor irrevocably grants, transfers and assigns to Trustee in trust, with Power of Sale, that real property in the State of California, County of Humboldt, described as: situated in the City of Somewhere and being:

Lot 31, Block A, Tract 1501, as recorded in Map Book 43, Page 291 of the official records of the County Recorder, on July 17, 1967, Humboldt County, California.

All sums secured hereby may be declared due and payable at the option of the payee herein upon the sale, conveyance, alienation, lease, succession, assignment or other transfer of the property described in the Deed of Trust Note given to secure payment of the indebtness referred to herein.

TOGETHER with the rents, issues and profits thereof, subject, however, to the right, power and authority hereinafter given to and conferred upon Beneficiary to collect and apply such rents, issues and profits.

FOR THE PURPOSE OF SECURING:

1. Payment of the indebtedness evidenced by one promissory note of even date herewith executed by Trustor in favor of Beneficiary or order in the principal sum of $75,000.00 and any additional sums and interest thereon hereafter loaned by Beneficiary to the then record owner of said property which loans are evidenced by a promissory note or notes.

2. Performance of each agreement of Trustor contained herein or incorporated by reference.

A. TO PROTECT THE SECURITY OF THIS DEED OF TRUST, and with respect to the real property above described, Trustor expressly makes each and all the agreements, and adopts and agrees to perform and be bound by each and all of the terms and provisions set forth in paragraphs 1 to 5 inclusive of Subdivision A of that certain Deed of Trust recorded May 16, 1952, in Book 208, Page 87, of Official Records, in the office of the Recorder of Humboldt County, California, which Subdivision A is and said agreements, terms and provisions are by this reference thereto, incorporated herein and made a part of this Deed of Trust for all purposes as fully as if set forth at length herein.

B. IT IS MUTUALLY AGREED that each and all of the terms and provisions set forth in paragraphs 1 to 9 inclusive of Subdivision B of said Deed of Trust recorded May 16, 1952, in said Book 208, Page 87, of Official Records, in the office of the Recorder of Humboldt County, California, are, and said Subdivision B is, by this reference thereto, incorporated herein and made a part of this Deed of Trust for all purposes as fully as if set forth at length herein, and said Subdivision B and each and all of the terms and provisions thereof shall inure to and bind the parties hereto.

C. THE UNDERSIGNED TRUSTOR requests that a copy of any notice of default and of any notice of sale hereunder be mailed to him at his address hereinbefore set forth.

John J. Borrower
JOHN J. BORROWER _____ Signature of Trustor

Alice M. Borrower
ALICE M. BORROWER _____ Signature of Trustor

STATE OF CALIFORNIA
COUNTY OF Humboldt } ss

On April 22, 199- before me, the undersigned, a Notary Public in and for said County and State, personally appeared
John J. Borrower and
Alice M. Borrower

known to me to be the person s whose name s are subscribed to the within instrument, and acknowledged to me that they executed the same.
WITNESS my hand and Official seal.

Jane Q. Notary
Notary Public in and for said County and State.
Jane Q. Notary

For Notary Seal or Stamp

NOTARY SEAL

Figure 7-3

WRAPAROUND DEED OF TRUST

A *wraparound deed of trust* (also called all-inclusive or overriding) is a financing device used to increase the lender's yield upon the sale of real property and to make it easier for the buyer to finance the purchase.

Example. An owner has a $100,000 property with an existing loan of $50,000 at 9 percent interest payable at $500 per month. The owner sells for $100,000, the buyer puts down $20,000 cash, and the seller carries a wraparound deed of trust for $80,000 at 12 percent payable at $900 per month. The buyer makes the $900 payments to the seller on the $80,000 wraparound loan, and the seller then makes the $500 payments on the $50,000 underlying loan, keeping the $400 difference ($900 − $500 = $400).

The seller's yield is increased because the seller receives 12 percent on $80,000, but only pays 9 percent interest on $50,000.

The buyer does not assume the seller's existing loan, but rather makes payments only on the wraparound deed of trust. The seller is responsible for all existing loans. By having the seller carry a wraparound deed of trust, the buyer avoids the new loan fees charged by institutional lenders.

A wraparound deed of trust is a complicated financing device that should only be used if all parties understand its details. Also adequate provisions should be inserted to protect the buyer's interest in case the seller fails to make the payments on the underlying loan(s) after receiving the buyer's payment on the wraparound deed of trust. Certain existing real estate loans may have enforceable due-on-sale clauses which prohibit the use of a wraparound deed of trust. A wraparound deed of trust can also be used to refinance a property . . . a lender makes a new wraparound loan and the lender agrees to make payments on the underlying existing loan(s).

A financing instrument may contain several other special clauses depending upon the operating policies of the lender. Borrowers should carefully read all documents to make certain that they completely understand what all clauses mean. This will help to maintain harmony between the lender and the borrower during the life of the loan.

Junior Deed of Trust Any trust deed other than a first is called a "junior deed of trust" or a "junior lien." When a buyer does not have enough cash down payment to cover the gap between the sales price and the first deed of trust loan, a *junior* (or second) *deed of trust* loan is frequently carried back by the seller.

Example. Sales price $190,000, buyer has $30,000 cash down payment and is willing to assume the seller's existing first deed of trust bank loan of $150,000. Therefore, $150,000 + 30,000 = $180,000. The buyer is short $10,000. To cover the gap the seller agrees to carry back a $10,000 promissory note secured by a second deed of trust. This can be illustrated as follows:

$190,000	Sales price
−150,000	First deed of trust
$ 40,000	Required
−30,000	Cash down payment
$ 10,000	Second deed of trust

Homeowner equity loans are another common example of the use of junior (second) deeds of trust. Many banks and finance companies advertise their homeowner loan programs, whereby the lender grants a loan based on the homeowner's increase in equity caused by inflation and appreciation of property values. These loans are usually secured by junior deeds of trust. Because junior trust deeds are less secure than first trust deeds, lenders usually demand a higher interest rate on junior deeds.

Taking Over a Seller's Existing Loan

The placement of a new real estate loan from an institutional lender requires the payment of loan fees, appraisal fees, credit report charges, and other loan closing costs.

In addition, the interest rate paid by the buyer is at the current prevailing market rate. If a buyer has enough cash downpayment and if legally possible, it is usually cheaper to take over the seller's existing loan, rather than obtain a new loan. Many of the loan costs are avoided, and in some cases the interest rate on the seller's loan is less than the prevailing interest rates on new real estate loans.

There are two ways a buyer can take over a seller's existing loan. A buyer can *assume* a seller's existing loan, or a buyer can purchase *subject to* a seller's existing loan. When a buyer *assumes* a seller's existing loan, the buyer agrees to take over the payments and to become personally liable for the debt. But when a buyer purchases *subject to* the existing loan, the buyer agrees to take over the payments, but not the primary liability for the debt; the seller remains personally liable. This distinction becomes important if a lender should sue for a deficiency judgment.

A *deficiency judgment* is where a lender sues a borrower after a foreclosure, when the proceeds from a foreclosure are not enough to cover the outstanding loan amount. An example would be: A real estate lender is owed $100,000; there is a default on the loan and the lender sells the property in foreclosure sale for $90,000. The amount owed was $100,000; the proceeds from the foreclosure were only $90,000; therefore, the deficiency is $10,000.

If the lender is allowed to sue for the $10,000 deficiency, the question arises, "Who shall be sued?" The answer is, "Whoever is personally liable for the debt." If a buyer has *assumed* a seller's existing loan, the action would be brought against the buyer as he or she is personally liable. On the other hand, if a buyer purchased *subject to* a seller's existing loan, the seller is still primarily liable and the deficiency action would be brought against the seller. Deficiency judgments on owner-occupied residential dwellings are difficult to obtain in California because of special laws protecting homeowners. But deficiency judgments are obtainable on FHA-insured and VA-guaranteed home loans, because these are federally backed loans and federal law supercedes state antideficiency laws.

Installment Sales Contracts (Land Contracts)

Another real estate financing instrument is an installment sales contract, also called a contract of sale, or agreement of sale. An *installment sales contract* is an agreement between the seller, called the *vendor,* and the buyer, called the *vendee,* where the buyer is given possession and use of the property. In exchange for possession and use, the buyer agrees to make regular payments to the seller. Legal title to the property remains with the seller until an agreed amount has been paid, at which time the seller formally deeds title to the buyer. In essence, under an installment sales contract, the seller becomes the lender. Outside lending institutions, such as banks or savings and loan associations, are not needed in such a transaction.

The lack of immediate title poses some risks for the buyer. If the seller should die, become bankrupt, or incompetent, or encumber the title during the contract, the buyer could become involved in legal entanglements.

Recent court cases have greatly restricted the ease by which a seller can remove a buyer if he or she defaults on the payments. A long, expensive court action may be needed to remove a defaulted buyer from possession. In light of the disadvantage for both the buyer and seller, installment sales contracts are no longer as popular as they were in the past.

7.2 FORECLOSURE PROCESS—TRUSTEE'S SALE

Borrowers default on repayment of loans for a variety of reasons, usually due to events beyond their control. Financial reversals such as loss of a business or job probably head the list, but other circumstances are closely related: death, disability, bankruptcy, dissolution of marriage, and poor budgeting. Unless arrangements can be made with the lender to work out a satisfactory schedule for repayment following default, foreclosure takes place. However, most lenders try to avoid foreclosure whenever possible and use it only as a last resort, since lenders are in the business of lending money and do not want to become involved in owning and managing real estate.

A borrower may be in default not only through delinquency on payments of principal and interest, but when there is a violation of other terms of the trust deed, such as, agreement to maintain the property and pay other liens in a timely manner, and so on. Regardless of the violation, lenders in California must follow a prescribed procedure in ousting the interests of the delinquent debtor. Here is a summary of the process.

TRUSTEE'S SALE (FORECLOSURE)

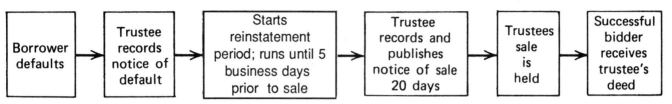

Trustee's Sale   Virtually all trust deeds contain a "power-of-sale" clause, which empowers the trustee, in the event of default by the trustor, to sell the property at public auction. While the provisions of the power-of-sale clause are a matter of contract and may vary from instrument to instrument, there are laws that specifically regulate foreclosures through trustee's sale. The statutory requirements are as follows:

1. *Notice of default.* After the beneficiary is reasonably certain that a trustor is unable to make good on the loan, the beneficiary orders the trustee to record a *notice of default* in the county where the property is located. This begins a reinstatement period. The notice must contain a correct legal description of the property, name of trustor, nature of the breach, and a statement to the effect that the party executing the notice of default has elected to sell the property in order to satisfy the obligation.

   Within ten days after filing the notice of default, a copy must be sent by registered or certified mail to the borrower, junior lienholders, and to anyone whose "request for notice" appears on record.

   During this reinstatement period, which runs until 5 days before the date of sale, the trustor (borrower) may reinstate the loan by paying all delinquent installments. The trustor must also pay foreclosure costs, and trustee's fees. This is referred to as the *right of reinstatement.*

2. *Notice of sale.* In addition to recording a notice of default, a trustee must also record a *notice of sale.* This notice of sale is filed if the borrower fails to reinstate the loan.

   The notice must contain a correct identification of the property, such as the street address or legal description. must be published in a newspaper of general circulation in the county or jurisdiction in which the property is located. The publication must appear at least once a week for 20 days, not more than seven days apart. Moreover, the notice must also be posted in a public place, such as a courthouse; and also on some conspicuous place on the property, such as the front door. The sale must be held in a public place, during business hours, on a weekday (Monday through Friday).

3. *Final sale.* Any person, including the trustor and beneficiary, may bid on the property via public auction. All bids must be in cash or its equivalent. However, the lender foreclosing can submit the amount owed the lender as a bid in lieu of cash.

Δ *trustee's deed* is issued to the highest bidder. Any surplus funds, that is, funds remaining after paying off the lender, foreclosure costs, and junior liens if any, are given to the trustor.

No right of redemption exists after a trustee's sale. The purchaser acquires all rights held by the former owner, becoming the successor in interest, and is entitled to immediate possession, subject to those having superior rights over the trust deed that was foreclosed.

Rights of Holders of Junior Trust Deeds

When a trustee's sale is held on behalf of a first trust deed lender, junior trust deeds can be eliminated. Therefore, it is important to examine what rights a junior trust deed holder has in the foreclosure process.

Assume that a homeowner has a first and a second trust deed loan against the property and is in default on the loans. If the first trust deed lender begins to foreclose, the second trust deed lender can step in and make the payments due on the first loan. This will stop the first lender from foreclosing. *The second trust deed lender then adds the payments made on first trust deed loan to the balance the borrower owes on the second trust deed loan.* The holder of the second trust deed loan then demands repayment from the borrower. If the borrower fails to repay, the holder of the second trust deed then forecloses under the trustee sale provisions of the second trust deed. The successful bidder at the trustee's sale becomes the owner of the property, subject to the first trust deed—that is, takes over the property and is required to make all future payments on the first trust deed loan. In short, a holder of a junior trust deed can stop the first from foreclosing on the first trust deed. This in turn will keep the second trust deed from being eliminated. The holder of the second trust deed will get either title to the property as the lone bidder at the trustee's sale, or cash from a third party who is the successful bidder at the trustee's sale on the second trust deed.

How does a holder of a second trust deed know when a borrower has defaulted on the first trust deed? A recent law requires that senior trust deed holders must send a certified copy of any notice of default and sale to all holders of junior trust deeds. To be doubly sure, a holder of a junior trust deed may also wish to record an instrument called a *request for copy of notice of default*. This places on public record a notice to the senior trust deed holder that the junior trust deed holder wishes to be informed when a default is declared on the first loan.

7.3 TRUTH-IN-LENDING, EQUAL CREDIT OPPORTUNITY, AND REAL ESTATE SETTLEMENT PROCEDURES ACT

> Real Estate Ads must comply with Regulation Z. If one financial term such as *interest* or *no money down* is mentioned, all financing terms—interest rate, payments, etc., must be stated in the ad.

In 1968, Congress passed the *Truth-in-Lending Law,* also called Regulation Z. The purpose of the law is to help borrowers understand how much it is costing to borrow money. The law requires all lenders to show loan costs in the same way. This allows borrowers to compare one lender's cost against the other.

The law requires lenders to quote the cost of borrowing, using what is called an *Annual Percentage Rate* (APR). The APR is *not* an interest rate, but rather a percentage rate that reflects the effective interest rate on the loan, including other prepaid financing charges such as loan fees, prepaid interest, and tax service fees.

Regulation Z requires a lender to give the borrower a disclosure statement showing a complete breakdown of all loan costs, plus other loan information. The law also provides that certain loans are rescindable within three business days. This means that borrowers have three days after they agree to a loan to cancel it if they wish. Generally, this rescindable right only applies to loans to refinance a borrower's home and to certain types of junior deeds of trust, including home improvement loans. First deeds of trust to purchase a home are not rescindable, nor are loans carried back by a seller of real estate.

Equal Credit Opportunity Act

On October 28, 1975, the Equal Credit Opportunity Act became effective. This act prohibits lenders from discrimination on the basis of race, color, religion, national origin, age, sex, marital status, or on the grounds of receipt of income from a public assistance program.

Some of the basic provisions of the act are:

1. A lender cannot ask if the borrower is divorced or widowed. The lender may ask if the borrower is married, unmarried, or separated. For purposes of the law, unmarried means single, divorced, or widowed.

2. A lender cannot ask about receiving alimony or child support unless the borrower is first notified that it need not be revealed. However, the lender may ask about obligations to pay alimony or child support.

3. A lender cannot ask about birth control practices or childbearing intentions or capabilities.

4. A lender must notify every borrower within 30 days of what action

has been taken on his or her loan application. In case of disapproval, the reason must be given if requested.

5. If the borrower requests, the lender must consider information provided by the borrower indicating that a bad history of a joint account does not reflect on his or her credit.

In short, the Equal Credit Opportunity Act assures that all qualified persons shall have equal access to credit. This law has been especially helpful in assuring women that they shall not be discriminated against because of their sex.

Real Estate Settlement Procedures Act

The Real Estate Settlement Procedures Act (RESPA) is a federal law that requires certain forms be provided regarding closing costs. The law applies whenever a person purchases an owner-occupied residence, using funds obtained from institutional lenders which are regulated by a federal agency. Virtually all banks, savings and loan associations, and most other lenders fall directly or indirectly under RESPA's rules. The one major exception would be real estate loans by private parties.

RESPA rules require a lender to furnish the borrower with a special information booklet and a good faith estimate of closing costs three days from the time the prospective borrower files an application for a real estate loan. RESPA rules prohibit any kickbacks or unearned fees from being listed as closing costs. The law states that only valid, earned, closing costs shall be charged the buyer or seller. Any violators can be punished by up to one year in jail and/or a $10,000 fine.

Most of the burden for implementing RESPA falls upon the real estate lender. However, escrow agents are also involved. RESPA requires the use of a Uniform Settlement Statement (HUD-1) which must itemize all closing charges. Upon request, the escrow agent must let the borrower-buyer inspect the Uniform Settlement Statement one day before the close of escrow. In addition, the escrow officer must see that all parties receive a copy of the Uniform Settlement Statement after the close of escrow.

7.4 REAL PROPERTY LOAN LAW

Another consumer-oriented law is the Real Property Loan Law found in Sections 10240-48 of the California Business and Professions Code (Article 7). This segment of the law is commonly called the "Mortgage Loan Broker Law." The purpose of this law is to protect borrowers who use the services of mortgage loan brokers. The law requires mortgage brokers to give a loan disclosure statement to all borrowers before they become obligated for the loan. The disclosure statement itemizes all closing costs, loan expenses, and commissions to be paid, thereby showing the borrower how much he or she will net from the loan.

Exceptions to the Mortgage Loan Broker Law

It is easier to state which lenders and what transactions are not covered by the law than to list those that are. Exempt from the Real Property Loan Law are: (As of 1/91)

1. Regulated institutional lenders, such as banks, savings and loan associations, credit unions, and finance companies.

2. Purchase money transactions where a seller carries back the loan as part of the sale price. However, if a seller carries back the loan for more than seven transactions in one year, the Mortgage Loan Broker Law does apply.

3. Loans secured by first trust deeds when the principal amount is $30,000 or more.

4. Loans secured by junior trust deeds when the principal amount is $20,000 or more.

Maximum Commissions

Mortgage loan brokers are limited in the percentage amount of commissions that they may charge, as shown in Table 7-1.

TABLE 7-1

Type of Loan	Percentage Commission			Exempt Transactions
	Less than two years	Two years but less than three	Three years and over	
First Trust Deeds	5%	5%	10%	Loans of $30,000 and over
Junior Trust Deeds	5%	10%	15%	Loans of $20,000 and over

As the table shows, the shorter the term of the loan, the less commission the broker may charge as a percentage of the face amount of the loan. On loans of $30,000 and over for first liens, and $20,000 for junior liens, the broker may charge as much as the borrower agrees to pay. Even for loans covered by the law, however, competition normally keeps rates below those allowed.

Other Costs and Expenses

Loan brokers are limited also to the amount of costs and expenses, other than commissions, that they may charge a borrower for arranging the loan. Such costs and expenses may not exceed 5 percent of the amount of the loan. However, if 5 percent of the loan is less than $390, the broker may charge up to that amount, provided that the charges do not exceed actual costs and expenses paid, incurred, or reasonably earned by the broker. Regardless of the size of the loan, the borrower cannot be charged more than $750 for miscellaneous costs and expenses, excluding commission, title and recording fees (1991).

Balloon Payments

A balloon payment is prohibited if (1) the term of the loan is for six years or less and (2) the loan is secured by the dwelling place of the borrower. Again, this provision does not apply to loans carried by sellers.

Insurance

A borrower is not required to purchase credit life or disability insurance as a condition for obtaining the loan. However, the lender may insist, for self-protection, that fire and hazard insurance be obtained on the property until the loan has been repaid. If licensed to sell such insurance, the broker may act as the agent for the borrower, but the borrower is not obligated to purchase the insurance coverage through the mortgage loan broker.

Miscellaneous Provisions

Mortgage brokers are prohibited from charging loan servicing or collection fees to be paid by the borrower. Late charges, if any, may not exceed $5 or 10 percent of the principal and interest part of an installment payment, whichever is greater. If the installment payment is made within ten days of its due date, however, no late charge can be assessed.

In case of early repayment of the loan, there can be no prepayment penalty against the borrower when the loan is over seven years old. During the first seven years, a borrower is allowed to pay up to 20 percent of the remaining principal balance of the loan during any 12-month period without a penalty. The remaining balance may then be subjected to a maximum prepayment penalty of six months' unearned interest.

Source: From *California Real Estate Finance,* Fourth ed., by Robert J. Bond, Alfred Gavello, Dennis J. McKenzie, and Carden Young (New York: John Wiley & Sons, Inc., 1990, p. 79).

USURY LAW

Many states have passed laws establishing the maximum rate of interest that can be charged on various types of loans. Interest rates that exceed the maximum rate are considered usurious and therefore illegal. In some instances if a lender is found guilty of usury, the borrower does not have to repay the interest due on the loan.

In California, the maximum rate is 10 percent or 5 percent above the Federal Reserve discount rate **whichever is the greater,** unless the lender is exempt from the law. California regulations exempt banks, savings and loan associations, and several other recognized lenders from the usury law. Any real estate transaction handled by a licensed broker is also exempt from the usury law. However, private lenders lending directly to a private borrower are not exempt. For example, real estate loans from institutional lenders can be at any rate agreed, while real estate loans from private lenders cannot be. There is at least one exception—sellers carrying back a purchase money deed of trust as part of their equity on a real estate sale can charge interest at any rate agreed—but this should be cleared with an attorney at the time of the transaction to make sure the law has not changed.

The pros and cons of usury laws are currently being debated. Proponents believe that usury laws protect consumers against lenders, while opponents believe usury laws restrict the supply of loan funds and drive some borrowers to illegal loan sharks. From time to time the federal government passes temporary laws that override state usury laws during periods of tight mortgage money.

SUMMARY

The financing of real estate usually involves a five-phase process consisting of the loan application, analysis, processing, closing, and servicing phases. In California the major instruments of finance are promissory notes and deeds of trust (trust deeds). Promissory notes can be straight notes which contain interest only payments or installment notes which have payments of principal and interest. The most common promissory note is the fully amortized installment note. Adjustable rate loans are becoming more popular in California.

Real estate loans in California are secured by deeds of trust, also called trust deeds. A deed of trust is a three-party instrument consisting of a trustor (borrower), trustee (title holder), and a beneficiary (lender). Upon the repayment of the loan, the trustee reconveys title back to the trustor. If the trustor (borrower) should default on the loan, the trustee forecloses on the property under what is called a trustee's sale.

Many promissory notes and deeds of trust contain special clauses that outline the duties and responsibilities of the borrower. Acceleration, alienation (due-on-sale), and prepayment penalty clauses are most common. Junior deeds of trust are used in many real estate transactions.

Installment sales contracts are no longer popular for the purchase and financing of real estate.

The Truth-in-Lending Act, the Equal Credit Opportunity Act, and the Real Estate Settlement Procedures Act (RESPA) are examples of federal laws designed to assure the proper disclosure and equal treatment of prospective real estate borrowers. The Real Property Loan Law is a California law that requires full disclosure when a borrower procures a loan through a mortgage loan broker. This law also regulates maximum commissions and closing costs that can be charged to borrower. The Real Property Loan Law does not apply to first deed of trust loans of $30,000 or more or second deed of trust loans of $20,000 or more.

Important Terms and Concepts

Acceleration clause

Adjustable rate loan

Alienation (due-on-sale) clause

Annual percentage rate (APR)

Balloon payment

Beneficiary

Deed of trust

Equal Credit Opportunity Act

Installment note

Installment sales contract

Junior deed of trust

Leverage

Prepayment penalty

Real Property Loan Act

RESPA

Straight note

Trustee   Trustor

Trustee's sale   Usury law

Truth-in-Lending Act

REVIEWING YOUR UNDERSTANDING

1. A fully amortized promissory note with equal payments to liquidate the debt would be a (an):
   (a) Straight note
   (b) Principal, plus interest note
   (c) Conventional note
   (d) Installment note

2. Sales price $120,000; $30,000 cash down; seller carries $90,000 loan; seller continues to pay on existing $50,000 bank loan against the property. The seller carry loan is a:
   (a) First deed of trust
   (b) Senior lien
   (c) Wraparound deed of trust
   (d) Institutional loan

3. Under a deed of trust (trust deed) the lender is the:
   (a) Beneficiary
   (b) Trustee
   (c) Trustor
   (d) Mortgagor

4. A due-on-sale clause is correctly called:
   (a) A subordination clause
   (b) An alienation clause
   (c) An esculation clause
   (d) A prepayment clause

5. Which real estate sale will make use of a junior lien?
   (a) All cash sale
   (b) Buyer puts 20 percent downpayment, obtains an 80 percent loan
   (c) Seller carries the first deed of trust
   (d) Buyer puts 10 percent down payment, obtains 80 percent loan, seller carries a 10 percent second deed of trust

6. Under which financing instruments is the seller known as the vendor?
   (a) Installment sales contract
   (b) Contract of sale
   (c) Agreement of sale
   (d) All of the above

7. Once a trustee records a notice of default, how much time does the borrower have to make up the delinquencies and stop the foreclosure?
   - (a) 5 days prior to sale
   - (b) 90 days prior to sale
   - (c) 21 days prior to sale
   - (d) 180 days prior to sale

8. The law that requires a lender to quote the cost of borrowing as an annual percentage rate is:
   - (a) Real Estate Settlement Procedures Act (RESPA)
   - (b) Truth-in-Lending Act
   - (c) Equal Credit Opportunity Act
   - (d) Fair Credit Reporting Act

9. Under the Real Property Loan Law, the maximum commission a mortgage broker can charge for a $9,000 junior trust deed loan, payable in 37 equal installments is:
   - (a) $1,350
   - (b) $900
   - (c) $450
   - (d) There is no maximum commission

10. Regarding question 9, what would be the maximum amount the borrower can be charged for actual fees and expenses, excluding commission, title and recording fees?
   - (a) $450
   - (b) $750
   - (c) $195
   - (d) No maximum amount

Appendix A
History of Court Cases and Legislation on the Due on Sale Clause

WELLENKAMP v. BANK OF AMERICA

The 1978 California Supreme Court decision in "Wellenkamp v. Bank of America" (21 Cal. 3d 943) held that savings and loan associations and banks could not exercise their due on sale clause unless they could prove that the new buyer was too great a risk. The lender's desire to increase the interest rate or charge an assumption fee was not grounds for exercising the due on sale clause.

After the *Wellenkamp* case, numerous additional cases were heard in the California court system. In time, the due on sale clause was held unenforceable in virtually all real estate transactions in California, including loans held by private lenders.

ALONG COMES FIDELITY FEDERAL SAVINGS & LOAN ASSOCIATION v. DE LA CUESTA (1982 U.S. 458)

After the 1978 *Wellenkamp* decision, federally chartered savings and loan associations in California took the position that the California Supreme Court decision did not affect their loans because they were chartered by the Federal Home Loan Bank, a federal agency, and therefore exempt from state laws. The regulations of the Federal Home Loan Bank did allow federal savings and loan associations to exercise the due on sale clause. The question became "What governs federal savings and loan associations—the California Supreme Court or the regulations of the Federal Home Loan Bank?"

In the Summer of 1982 that question was answered. The United States Supreme Court ruled, in "Fidelity Federal Savings and Loan Association v. de la Cuesta" (1982 U.S. 458), that the Federal Home Loan Bank regulations allowing the due on sale clause superceded the California Supreme Court *Wellenkamp* decision. Federally charted savings and loan associations did have the right to exercise the due on sale clause. However, national banks and state-chartered savings and loan associations in California were still bound by the decision and could not enforce their due on sale clause. Immediately after the U.S. Supreme Court *de la Cuesta* decision, many California state-chartered savings and loan associations filed to become federally chartered institutions in an attempt to take advantage of the *de la Cuesta* decision.

ENTER THE GARN BILL

The controversy over the due on sale clause for state-chartered savings and loan associations and all banks was finally settled on October 15, 1982 with the enactment of the Depository Institutions Act of 1982, known as the Garn Bill. The key features of this bill were:

1. It allowed for continued assumability of state-chartered savings and loan association and bank loans originated during a "window period." The window period is the period of time beginning with the *Wellenkamp* case and ending on October 15, 1982.

2. Loans originated after October 15, 1982 by all banks, savings and loan associations, credit unions, and private lenders can carry enforceable due on sale clauses.

3. States had three years from October 15, 1982 to enact legislation on the future assumability of "window period" loans. If the state failed to act, all window period loans would become due upon sale when the three years were up, provided the note had the clause.

Controversy Ends

Per the Garn Bill, effective October 15, 1985, *all* due on sale clauses are enforceable in California.

CONFUSED???

It is strongly suggested that, before you buy or sell a property, you consult with an attorney and a real estate professional and have the impact of the current law and practices of the due on sale clause clearly explained to you.

Appendix B
Leverage

EQUITY CAPITAL

BORROWED CAPITAL

Leverage can be described as using a small amount of your money (equity capital) and a large amount of someone else's money (borrowed capital) to buy real estate. Leverage can be advantageous if the property increases in value.

For example, assume that you can purchase a home for $100,000 and resell it later for $150,000. If you pay $100,000 all cash and sell the property for $150,000, you would realize a $50,000 gain or a 50 percent return on your investment.

All-cash Transaction

$150,000	Resale price			
−100,000	Purchase price	$ 50,000	Gain	= 50%
$ 50,000	Gain	$100,000	Investment	

On the other hand, if you could obtain a $90,000 real estate loan, you would only need to invest $10,000 as a downpayment. If you resell the property for $150,000 and pay off the $90,000 loan, you would have a $50,000 gain or a 500 percent return on your investment.

Leverage Transaction

$100,000	Purchase price	$150,000	Resale price	
− 90,000	Loan	− 90,000	Loan	
$ 10,000	Downpayment	$ 60,000		
	(investment)	− 10,000	Downpayment	
		$ 50,000	Gain	

$$\frac{\$50,000 \text{ Gain}}{\$10,000 \text{ Investment}} = 500\%$$

Of course the percentage return will be reduced by income taxes paid, closing costs, and interest paid on the loan, but they have been omitted in order to stress the impact of leverage.

PITFALLS! Leverage can work in reverse if the value of the property declines. Let us see what happens if the property in our example has declined in value by 10 percent upon resale.

All-cash Transaction

$100,000	Purchase price			
− 90,000	Resale price	$ 10,000	Loss	= 10%
$ 10,000	Loss on resale	$100,000	Invested	Loss on invest- ment

Leverage Transaction

$90,000	Resale price			
− 90,000	Loan	0	Gain	= −100%
0	Gain	$10,000	Invested	Loss on invest- ment

If you paid $100,000 all cash, your loss is 10 percent, but if you paid $100,000 by borrowing $90,000 and putting $10,000 as down payment and the property resold for only $90,000, you were just able to repay the lender, and you lost all of your $10,000 downpayment!

Chapter 8

Part I: Real Estate Lenders and Government-Backed Housing Programs

Preview This chapter has been divided into two parts. Part I covers the principal types of real estate lenders found in California. Part II discusses government's role in real estate finance, stressing the main points of the FHA, VA, and Cal-Vet programs. When you have completed this chapter you will be able to:

1. *Compute the multipliers and ratios used by many real estate lenders to qualify borrowers.*

2. *List three institutional and noninstitutional real estate lenders.*

3. *Describe how private mortgage insurance has changed real estate lending practices in California.*

4. *Discuss the main characteristics of FHA-insured, VA-guaranteed, and Cal-Vet loans.*

5. *Define the secondary mortgage market and discuss the role played by government agencies in this market.*

8.1 QUALIFYING FOR A REAL ESTATE LOAN

When qualifying a borrower, a lender tries to determine if a borrower will make his or her loan payments in the future. To make this determination, a loan officer analyzes two major characteristics:

1. *Capacity to pay.* To determine capacity to pay, these questions must be asked: Does the borrower make enough money to make the payments? And, if so, is it a stable source of income? Does the borrower have enough cash to buy this property? What other assets does the borrower have? The answers to these questions all affect the borrower's capacity to pay.

2. *Desire to pay.* The desire to pay is the other major factor a lender must analyze. A person may have the capacity to pay but lack the desire to do so. The desire to pay is just as important, but it is more difficult to measure. The desire to pay is generally reflected by the past credit history of a borrower.

Old Rule of Thumb Is Inadequate

"A home should not cost more than 2½ times a buyer's (borrower's) gross income." This old lender's rule is inadequate. The rule ignores the real issue—the buyer's ability to pay the monthly housing payment. This rule also ignores the issue of a buyer's personal debts. Isn't a buyer who is free of debt able to pay more for housing than a buyer heavily in debt? Many lenders today recognize that the 2½ times the gross income rule is riddled with errors and pitfalls.

Use of Multipliers and Ratios

Most lenders qualify borrowers by using income multipliers or ratios. The ratios can vary from lender to lender; however, the traditional 4:1 multiplier has been used by conventional real estate lenders for many years.

A 4:1 multiplier simply means that the monthly income of the borrower should be four times the monthly housing payment. Thus if the monthly housing payment (principal, interest, taxes, and insurance) will be $950, four times this amount ($950 × 4) or $3,800 should be the borrower's gross monthly income. When converted to a ratio, the 4:1 multiplier means that a borrower's monthly housing payment should not exceed 25 percent of the borrower's gross monthly income. Gross income must include all the stable income of the borrower and co-borrowers, such as a spouse's income, alimony payments, and public assistance payments, as well as regular wages, commissions, and salaries.

Trend Toward More Liberal Ratios

Recently there has been a move toward use of 3.5:1 multipliers. This means that the borrower's monthly housing payments should not exceed 30 percent of the borrower's gross income. Lenders now recognize that due to rapid increases in the price of housing, more of a borrower's income must be used to cover housing payments. Therefore, if a borrower's monthly housing payment (principal, interest, taxes, and insurance) will be $950, three and one-half this amount or $3,325 should be the borrower's gross monthly income. Contrast this $3,325 with the $3,800 required above when a lender uses the 4:1 multiplier and you can see that the lower the ratio, the less gross income is needed to qualify for a real estate loan.

Debts

The lender must also consider a borrower's debts in order to determine the capacity to pay. A borrower's debts may be short-term or long-term. Short-term debts usually are ignored and long-term debts are counted. The definition of long- versus short-term debts can vary depending upon the lender. However, many lenders consider long-term debts to be obligations that exist for ten months or more.

When considering debts, conventional lenders traditionally have used the following guidelines: The monthly housing payment + long-term debts = total monthly expenses. The total monthly expenses should not exceed 33 percent to 38 percent of the borrower's gross monthly income.

Example. $950 monthly housing expense + $150 long-term monthly debts = $1,100 × 3 = $3,300 the gross monthly income required from the borrowers.

Summary of Qualifying Guidelines

1. (Principal + interest + taxes + insurance) = monthly housing payments ÷ gross monthly income =_____percent. This rate should not exceed 25 percent to 30 percent.

2. Monthly housing payments + long-term monthly debts = total monthly expenses ÷ gross monthly income =_____percent. This ratio should not exceed 33 percent to 38 percent.

Most real estate lenders require that the borrower(s) must qualify under both these tests. Some borrowers can qualify on the first test, but not on the second, because they are too heavily in debt.

Note: These guidelines can vary from lender to lender, thus consumers and real estate agents should contact local lenders to obtain specific guidelines.

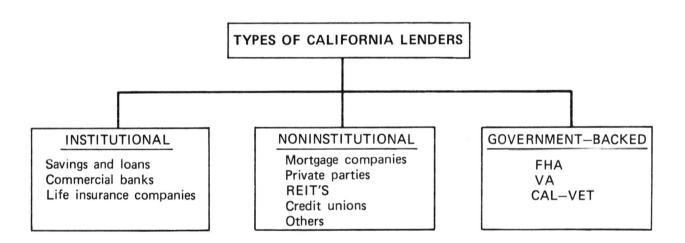

8.2 INSTITUTIONAL LENDERS

An institutional lender is a financial depository that pools funds of clients and depositors and then invests these funds. In California, there are three types of institutional lenders: commercial banks, savings and loan associations, and life insurance companies. All three of these institutionals pour billions of dollars into California real estate loans. Before studying institutional lenders, we need to review the characteristics of the California mortgage market and the concept of savings funds forming the pool for borrowing.

The California Mortgage Market

The characteristics of the California mortgage market can be summarized as follows:

1. *High demand.* Because of the diversified industry and economic growth, California has traditionally needed large amounts of mortgage funds.

2. *Population growth.* California is the most populous state, and continues to attract in migration. High population means high demand for housing.

3. *Financial institutions.* California has many of the nation's largest banks and savings and loan associations.

4. *Loan correspondents.* California has many experienced mortgage companies who represent out-of-state life insurance companies and other lenders who are eager to invest in California real estate loans.

5. *Title and escrow companies.* Title insurance and escrow companies originated in California. Many of the nation's largest are in California and provide fast and efficient service for real estate lenders.

6 *Use of deeds of trust.* The deed of trust is used rather than the mortgage instruments for securing real estate loans. Deeds of trust give lenders more flexibility than mortgages.

7. *Active secondary market.* Existing real estate loans are sold to out-of-state purchasers. These include mutual savings banks, which are not located in California, but make the capital available through secondary purchases.

Savings Form the Pool for Borrowing

Individual income can be taxed, spent, or saved. For most people taxes are taken out first; the remainder is then used for consumer expenditures. If any funds remain after consumer expenditures, they are saved (or invested, which is a form of saving). Sometimes, we spend more than we earn; therefore, we need to borrow. Where do the funds come from when we borrow? (Answer: someone else's savings.) If all income was taxed or spent, there wouldn't be any savings to borrow and it would be impossible to obtain a loan. Thus, it can be said that all private funds for loans, including real estate loans, can be traced back to some form of savings. With this background, let us turn our attention to the characteristics of institutional real estate lenders.

Commercial Banks

Commercial banks operate under a license or charter from either the state or federal government. As far as real estate loans are concerned, there is little difference between a state and national bank.

Commercial banks are the primary source for short-term construction financing, where the builder or developer has a "take-out" commitment from some other lender—most often a savings and loan association—for the permanent mortgage loan. Large commercial banks play a major role in financing business and commercial properties, while some smaller banks deal exclusively with home loans.

Bankers may make conventional real estate loans up to 90 percent of appraised value, for as long as 30 years on single-family dwellings. Most banks will require private mortgage insurance on loans whose loan-to-value ratio is in excess of 80 percent. Bankers are usually authorized to grant FHA-insured and VA-guaranteed loans.

OTHER CHARACTERISTICS OF BANK REAL ESTATE LOANS

The chief characteristics of bank real estate loans are:

1. Strong collateral is required, and a favorable previous relationship between bank and borrower is preferred.

2. Interest rates are usually in the medium range, between the higher rates charged by some S & Ls, and the rates charged by life insurance companies.

3. The property offered as collateral is usually situated in close proximity to the bank, or one of its branches.

4. Commercial banks are active seekers of home improvement and homeowner's equity loans, even though they constitute a junior lien against the property.

Savings and Loan Associations

A savings and loan association is a financial institution that accepts savings from the public, and invests these savings in real estate trust deeds and mortgages. The majority of S & L loans are in residential properties, mainly single-family dwellings.

A savings and loan association is also classified as either a state-chartered of federally-chartered institution. As far as real estate lending is concerned, there is very little difference.

LENDING CHARACTERISTICS OF SAVINGS AND LOAN ASSOCIATIONS

Chief lending characteristics are:

1. Under certain conditions 90 percent to 95 percent loan-to-value ratio loans are obtainable if they are covered by private mortgage insurance.

2. Most savings and loan associations limit their loans to 30 years.

3. Interest rates are ordinarily the highest among the institutional real estate lenders. This is due to the large demand for loans and to the higher risks associated with higher loan-to-value ratios. Lately, however, increasing rates charged by banks and life insurance companies have resulted in a more competitive position for S & Ls.

4. Their prime real estate loan is on a single-family, owner-occupied dwelling, but in a favorable market S & L's will also grant mobile home loans and apartment loans.

5. Combination loans that combine construction and long-term take out financing are common.

Life Insurance Companies

Life insurance companies are another important source for real estate financing, particularly for large commercial properties like shopping centers and office buildings. They also provide a significant amount of money for new housing subdivisions. In general, life insurance companies have broad lending powers.

LENDING CHARACTERISTICS OF LIFE INSURANCE COMPANIES

The chief lending characteristics of life insurance companies are:

1. Loan-to-value ratios are usually on the conservative side, generally in the 66⅔ to 75 percent range for conventional financing.

2. Long payback terms, usually 30 years, are common.

3. Interest rates and other fees on conventional loans have traditionally been the lowest among the institutionals, though in recent times they have been steadily climbing. Prepayment penalties, as a rule, are also among the lowest.

4. Insurance companies prefer to grant large commercial and industrial real estate loans.

5. "Loan correspondents," such as mortgage companies, are widely used as agents of insurance companies. In this way the insurance company is relieved of the burden of originating and processing loans, as well as some administrative and service functions.

8.3 NONINSTITUTIONAL LENDERS

Institutional lenders such as commercial banks, savings and loan associations, and life insurance companies are highly regulated by state and federal agencies. Noninstitutional lenders are lenders whose real estate activities are not as strictly regulated. Major noninstitutional lenders include private parties, mortgage companies, real estate investment trusts, and credit unions.

Private Lenders

Private lenders are individuals who invest their savings in real estate loans. Private persons can invest directly by granting loans to borrowers, or they can invest indirectly by turning to mortgage brokers who find borrowers for the private lender. Sellers frequently become private lenders when they carry back trust deeds in order to facilitate the sale of their property. The prime motivation of private lenders is to earn a higher yield, with some degree of safety, than they might otherwise receive with more conventional investments. Many private lenders are becoming investors by entering into partnership with young home buyers in the purchasing *and* financing of homes. Effective July 1, 1983 on seller carry loans on one to four residential units both the buyer and seller must be given complete disclosure in writing on a variety of financial items such as balloon payments, balances on senior loans and so on. Most real estate brokers have pre-printed forms that act as a checklist.

CHARACTERISTICS OF PRIVATE LENDERS

Private lenders generally have some common characteristics, regardless of whether the loan is made directly by the individual, or indirectly through a loan broker:

1. Most private lenders operate in the second trust deed market. Frequently these loans are seller carry-back seconds that thereafter are sold to investors, usually at a discount, when the seller needs cash.

2. Most loans are on single-family dwellings because this type of property is most familiar to the typical private investor, and also because the size of the loan is usually small.

3. The term of a private loan is usually short and often calls for a balloon payment. Three to six years are the most common maturities.

Mortgage Companies

Mortgage companies are another type of noninstitutional real estate lender. When a mortgage company represents a life insurance company, bank, savings and loan association, or other lender, it is called a *mortgage or loan correspondent*. It "corresponds" on behalf of its principal(s) in dealing with prospective borrowers. The mortgage correspondent is paid a fee in exchange for originating, processing, closing, and servicing loans. A loan correspondent serves a valuable function in the field of real estate financing for lenders whose headquarters or principal offices are located great distances from the properties on which they make loans.

LENDING CHARACTERISTICS OF MORTGAGE COMPANIES

Mortgage companies that do not use their own funds are subject in their lending activities to the same restrictions that govern their principal(s). Thus, if a California mortgage correspondent or banker represents an Eastern life insurance company, the correspondent would have the same loan-to-value limitations placed on its loans as the insurance company.

Those mortgage companies using their own funds, on the other hand, have some special restrictions placed upon them. In California they must be licensed real estate brokers. Even though they are not lending money belonging to third parties, they are subject to the Real Property Loan Law when they make loans that are not specifically exempt under that law. They are also subject to some lending and other business regulations. Otherwise mortgage companies are free to deal pretty much as they wish, making loans that institutional lenders would ordinarily turn down, and at whatever terms mutually agreed upon by borrower and lender.

Real Estate Investment Trusts

The *real estate investment trust* (or REIT) is a creature of the federal tax law. It was created in 1960 with the goal of encouraging small investors to pool their resources with others in order to raise venture capital for real estate transactions. It has been called the "mutual funds" of the real estate business. Just as mutual funds invest in a diversified portfolio of corporate stocks and bonds, REITs invest in a diversified portfolio of real estate and mortgage investments.

To qualify as a trust, there are many tests which must be met, such as the requirements that at least 95 percent of the REIT's ordinary income be distributed to the investors to qualify for favorable tax treatment. The legal ramifications of REITs are beyond the scope of this course; anyone interested in forming or participating in REITs should seek legal counsel.

Credit Unions

A *credit union* is a mutual, voluntary, cooperative organization of people who agree to save their money together in order to provide money for loans to each other. There are many credit unions throughout the United States, and their numbers are growing rapidly.

For the most part, credit union lending in the field of real estate has been short-term, but law changes now allow long-term real estate loans. In the near future, credit union funds could become a significant force in real estate financing, pumping millions of dollars into local real estate markets.

Syndicates, pension funds, trust funds, and various types of endowment funds are also noninstitutional real estate lenders. But their lending practices are beyond the scope of this course.

8.4 PRIVATE MORTGAGE INSURANCE

What is *private mortgage insurance?* It is insurance that is used to guarantee to lenders the payment of the upper portion of a conventional loan, if the borrower defaults and a deficiency occurs at the foreclosure sale.

Mortgage Guaranty Insurance is sold by private insurance companies, and in the lending business, they are referred to as PMI's. One reason for the growth of PMI companies was that lenders and builders had become unhappy with the Federal Housing Administration (FHA) because of the red tape and the artificially low interest rate set by the government. Due to the low FHA interest rate, builders had to pay high discounts (points) to sell their houses. To avoid these problems, builders and lenders turned to conventional mortgages insured by the PMI companies.

Coverage and Cost of Private Mortgage Insurance

Private mortgage insurance is available on one- to four-unit dwellings. It generally covers the top 20 to 25 percent of the loan amount, based on the value of the property. For example, if a home sold for $180,000 and the loan was 90 percent, the loan would be $180,000 × 90% = $162,000 loan. The private mortgage insurance coverage would be 20% × $162,000 loan = $32,400 insurance coverage to the lender.

The initial insurance premium fee varies with PMI companies, but it is usually paid by the borrower. In addition, there is an annual premium of one-quarter of one percent on the remaining principal balance. This premium is added to the borrower's monthly payment.

There are other variations of fees and annual premiums. There are also plans whereby you can pay one fee at the time of closing and no annual premium. However, the plan cited above is by far the most widely used.

Part II FHA, VA, Cal-Vet Loans and The Secondary Mortgage Market

8.5 GOVERNMENT'S ROLE IN REAL ESTATE FINANCING

Government has become heavily involved in helping Americans acquire decent housing. There are many government housing programs, but in this text only FHA-insured, VA-guaranteed, and Cal-Vet loan programs are discussed.

Federal Housing Administration (FHA)

The FHA, a part of the Department of Housing and Urban Development (HUD), was established in 1934 to improve the construction and the financing of housing. Since its creation, FHA has had a major influence on real estate financing. Some of today's loan features that are taken for granted were initiated by FHA.

The FHA is not a lender—*it does not make loans.* Approved lenders such as mortgage companies, savings and loan associations, insurance companies, and banks make the loans. However the loans must be granted under FHA guidelines. Once the loan is granted, if the borrower defaults on the loan, FHA insures the lender against foreclosure loss.

The FHA collects a fee for this insurance, which is called *mutual insurance policy (MIP).* The cost is paid as a lump sum upon organization of the FHA-backed loan. This fee used to be paid monthly. But FHA changed the regulations in November 1983. Now all new MIP fees are paid up front in cash or financed as part of the loan.

This insurance should not be confused with credit life insurance. FHA's mutual insurance policy does not insure the borrower's life. Mutual insurance policy is used by FHA to reimburse a lender if the borrower defaults on mortgage payments, and the foreclosure results in a loss for the lender.

ADVANTAGES AND DISADVANTAGES OF FHA-INSURED LOANS

Advantages of an FHA loan:

1. *Low downpayment.* The main advantage of an FHA insured loan is the low downpayment required. It used to be that FHA interest rates were set below the conventional rates. But deregulation in 1983 allowed the FHA interest rate to float with the market. Therefore sellers are no longer required to pay discount points to increase the lender's yield.

2. *No prepayment penalty.* An FHA insured loan does not allow a prepayment penalty.

3. *Under some circumstances, FHA insured loans are assumable.* FHA insured loans do not allow alienation clauses (due-on-sale

clauses). This makes it possible to buy property, and with FHA approval, takeover the seller's existing FHA insured loan. At one time all FHA insured loans were assumable without requiring a credit and/or income check. But beginning with FHA insured loans originated 12/15/89 on, all assumptions must be approved by FHA. In addition, non-owner occupied assumptions are prohibited on FHA insured loans originated 12/15/89 on. Under some circumstances, FHA insured loans dated before 12/15/89 can still be taken over without formal FHA approval. See a qualified loan representative for details.

4. *All cash to the seller.* New FHA-insured loans cash out the seller. In today's up and down real estate market, many sellers must carry a second in order to help finance a conventional loan for a buyer. Under FHA terms, the high loan-to-value ratio gives the seller all cash.

5. *Minimum property standards and independent appraisals.* Many buyers prefer the FHA program because FHA makes an independent appraisal of the property. Buyers feel they can rely on that appraisal, since it is prepared independently of the seller or the real estate agent. Also FHA will not allow a lender to grant a loan unless the property meets FHA housing standards.

DISADVANTAGES OF FHA LOANS

1. *Red tape and processing time.* The FHA is a large federal agency; therefore, you may experience the usual problems of dealing with a bureaucracy. It takes longer to process an FHA loan than a conventional loan.

2. *Repairs on existing property.* When FHA makes an appraisal on an existing property, it also checks for repairs it feels are necessary. FHA will then require that these repairs be made before the property is approved. Sellers may not wish to make these repairs and refuse to sell to an FHA-insured buyer.

Federal Housing Administration Programs

Here are some general rules that apply to all FHA programs:

1. FHA will approve loans on one- to four-unit dwellings, units in planned unit developments (PUDs), condominiums, and mobile homes.

2. The maximum loan fee is one percent of the loan amount, and the buyer normally pays this fee.

3. No secondary financing is allowed with a new FHA insured loan.

4. The maximum term is 30 years or three-quarters of the remaining economic life of the property, whichever is less.

5. FHA requires that monthly payments include principal and interest, property taxes, and hazard insurance premiums.

6. There is no maximum purchase price. The buyer can pay more than the FHA appraisal. However, the loan is based on the FHA appraisal if it is lower than the sale price.

7. The interest rates on FHA-backed loans now float with the market instead of being fixed by FHA.

8. FHA appraisals are good for six months on existing property, one year on new construction.

9. FHA requires a certification that the property has no evidence of termite infestation or other structural pest problems. Certification must be obtained from a recognized structural pest control company.

How to Calculate FHA-Insured Loan Amounts

FHA calculates loan amounts differently than other lenders. A conventional lender will figure its loan on the sales price (or appraised value if it is lower). The FHA bases its loan on what is called acquisition cost.

Acquisition cost is sales price (or FHA value if lower) plus nonrecurring closing costs the buyer is paying. Nonrecurring closing costs are a one-time cost that the borrower pays at close of escrow. They usually consist of title policy costs, fees for escrow, loan fee, appraisal fee, termite inspection report, recording and notary fees, and credit report charges.

The FHA adds these costs to the sales price to arrive at a true cost of acquisition. By calculating the loan based on both the sales price and closing cost, the FHA is helping the borrower finance part of the nonrecurring closing costs.

The FHA realizes that if you had to figure the closing costs, item by item on every sale, it would be difficult, so they have simplified the whole procedure. The FHA estimates various closing costs for different geographical areas according to an area's local customs and usage. Estimates are printed on schedules that are updated periodically and can be obtained from a local FHA office.

FHA appraisals will indicate both the value of the property and the closing costs. For example, assume that an FHA appraised value of a condo is $90,000 and the nonrecurring closing costs are $1,800. To figure acquisition cost, add the appraised value to the nonrecurring closing cost. In this case, it is $91,800. The maximum loan amount would then be computed using this $91,800 acquisition cost instead of the $90,000 appraised value. If the buyer does not pay the nonrecurring closing costs, they cannot be added to the sales price to get acquisition cost.

What if the FHA value differs from the sales price? The rule is: A loan is based on FHA value or sales price, whichever is the lesser, plus nonrecurring closing costs the buyer is paying.

CALCULATING DISCOUNT POINTS FOR VA LOANS

Under VA terms a lender is limited by law as to the maximum interest rate that they can charge a borrower. If this fixed rate is not sufficient to cope with today's cost of overhead and profit, a lender simply refuses to grant a loan under VA terms. Under these circumstances VA will allow a lender to charge the seller a discount fee to increase the lender's yield and thereby encouraging the lender to grant a loan under VA terms.

Example. Assume home appraisal is $140,000; the maximum VA-insured loan available is $140,000; current VA interest rate 10%, but lenders can get 11% interest on nongovernment-backed real estate loans.

To entice the lender to make the VA-backed loan, the government will allow the lender to charge the seller a fee which is a percentage based on the loan amount. (Of course sellers have to agree!) This fee is called a "mortgage discount" or points.

As a rule of thumb, points are calculated as follows: each one percent of discount (1 point) is equal to one-eighth of one percent interest. For a lender to increase the yield on a loan by one percent, it is necessary for the lender to charge 8 percent or eight points of the loan amount, which is deducted from the seller's net proceeds from the sale. Once again it should be stressed that the seller is made aware of this *before* accepting the buyer's offer to purchase the home.

Thus, in our example:

$$11\% - 10\% = 1\% = 8/8 = 8 \text{ points, or } 8\%$$

Therefore,

$140,000 loan amount $\times 8\%$ = $11,200 discount fee the seller must pay to the lender!

Without this discount, or point system, there would be few lenders who would lend at the government-controlled interest rates, when other interest rates are considerably higher. Lenders would simply place their funds elsewhere.

Formula for Computing VA points

⅛ difference between the VA interest rate and the conventional loan amount rate equal 1% or 1 point of the loan amount.

Special Note: Under VA rules, the buyer can only pay a 1% loan origination fee a 1.875% funding fee. *The discount points are paid by the seller.*

FHA Programs
The National Housing Act of 1934 created the Federal Housing Administration. The act has eleven subdivisions or "Titles" with further subdivisions called "Sections."

This chapter only deals with two of the sections under Title II of the act, since these are the most important to the average consumer or real estate agent.

SECTION 203b
Under the 203b program:

1. Anyone who is financially qualified is eligible.

2. Loans are available on properties from one to four units.

3. The maximum loans (1990) for high cost areas in California are: single-family dwelling, $124,875; two-family unit, $140,660; three-family dwelling, $170,200 and four-family dwelling, $197,950. To compute the maximum loan on a property, the formula is: 97 percent of the first $25,000, and 95 percent of the remainder to the maximum loan allowed. Maximum FHA loan amounts may vary depending on the median price of homes in an area. The figures given are for high price areas in California. Other areas within the state may have lower maximum FHA loan amounts.

Example.

Sales price and FHA appraisal	$100,000
Nonrecurring closing cost (use FHA estimate)	1,500
Acquisition cost	$101,500

Maximum loan is:
97% of $25,000 = $24,250
95% of $76,500 = $72,675
$101,500 $96,925

Using this formula, the maximum loan is $96,900, as FHA rounds down to the nearest $50.

SECTION 245GPM
This section provides for a graduated payment mortgage (GPM), which is designed to help the young family who would have difficulty making normal payments but whose income is expected to increase. Monthly mortgage payments start low and rise for the first five to ten years, and then become fixed for the remaining term of the mortgage.

Under this program:

1. Anyone is eligible.

2. Loans are available only on single-family dwellings, planned urban developments, or condominiums.

3. The downpayment requirements are roughly 10% down to the maximum loan allowed. The actual calculations are complicated and therefore beyond the scope of this course. See your local lender for specific details.

During the initial years of the 245 GPM mortgage, the monthly payments cover only part of the interest due. Therefore, the deferred (unpaid) interest is added to the principal balance, which increases during the early years.

Under this program, the buyer has a choice of five repayment plans. Three of the plans permit mortgage payments (not the interest rate) to increase at a rate of 2.5, 5, or 7.5 percent over the first five years. The other two plans permit payments to increase 2 or 3 percent over the first ten years. Starting at the sixth year for the five-year plan, and the eleventh year for the ten-year plan, the payments will be level for the remaining term of the mortgage.

Note Congress in the past has considered a bill which will change the 245 program downpayment to match the FHA 203b downpayment requirement. For details consult your broker.

Example. Under the GPM Plan shown below, mortgage payments would increase 7.5 percent each year for five years before leveling off.

Assume: Mortgage Amount $50,000
         Interest Rate   9 percent
         Term   30 years

Mortgage Payment Each Month

Year	Regular 203b Loan	GPM Loan
1	$402.50	$303.94
2	402.50	326.74
3	402.50	351.24
4	402.50	377.59
5	402.50	405.96
6	402.50	436.35
7	402.50	436.35
Remaining payments (life of loan)	402.50	436.35

As you can see, under the 245 plan, payments start out lower than the regular 203b plan, but then increase over a seven-year period, and eventually level off approximately $35 higher per month for the remaining period of time.

Veterans Administration (G.I.) Loans

In 1944, Congress passed the G.I. Bill of Rights to provide benefits to veterans, including provisions for making real estate loans.

Like the FHA, the VA is not a lender. However, if no approved private lender is located in the area, the VA will make direct loans under certain conditions. Generally, the VA operates the same as the FHA; however, one difference is that the VA *guarantees* a portion of the loan, while the FHA *insures* the loan. Currently (June 1990); the maximum guarantee on a VA loan to a lender is $46,000 or 50 percent of the loan amount, whichever is less. For homes priced less than $144,000, $36,000 is the maximum guarantee. Whether a loan is insured or guaranteed is important only if foreclosure takes place. In foreclosure cases the VA has two options:

1. It can pay the lender the balance on the loan and take back the property.

2. It can let the lender keep the property and pay it the amount of the guarantee.

Under FHA, the lender is always paid off and the property is taken back by the FHA.

ADVANTAGES AND DISADVANTAGES OF VA (G.I.) LOANS

Advantages of VA Loans

1. *No downpayment.* The VA does not require a borrower to make any downpayment on loans up to $184,000 if the borrower pays the VA appraised value for the property.

2. *Lower interest rate.* VA-set interest rates on VA-guaranteed loans are almost always less than the going conventional rates.

3. *No prepayment penalty.*

4. *Appraisal.* VA appraisals are made by independent professional appraisers who work for the VA on a fee basis. The buyer is not allowed to pay more than that value unless he or she agrees. This is a real protection for a buyer who is not aware of property values. VA appraisals are called "certificate of reasonable value" (CRV).

Disadvantages of VA Loans

1. *Credit worthiness qualification.* Effective March 1, 1988 VA loans are no longer automatically "assumable or subject to." VA requires a credit worthiness qualification before an existing loan can be taken over by a new buyer. The fee can be as high as $500.

2. *Seller must pay discounts* (points). The VA point system is explained on page 156.

3. *Red tape and processing time.* Processing time, inflexibility, and paperwork are the usual problems in dealing with a large government agency.

4. *Repairs on existing property.* The VA requires repairs that it feels are necessary. However, in practice, VA does not usually require as many repairs as the FHA.

Who Is Eligible for VA Loans?

There are specific rules that determine whether a veteran is eligible for a loan. Not everyone who has served in the armed forces is eligible. Before 1970, a veteran's eligibility expired a number of years after discharge. Today, there is no termination date. Also a veteran can use his or her VA loan more than once.

To be eligible, the veteran must have a discharge or release that is not dishonorable and have served a minimum number of days depending upon the time period in the service. The usual minimum is 181 days of active duty.

Those who served less than the required time but were released or discharged due to a service-connected disability are also eligible for VA loans. In addition, many other classifications of veterans may be eligible for a VA-guaranteed loan.

General Information on VA Loans

1. *Type of property.* The VA will guarantee loans on properties from one to four units and units in planned unit developments (PUDs), condominiums, and mobile homes.

2. *Interest rate.* The interest rate cannot exceed the maximum rate as established by the VA.

3. *Loan fee.* The loan origination fee paid by the borrower cannot exceed one percent of the loan amount.

4. *Funding fee.* A 1.875% fee paid by the borrower for granting the loan.

5. *Terms of loan.* The maximum term is 30 years.

6. *Downpayment.* The VA does not require a downpayment on loans to $184,000. The veteran is frequently allowed to borrow the full amount of the purchase price. What happens if the VA appraises the property for less than the purchase price? The loan amount cannot exceed the appraisal. The difference between the purchase price and the appraisal has to be paid by the borrower in cash.

7. *Maximum loan.* There is no maximum loan amount on a VA loan. This does not mean you can obtain a no-downpayment VA loan in any amount. Since the VA only guarantees a portion of the loan, lenders limit the amount they will lend on VA loans. Many lenders will not lend more than four times the guarantee. Thus, $46,000 guarantee x 4 = $184,000 maximum VA loan. VA regulations change from time to time regarding loans in excess of $184,000 and secondary financing. Check your local lender.

8. *Occupying the property.* The veteran must occupy the property. The VA does not have a program for veterans who do not intend to occupy the property.

9. *Monthly payments.* Included are principal, interest, property taxes, and hazard insurance premiums.

10. *Appraisal.* The VA appraisal is called "certificate of reasonable value" (CRV). To the VA, reasonable value means current market value.

11. *Structural pest control report.* The VA requires that a report be obtained from a recognized structural pest control company. The work must be done and the veteran must certify that the work has been done satisfactorily.

Cal-Vet Loans

The Cal-Vet program is administered by the State of California Department of Veteran Affairs, Division of Farms and Home Purchases. The veteran (buyer) deals directly with this agency. There is no other lender involved, the state makes the loan to the veteran directly. The money is obtained from the sale of State Veteran Bonds.

Who Is Eligible for Cal-Vet Loans?

To qualify, a veteran must meet these requirements.

1. Ninety days active duty.

2. Honorable discharge.

3. Served within one of these periods: World War II (December 7, 1941 to December 31, 1946); Korean War (June 27, 1950 to January 31, 1955); Vietnam War (August 5, 1964 to May 7, 1975). (There are special dates in between these years in which a veteran may qualify.)

4. Be a native of California or have been a resident of California when the veteran entered the service.

General Information About Cal-Vet Loans

1. *Property.* Cal-Vet has generally the same property standards as FHA and VA. The property must be a single-family dwelling or a unit in a planned unit development, condominium, or mobile home.
   Cal-Vet requires both a structural pest control report and a roof inspection.

2. *Maximum loan.* The maximum loan (as of June 1990) is $125,000 for a home and $200,000 for a farm.

3. *Downpayment.* The downpayment required is 5 percent, if the sales price and appraised value exceeds $35,000. On properties where the sales price is $35,000 or less the down payment is reduced to 3 percent.

4. *Term of loan.* Legal maximum is 40 years, but most loans are approved for a term of 25 years.

5. *Interest rate.* The interest rate is variable. The rate is checked periodically to determine if a change is necessary. The cost of the bonds and of running the program determine the interest rate.

6. *Secondary financing.* This is permitted under special circumstances. However, the provisions are too complex to be covered in this text.

7. *Prepayment penalty.* If the loan is paid off within five years, the penalty is six months interest on original loan amount. There is no penalty after five years.

8. *Occupancy.* The veteran must occupy the property.

9. *Monthly payments.* Principal and interest, taxes, fire, disability, and life insurance premiums are included in monthly loan payments.

10. *Title to property.* When a property is being financed with a Cal-Vet loan, title is first conveyed to the Department of Veterans Affairs by the seller. The department then sells the property to the veteran under a land contract of sale. The department continues to hold title until the veteran has paid the loan in full.

ADVANTAGES AND DISADVANTAGES OF CAL-VET LOANS

The main advantages of Cal-Vet loans are low interest rate, inexpensive life and fire insurance, and low closing costs.

One disadvantage is the $125,000 maximum loan amount. Another disadvantage is the time required to process a loan. In the past, it has varied from 30 days to six months and, in some cases, even longer. In most real estate transactions, a buyer does not have that much time to arrange financing. Cal-Vet realizes this is a problem. Therefore, Cal-Vet will allow the veteran to purchase the property with interim financing as long as the veteran makes application for the Cal-Vet loan to the Department of Veterans Affairs before he or she takes title. When the Cal-Vet loan is approved, the interim loan is paid off.

Comparison of Government-Backed Loans as of June 1990

	Federal Housing Administration	*Veterans Administration (GI)*	*Cal-Vet*
Purpose of loan	1–4 units	1–4 units	single-unit dwelling, farms
Eligibility	any U.S. resident	U.S. veteran	California veterans
Maximum purchase price	none	none	none
Maximum loan for high cost areas	1 unit $124,875 2 units, $140,660 3 units, $170,200 4 units, $197,950	none by VA; lenders limit loan amount	$125,000, home; $200,000, farm
Downpayment	Section 203b, 3% of first $25,000 acquisition cost and 5% of remainder to maximum loan	none, but loan limited to CRV	5% of appraisal if over $35,000; 3% if $35,000 or under
Maximum term	usually 30 years	usually 30 years	legally 40 years but usually 25 years
Interest rate	market rate	legally imposed rate	variable rate regulated by state
Prepayment penalty	none	none	6 months interest if paid during first 5 years on original loan amount

8.6 SECONDARY MORTGAGE MARKET

The secondary mortgage market is a market where existing real estate loans are bought and sold—in other words, lenders sell their loans to other lenders and investors. The secondary mortgage market should not be confused with secondary financing. Secondary financing is a loan secured by a second or junior deed of trust, while a secondary market is the sale of an existing loan by one lender to another lender or investor.

SECONDARY MARKET

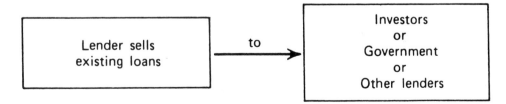

Purpose of the Secondary Mortgage Market

FLOW OF MONEY

Why do lenders need a secondary market? Why don't they just make a loan and keep it? That would be fine if every lender always had a perfect balance between the demand for loans and its supply of money. However, in the real world, this balance rarely exists. For example, a lender in California may have more demand for loans than it can meet. Another lender in Texas might have the opposite problem—surplus funds because of lack of demand in Texas. The solution to this problem is to have the Texas lender buy loans from the California lender. Both would be satisfying their needs. The Texas lender would be putting idle money to work and the California lender would obtain additional funds to use to make new loans. Thus, one of the main purposes of the secondary market is to shift mortgage funds to areas where they are needed.

STABILIZE THE MORTGAGE MARKET

The mortgage market is never static; rather it moves through cycles of tight and loose money. Another purpose of the secondary market is to help stabilize the mortgage market. The market can be stabilized by providing funds to buy loans during tight money periods and providing loans to be purchased during loose money periods. Three main organizations help to stabilize the mortgage market:

1. Federal National Mortgage Association

2. Federal Home Loan Mortgage Corporation

3. Government National Mortgage Association

In the late 1970s and early 1980s the United States went through a tight money cycle, so severe it was called a "credit crunch." The crunch was caused by the high rate of inflation. To combat the inflation, the Federal Reserve Board clamped down on the money supply. As a result, interest rates on short-term investments soared and savers withdrew their deposits from savings institutions to take advantage of the higher rates they could get elsewhere. Money for real estate loans became very scarce. To support the mortgage market, these three organizations often pour money into the market. They do it by purchasing billions of dollars of loans from lending institutions. With the money they receive from the sale of their existing loans, lending institutions are able to make new real estate loans. This action helps to ease the credit crunch in the housing market.

Government Agencies and the Secondary Mortgage Market

FEDERAL NATIONAL MORTGAGE ASSOCIATION

The Federal National Mortgage Association is usually called by its nickname "Fannie Mae." Established in 1938 by the U.S. Congress, its main job is to provide a secondary market for mortgages. Fannie Mae remained a part of the federal government until 1968, when it became a private corporation. Its main function today is still to maintain a secondary market.

In order to maintain a secondary market, Fannie Mae buys and sells mortgages. Where does it get the money to do this? It borrows money in the capital market by selling notes and bonds. Fannie Mae can usually obtain a more favorable rate than another corporate borrower because its obligations carry the indirect backing of the U.S. Government.

What type of loans can Fannie Mae buy and sell? Until 1972, it only purchased FHA and VA loans; in 1972, it began purchasing conventional loans. Fannie Mae will purchase conventional loans on one- to four-unit dwellings, units in planned unit developments, and condominiums. Fannie Mae buys only conventional loans that are generally marketable to private lending institutions. Therefore, any conventional loan Fannie Mae approves should meet the usual standards of a conventional lender.

FEDERAL HOME LOAN MORTGAGE CORPORATION

The Federal Home Loan Mortgage Corporation, known as "Freddie Mac," was created in 1970 under the Emergency Home Finance Act. Freddie Mac is a subsidiary of the Federal Home Bank Board which supervises the federally chartered S & Ls. The main function of Freddie Mac is to provide a secondary mortgage market for the savings and loan associations.

Freddie Mac can buy loans from S & Ls that are members of the Federal Home Loan Bank system or from financial institutions whose deposits are insured by an agency of the federal government. Banks, for example, can sell loans to Freddie Mac.

Freddie Mac buys FHA, VA, and conventional loans. It purchases conventional loans on one- to four-unit buildings, units in planned unit developments, and condominiums.

GOVERNMENT NATIONAL MORTGAGE ASSOCIATION

The Government National Mortgage Association also has a nickname, "Ginnie Mae" and is a wholly owned corporation of the U.S. Government. It was created in 1968 when Fannie Mae became a private corporation. At the time, Fannie Mae was relieved of two of its duties which were given to Ginnie Mae. These were:

1. The management and liquidation of certain mortgages previously acquired by the U.S. Government.

2. Special assistance functions, including the development of a mortgage-backed security program.

By directly and indirectly providing low-interest rate loans, Ginnie Mae encourages people to buy new homes. The increased demand for new homes results in more work and jobs for the construction industry.

The real impact of Ginnie Mae is in its mortgage-backed security program. This program was established to attract new money into the housing market. The mortgage-backed security was created to make investing in mortgages as simple as buying stocks and bonds. Under this mortgage program, an investor will purchase a pool of mortgages and receive a certificate. There is no need to examine each mortgage. All of the time-consuming paper work is eliminated. Since Ginnie Mae is a federal corporation, its guarantee is backed by the "full faith and credit" of the U.S. Government.

In short, the Ginnie Mae programs in the secondary mortgage market have added to the funds made available for real estate borrowers.

SUMMARY
Three institutional real estate lenders are savings and loan associations, commercial banks, and life insurance companies. The greatest bulk of residential home loans are made by savings and loan associations. Noninstitutional real estate lenders include private lenders, mortgage companies, REITs, pension funds, and credit unions.

To determine if a borrower qualifies for a real estate loan, lenders use multipliers and ratios of income to monthly housing payments. The common ratios are monthly housing payments divided by the gross monthly income, and total monthly expenses divided by the gross monthly income.

The use of private mortgage insurance (PMI) has increased in recent years. The main advantage for real estate borrowers is that the use of PMI has greatly lowered the down payment needed to purchase a home.

Government has taken an active role in the field of real estate finance. On the federal level the Federal Housing Administration (FHA) has several programs. The 203b program has historically been the most popular, but recently the 245 Graduated Payment Mortgage program has zoomed into prominence. The Veterans Administration (VA) has a no down payment program for qualified veterans. However, the slow processing time and red tape, coupled with VA need for sellers to pay discount points, has discouraged many sellers from selling to VA approved buyers.

The State of California's Cal-Vet loan program has been a huge success, with demand usually exceeding the supply of loans available. The extremely low interest rate paid by the California veteran is the main attraction.

The secondary mortgage market consists of real estate lenders who sell existing mortgages to other real estate lenders. The main purpose of the secondary mortgage market is to help strike a balance between the demand for real estate loans and the supply of money available for real estate loans. The Federal National Mortgage Association, the Federal Home Loan Mortgage Corporation, and the Government National Mortgage Association all participate in this secondary mortgage market.

Important Terms and Concepts

Cal-Vet loans

Commercial banks

Credit unions

Discount points

Federal Home Loan Mortgage Corporation (Freddie Mac)

Federal Housing Administration (FHA)

Federal National Mortgage Association (Fannie Mae)

Government National Mortgage Association (Ginnie Mae)

Graduated payment mortgages (FHA 245 GPM)

Institutional Lenders

Life insurance companies

Loan qualification ratios

Mortgage companies

Noninstitutional lenders

Private lenders

Private mortgage insurance (PMI)

Real estate investment trust (REIT)

Savings and loan associations

Secondary mortgage market

Veterans Administration (VA)

203b Program (FHA)

REVIEWING YOUR UNDERSTANDING

1. A borrower's total monthly housing payments will be $1,000. The borrower's other long-term debts are $300 per month. The borrower's gross monthly income is $3,600. What are the borrower's qualifying ratios?
   (a) 25% and 33.3%
   (b) 27.8% and 36.1%
   (c) 30% and 38.9%
   (d) 31.2% and 37.3%

2. Which of the following is a noninstitutional lender?
   (a) Commercial bank
   (b) Life insurance company
   (c) Credit union
   (d) Savings and loan association

3. In California, which lender has the largest percentage of residential real estate loans?
   (a) Savings and loan associations
   (b) Commercial banks
   (c) Mortgage companies
   (d) Credit unions

4. Which real estate lender frequently acts as a loan correspondent for other lenders?
   (a) Pension funds
   (b) Mortgage companies

(c) Real estate investment trusts

(d) Private lenders

5. The use of private mortgage guaranty insurance permits lenders to make up to what percent loans on owner-occupied homes?
    (a) 80 percent
    (b) 90 percent
    (c) 95 percent
    (d) 100 percent

6. If the VA allowed interest rate is 12 percent, but a lender wishes a rate of 12¾ percent, how many points difference are there between these two rates?
    (a) ¾ points
    (b) 3 points
    (c) 4 points
    (d) 6 points

7. Which FHA program has graduated payments during the early years of the loan?
    (a) 203b
    (b) 221d
    (c) 245
    (d) 220

8. Which statement is true about a VA-guaranteed loan?
    (a) The buyer pays the discount points.
    (b) The downpayment requirement is 3 percent of the first $25,000 and 5 percent of the remainder.
    (c) There is no mutual mortgage insurance.
    (d) The maximum loan amount for a home is $60,000.

9. Which government program charges the homeowner the lowest interest rate?
    (a) Cal-Vet
    (b) FHA 203b
    (c) FHA 245
    (d) VA

10. A secondary mortgage market is where:
    (a) Second loans are placed against real estate.
    (b) Existing real estate loans are bought and sold to other lenders or investors.
    (c) An insurance company guarantees the loan payments.
    (d) Mortgage brokers arrange loans to borrowers.

11. "Fannie Mae" refers to:
    (a) Government National Mortgage Association
    (b) Federal National Mortgage Association
    (c) Federal Home Loan Mortgage Corporation
    (d) Department of Veterans Affairs

12. Which government program requires the least downpayment for the purchase of a owner-occupied $140,000 home?
    (a) FHA 203b
    (b) FHA 245
    (c) Cal-Vet
    (d) VA

13. Sales price and FHA appraisal is $103,000. Nonrecurring closing cost comes to $1,500. The maximum FHA 203b loan will be:
    (a) $ 99,775
    (b) $104,500
    (c) $101,400
    (d) $ 98,500

14. Under a Cal-Vet loan, title to the real property rests with the:
    (a) Institutional lender
    (b) Borrower
    (c) Department of Veterans Affairs
    (d) Buyer

15. Which of the following statements is false?
    (a) The higher the qualifying ratios, the more income a borrower needs to qualify for a real estate loan.
    (b) Savings form the pool for borrowing.
    (c) Life insurance companies specialize in making individual homeowner loans.
    (d) Private lenders, who grant hard money loans to private individuals, are not exempt from usury laws.

Chapter 9
Real Estate Appraisal

Preview

An appraisal is an essential part of a real estate transaction. Many times the decision to buy, sell, or grant a loan on real estate hinges upon a real estate appraiser's estimate of its value. When you have completed this chapter you will be able to:

1. *Define appraisal, and then list four elements and forces that influence value.*

2. *Distinguish between utility value and market value.*

3. *Define depreciation; outline the causes of depreciation and then describe how to calculate depreciation.*

4. *Discuss the three approaches or methods used to determine value; outline the steps in each approach; define gross multipliers.*

9.1 APPRAISAL CONCEPTS

An *appraisal* is defined as an estimate or opinion of value. Real estate appraisals are needed to:

1. Set sales prices on property.

2. Estimate real estate loan values.

3. Determine values for real property taxes.

4. Help set premiums on fire insurance policies.

Other reasons include determining inheritance taxes and values for government acquisition. Real estate appraisal is not an exact science; therefore, the accuracy of an appraisal is related to the skill, experience, and judgment of the appraiser. In 1991, per federal law, all states must issue guidelines and qualifications to become a certified appraiser. After this date government type real estate loans and certain loans sold in the secondary market must be appraised by state certified appraisers.

There are several professional estate appraisal organizations in the United States. Two of the largest appraisal trade associations are the American Institute of Real Estate Appraisers (AIREA), which issues the widely recognized designation, MAI (Member of the Appraisal Institute), and the Society of Real Estate Appraisers, which issues the designation SRPA.

Market Value

Although there are various types of value—sales value, loan value, tax value, and insurance value—two major categories of value are *value in use* (utility value) and *market value.* Value in use refers to the value of property to an owner or user of real estate. The value of property to an owner may be emotional, as well as economic, thus, value in use is also known as *subjective value.*

On the other hand, *market value* is value in exchange as determined by supply and demand in the real estate market. Market value is also referred to as *objective value.* Between utility and market value, without question most appraisals are for the purpose of establishing market value. *Market value* can be briefly defined as "the highest price in terms of money for which a property would sell in the open market, seller not being obligated to sell, the buyer not being obligated to buy, allowing a reasonable length of time to effect the sale." This also assumes that both the buyer and seller are fully knowledgeable persons. In short, when a buyer or seller asks the question "What is the property worth?" they are asking for an estimate or opinion of market value as of a certain date.

Market Value Versus Price Paid

Price paid may or may not be the same as market value. A person could pay a price of $100,000 for a condo which has a market value of $90,000, or just the opposite—pay a price of $90,000 for a condo with a market value appraisal of $100,000. On the other hand, a person may pay $100,000 for a condo valued at $100,000. The key point is this: Price trends establish market values, but for any single sale, the price paid may be equal to, higher, or lower than market value.

Essential Elements of Value

For property to have value four elements or characteristics must be present. These are: (1) utility, (2) scarcity, (3) demand, and (4) transferability.

Utility refers to usefulness—the more useful a property, the greater its potential value. Scarcity means lack of abundance. When utility exists, the more scarce an item, the greater its value. Demand refers to the desire to own real estate, coupled with the financial ability to buy. Assuming a scarce number of properties for sale, the greater the number of ready, willing, and able buyers (demand) the greater the likelihood that the property offered for sale will increase in value. Transferability refers to the ability to transfer identifiable ownership. A beautiful home on the California coast may be a scarce commodity, with great utility and high demand. But if the property's title is clouded and uncertain, not many people will be willing to buy this home. The clearer the title, the more valuable the property. When a title is clouded, the property is less valuable.

Utility, scarcity, demand, and transferability are the essential elements of value. If all are present in a favorable combination, a property's value may increase. If one or more elements are missing, a property's value may be stagnant or even decline.

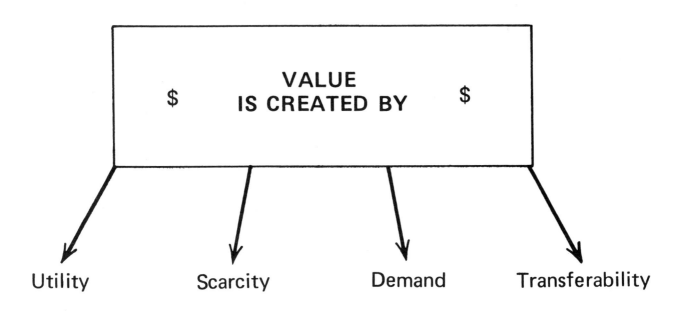

THEN

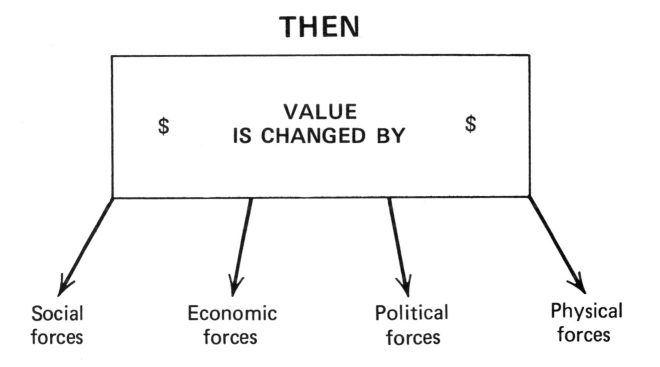

Four Forces that Influence Value

Once a property's value has been established, there are four forces that can change its value. These forces are:

1. *Social forces* such as changes in population, marriage trends, family size, and attitudes toward education, recreation, and life styles.

2. *Economic forces* which include changes in income levels, employment opportunities, the cost of money and credit, taxes, and the availability of energy and natural resources.

3. *Political forces* such as changes in zoning, building codes, construction moritoriums, government housing programs, and pro-growth or no-growth government philosophy.

4. *Physical forces* that affect the physical aspects of the property, such as size and shape of the parcel, the location, climate, and soil conditions.

These four forces continually bombard every parcel of real estate and cause values to shift either positively or negatively. Which of these forces is the single most important? There is no simple answer! This is where the skill, experience, and judgment of an appraiser comes in. However, there is an old saying that states "The three most important factors of value are location, location, location."

Basic Principles of Valuation

Appraisal theory and practice is based upon several principles or assumptions:

1. *Principle of highest and best use.* The best use of land is that use which produces the greatest net return to the land.

2. *Principle of change.* Real estate values are constantly changing due to social, economic, political, and physical forces within a region, city, and neighborhood.

3. *Principle of supply and demand.* The interaction of supply and demand cause real estate values to change—for example, assuming a fixed supply of homes for sale, an increase in demand should cause prices to increase.

4. *Principle of substitution.* The value of a property tends to be influenced by the price of acquiring an equally desirable substitute property—for example, the value of Property A is somewhat determined by the value of comparable properties B, C, and D.

5. *Principle of conformity.* In a residential neighborhood, the maximum value will be found where there is a high degree of conformity—such as homes of similar design, architecture, and upkeep.

Several other principles are the principles of progression, regression, contribution, anticipation, competition, and surplus productivity.

But these are beyond the scope of this book. For specific details consult any appraisal textbook.

What needs to be emphasized here is that all of the above principles form the theoretical foundation upon which real estate appraisers rely to estimate value.

9.2 DEPRECIATION

Depreciation is defined as a loss in value from any cause. Depreciation is usually measured as the difference between the new replacement cost of a building or improvement, and its value as of the date of the appraisal. If an existing building (excluding land) is appraised at $80,000, but its replacement cost if it were destroyed and needed to be rebuilt is calculated to be $100,000, the difference ($100,000 − $80,000) of $20,000 is depreciation.

Causes of Depreciation

The causes or reasons for a loss in real estate value can be grouped into three categories.

1. *Physical deterioration.* A loss in value caused by: (a) wear and tear from use, (b) deferred maintenance, lack of upkeep, (c) damage by termites, dry rot, and so on, and (d) weather conditions. A rundown home, in need of paint and repairs, is an example of depreciation caused by physical deterioration.

2. *Functional obsolescence.* A loss in value caused by: (a) unpopular floor plan and layout, (b) lack of updated, modern appliances and equipment, and (c) poor or unpopular architectural design and style. A three-bedroom, one-bath home with a wall heater and single-car garage is an example of depreciation caused by functional obsolescence. Why? Because most buyers of three-bedroom homes prefer one and one-half or two bathrooms, two-car garage, and a forced-air heating system. Therefore, all other things being equal, the three-bedroom, one-bath home noted above will usually sell at a lower price.

3. *Economic and social obsolescence.* A loss in value resulting from: (a) zoning and other government actions, (b) misplaced improvements—such as a home built next to an all-night service station, and (c) a drop in demand for real estate, or overbuilding, creating an excessive supply of homes. An example of economic obsolescence would be a neighborhood street, recently declared a truck route, whose increased traffic brings noise and fumes into the area. This could cause home values to decline. In short, economic obsolescence is caused by factors outside the boundaries of the property—items beyond the control of the owners.

Curable Versus Incurable Depreciation

Physical deterioration and functional obsolescence can be classified as curable or incurable. *Curable* means that if repairs and/or remodeling are undertaken, the expense incurred will be less than the value added to the property—that is, you spend $15,000 on repairs and add $17,500 in increased value.

Incurable depreciation means the cost to repair or remodel exceeds the value added to the property—that is, you spend $15,000 on repairs and only add $10,000 in increased value.

Physical deterioration and functional obsolescence can be classified as curable or incurable per the guidelines noted above. However, economic obsolescence is almost always considered incurable, because the loss in value is caused by negative factors outside the property's boundaries. Therefore, it is assumed that these negative factors are beyond the control of any single property owner.

Accrued Depreciation Versus Recapture for Depreciation

Accrued depreciation is the loss in value that has already occurred in a building. Recapture for depreciation is an estimate for depreciation that will occur in the future. Accrued (past) depreciation is used in an appraisal technique called the cost approach. A recapture for depreciation is used in an appraisal technique called the income approach. The approaches to value will be discussed in the next section of this chapter.

An Additional Word about Depreciation

Depreciation for appraisal purposes is different from depreciation for income tax purposes. The appraiser looks at depreciation as being an actual decline in value. An accountant, for income tax purposes, uses *book depreciation* as a basis for an income tax deduction. The two concepts are not the same. The accountant uses a theoretical figure allowed by the Internal Revenue Service, while an appraiser uses economic analysis to arrive at an actual decline in value.

Appreciation is an increase in value which can result from inflation or from the interaction of supply and demand forces. All real estate improvements suffer some form of depreciation, but simultaneously many properties are appreciating. The question then becomes: Is the rate of appreciation exceeding the rate of depreciation? If so, overall value of the property increases. But if the rate of depreciation is exceeding appreciation, the overall value of the property decreases.

9.3 APPRAISAL METHODS

When an appraiser is hired, the appraiser's estimate of value is submitted as a report. Three common types of appraisal reports are: (1) letter form appraisal report, (2) short-form appraisal report, and (3) narrative appraisal report.

The *letter form* is the least comprehensive report. It is used when a client is familiar with the area and therefore does not need appraisal details. The appraiser merely submits the estimate of value on company letterhead.

The *short-form* report is most commonly used by real estate lenders when appraising property for loan purposes. The short-form report consists of check sheets and spaces to be filled in by the appraiser.

In recent years there has been a tendency to standardize the short-form report using guidelines established by government-backed agencies that operate in the secondary mortgage market (see Figure 9-1).

The *narrative report* is the most comprehensive appraisal report. It is a complete documentation of the entire appraisal process, including computation, maps, photographs, and detailed analysis. This report is used in court cases, condemnation proceedings, and for expensive commercial and industrial properties. Due to its size, detail, and cost, a narrative appraisal report is *not* commonly used in the home real estate market.

Appraisal Process

As in many other professional occupations, real estate appraisers have developed a system for conducting their work. The appraisal of real estate can be viewed as a series of steps, with each step logically following the preceding, until a final estimate of value is reached. Figure 9-2 is a flowchart of the real estate appraisal process.

As shown in Figure 9-2, the appraiser starts with a definition of the problem (What is the reason for the appraisal? Why does the client need the appraisal?). Then the needed data are gathered and classified. The data are run through three approaches or techniques of analysis called the *cost, market,* and *income approaches.* A separate value is arrived at under each approach, and then these three values are correlated. From this correlation, one final estimate of value is given to the client.

Although this appraisal process has its roots in scientific analysis, the appraisal of real estate is still somewhat judgmental. Therefore, the accuracy of the appraisal depends not only on the data gathered, but also upon the judgment, skill, and experience of the person doing the appraisal.

Three Approaches to Value

COST APPROACH

The cost approach to value comprises four basic steps:

1. *Estimate the value of the land.* Compare recent lot sales prices.

2. *Estimate the current replacement costs of the improvements.* Building square footage × cost per square foot; also estimate price of fencing, cement work, landscaping.

3. *Estimate and then subtract accrued depreciation to arrive at present value of the improvement.* Current replacement cost new, less depreciation = present value of the improvements.

4. *Add value of land to present value of the improvements.* Land value + present value of improvements = estimate of value.

To estimate the value of the land, appraisers usually compare recent vacant lot sales, adjusting their estimates for the differences in location, topography, size, shape, and so on.

To estimate the current replacement cost of buildings, appraisers first measure the square footage (exterior length × width). Then

RESIDENTIAL APPRAISAL REPORT

File No. 1234

To be completed by Lender

Borrower	John J. Borrower and Alice M. Borrower
Census Tract	17
Map Reference	98-235

Property Address **2003 Elm Street**

| City | Somewhere | County | Acme | State | California | Zip Code | 95500 |

Legal Description **APN 13-063-07, Lot 1, Blk.2, Tr. 1731, Bk. 1047, Page 17**

Sale Price $ **121,000** Date of Sale **7/22/8—** Loan Term **30** yrs Property Rights Appraised [X] Fee [ ] Leasehold [ ] DeMinimis PUD

Actual Real Estate Taxes $ **560** (yr) Loan charges to be paid by seller $ **none** Other sales concessions **none**

Lender/Client **First Acme Bank** Address **2910 F Street, Somewhere, CA.95500**

Occupant **vacant** Appraiser **R.J. Good** Instructions to Appraiser **Mr. Owner**

NEIGHBORHOOD

Location	[X] Urban	[ ] Suburban	[ ] Rural
Built Up	[X] Over 75%	[ ] 25% to 75%	[ ] Under 25%
Growth Rate	[ ] Fully Dev. [ ] Rapid	[ ] Steady	[X] Slow
Property Values	[X] Increasing	[ ] Stable	[ ] Declining
Demand/Supply	[ ] Shortage	[X] In Balance	[ ] Over Supply
Marketing Time	[ ] Under 3 Mos.	[X] 4–6 Mos.	[ ] Over 6 Mos.

Present Land Use **90** % 1 Family **5** % 2-4 Family **5** % Apts ___ % Condo ___ % Commercial
___ % Industrial ___ % Vacant ___ %

Change in Present Land Use [X] Not Likely [ ] Likely (*) [ ] Taking Place (*)
(*) From _____ To _____

Predominant Occupancy [X] Owner [ ] Tenant ___ % Vacant
Single Family Price Range $ **115,000** to $ **135,000** Predominant Value $ **125,000**
Single Family Age **new** yrs to **25** yrs Predominant Age **15** yrs

	Good	Avg.	Fair	Poor
Employment Stability	[ ]	[X]	[ ]	[ ]
Convenience to Employment	[ ]	[X]	[ ]	[ ]
Convenience to Shopping	[ ]	[X]	[ ]	[ ]
Convenience to Schools	[X]	[ ]	[ ]	[ ]
Adequacy of Public Transportation	[X]	[ ]	[ ]	[ ]
Recreational Facilities	[X]	[ ]	[ ]	[ ]
Adequacy of Utilities	[X]	[ ]	[ ]	[ ]
Property Compatibility	[ ]	[X]	[ ]	[ ]
Protection from Detrimental Conditions	[ ]	[X]	[ ]	[ ]
Police and Fire Protection	[ ]	[X]	[ ]	[ ]
General Appearance of Properties	[ ]	[X]	[ ]	[ ]
Appeal to Market	[ ]	[X]	[ ]	[ ]

Note: FHLMC/FNMA do not consider the racial composition of the neighborhood to be a relevant factor and it must not be considered in the appraisal.

Comments including those factors, favorable or unfavorable, affecting marketability (e.g. public parks, schools, view, noise) **Greater than average traffic flow as Elm Street is a main arterial street running East and West. Near excellent regional park.**

SITE

Dimensions **50 x 110** **5,500** Sq. Ft. or Acres [X] Corner Lot

Zoning classification **R 1** Present improvements [X] do [ ] do not conform to zoning regulations

Highest and best use [X] Present use [ ] Other (specify) _____

	Public	Other (Describe)	OFF SITE IMPROVEMENTS		Topo	level
Elec.	[X]		Street Access: [X] Public [ ] Private		Size	typical
Gas	[X]		Surface **asphalt**		Shape	rectangular
Water	[X]		Maintenance: [X] Public [ ] Private		View	wooded
San.Sewer	[X]		[X] Storm Sewer [X] Curb/Gutter		Drainage	adequate
	[ ] Underground Elect. & Tel.		[X] Sidewalk [X] Street Lights		

Is the property located in a HUD Identified Special Flood Hazard Area? [X] No [ ] Yes

Comments (favorable or unfavorable including any apparent adverse easements, encroachments or other adverse conditions) **Level corner lot, cross street is a deadend street, attractive redwood setting behind subject lot**

IMPROVEMENTS

[X] Existing [ ] Proposed [ ] Under Constr. No. Units **1** Type (det, duplex, semi/det, etc.) **SFD** Design (rambler, split level, etc.) **ranch** Exterior Walls **wood siding**

Yrs. Age: Actual **24** Effective **16** to **18** No. Stories **1**

| Roof Material **T and G** | Gutters & Downspouts [ ] None **GI downspouts** | Window (Type) **fixed and louvered** [ ] Storm Sash [X] Screens [ ] Combination | Insulation [X] None [ ] Floor [ ] Ceiling [ ] Roof [ ] Walls |

[ ] Manufactured Housing

Foundation Walls **concrete perim.**

[ ] Slab on Grade [X] Crawl Space

BSMT **0** % Basement [ ] Floor Drain Finished Ceiling
[ ] Outside Entrance [ ] Sump Pump Finished Walls
[ ] Concrete Floor ___ % Finished Finished Floor
Evidence of: [ ] Dampness [ ] Termites [ ] Settlement

Comments _____

ROOM LIST

Room List	Foyer	Living	Dining	Kitchen	Den	Family Rm.	Rec. Rm.	Bedrooms	No. Baths	Laundry	Other
Basement											
1st Level		1	1	1				3	2		
2nd Level											

Finished area above grade contains a total of **6** rooms **3** bedrooms **2** baths, Gross Living Area **1,518** sq. ft. Bsmt Area **0** sq. ft.

INTERIOR FINISH & EQUIPMENT

Kitchen Equipment [ ] Refrigerator [X] Range/Oven [X] Disposal [X] Dishwasher [X] Fan/Hood [ ] Compactor [ ] Washer [ ] Dryer

HEAT Type **FA** Fuel **NG** Cond. **ave.** AIR COND [ ] Central [ ] Other [ ] Adequate [ ] Inadequate

Floors	[X] Hardwood [X] Carpet Over
Walls	[X] Drywall [ ] Plaster
Trim/Finish	[ ] Good [X] Average [ ] Fair [ ] Poor
Bath Floor	[ ] Ceramic [X] v. lino.
Bath Wainscot	[ ] Ceramic [X] wall paper

Special Features (including energy efficient items) **ceramic showers and tub**

ATTIC: [ ] Yes [X] No [ ] Stairway [ ] Drop-stair [ ] Scuttle [ ] Floored
Finished (Describe) [ ] Heated

CAR STORAGE: [X] Garage [ ] Built-in [X] Attached [ ] Detached [ ] Car Port
No. Cars **2** [X] Adequate [ ] Inadequate Condition **ave.**

PROPERTY RATING

	Good	Avg.	Fair	Poor
Quality of Construction (Materials & Finish)	[ ]	[X]	[ ]	[ ]
Condition of Improvements	[ ]	[X]	[ ]	[ ]
Rooms size and layout	[ ]	[X]	[ ]	[ ]
Closets and Storage	[ ]	[X]	[ ]	[ ]
Insulation—adequacy	[ ]	[ ]	[ ]	[X]
Plumbing—adequacy and condition	[ ]	[X]	[ ]	[ ]
Electrical—adequacy and condition	[ ]	[X]	[ ]	[ ]
Kitchen Cabinets—adequacy and condition	[ ]	[X]	[ ]	[ ]
Compatibility to Neighborhood	[ ]	[X]	[ ]	[ ]
Overall Livability	[ ]	[X]	[ ]	[ ]
Appeal and Marketability	[ ]	[X]	[ ]	[ ]

Yrs Est Remaining Economic Life **35** to **40** . Explain if less than Loan Term

FIREPLACES, PATIOS, POOL, FENCES, etc. (describe) **No fireplace, good fencing, 40 sq. ft. storage shed in good condition**

COMMENTS (including functional or physical inadequacies, repairs needed, modernization, etc.) **New roof installed last year, recent upgrading of landscaping**

Figure 9-1

VALUATION SECTION

Purpose of Appraisal is to estimate Market Value as defined in Certification & Statement of Limiting Conditions (FHLMC Form 439/FNMA Form 1004B). If submitted for FNMA, the appraiser must attach (1) sketch or map showing location of subject, street names, distance from nearest intersection, and any detrimental conditions and (2) exterior building sketch of improvements showing dimensions.

COST APPROACH

Measurements		No. Stories	Sq. Ft.	
24 x 64	x	1	= 1,536	
x	x		= - 18	
x	x		=	
x	x		=	
x	x		=	

Total Gross Living Area (List in Market Data Analysis below) 1,518
Comment on functional and economic obsolescence: none

ESTIMATED REPRODUCTION COST – NEW – OF IMPROVEMENTS:

Dwelling 1,518 Sq. Ft. @ $ 63 = $95,634

Extras storage shed 40sfx $14 = 560

Special Energy Efficient Items _____ = _____

Porches, Patios, etc. _____ = _____

Garage/Car Port 456 Sq. Ft. @ $ 20 = 9,120

Site Improvements (driveway, landscaping, etc.) = 2,550

Total Estimated Cost New . . . . = $107,864

Less

	Physical	Functional	Economic
Depreciation	$16,519	$	$

= $(16,519)

Depreciated value of improvements . . . . . . = $ 91,345

ESTIMATED LAND VALUE = $ 30,000
(If leasehold, show only leasehold value) 121,345

INDICATED VALUE BY COST APPROACH . . . $121,300

MARKET DATA ANALYSIS

The undersigned has recited three recent sales of properties most similar and proximate to subject and has considered these in the market analysis. The description includes a dollar adjustment, reflecting market reaction to those items of significant variation between the subject and comparable properties. If a significant item in the comparable property is superior to, or more favorable than, the subject property, a minus (-) adjustment is made, thus reducing the indicated value of subject; if a significant item in the comparable is inferior to, or less favorable than, the subject property, a plus (+) adjustment is made, thus increasing the indicated value of the subject.

ITEM	Subject Property	COMPARABLE NO. 1		COMPARABLE NO. 2		COMPARABLE NO. 3	
Address	2003 Elm St.	704 Pine St.		1128 Wood St.		1318 Oak St.	
Proximity to Subj.		¼ mile		½ mile		1¼ mile	
Sales Price	$121,000	$126,000		$125,500		$124,250	
Price/Living area	$	$		$		$	
Data Source	lender	appraiser		appraiser		appraiser	
	DESCRIPTION	DESCRIPTION	+(-)$ Adjustment	DESCRIPTION	+(-)$ Adjustment	DESCRIPTION	+(-)$ Adjustment
Date of Sale and Time Adjustment		3/8-	+1000	2/8-	+1500	4/8-	+500
Location	good(traffic)	equal		equal		equal	
Site/View	ave.	equal		equal		equal	
Design and Appeal	ranch/ave.	equal		equal		equal	
Quality of Const.	ave.	equal		superior	-2000	very superior	-3000
Age	24	21		20		23	
Condition	ave.	superior	-2000	equal		equal	
Living Area Room Count and Total	Total 6 / B-rms 3 / Baths 2	Total 6 / B-rms 3 / Baths 2	-2000	Total 7 / B-rms 3 / Baths 2	-1000	Total 6 / B-rms 3 / Baths 2	
Gross Living Area	1,518 Sq.Ft.	1,710 Sq.Ft.		1,600 Sq.Ft.		1480 Sq.Ft.	
Basement & Bsmt. Finished Rooms							
Functional Utility	ave.	ave.		ave.		ave.	
Air Conditioning							
Garage/Car Port	A 2G	A 2G		A 3G	-1500	A 2G large	-100
Porches, Patio, Pools, etc.	storage	storage		storage		storage	
Special Energy Efficient Items	none	insulation	-1500	insulation	-15,00	insulation and small collector	-2000
Other (e.g. fireplaces, kitchen equip., remodeling)	R/O	R/O		R/O		R/O	
Sales or Financing Concessions	conv.	conv.		conv.		conv.	
Net Adj. (Total)		☐ Plus; ☒ Minus $ 4,500		☐ Plus; ☒ Minus $ 4,500		☐ Plus; ☒ Minus $ 4,600	
Indicated Value of Subject		$121,500		$121,000		$119,650	

Comments on Market Data: comparable 1 and 2 nearest to subject property

INDICATED VALUE BY MARKET DATA APPROACH . . . $121,000

INDICATED VALUE BY INCOME APPROACH (If applicable) Economic Market Rent $ 575 /Mo. x Gross Rent Multiplier 125 = $121,875

This appraisal is made ☐ "as is" ☒ subject to the repairs, alterations, or conditions listed below ☐ completion per plans and specifications.

Comments and Conditions of Appraisal: structural pest control clearance

Final Reconciliation: each of the approaches supports the final conclusion

Construction Warranty ☐ Yes ☒ No   Name of Warranty Program _____ Warranty Coverage Expires _____

This appraisal is based upon the above requirements, the certification, contingent and limiting conditions, and Market Value definition that are stated in

☒ FHLMC Form 439 (Rev. 10/78)/FNMA Form 1004B (Rev. 10/78) filed with client Nov. 14 198- ☐ attached.

I ESTIMATE THE MARKET VALUE, AS DEFINED, OF SUBJECT PROPERTY AS OF 8/17 198- to be $ 121,000

Appraiser(s) _RJ-_____ Class III   Review Appraiser (If applicable) _____
J. Helper   Class II   ☐ Did ☐ Did Not Physically Inspect Property

THE APPRAISAL PROCESS

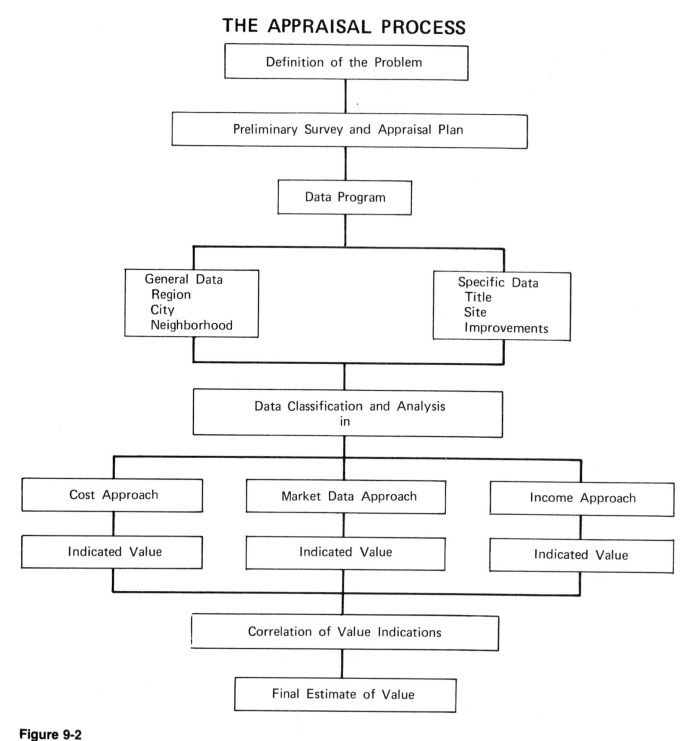

Figure 9-2

Source: From *Reference Book,* California Department of Real Estate.

based upon the construction quality of the building they are appraising, appraisers obtain estimates from local contractors regarding construction costs per square foot. In addition to local contractors, square foot costs and other construction information can be obtained by subscribing to cost estimating publications. Once accurate costs per square foot are obtained, the appraiser multiplies this figure times the square footage of the building. Figures for fencing, cement work, and landscaping are then added to arrive at the current replacement cost of the improvement.

To estimate accrued depreciation, appraisers can use several techniques. The two most common methods of determining depreciation are the straight-line/age-life method and the cost-to-cure/observed condition method. The *straight-line/age-life method* assumes that depreciation occurs annually at an even rate over the estimated life of the improvement. For example, if a new building has an estimated life of 50 years, the straight-line/age-life method would assume a rate of depreciation of 2 percent per year (100% ÷ 50 year life = 2%). Thus, if an appraiser were appraising a building with an effective age of ten years, the subtraction for depreciation would be 20 percent of the current replacement cost (10 years × 2% per year = 20%).

To estimate accrued depreciation using the *cost-to-cure/observed condition method* requires the appraiser to carefully observe physical, functional, and economic depreciation; then the appraiser estimates what it would cost to cure this depreciation. If some of the depreciation is incurable, the appraiser estimates the permanent loss in value. The sum of the cost to cure, plus the permanent loss in value equals the estimated depreciation.

Once the accrued depreciation has been estimated, this figure is subtracted from the current replacement cost to arrive at the present value of the improvements.

The final step in the cost approach is the easiest. The estimated value of the land is added to the estimated present value of the improvements to arrive at the estimated value of the total real property.

ADVANTAGES VERSUS DISADVANTAGES OF THE COST APPROACH

The cost approach is appropriate for appraising newly constructed buildings, and unique, special purpose properties and public buildings such as schools and libraries. The cost approach usually sets the highest limits on value, with the thought being that the most a person will pay for real property is what it would cost to replace the property.

On the negative side, the cost approach does not always measure the individual amenities of the property, such as location, or outside influences like neighborhood surroundings. Also it is difficult to accurately convert depreciation into dollar figures. Thus, on older properties the likelihood of errors in estimating depreciation increases with the age of the building.

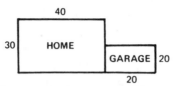

40

30 | HOME

GARAGE | 20

20

Cost New per Square Foot
Home = $80 per sq. ft.
Garage = $25 per sq. ft.

Depreciation Information
Estimated life new = 50 years

Land Value
$70,000 based on recent comparable sales

Present effective age = 10 years

Solution

EXAMPLE USING COST APPROACH

```
  30 ft.
× 40   ft.          (Home)
1,200 sq. ft.
```

```
1,200 sq. ft.
×  $80    per sq. ft.
$96,000 replacement value of home
```

```
  20 ft.
× 20   ft.          (Garage)
400 sq. ft.
```

```
  400 sq. ft.
× $25    per sq. ft.
10,000 replacement value of garage
```

```
 $96,000 replacement value of home
+10,000 replacement value of garage
$106,000 before depreciation
```

Depreciation

$$\frac{100\%}{50 \text{ yrs.}} = 2\% \text{ depreciation per year} \times 10 \text{ years} = 20\%$$

($106,000 × 20% depreciation = $21,200 depreciation)

```
 $106,000 before depreciation
 −21,200 depreciation
 $ 84,800 present value of improvement
 +70,000 land
 $154,800 estimate of value
```

INCOME APPROACH

The *income approach* to value is based on the premise that a property is worth the present value of the future income to be produced by the property. In other words, what an investor should be willing to pay today for a property is directly related to what the investor expects to receive from the property in the future. Financial analysts have developed a technique called *capitalization* which mathematically computes the present value of the future income produced by real estate.

The determination of the value by the income approach can be viewed as a series of steps:

1. Estimate gross annual income.

2. Estimate vacancies and uncollectible rents and subtract this from gross annual income to arrive at effective gross income, also called gross operating income.

3. Estimate annual expenses and subtract these from effective gross income to arrive at net operating income.

4. Select the proper capitalization rate.

5. Divide the capitalization rate into net operating income to arrive at the estimate of value.

These steps can be summarized as follows:

	Gross annual income
Less	— Vacancy factor and uncollectible rents
Equals	Effective gross income
Less	— Annual expenses
Equals	Net operating income

$$\frac{\text{Net operating income}}{\text{Capitalization rate}} = \text{Estimate of property's value}$$

EXPLANATION OF THE INCOME APPROACH

Gross annual income is the maximum amount of income a property can expect to make if fully occupied 100 percent of the time and assuming rents are at the going market rate. Appraisers recognize that 100 percent occupancy all the time is unrealistic. Vacancies and turnovers will occur. Also some tenants will skip out on their rent. Therefore, appraisers subtract an estimate for vacancies and uncollectibles to arrive at *effective gross income.*

After computing effective gross income the appraiser totals the annual operating expenses. Operating expenses are the costs of running and maintaining the property. Examples include:

Property taxes

Insurance premiums

Repairs

Maintenance

Management fees

Supplies

Utilities

Accounting and legal advice

Advertising

Reserves for replacement

Real estate loan payments and income tax depreciation deductions are *not* considered operating expenses because they are not used to run the building. Therefore they are not deducted to arrive at net income.

Once annual operating expenses are calculated, they are subtracted from the effective gross income to arrive at net operating income. *Net operating income* is the income the property produces after deducting operating expenses, but before real estate loan payments.

The next step in the income approach is to select the appropriate capitalization rate. A *capitalization rate* can be defined as the rate necessary to attract an average investor to invest in the property being appraised. The capitalization rate reflects a return on the funds invested, as well as a return (recapture) of the investment. The determination of the appropriate capitalization rate is the most difficult aspect of the income approach to value. The techniques for the selection of a capitalization rate are complex and beyond the scope of this book. For our purpose visualize the capitalization rate as being the rate that other like properties are returning to their owners.

The final step in the income approach is to divide the capitalization rate into net operating income to arrive at an estimate of value.

$$\frac{\text{Net operating income}}{\text{Capitalization rate}} = \text{Estimate of value}$$

The income approach to value is appropriate for income-producing properties such as large apartment buildings, commercial office buildings, and retail stores.

MARKET APPROACH

The market approach to value is based on the principle of substitution. The *principle of substitution* states that a buyer should not pay more for a home than the price it takes to acquire a comparable home. Therefore, the market approach is also known as the *comparison approach to value*.

To apply the market approach, an appraiser gathers data on current sales of properties that are similar to the property being appraised. Ideally, the comparable properties should be in the same neighborhood and be similar in size, style, quality, and contain similar internal characteristics as the subject property.

Each comparable used must also be what is called a *market sale*. A market sale is a sale in which a property is sold using normal financing techniques, and the buyer and the seller were fully informed and knowledgeable about the real estate market. If either the buyer or the seller were under any duress or strain, such as divorce, death in the family, or financial reversals, the appraiser will discard the sale as not being a good comparable sale. For the market approach to be valid the sales used for comparison must reflect normal market conditions, not sales sold under abnormal circumstances.

EXAMPLE USING INCOME APPROACH

A 15-unit apartment with fair market rents of $700 per unit. The estimated factor for vacancies and uncollectibles is 5 percent. Annual operating expenses include:

Property taxes	$9,450
Insurance	$1,000
Management & accounting	$10,000
Repairs and others	$12,000

The capitalization rate selected by the appraiser is 10 percent.

Solution

Gross annual income	$126,000	($700 x 15 units x 12 months)
Less vacancies and uncollectibles	−6,300	($126,000 × 5%)
Effective gross income	$119,700	
Less annual expenses	−32,450	($9,450 + 1,000 + 10,000 + 12,000)
Net operating income	$87,250	

$$\frac{\text{Net operating income}}{\text{Capitalization rate}} \qquad \frac{\$87,250}{10\%} = \$872,500 \quad \text{Estimate of value}$$

If the capitalization rate selected had been 9 percent, the value would be:

$$\frac{\$87,250}{9\%} = \$969,444$$ If the capitalization rate were 11 percent, the value would be $\frac{\$87,250}{11\%} = \$793,181$. Observe this rule: *The higher the capitalization rate, the lower the value.* Therefore, you can see that the selection of the appropriate capitalization rate is very critical! *The selection of an inappropriate capitalization rate can greatly distort value.*

Once the comparable properties are selected (three properties are usually the minimum; five are better), the appraiser then makes adjustments for the differences between the comparable properties and the property being appraised. In essence what the appraiser does is take sales prices of the comparable properties and adjust these prices to reflect what the comparable properties would have sold for if they had the characteristics of the subject property. The results of this process will produce an indicated market value range for the property being appraised.

Assume that the subject property is a medium quality, 25-year old, three-bedroom home, which has a two-car garage. The square footage of the home is 1,300 square feet. The appraiser locates three similar homes that have recently sold in the neighborhood at fair market prices. All have identical square footage and number of rooms.

Comparables

Data	Comparable A	Comparable B	Comparable C
Price paid	$173,900	$171,500	$166,000
Location	better than subject property	equal to subject property	equal to subject property
Lot size	equal to subject property	larger than subject property	smaller than subject property
Overall condition	better than subject property	equal to subject property	worse than subject property

EXAMPLE USING MARKET APPROACH

Dollar Adjustment Factors per the Opinion of the Appraiser

Location difference	$1,000
Lot size difference	$1,500
Overall condition difference	$3,000

Adjustments

Data	Comparable A	Comparable B	Comparable C
Price paid	$173,900	$171,500	$166,000
Location	−1,000	0	0
Lot size	0	−1,500	+1,500
Overall condition	−3,000	0	+3,000
Price comparables would have sold for if they were like the subject home	$169,900	$170,000	$170,500

VALUE RANGE   If the comparables in the example above were near the location of the subject home and had the same lot size and overall condition of the subject home, the comparables A, B, C would have sold for somewhere between $169,900 and $170,500; these figures reflect the indicated market value range.

VALUE CONCLUSION   Subject home should sell for somewhere between $169,900 and $170,500. Final estimate is $170,000, as Comparable B is most comparable in the opinion of the appraiser.

This example is a highly simplified example of the market approach, but it does show the basic concept of how the market approach attempts to adjust known comparable sales to reflect what the comparables should have sold for if the comparables had the characteristics of the subject property. As consumers, people use an informal market approach when they shop for automobiles, furniture, clothes, and most other types of consumer purchases. When it comes to real estate, appraisers simply formalize the process by reducing the comparative facts to writing.

The market approach to value is not used when appraising all types of real estate, but it is an excellent approach to use when appraising homes, especially when the local home market is highly active with many comparable sales in the immediate neighborhood.

USE OF GROSS MULTIPLIERS   Appraisers have designed a method for quickly obtaining a rough estimate of value using what are called gross monthly rent multipliers (GMRM), also known as gross rent multipliers (GRM). A *gross monthly rent multiplier* is a ratio between sales price and rental rates. The gross monthly rent multiplier is found by dividing the sales price of a home by its monthly rent.

Example.
Sales price
Monthly rental rate $\dfrac{\$170{,}000}{\$1{,}000} = 170$ Gross monthly rent multiplier

An appraiser does this for many sales until a trend develops. When asked to conduct an appraisal on a home, the appraiser will do a complete market approach to arrive at an estimate of value. To recheck the results of the market approach, the appraiser may also do a cost approach and an income approach. For a home, a full-blown income approach is not needed, so the gross monthly rent multiplier approach often is used instead.

The appraiser will locate comparable homes, determine their gross monthly multipliers, then select the most appropriate multiplier. Next, the appraiser will determine the fair market rent of the subject home. Then the gross monthly multiplier is multiplied by the fair market rent to arrive at an estimate of value.

Example.   After carefully selecting comparable sales, the appraiser determines that the gross monthly rent multiplier should be 170. The fair market rent of the home is $1,100. Therefore, gross monthly rent multiplier x monthly rent = estimate of value.

$$170 \times \$1,100 = \$187,000 \text{ Estimate of value}$$

CORRELATION AND FINAL ESTIMATE OF VALUE

The process of bringing together the three indications of value derived through the market, cost, and income approaches is the final step in the appraisal process. This process is called *correlation,* or *reconciliation.* When reconciling, the appraiser gives full consideration to each approach; then based on judgment and experience, arrives at one final value or price. *Correlation or reconciliation is not the averaging of the three approaches!*

Averaging gives equal weight to each approach and this is wrong. For any given property one of the approaches is better and should be given more weight.

The final value estimate is not given in odd dollars and cents. The final estimate of value usually is rounded to the nearest $100, $500, or $1,000, depending upon the value of the property.

SUMMARY

An appraisal is defined as an estimate or opinion of value. Although there are many types of value, the value sought most often is the market value.

For a property to have value, four elements are necessary: utility, scarcity, demand, and transferability. Once value has been established, social, economic, political, and physical forces cause value to change.

Appraisal theory rests on certain principles such as highest and best use, change, supply and demand, substitution, conformity, plus several others.

Depreciation is defined as a loss in value from any cause. Depreciation of real estate is caused by physical deterioration, functional obsolescence, and economic obsolescence.

Depreciation can be classified as curable or incurable or as accrued or accrual for depreciation.

The appraisal process can be viewed as a series of steps leading to a final estimate of value. The appraisal techniques include the cost approach, income approach, and market approach. In certain instances the gross monthly rent multiplier technique is also used to estimate value.

The selection of a single final estimate of value is called correlation or reconciliation. Final value conclusions are submitted in written reports, which may be a letter form report, a short-form report, or a narrative report.

Important Terms and Concepts

Appraisal

Appreciation

Correlation (reconciliation)

Gross monthly rent multipliers (GMRM)

Income approach

Cost approach

Depreciation

Economic and social
obsolescence

Elements of value

Functional obsolescence

Market approach

Market value

Physical deterioration

Principles of substitution

Value in use (utility value)

1. An appraisal is defined as:
   (a) Market price
   (b) An estimate of value
   (c) Loan value
   (d) Actual selling price

2. For most home buyers, the value they would like to know is:
   (a) Market value
   (b) Tax value
   (c) Insurance value
   (d) Resale value

3. The best use of land is that use which produces the greatest net
   return to the land. This is the:
   (a) Principle of change
   (b) Principle of substitution
   (c) Principle of conformity
   (d) Principle of highest and best use

4. Loss in value in a home due to a poor floor plan is called
   (a) Physical determination
   (b) Functional obsolescence
   (c) Economic obsolescence
   (d) Book depreciation

5. The most comprehensive type of appraisal report is the:
   (a) Letter form
   (b) Short-form
   (c) Narrative
   (d) Negotiated

6. For existing residential homes, the best appraisal approach is
   usually the:
   (a) Market approach
   (b) Income approach
   (c) Cost approach
   (d) Capitalization approach

7. Given: land is valued at $35,000; cost new per square foot: home
   $80, garage $25; Estimate life: new 50 years, present effective
   age, ten years. What is the estimated value of the property?
   (a) $110,400

(b) $163,000
(c) $173,000
(d) $145,400

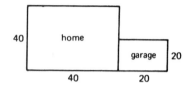

8. Find the value, by use of the income approach (round to nearest $100). Given: four-unit apartment rents for $500 per unit per month; vacancy factor 5 percent; annual expenses $8,000; capitalization rate 10 1/2 percent.
(a) $141,000
(b) $164,900
(c) $250,000
(d) $173,500

9. Gross monthly multiplier is 125 and fair market rent of condo is $575. The estimate of value is:
(a) $71,875
(b) $70,000
(c) $57,500
(d) $125,000

10. One of the last steps in the appraisal process is known as reconciliation or:
(a) Averaging the three values
(b) Correlation
(c) Establishing the median value
(d) Discounting the values to a single value

Chapter 10

The Role of Escrow and Title Insurance Companies

Preview
Closing a real estate transaction is a highly technical process. Escrow and title insurance companies provide valuable services that help consumers and real estate agents to smoothly and efficiently close a real estate transaction. When you have completed this chapter you will be able to:

1. Define "escrow," and list the legal requirements for a valid escrow.

2. Describe the basic services provided by title insurance companies.

3. Explain the difference between a CLTA standard and an ALTA extended coverage policy of title insurance.

4. Explain various closing costs and indicate who normally pays for each closing cost.

10.1 ESCROWS

Definition of Escrow

In a real estate sale, an *escrow* is that operation in which a neutral third party acts as the closing agent for the buyer and the seller. The escrow officer assumes the responsibility of handling all the paperwork and disbursement of funds to close out a real estate transaction. The Civil Code defines an escrow as:

> A grant may be deposited by the grantor with a third person, to be delivered on the performance of a condition, and, on delivery by the depository, it will take effect. While in the possession of the third person, and subject to condition, it is called an escrow.

Escrows can be used for a variety of business transactions, such as sale or exchange of real estate, sale or encumbrance of personal

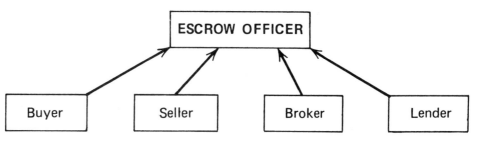

property, sale or pledging of securities; sale of assets of a business (bulk sale), sale of a promissory note secured by a deed of trust, and the transfer of liquor licenses. By far the most common reason for the use of an escrow is to handle the sale and transfer of real estate. The clerical aspects of transferring title to real estate are detailed and complicated; therefore, buyers, sellers, lenders, and real estate agents prefer to use trained escrow officers.

Legal Requirements for a Valid Escrow

There are two essential requirements for a valid escrow:

1. There must be a binding contract between the seller (grantor) and the buyer (grantee).
2. There must be the conditional delivery of transfer instruments and monies to a neutral third party.

The binding contract can be in any legal form, such as a deposit receipt, agreement of sale, exchange agreement, or mutual instructions from the buyer and the seller. The escrow instructions signed by the buyer and seller supplement the terms of the original purchase agreement, and the two contracts are interpreted together. If there is a conflict between the purchase contract and the escrow instructions, the usual rule is that the most recent contract prevails. In most cases, this would be the signed escrow instructions.

Confidentiality of Escrows

Escrow instructions are confidential. Only the principals and their agents in the transaction are entitled to see the escrow instructions, and then, only insofar as the instructions pertain to mutual items in the transaction. For example, both the buyer and the seller are entitled to see each other's escrow instructions regarding the sales price, downpayment, and other terms of the sale. But how much the seller is netting from the sale is no business of the buyer. Likewise, the buyer's financing arrangement with an institutional lender is no business of the seller who is cashing out of the transaction.

If the escrow holder receives conflicting instructions from the principals, the escrow officer simply refuses to proceed until the parties settle their differences. An escrow officer cannot give legal advice and may bring an action in court forcing the principals in the escrow to litigate their differences. This legal action is called an *interpleader action*.

Status of the Escrow Holder

The escrow agency is considered a limited one. The only obligations to be fulfilled by the escrow holder are those set forth in the instructions connected with the transaction. Before a real estate sale is recorded, the escrow officer is the dual agent for both the buyer and the seller. After the deed is recorded, the escrow officer becomes the individual agent for each party.

This distinction is important, especially if an unethical escrow officer should steal money from the escrow company. If the escrow officer embezzles the money before the seller is entitled to it, the buyer suffers the loss. But if the money is embezzled after the seller has become entitled to it, the loss falls on the seller, since it is now considered to be the seller's money.

Regulation of Escrow Holders

Title insurance companies, banks, savings and loan associations, trust companies, or attorneys can handle escrows without obtaining an escrow license. However, independent escrow companies must be incorporated and can handle escrows only after obtaining a special license from the California Corporations Commissioner. Independent escrow companies have flourished in Southern California, while title insurance companies and financial institutions handle most of the escrows in Northern California.

Who Decides Which Escrow Company to Use?

The selection of an escrow company is negotiated between the buyer and seller. The real estate agent cannot dictate which escrow company to use. If a real estate agent has a financial interest in an escrow company, the law requires the agent to disclose this interest to the buyer and the seller before a final selection is made. *Real estate brokers can legally handle escrows without obtaining a special escrow license if the broker is an agent for the buyer or the seller in the transaction.*

Once an escrow company is selected, who pays for the fee? The payment of the escrow fee is an item that is negotiable between the buyer and the seller. The decision as to who pays this fee will vary throughout the state. In some geographic areas the seller usually pays; in other areas the buyer usually pays; in some areas the fee is split between the buyer and the seller.

Services Provided by Escrow Holders

For a fee the escrow holder carefully collects, prepares, and safeguards the instructions, documents, and monies required to close the transaction. Upon receipt of written instructions from all parties (that is, buyer, seller, lender, real estate agent), the escrow instructions are compared to determine if the parties are in mutual agreement.

When the parties are in agreement and all instruments and monies have been deposited, the escrow officer then sees that title is transferred. The following are some of the services performed by an escrow company:

1. Prepares buyer's and seller's escrow instructions; prepares deed and other needed documents, such as promissory notes and deeds of trust.

2. Requests the demand for payoff for the seller's loan from the lending institution; or in the case of an assumption, requests a beneficiary statement from the lending institution.

3. Collects the structural pest control report and the notice of work completed, if any.

4. Collects the required fire insurance policy.

5. Balances the accounting details, including adjustments and pro-rations of the taxes, interest, insurance, and assessments and rents, if any.

6. Verifies that the appropriate documents are recorded.

7. Collects the balance of monies required to close the transaction.

After transfer has occurred, the escrow file is audited. The escrow officer then disburses the monies, issues itemized closing statements to all parties, and orders the title insurance policy.

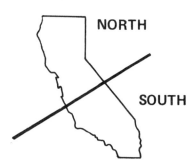

NORTH VERSUS SOUTH

Escrow practices differ between Southern and Northern California. In Southern California, independent escrow companies are common and they handle a considerable amount of the real estate transactions. Title insurance companies provide the title services, but the escrow companies do the actual closing of the sale. Banks and savings and loan associations also provide extensive escrow services in Southern California.

In Northern California, most escrows are handled by title insurance companies that have extensive escrow departments with many branch offices. In recent years, independent escrow companies have attempted to make inroads in the Northern California real estate market.

One other point of difference has to do with the timing of the signing of escrow instructions. In Southern California, it is common to have the buyer and seller sign escrow instructions shortly after they sign their purchase agreement and receipt for deposit. This may be 30 or 60 days before the actual close of escrow. In many Northern California counties, escrow instructions are not signed until a day or two before the actual close of escrow.

Termination of Escrows

Escrows are usually terminated by completion of the sale, and in the case of a refinance, upon completion of the loan process. If the transaction is not completed, the escrow may then be canceled by mutual agreement of all parties. The escrow company is entitled to receive partial payment of escrow fees for services rendered to date.

It has been held that all the conditions required by escrow instructions must be performed within the time limit set forth in the escrow agreement, and the escrow officer has no authority to enforce or accept the performance after the time limit provided in the instructions. When the time limit provided in the escrow has expired and neither party to the escrow has performed in accordance with the terms, the parties are entitled to the return of their respective papers and documents from the escrow officer. See page 196 for summary.

Escrows and RESPA

The Real Estate Settlement Procedures Act (RESPA) is a federal law that requires certain forms be provided regarding closing costs. The law applies whenever a person purchases an owner-occupied residence, using funds obtained from institutional lenders, regulated by a federal agency. Virtually all banks, savings and loan associations, and most other lenders fall directly or indirectly under RESPA's rules. The one major exception would be real estate loans by private parties—they are usually exempt from RESPA.

RESPA rules require a lender to furnish the borrower with a special information booklet and a good faith estimate of closing costs when the prospective borrower files an application for a real estate loan. RESPA rules prohibit any kickbacks or unearned fees to be listed as closing costs. The law expressly states that only valid, earned, closing costs shall be charged the buyer or seller. Any violators can be punished up to one year in jail and/or a $10,000 fine.

Most of the burden for implementing RESPA falls upon the real estate lender. However, escrow agents are also involved. RESPA requires the use of a Uniform Settlement Statement (HUD-1) which must itemize all closing charges. Upon request, the escrow agent must let the borrower-buyer inspect the Uniform Settlement Statement one day before the close of escrow. In addition, the escrow officer must see that all parties receive a copy of the Uniform Settlement Statement after the close of escrow.

10.2 TITLE INSURANCE COMPANIES

Title insurance companies are incorporated businesses that provide these basic services:

1. Search and gather public records relating to the legal title of real property.
2. Examine and interpret the title records that have been gathered.

An escrow holder is a neutral third party who, for a fee, will handle the paperwork involved in transferring title and/or in placing a new loan on real property. Escrow companies are licensed by the State of California. However, banks, savings and loan associations, attorneys, and title insurance companies can act as escrow holders without obtaining a special license. A real estate broker can act as an escrow holder only if the broker is an agent for either the buyer or the seller.

ESCROWS—SUMMARIZED

Technical Reasons for an Escrow

1. To provide a custodian for funds and documents who can make concurrent delivery.

2. To provide a clearinghouse for payments.

3. To provide an agency for computing prorations.

Essentials of a Valid Escrow

1. Must have a binding contract between buyer and seller.

2. Must have conditional delivery of transfer instruments to a third party.

Termination of an Escrow

1. By full performance and closing.

2. Mutual cancellation by the parties.

3. Revocation by a party.

Examples of typical escrow and title insurance fees are shown on page 201

3. Insure an owner or lender against financial loss due to certain unreported defects in the title.

Title Search   A title search can be conducted in one of two ways. The first is the "courthouse search." Under this method, a title person goes to the county courthouse and searches through the public records, seeking information pertaining to a particular property under examination. The title searcher then reproduces the information and presents the items to a title examiner for interpretation.

The second method is for a title company to maintain its own "title plant." A title plant is really a condensed courthouse where records affecting real property are copied, usually microfilmed or computerized, and filed for future reference. When a title search is ordered, the title person has only to select from the title plant the needed information. This reduces the need for frequent trips to the county courthouse, thereby saving valuable time for the title company and the customer.

Title Examination

The actual examination and interpretation of the title is done by a highly skilled title examiner (not an attorney) whose task is to review each document and create what is known as a chain of title. A *chain of title* is a history of all of the title transfers, beginning with the document originally transferring title from the government to private ownership and ending with the document vesting title in the current owner.

In addition to identifying the correct owner, the title examiner determines what and how various encumbrances, such as taxes, deeds of trust, easements, and so on, affect the ownership. When the examination is complete the data is compiled into a *preliminary title report* which lists the owner(s) name, the legal description of the property, the status of property taxes and special assessments, and the various encumbrances against the property. This preliminary title report does not insure, but is the basis upon which a title company is willing to insure the owner's title.

Title Insurance

In the early days of California, title insurance did not exist. Land holdings were large and population sparse. Property frequently was transferred simply by the delivery of a symbol in the presence of a witness.

As population and migration increased, land holdings were divided and sold to incoming strangers. Boundaries became confused and it was difficult to identify ownerships. To combat this confusion, when California became a state in 1850, the legislature enacted recording statutes. These recording statutes created depositories, namely the county recorder's office, to collect and file title documents for public use. Soon the recorder's offices became too complex for many laypeople to use. Specialists called *abstractors* began searching and compiling courthouse records. For a fee, these abstractors would publish their findings on a specific parcel of land.

To protect the public, the need arose for a system to guard against the errors, omissions, and incorrect judgments that abstractors might make. This need for additional assurance led to the concept of title insurance.

Today, a title insurance policy insures the ownership of land and the priority of a lien (deed of trust, contract of sale, and so on) subject to the encumbrances revealed in the title examination. The owner and/or lender is insured that a thorough search has been made of all public records affecting a particular property.

Types of Title Insurance Policies

Title insurance policies are divided into two basic groups, the *standard policy* and the *extended coverage policy.* The standard policy is the most widely used and can be divided into three subtypes:

1. *Standard owner's policy,* which insures the owner for the amount of the purchase price.

2. *Standard lender's policy,* which insures the lender for the amount of the loan.

3. *Standard joint protection policy,* which co-insures the owner and lender under one policy.

The standard policy is frequently referred to as a *CLTA policy.* CLTA stands for California Land Title Association, a state trade association for title insurance companies.

Included in the standard coverage policy is the assurance that title is free and clear of all encumbrances of public record, other than the items revealed in the title examination and listed as exceptions in the title policy. Under the standard policy, the title company does not make a physical inspection of the property and therefore excludes from coverage unrecorded items which could affect the title. For example, unrecorded easements are excluded, as well as the rights of parties in possession other than the owner, such as tenants or squatters. Also excluded from standard policy coverage are zoning and other government ordinances affecting the use of the property, non-declared assessments, and some items regarding mining and water claims.

EXTENDED COVERAGE POLICY

The extended coverage policy was established for real estate lenders. This policy requires the title company to make a physical inspection of the property and insures against certain unrecorded title risks excluded under the standard policy. In some cases the extended coverage policy is requested and issued to individual owners, but it can be expensive. The extended coverage policy is commonly referred to as an *ALTA policy.* ALTA stands for American Land Title Association, a national trade association for title insurance companies.

How Much Does Title Insurance Cost?

Title insurance premiums, like most other types of insurance premiums, are calculated based upon the dollar amount of insurance coverage. Owner's title policies are issued for the purchase price of the property, while lender's title policies are issued for the loan amount. Therefore, owners of more expensive property pay higher title fees than owners of less expensive property. Title fees are established by title companies themselves, not any government agency. Competition keeps rates between title companies comparable.

TITLE INSURANCE PROCESS

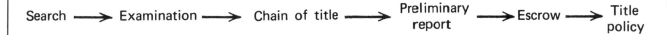

Search ⟶ Examination ⟶ Chain of title ⟶ Preliminary report ⟶ Escrow ⟶ Title policy

TITLE INSURANCE SUMMARIZED

A title insurance policy insures that a thorough examination has been made of all public records affecting the property in question, that the owner has acquired ownership free from title defects of public record, subject only to the encumbrances revealed in the title examination and the exceptions recited in the title insurance policy. It means that the owner has a marketable title that can be transferred to others.

Standard Coverage Policy (CLTA)

1. Risks normally insured against:
   (a) most matters disclosed by public records
   (b) certain off record risks such as forgery, or incompetence of parties.

2. Risks not normally insured against:
   (a) matters not disclosed by public records
   (b) zoning and other government ordinances regarding the use of the property
   (c) certain mining and water claims
   (d) defects known to the insured before the property was purchased and not revealed to the title company before the sale.

Extended Coverage Policy (ALTA)

1. Risks covered:
   (a) all those listed under the standard coverage policy, *plus*
   (b) unperfected mechanic's liens
   (c) unrecorded physical easements
   (d) facts a correct survey would show
   (e) certain water claims
   (f) rights of parties in possession, including tenants and owners under unrecorded instruments.

2. Risks not normally covered:
   (a) zoning and other government ordinances affecting the use of the property
   (b) defects known to the insured before the property was insured but not revealed to title company by the insured.

For an additional charge, an insured can purchase *special endorsements* to cover items normally excluded under the CLTA or ALTA policies.

Unlike other forms of insurance—such as automobile, fire, or life insurance which require annual premiums—a title insurance fee is paid only once. The title policy stays in force as long as the owner retains title to the property. Once title is transferred, the title policy coverage ceases, and the new owner must obtain his or her own title insurance policy (see page 201 for an example of title insurance fees).

Who Pays for the Title Insurance?

The payment of the owner's policy fee is a negotiable item between the buyer and the seller. However, in different geographical areas the method of payment varies. In some areas it is customary to split the title fee between the buyer and the seller. In some areas the seller normally pays the title fee, while in others the buyer pays. The payment of the lender's policy title fee is almost always paid by the borrower-buyer.

Who Decides Which Title Insurance Company to Use?

This is another negotiable item between the buyer and seller. The usual custom is for the party paying for the title fee to select the title company. Real estate regulations prohibit a real estate agent from dictating which title insurance company to use. If the real estate agent should happen to have a financial interest in the title company selected, the agent must disclose this fact to both the buyer and seller.

EVOLUTION OF TITLE PROTECTION

FIRST CAME

Abstract of Title
A summary of title prepared by an early day specialist, with no guarantees on accuracy.

THEN

Certificate of Title
A certificate stating the name of the owner and a list of encumbrances. No guarantee on accuracy.

THEN

Guarantee of Title
A title search in which an abstract company guaranteed the accuracy of the search.

AND TODAY

Title Insurance
Creation of an insurance company that issues a title policy and insures the accuracy of results. If insured suffers an insured loss, a claim is filed similar in nature to any other type of insurance.

TYPICAL ESCROW AND TITLE INSURANCE FEES

Sales Price	Escrow Fee	Title Insurance Fee	Combined
$ 50,000	$ 500	$ 375	$ 875
100,000	500	550	1,050
150,000	600	725	1,325
200,000	700	875	1,575
250,000	800	1,025	1,825
300,000	900	1,175	2,075
350,000	950	1,300	2,250
400,000	1,000	1,425	2,425
450,000	1,050	1,550	2,600
500,000	1,100	1,675	2,775

For illustrative purposes only. Fees vary from company to company.

10.3 CLOSING COSTS

Closing costs refer to the expenses paid by a buyer and the seller upon the sale of property. Some people attempt to estimate closing costs by using simple rules of thumb such as "3 percent of the sales price" or some other rough figure. However, rules of thumb are inaccurate. The only sure way to determine actual closing cost is to list and price each individual item.

It must be stressed that the payment of the closing costs is a negotiable topic between the buyer and seller. There is no law requiring that certain closing costs are the responsibility of the buyer or the seller. The only exception deals with government-backed loans where regulations prohibit the buyer from paying certain closing costs, such as loan discount points. However, by custom, certain closing costs are typically paid by the buyer, while other costs are usually paid by the seller.

Buyer's Closing Costs

For the buyer (borrower) closing costs can be divided into two categories: (1) nonrecurring closing costs and (2) recurring closing costs.

Nonrecurring closing costs are one-time charges paid upon the close of escrow. Recurring closing costs are prepaid items that the buyer pays in advance to help offset expenses that will continue as long as the buyer owns the property.

Humboldt Land Title Company

SIXTH & I STREETS · P. O. BOX 102 · EUREKA, CALIFORNIA 95501 · TELEPHONE 443-0837 AREA CODE 707

TO: Mr. and Mrs. Buyer
123 Elm Street
Somewhere, CA. 95500

ESCROW # 36139DM

Small 2 Bedroom Home

DATE January 13, 199-

PROPERTY: 123 Elm Street, Somewhere, CA. 95500	DEBITS	CREDITS
CONSIDERATION OR SALES PRICE	$ 89,500.00	$
Paid outside of Escrow		
Deposits to escrow		11,200.00
By First Trust Deed in favor of First Acme Bank		80,550.00
By Second Trust Deed		
PRO-RATIONS MADE AS OF January 13, 198-		
Taxes for one-half year $360 paid to June 30, 198-	334.00	
$83,000 Fire Ins. expires: Prem. $pd outside escrow		
Rent @ $ paid to:		
Trust Fund $180 impounds	180	
Interest on $ 80,550 @ 11½ % paid to: 1/30/8-	427.92	
Commission Paid To:		
Commission Paid To:		
Loan Escrow Fee		
Alta Title Policy $79.80 Insp. Fee $10.00 Total =	89.80	
Clta Title Policy $ Escrow Fee $61.50 (½) Total =	61.50	
Real Property Transfer Tax		
Recording Deed(s)	3.00	
Recording Trust Deed(s)	3.00	
Recording		
Reconveyance Fee		
Drawing Deed(s)		
Drawing Trust Deed(s)		
Taxes Paid		
PRINCIPAL OF ENCUMBRANCE PAID TO		
Interest @ From Thru		
Loan Fee to First Acme Bank	905.50	
Tax Service Fee	15.00	
Ajax Pest Control Company-inspection fee	75.00	
Balance due HUMBOLDT LAND TITLE COMPANY		
Balance due YOU for which our check is enclosed	155.28	
TOTALS	$ 91,750.00	$ 91,750.00

HLT CO/ES1

ESCROW STATEMENT

Courtesy of Humboldt Land Title Company.

Humboldt Land Title Company

SIXTH & I STREETS · P. O. BOX 102 · EUREKA, CALIFORNIA 95501 · TELEPHONE 443-0837 AREA CODE 707

TO:
Mr. and Mrs. Seller
793 Tan Oak Street
Somewhere, CA. 95500

ESCROW #36138DM

DATE January 13, 199-

Small 2 Bedroom Home

PROPERTY: 123 Elm Street, Somewhere, CA. 95500	DEBITS	CREDITS
CONSIDERATION OR SALES PRICE	$	$ 89,500.00
Paid outside of Escrow		
Deposits		
By First Trust Deed		
By Second Trust Deed		
PRO-RATIONS MADE AS OF January 13, 198-		
Taxes for one-half year $360 paid to June 30, 198-		334.00
$ Fire Ins. expires: Prem. $		
Rent @ $ paid to:		
Trust Fund $		
Interest on $ @ paid to:		
Commission Paid To: Superior Realty Company(6%)	5,370.00	
Commission Paid To:		
Loan Escrow Fee		
Alta Title Policy $ Insp. Fee $ Total =		
Clta Title Policy $373.00 Escrow Fee $ 61.50 (½) Total =	434.50	
Real Property Transfer Tax	98.45	
Recording Deed(s)		
Recording Trust Deed(s)		
Recording Deed of Reconveyance	3.00	
Reconveyance Fee Acme Company	25.00	
Drawing Deed(s)		
Drawing Trust Deed(s)	10.00	
Taxes Paid		
PRINCIPAL OF ENCUMBRANCE PAID TO First Acme Savings & Loan	53,119.47	
Interest @ 9½ % From 1/1/8- Thru 1/13/8-	177.43	
prepayment penalty	1,965.42	
Ajax Pest Control Company- work completed	850.00	
Balance due HUMBOLDT LAND TITLE COMPANY		
Balance due YOU for which our check is enclosed	27,780.73	
TOTALS	$ 89,834.00	$ 89,834.00

HLT CO/ES1

ESCROW STATEMENT

Nonrecurring Closing Costs Usually Paid by the Buyer

1. *Loan origination fee.* A fee charged by a lender to cover the expenses for processing a loan. The fee is usually quoted as a percentage of the loan amount. For example, a 1½ percent loan fee for a $80,000 loan would be 1½% × $80,000 = $1,200 loan fee.

2. *Appraisal fee.* A fee charged by an appraiser for giving an estimate of property value. The fee for a simple appraisal will vary throughout the state, with $200 or more being a typical charge for a single-family residence. Appraisal fees for income properties such as apartments or office buildings are considerably higher.

3. *Credit report fee.* Before a lender grants a loan, the borrower's credit is checked at a credit agency. The credit report usually costs from $15 to $30.

4. *Structural pest control inspection fee.* A fee charged by a licensed inspector who checks for termites, fungus, dry rot, pests, and other items that might cause structural damage. For a home in an urban area the fee is usually from $75 to $125.

5. *Tax service fee.* A fee paid to a tax service company that, for the life of the loan, each year reviews the tax collector's records. If a borrower fails to pay the property taxes, the tax service company reports this to the lender, who can then take steps to protect the loan against a tax foreclosure sale. This fee usually runs from $15 to $25.

6. *Recording fees.* This covers the cost of recording the deed, deed of trust, and other buyer related documents. Most counties charge $3 to record a single-page document.

7. *Notary fees.* Signatures on documents to be recorded must be notarized. Notary publics typically charge from $1 to $3 per signature.

8. *Assumption fee.* A fee paid to a lender if the buyer "assumes"—that is, agrees to take over and continue to pay the seller's existing loan.

9. *Title and escrow fees.* Fees in buyer pays areas—areas where it is customary for the buyer to pay the title and escrow fees.

Recurring Closing Costs Usually Paid by the Buyer

1. *Hazard insurance.* A one-year premium for insurance against fire, storm, and other risks. The minimum coverage is the amount of the real estate loan, but buyers are advised to purchase greater amounts if they make a large downpayment toward the purchase price. Many owners purchase comprehensive homeowner's packages.

2. *Tax proration.* The property tax year runs from July 1 through June 30 of the following year. If the seller has prepaid the taxes, the buyer reimburses the seller for the prepaid portion. Prorations were discussed in detail in Chapter 6.

3. *Tax and insurance reserves.* This is also known as an impound account or trust account. If a buyer's (borrower) monthly loan payment is to include taxes and insurance, as well as principal and interest, the lender sets up a reserve account. Depending upon the time of the year (the date taxes and insurance are due relative to the date escrow closes), a lender will want the buyer to prepay one to six months of taxes and insurance premiums into this reserve account. Once an adequate reserve account is established, the buyer forwards tax and insurance bills to the lender for payment.

4. *Interest due before the first loan payment.* Interest on real estate loans is typically paid in arrears. For example: escrow closes September 15, with the first loan payment due November 1. The payment due November 1 covers the interest due for the month of October. How is the interest from September 15 to September 30 collected? It is collected in advance at close of escrow and is called prepaid interest. If escrow closed on the first of a month, there would be no prepaid interest if the first payment was due the first of the following month.

Seller's Closing Costs

The closing costs paid by a seller are one-time, nonrecurring expenses. After the close of escrow the seller is divested of ownership and therefore has no recurring expenses attached to ownership such as property taxes and hazard insurance. Again it must be emphasized that the payment of a particular closing expense is negotiable between the buyer and seller. This list below is merely a guideline to closing costs usually paid by the seller as the result of custom and/or agreement.

Closing Costs Usually Paid by the Seller

1. *Transfer tax.* A tax charged when title is transferred. The state has a documentary transfer tax that is computed at $1.10 per $1,000 (or 55¢ per $500 or fraction thereof) of the sales price. For example, if a $90,000 home is sold for cash, the state documentary transfer tax would be $90,000 sales price ÷ 1,000 = 90 × $1.10 = $99 tax.

    For a more detailed explanation of the state documentary transfer tax see Chapter 6. In addition to the state documentary transfer tax, some cities in California have enacted a municipal transfer tax that must be collected at the close of escrow.

2. *Prepayment penalty.* A charge by a lender when a borrower pays off a loan before the required due date. Many times when a prop-

erty is sold, the buyer obtains financing to cover the sales price. In the process the seller's existing mortgage is paid off to make way for the buyer's new mortgage. If the seller's mortgage has a prepayment clause, the seller pays this penalty as a closing cost. Not all loans have prepayment penalties, and recent state laws prohibit a lender from charging a prepayment penalty on an owner-occupied home, if the loan has been on the books for more than five years.

FHA and VA loans do not have prepayment penalties. Cal-Vet loans have a prepayment penalty if the loan is paid off within five years. After five years there is no prepayment penalty on Cal-Vet loans.

Although prepayment penalties vary, a typical penalty is six-months interest on the outstanding loan balance at the time of payoff, after subtracting 20 percent of the original loan amount. (See Chapter 7 for details).

3. *Structural pest control work.* Customarily the buyer pays for the structural pest control inspection fee, and the seller pays for corrective work.

4. *Real estate brokerage commission.* The commission is normally quoted as a percentage of the sales price. A 6 percent commission with a sales price of $80,000 would be a $4,800 closing cost for the seller.

5. *Discount points.* On some government-backed loans (FHA and VA), the seller pays discount points to increase a lender's yield on a loan. The seller pays points because regulations prohibit a buyer on some government-backed loans from paying more than a certain fixed interest rate. One point is equal to 1 percent of the buyer's loan amount.

6. *Recording fees.* Fees for recording seller oriented documents such as a deed or reconveyance.

7. *Notary fees.* Fees for notarizing the seller's signatures on documents to be recorded.

8. *Title and escrow fees.* In seller pays areas—areas where it is customary for the seller to pay the title and escrow fees.

Summary of Closing Costs

BUYER USUALLY PAYS

1. Loan origination fee.
2. Appraisal fee.
3. Credit report.
4. Structural pest control inspection fee.
5. Tax service.
6. Recording fees.

7. Notary fees.

8. Assumption fee.

9. Title and escrow fees in buyer pays areas.

10. Hazard insurance.

11. Interest on loan before first payment.

SELLER USUALLY PAYS

1. Transfer tax.

2. Prepayment penalty.

3. Structural pest control work fee.

4. Real estate brokerage commission.

5. Discount points on government-backed loans.

6. Recording fees.

7. Notary fees.

8. Title and escrow fees in seller pays areas.

The following is usually prorated between the buyer and seller:

1. Property taxes.

2. Interest if loan is assumed by buyer.

3. Hazard insurance if existing policy is assumed by buyer.

4. Rents if the property is tenant-occupied income property.

SUMMARY   An escrow is that operation in which a neutral third party acts as the closing agent in a real estate transaction. To be valid, an escrow requires a binding contract and a conditional delivery of transfer instruments. Escrow companies must comply with the Federal Real Estate Settlement Procedures Act (RESPA).

Title insurance companies, banks, savings and loan associations, attorneys, and independently licensed companies can handle escrows. Real estate brokers can handle escrows if they are an agent in the transaction.

Title insurance companies search and gather public title records, examine and interpret the records, and then issue policies of title insurance. The two major types of title insurance policies are the CLTA standard and the ALTA extended coverage policies. Certain items are not included in title insurance coverage and therefore consumers should be aware that these excluded items are their own responsibility.

Closing costs can be classified as recurring and nonrecurring. Recurring closing costs are prepaid items that the buyer pays in advance to help offset expenses that will continue as long as the buyer owns the property. Nonrecurring closing costs are one-time charges paid upon the close of escrow.

The payment of escrow fees, title insurance, and closing costs is an item of negotiation between the buyer and the seller. However, by custom, certain closing costs are typically paid by the buyer, while other costs are usually paid by the seller. This custom varies through the State of California. Escrow and closing practices differ between Northern and Southern California.

Important Terms and Concepts

Abstractor	Extended coverage policy
ALTA policy	Nonrecurring closing costs
Beneficiary statement/demand	Preliminary title report
Chain of title	Recurring closing costs
CLTA policy	Standard policy
Escrow	

REVIEWING YOUR UNDERSTANDING

1. For an escrow to be binding there must be a:
   (a) Conditional delivery of transfer instruments
   (b) Contract between the parties
   (c) Neutral third party
   (d) All of the above

2. Which of the following must have an escrow license?
   (a) Title insurance companies
   (b) Independent escrow companies

   (c) Real estate brokers if they handle escrows in which they are also the agent

   (d) All of the above must have an escrow license

3. A history of all title transfers of a particular parcel of land is called a
   (a) Preliminary title report
   (b) Chain of title
   (c) Abstract of title
   (d) Guarantee of title

4. A CLTA title policy is also known as a
   (a) Extended coverage policy
   (b) ALTA coverage policy
   (c) Standard coverage
   (d) All-inclusive policy

5. Which of the following is a nonrecurring closing cost?
   (a) Title insurance fee
   (b) Real property tax proration
   (c) Interest on new real estate loan
   (d) Hazard insurance premium

6. A title insurance policy especially designed for lenders which requires the title company to make a physical inspection of the property is called a:
   (a) CLTA standard policy
   (b) Joint protection policy
   (c) All-inclusive policy
   (d) ALTA extended coverage policy

7. Annual real property taxes of $720 are paid for the current fiscal year. Escrow closes April 1 and the taxes are to be prorated. Therefore the:
   (a) Seller will be charged (debited) $180
   (b) Seller will be credited $180
   (c) Buyer will be credited $180
   (d) Buyer will be debited $540

8. The sales price is $90,000 with buyer obtaining a new VA-guaranteed loan. The seller agrees to pay off her existing $50,000 FHA-insured loan. The seller also agrees to pay the state documentary transfer tax which is:
   (a) $44
   (b) $55
   (c) $88
   (d) $99

9. Although the payment of closing cost is negotiable between the buyer and seller, the buyer usually pays for the:
   (a) Loan origination fee

(b) Broker's commission

(c) Prepayment penalty

(d) Discount points on FHA-insured loans

10. Sales price $80,000, buyer pays all cash, seller pays off old loan of $45,000. Seller also pays 5 percent broker commission, state documentary transfer tax, $300 prepayment penalty, plus $500 in other closing costs. How much will the seller net from escrow?

(a) $35,000

(b) $30,112

(c) $49,888

(d) $45,000

Chapter 11
Landlord and Tenant Relations

Preview   The relationship between landlords and tenants can be calm and enjoyable or it can be turbulent, with frustrations and confusion on both sides. The California legislature is constantly passing laws related to landlords or tenants. Many problems between landlords and tenants are caused by a lack of understanding of the legal rights and duties of each party. When you complete this chapter, you will be able to:

1. *Define a lease, and then list four types of leasehold estates.*

2. *Outline the requirements needed for a valid lease or rental agreement.*

3. *Explain the difference between a sublease and an assignment of a lease.*

4. *Discuss the duties and responsibilities landlords and tenants owe to each other.*

5. *Describe how tenants can be evicted lawfully.*

6. *Explain the services provided by professional property managers.*

11.1 LEASES   A lease is a contract between an owner, called a *lessor* or *landlord* and a *lessee* or *tenant*. A tenant is given the right to possess and use the landlord's property in exchange for *rent*. California law requires that all leases for more than one year must be in writing to be valid.

Rental agreements for one year or less need not be in writing to be valid. However, a prudent person should reduce all rental and lease agreements to writing.

Types of Leasehold Estates   In Chapter 2, a distinction was made between a *freehold estate* and a *less-than-freehold estate*. It was stated that a freehold estate is an interest in real property as an owner, while a less-than-freehold estate is an interest in real property as a tenant. Less-than-freehold estates are also known as *leasehold estates*. There are four types or classifications of leasehold estates:

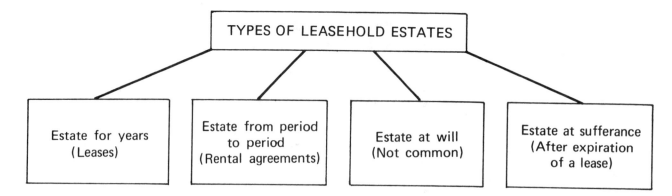

TYPES OF LEASEHOLD ESTATES			
Estate for years (Leases)	Estate from period to period (Rental agreements)	Estate at will (Not common)	Estate at sufferance (After expiration of a lease)

1. *Estate for years.* A leasehold that continues for a fixed time span. The term "estate for years" is misleading because the fixed time span can be for a single day, week, month, year, or years. Therefore, a signed lease for five years, and a signed lease for one month may both be "estates for years."

2. *Estate from period to period (periodic tenancy).* A leasehold that continues from period to period (day, week, month, year) with no specified termination date. Each party agrees to renew or terminate at the end of each period. A month-to-month rental agreement is an example of an estate from period to period.

3. *Estate at will.* A leasehold that can be terminated without notice at any time by the lessor or the lessee. An estate at will has no definite termination date listed in the lease. The California legislature has passed laws stating that both the lessor and the lessee must give advance notice prior to the termination of an estate at will.

4. *Estate at sufferance.* A leasehold where a lessee retains possession of the land after the expiration of a lease. For example, a lessee has a five-year lease which expired today. The lessor and the lessee have not decided upon renewal terms. Under these circumstances the lessee's estate for years is converted to an estate at sufferance until a decision is made about the future rights of the lessee. The landlord can enter into another lease agreement or ask the lessee to leave.

Requirements for a Valid Lease

For a lease to be valid, it must:

1. Be in writing, if the term is for more than one year. Any alterations must also be in writing.

2. Contain the names of the lessor and lessee.

3. Contain a sufficient description of the property. In some cases a street address is sufficient for a simple residential lease. In other cases, it may be wise to include a complete legal description in addition to the common street address.

4. Show the amount of rent and the manner of payment. An example might be a rent of $30,000, payable $500 per month for five years.

5. State the duration or time period the lease is to run, or in the case of a periodic tenancy, the periods involved. According to law, urban property cannot be leased for more than 99 years and rural agricultural land for more than 51 years.

6. Be signed by the lessor. Technically, a lessee need not sign the lease to make it valid. The lessee's possession of the property is considered to be acceptable of the agreement. However, to eliminate misunderstanding, a landlord should insist that the tenant sign the lease.

7. Have a lessor and a lessee who are legally able to contract.

8. Have any renewal provisions in boldface type. A renewal provision is a clause that automatically extends the lease if the lessee remains in possession after expiration of the lease.

See page 215, for a sample residential rental agreement form.

Other Provisions

Although not legally required, a lease should also state who is responsible for utilities and maintenance. If there are special rules, regarding noise, guests, parking, pets, and so on, they should be noted in the rental agreement. The intended use of the property should be specified as well as the maximum number of tenant occupants per rental unit. A lease should also note the right, if any, the tenant may have to remove fixtures attached by the tenant.

Security Deposits

On a residential rental, a security deposit cannot exceed more than two months' rent on unfurnished dwellings, or three months' rent on furnished units. The security deposit must be refunded within 14 days after the tenant vacates the property.

However, the security deposit can be used to offset back rent, damages caused by the tenant, or to clean the premises left dirty by the tenant. If an offset is used, the landlord must provide the tenant with an itemized statement showing all charges within 14 days after the tenant vacates. *No security deposit can be labeled as nonrefundable.*

The landlord is still allowed to collect the first month's rent in addition to the security deposit noted above.

Assignment versus Sublease of the Lease

An *assignment* of a lease transfers the entire leasehold interest to another party, including the prime liability and responsibility to make payments to the lessor (landlord). Figure 11-1 illustrates an assignment of a lease.

Under an assignment the original lessee A is removed from the transaction and all rights and duties pass to assignee B. Assignee B is now primarily liable for the lease.

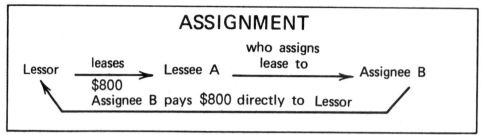

Figure 11.1

A *sublease* transfers only a part of the term of the lessee to a sublessee. The original lessee is still liable to the lessor (landlord) for the terms and conditions of the lease. Figure 11-2 illustrates a sublease.

Sublessee B pays lessee A who pays the lessor. In essence there are two contracts. The original lease between lessor and lessee A, and another contract between lessee A and sublessee B. Each contract stands alone. If sublessee B does not pay lessee A, lessee A must still pay the lessor. In Figure 11-2, lessee A is said to hold a "sandwich lease." In other words, lessee A is wedged between the lessor and the sublessee.

A lessor may insert a clause in the lease prohibiting any assignment or sublease without the prior written approval of the lessor.

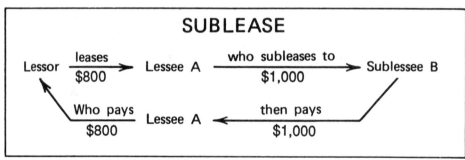

Figure 11.2

RESIDENTIAL RENTAL AGREEMENT

(Month To Month Tenancy)

THIS IS INTENDED TO BE A LEGALLY BINDING AGREEMENT — READ IT CAREFULLY

CALIFORNIA ASSOCIATION OF REALTORS® STANDARD FORM

Somewhere , California March 28 19 9-

Ralph R. Owner , Landlord, and
Sue J. Occupant Tenant, agree as follows:

1. Landlord rents to Tenant and Tenant hires from Landlord those premises described as: Apartment 15 at
2003 Evergreen Avenue, Somewhere, CA. 95500

together with the following furniture, and appliances, if any, and fixtures: Evans Stove model P2. , GM refrigrator
model G9

(Insert "as shown on Exhibit A attached hereto" and attach the exhibit if the list is extensive.)

2. The term shall commence on April 1, , 19 8- , and shall continue from month to month. This rental agreement may be terminated at any time by either party by giving written notice 30 days in advance.
Tenant agrees to pay $675. rent per month payable in advance on the first day of each month and $ 25.00 representing prorated rent from date of possession.

3. The rent shall be paid at 689 Nice Street, Somewhere, CA. 95500
or at any address designated by the Landlord in writing.

4. $675 as security has been deposited. Landlord may use therefrom such amounts as are reasonably necessary to remedy Tenant's defaults in the payment of rent, to repair damages caused by Tenant, and to clean the premises if necessary upon termination of tenancy. If used toward rent or damages during the term of tenancy, Tenant agrees to reinstate said total security deposit upon five days written notice delivered to Tenant in person or by mailing. Security deposit or balance thereof, if any, together with an itemized accounting, shall be mailed to Tenant at last known address within 14 days of surrender of premises.

5. Tenant agrees to pay for all utilities and services based upon occupancy of the premises and the following charges:

except water, sewer, and garbage
which shall be paid for by Landlord.

6. Tenant has examined the premises and all furniture, furnishings and appliances if any, and fixtures contained therein, and accepts the same as being clean, in good order, condition, and repair, with the following exceptions: no exceptions

7. The premises are rented for use as a residence by the following named persons: Sue J. Occupant

No animal, bird, or pet except no exceptions
shall be kept on or about the premises without Landlord's prior written consent.

8. Tenant shall not disturb, annoy, endanger or interfere with other Tenants of the building or neighbors, nor use the premises for any unlawful purposes, nor violate any law or ordinance, nor commit waste or nuisance upon or about the premises.

9. Tenant agrees to comply with all reasonable rules or regulations posted on the premises or delivered to Tenant by Landlord.

10. Tenant shall keep the premises and furniture, furnishings and appliances, if any, and fixtures which are rented for his exclusive use in good order and condition and pay for any repairs to the property caused by Tenant's negligence or misuse or that of Tenant's invitees. Landlord shall otherwise maintain the property. Tenant's personal property is not insured by Landlord.

11. Tenant shall not paint, wallpaper, nor make alterations to the property without Landlord's prior written consent.

12. Upon not less than 24 hours advance notice, Tenant shall make the demised premises available during normal business hours to Landlord or his authorized agent or representative, for the purpose of entering (a) to make necessary agreed repairs, decorations, alterations or improvements or to supply necessary or agreed services, and (b) to show the premises to prospective or actual purchasers, mortgagees, tenants, workmen or contractors. In an emergency, Landlord, his agent or authorized representative may enter the premises at any time without securing prior permission from Tenant for the purpose of making corrections or repairs to alleviate such emergency.

13. Tenant shall not let or sublet all or any part of the premises nor assign this agreement or any interest in it without the prior written consent of Landlord.

14. If Tenant abandons or vacates the premises, Landlord may at his option terminate this agreement, and regain possession in the manner prescribed by law.

15. If any legal action or proceeding be brought by either party to enforce any part of this agreement, the prevailing party shall recover in addition to all other relief, reasonable attorney's fees and costs.

16. Time is of the essence. The waiver by Landlord or Tenant of any breach shall not be construed to be a continuing waiver of any subsequent breach.

17. Notice upon Tenant shall be served as provided by law. Notice upon Landlord may be served upon Manager of the demised premises
2003 Evergreen Avenue, Somewhere , Ca. 95500
at address noted above . Said Manager is authorized to accept service on behalf of Landlord.

18. Within 10 days after written notice, Tenant agrees to execute and deliver a certificate as submitted by Landlord acknowledging that this agreement is unmodified and in full force and effect or in full force and effect as modified and stating the modifications. Failure to comply shall be deemed Tenant's acknowledgement that the certificate as submitted by Landlord is true and correct and may be relied upon by any lender or purchaser.

19. The undersigned Tenant acknowledges having read the foregoing prior to execution and receipt of a copy hereof.

Landlord *Ralph R Owner* Ralph R. Owner   *Sue J. Occupant* Sue J. Occupant Tenant

Landlord Tenant

$ $ $ $ $ $ $ $

TYPES OF RENTAL PAYMENTS

Gross lease. Tenant pays flat rental amount, and the landlord is responsible for taxes, maintenance, and insurance.

Triple net lease. Tenant pays rent and tenant also pays the landlord's property taxes, maintenance, and hazard insurance. This type of lease is used when leasing commercial property on a long-term basis.

Percentage lease. Rent is based on a percentage of the tenant's gross sales—sometimes uses a combination flat rent, plus a certain percentage of the tenant's gross sales. Usually the higher the tenant's gross sales the smaller the percentage. The lower the tenant's sales volume, the higher the percentage.

Extension of a lease. The continuation of an old lease would be an extension. For example, an existing lease is about to expire so the lessor and lessee agree to extend the lease for one year using the same terms and conditions.

Renewal of a lease. This occurs when the existing lessor and lessee renegotiate a new lease upon the expiration of the existing lease. The terms and conditions are frequently different than the terms of the old lease.

Escalator clause. Landlord is allowed to increase the rent during the term of the lease if costs increase. Frequently tied to the consumer price index or wholesale price index.

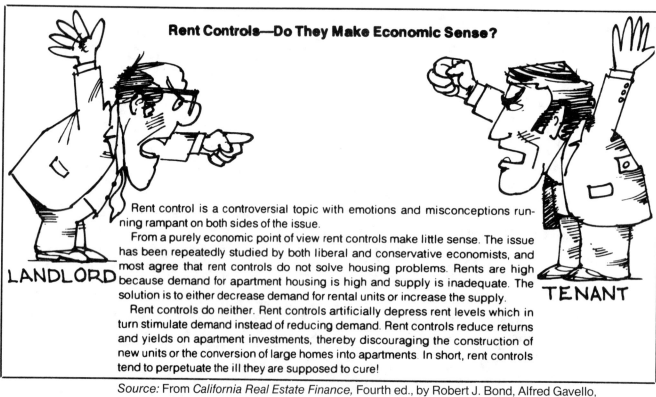

Rent Controls—Do They Make Economic Sense?

LANDLORD

TENANT

Rent control is a controversial topic with emotions and misconceptions running rampant on both sides of the issue.

From a purely economic point of view rent controls make little sense. The issue has been repeatedly studied by both liberal and conservative economists, and most agree that rent controls do not solve housing problems. Rents are high because demand for apartment housing is high and supply is inadequate. The solution is to either decrease demand for rental units or increase the supply.

Rent controls do neither. Rent controls artificially depress rent levels which in turn stimulate demand instead of reducing demand. Rent controls reduce returns and yields on apartment investments, thereby discouraging the construction of new units or the conversion of large homes into apartments. In short, rent controls tend to perpetuate the ill they are supposed to cure!

Source: From *California Real Estate Finance,* Fourth ed., by Robert J. Bond, Alfred Gavello, Dennis J. McKenzie, and Carden Young (New York: John Wiley & Sons, Inc., 1990, p. 361).

11.2 DUTIES AND RESPONSIBILITIES OF LANDLORDS AND TENANTS

Landlord's Duties and Rights

In exchange for rent, a landlord surrenders use and possession of the property to a tenant. Under this arrangement a landlord owes the tenant certain duties and responsibilities which include:

1. If the property is residential, there is an *implied right of habitability.* The landlord in essence guarantees that the dwelling meets minimum housing and health codes.

2. Landlords have the right to periodically inspect the property, but they must give *advance notice.* Most lease agreements state that the landlord must give 24 or 48 hours notice. In cases of emergency, to protect the property, a landlord is allowed to enter the premises without giving advance notice.

3. With residential property, a landlord is usually held liable for injuries resulting from unsafe conditions in common areas such as stairwells, hallways, and the surrounding grounds. If the defects or dangers are caused by tenant negligence, then the liability for injuries may shift from the landlord to the tenant. On nonresidential structures, the liability for keeping the premises safe is frequently shifted from landlord to tenant via the use of triple net lease terms.

4. A landlord is not allowed to interfere with the tenant's use and quiet enjoyment of the property. If the tenant is abiding by the terms of the rental agreement, frequent and uncalled for intrusions by a pesty landlord can be grounds for the tenant to cancel the rental agreement and possibly seek damages in court.

5. According to state law, a landlord cannot refuse to rent to a tenant based on: (a) race, color, national origin, (b) religion or creed, (c) sex or marital status, and (d) physical handicap, unless it can be proven that the building poses a danger to the handicapped person.

    In 1982 the California Supreme Court ruled that Landlords *cannot* refuse to rent to families with children. Certain senior citizen housing projects are exempt from this decision.

6. Under current law (1990), a landlord can terminate a month-to-month rental agreement by serving the tenant with a 30-day notice. The landlord does not need to give the tenant a reason, nor does the tenant need to be in violation of the terms of the rental agreement. However, if the tenant can prove that the landlord's actions are unfair, based upon the antidiscriminatory laws noted above, the tenant can sue the landlord. Also, it must be stressed that if a tenant has a signed lease for a specified duration (estate for years) a landlord cannot force the tenant (lessee) to leave unless the tenant violates the terms of the lease agreement.

Tenant's Duties and Rights

A tenant owes a landlord certain duties and responsibilities. In turn, a tenant has certain rights. Tenant duties and rights are summarized below.

1. Tenants are expected to pay the rent when due and not damage the property beyond normal wear and tear.

2. Tenants who have month-to-month rental agreements are required to give at least a 30-day notice before vacating the property. A landlord can sue for 30 days rent if a tenant fails to give the landlord a 30-day notice before vacating.

3. Tenants can be held liable for injuries to guests or customers due to unsafe conditions caused by the tenant's negligence. Tenants should purchase their own renter's insurance policy to protect their valuables in case of fire, storm damage, and theft. Most renter's insurance policies also provide personal liability protection for the tenant.

4. Tenants have a duty not to interfere with the rights of other tenants.

5. A tenant has the right to use and enjoy the property. If the tenant is unreasonably bothered by the landlord or another person, the tenant has the right to abandon the property and pay no further rent. This process is called *constructive eviction.*

6. In California, all residential rentals must meet minimum housing and health codes. The responsibility for meeting the codes rests with the landlord. If the property falls below standards due to damage or negligence caused by the tenant, the landlord can bring legal action against the tenant. On the other hand, if through no fault of the tenant, the dwelling falls below housing codes, the tenant can demand that the landlord make the needed repairs. If the landlord refuses, the tenant can abandon the property and not be liable for future rent. The tenant may elect to use a rental offset procedure outlined in the California Civil Code.

Rental Offset If a residential landlord refuses to make needed repairs, Section 1942 of the Civil Code allows a tenant to spend up to one month's rent to make the repairs. The paid repair bill can then be used to offset the next month's rent. The basic rules are:

1. The tenant must give the landlord written notice and adequate time to make the repairs.

2. If the landlord refuses, the tenant may spend up to one month's rent on the repairs, then deduct the cost of repairs from the following month's rent.

3. A tenant can use a rental offset *only twice per year* and only for needed repairs, not decorative changes. In most cases, a tenant cannot charge for his or her own labor, only repair parts. However, if a trades person makes the repairs, both parts and labor can be used for the offset. If a tenant spends more than one month's rent, the excess cannot be applied against subsequent rental payments.

Current law prohibits a landlord from taking retaliatory action, such as serving an eviction notice or raising the rents, for a period of 180 days after the tenant's use of the rental offset.

Rental Payments to Neutral Escrow

In some instances, needed repairs may exceed one month's rent and tenants may be reluctant to use the limited offset provisions noted above. Under these circumstances, it *might be possible* for the tenants to make their rental payments to a neutral escrow, with instructions to deliver the rents to the landlord after the property has been brought up to minimum housing standards. *Caution: this is a recent concept and should never be exercised without the advice of an attorney.*

11.3 EVICTION AND OTHER TERMINATIONS OF RENTAL AGREEMENTS

Eviction occurs when a tenant is dispossessed by process of law. It must be stressed that the eviction process is a legal procedure in court. Landlords cannot resort to "self help" actions such as changing the locks, shutting off utility services, seizing the tenant's property in lieu of rent, or threatening the tenants with bodily harm. If a landlord commits an illegal act, such as the ones noted above, the tenant can sue the landlord.

Unlawful Detainer Action

The process of removing a tenant from possession involves a series of steps.

1. Landlord serves a tenant with a three-day or 30-day notice depending upon the circumstances.

2. If the tenant fails to abide by the notice, the landlord files an unlawful detainer action in court.

3. If the landlord wins, the court awards the landlord a judgment. The landlord then asks for a writ of possession authorizing the sheriff to evict the tenant.

4. The sheriff sends tenant eviction notice; if tenant fails to leave, the sheriff then physically removes the tenant.

Three-Day versus 30-Day Notice

A tenant is served a three-day notice when the tenant has defaulted on rent or has violated other terms of the rental agreement. A 30-day notice is served when the tenant has not violated the rental agreement, but the landlord wants the tenant to leave. If the tenant has a fixed term lease (estate for years) a landlord cannot serve a notice unless the terms of the lease have been violated by the lessee. The exception being, serving notice to the lessee that the lease will not be renewed upon expiration. See the sample three-day serving notice and how it must be served.

SERVING NOTICE

THREE-DAY NOTICE

To _____

_____

_____

NOTICE TO PAY RENT
OR SURRENDER POSSESSION

NOTICE IS HEREBY GIVEN that, pursuant to the agreement by which you hold possession of the above-described premises there is now due and unpaid rent for said premises in the total sum of $_____, being the rent that became due on_____for the period from_____, at a monthly rental of $_____.

WITHIN THREE DAYS after service of this notice on you, you are required to pay said rent in full, or to deliver up possession of said premises to the undersigned, or legal proceedings will be commenced against you to recover possession of said premises, to declare said agreement forfeited, and to recover TREBLE RENTS AND DAMAGES for the unlawful detention of said premises.

Dated:_____

Signed:_____

The notice must be:

1. Personally delivered to the tenant(s).

OR

2. If the tenant(s) is absent, leave copy with someone of suitable age; then mail a copy to the tenant(s) at place of residence.

OR

3. If no one is home, copy may be affixed in a conspicuous place on the property; then mail a copy to the tenant(s).

Slipping the notice under the door or putting it in the mailbox is not sufficient delivery. Also it is a good idea to have the notice served by someone other than the landlord. If the sheriff, marshall, or constable serves the notice it will have the maximum impression on the tenant(s).

Small Claims versus Municipal Court

Small claims courts can hear unlawful detainer actions on residential properties only. The amount of the rent cannot be more than a designated amount, which is subject to change from year to year.

Municipal courts can hear unlawful detainer actions for larger amounts than small claims courts. In addition, municipal courts can hear cases involving nonresidential real estate.

Most landlords bring unlawful detainer actions in municipal court even if they fall within the jurisdiction of small claims court. Small claims courts do not allow attorneys, which is a cost savings. However, small claims court calendars are crowded and frequently it takes a long time to hear a case. In municipal court, unlawful detainer actions have a priority on the court's calendar and an early hearing is usually granted. An attorney generally is needed for a municipal court action. But the cost of an attorney for municipal court may be less than the rents lost, due to the delays of the small claims court.

Sheriff Evicts the Tenant

After a writ of possession has been granted the landlord, the sheriff sends the tenant an eviction notice. After approximately five days, if the tenant has not left, the sheriff physically removes the tenant, but not the tenant's possessions. The tenant's possessions are impounded according to the lien laws (see Figure 11-4 for details).

Delays and Appeals

With an increasing awareness of tenant's rights, many tenant action groups have effectively designed delay and appeal processes that can extend an unlawful detainer action for many months. This dramatically increases the landlord's cost both in attorney time and lost rents.

From the landlord's point of view, the best way to protect oneself is to make sure that a lawful, careful screening takes place before a tenant moves in. Once an unethical tenant moves in, it can become very expensive to have the tenant removed.

Termination of Lease

Few leases or rental agreements are ever terminated because of eviction. Most leases are terminated for the following reasons:

1. *Expiration of time.* The time period for the lease is up and new terms are not negotiated.

2. *Mutual consent.* The lessor and lessee agree to terminate the lease with no additional liability on either side.

In addition, leases can be terminated because of destruction of the premises, government action, such as condemnation, or a breach of terms and conditions by the lessor or lessee.

```
Mr. Ralph A. Tenant                          Court # 738472
_____                              _____
              plaintiff                      Acme Municipal
                                             _____
          vs.                                                  court

Mr. Irving Q. Landlord                       Sheriff's File 2479
_____                                    _____
              defendant

          TO: Ralph A. Tenant
              _____

              110 Pleasant Way, Apt. No. 3
              _____

              Somewhere, CA. 95500
              _____
```

By virtue of a WRIT OF POSSESSION/RESTITUTION issued out of the above Court, you are hereby ordered to vacate the premises described in the Writ, as follows: Apartment No. 3
                 110 Pleasant Way
                 Somewhere, CA. 05500

FINAL NOTICE IS HEREBY GIVEN that possession of the above described property must be delivered to the Plaintiff on or before _____ , the

__15th__ day of __June_____ , 19_9-__, at _12:00__ A.M.

Should you fail to vacate the premises within the allotted time, I will immediately enforce the Writ by removing you from the premises. **All personal property upon the premises at that time will be turned over to the plaintiff/landlord, who must return said personal property to you upon your payment of the reasonable cost incurred by the plaintiff/landlord in storing the property from the date of eviction to the date of payment. If the property is stored on the landlord's premises, the reasonable cost of storage is the fair rental value of the space necessary for the time of storage. If you do not pay the reasonable storage cost within fifteen (15) days, the landlord may either sell your property at a public sale and keep from the proceeds of the sale the costs of storage and of the sale, or, if the property is valued at less than $100.00, the landlord may dispose of your property or retain it for his own use.**

June 10, _____ , 199-   John Jones, SHERIFF

                                         by: _____
                                                    DEPUTY   P.I.N.

Figure 11-4

MOBILE HOME PARK TENANTS

A mobile home park is usually a development, where lots are rented to mobile home owners. The tenants own their mobile homes, but they are tenants of the land. In California, there are special laws for mobile home park tenants that differ from the typical landlord/tenant laws.

A mobile home tenant in a park *cannot be evicted unless the tenant:*

1. Fails to comply with local and state laws.

2. Annoys other tenants.

3. Fails to abide with reasonable park rules.

4. Fails to pay the rent.

If the mobile home park is condemned by government, or the use changes, a tenant is required to leave.

If the mobile home cannot be moved without a permit, the law requires that a tenant must have a reasonable notice to vacate. The tenant cannot be required to move to merely make space available for a person to purchase a mobile home from the park owner. In addition, there are many other special rules that apply to tenants in mobile home parks.

11.4 PROPERTY MANAGEMENT

As an investment, real estate offers a hedge against inflation, income tax advantages, and in some cases provides an annual cash income. However, real estate needs managerial attention and this frequently discourages investors who do not wish to be bothered by tenants. An alternative might be to employ a professional property manager.

Field of Property Management

Property management is a specialty within the real estate business. Property managers represent owners by screening tenants, negotiating rental agreements, hiring personnel to maintain the building and grounds, and hiring on-site residential managers. California rules state that an apartment building or complex with 16 or more rental units must have an on-site residential manager. In addition, property managers are responsible for rent collection and the keeping of accounting records for income tax purposes.

Property managers range from real estate brokers who handle a few properties for their clients to large corporate firms who manage hundreds of units, including commercial properties such as office buildings and shopping centers.

A property manager must be a licensed real estate broker. Key employees of the property management company must be bonded. The Institute of Real Estate Management, affiliated with the National

Association of Realtors issues the nationally recognized designation, Certified Property Manager (CPM). The CPM designation is achieved after meeting rigorous educational and experience requirements.

Compensation

Property management firms are usually paid a percentage of the rents collected. The percentage is negotiable and varies from firm to firm. For a large structure with many rental units, the fee may be as low as one percent or 2 percent of gross rents collected. On small units such as rental homes and duplexes, the fee may be 10 percent or more. The fee for renting resort properties may be 20 percent or even 25 percent of rents collected.

Property management fees do not include the cost of maintenance, but rather the management of the property. If maintenance or repairs are needed, the manager sees that the work is done, but the bill is paid by the property owner, or deducted from the rent proceeds.

When a property manager is hired, the manager and the owner sign a management contract. This contract designates the property manager as the owner's agent and lists all the duties and responsibilities of the parties. To be enforceable, the management contract must meet the legal requirements of California contract law.

SUMMARY

A lease is a contract between an owner called the lessor and a tenant called the lessee. A lessee is given possession in exchange for rent. Leases for more than one year must be in writing to be valid.

Types of leasehold estates are: estate for years, estate from period to period, estate at will, and estate at sufferance. Leases on urban property cannot exceed 99 years, while leases for agricultural land cannot exceed 51 years. Security deposits on residential properties cannot exceed two months' rent on unfurnished dwellings and three months' rent on furnished dwellings.

An assignment of a lease transfers the entire leasehold interest to another person, while a sublease transfers only a part of the leasehold interest to a sublessee.

Rental payments can be paid on a gross, net, or percentage basis. An escalator clause allows the landlord to raise the rent during the term of the lease.

A landlord's duties and rights may include an implied condition of habitability, advance notice prior to inspection, 30-day advance notice when ordering the tenant to vacate, and an obligation not to discriminate when renting property.

A tenant's duties and rights include paying the rent when due, not damaging the property, giving the landlord 30 days notice when vacating. Under certain conditions, a tenant can use a rent offset for repairs if the property falls below minimum housing standards.

Eviction occurs when a tenant is dispossessed by process of law.

The tenant must be served with either a three-day or a 30-day notice depending upon the circumstances.

The action suing for eviction is called unlawful detainer action. If a writ of possession is granted, the sheriff evicts the tenant. Delays and appeals by a tenant can extend the eviction process by several months.

In addition to eviction, leases can be terminated by expiration of time, mutual consent, destruction of the premises, government action, or breach of terms and conditions.

Property management is a specialty within the real estate business. Property managers represent owners by finding tenants, caring for the property, and maintaining proper accounting records. Property managers are usually paid a fee based upon the rents collected.

Important Terms and Concepts

Assignment of lease

Certified property manager (CPM)

Estate at sufferance

Estate for years

Estate from period to period

Eviction notices

Gross lease

Less-than-freehold estate

Lessee

Lessor

Net lease

Percentage lease

Refundable security deposit

Rental offset

Sandwich lease

Sublease

Unlawful detainer action

REVIEWING YOUR UNDERSTANDING

1. Ms. Brown leases her summer cabin to Mr. Greene for the months of June, July, and August of a designated year. Mr. Greene has an estate:
   (a) For years
   (b) From period to period
   (c) At sufferance
   (d) Of monthly rental

2. Urban property cannot be leased for more than:
   (a) 99 years
   (b) 51 years
   (c) 15 years
   (d) There is no time limit

3. An assignment of a lease differs from a sublease in that an assignment:
   (a) Transfers liability to the new occupant

(b) Involves two lease contracts: (1) lessor to lessee and (2) lessee to sublessee
(c) Requires that the original lessee is still primarily liable to the lessor
(d) None of these are correct

4. Under which lease does the tenant pay rent, property taxes, maintenance, and hazard insurance?
   (a) Gross lease
   (b) Triple net lease
   (c) Flat lease
   (d) Escalator lease

5. A residential tenant may expect the landlord to make necessary repairs to keep the dwelling habitable. If the landlord does not, the tenant may make repairs and offset the rent up to:
   (a) $700 maximum
   (b) One month's rent
   (c) Reasonable cost
   (d) $1,000 maximum

6. It is illegal to screen and eliminate potential tenants based on:
   (a) Marital status, sex
   (b) Race, color, creed
   (c) Religion, physical handicap
   (d) All of the above

7. If a tenant has violated the terms of the rental agreement or lease, before the tenant can be evicted the tenant must be served a:
   (a) One-day notice
   (b) Three-day notice
   (c) 30-day notice
   (d) 60-day notice

8. If an unfurnished apartment rents for $600 per month, the maximum security deposit the landlord may ask for is:
   (a) $100
   (b) $500
   (c) $600
   (d) $1,200

9. The legal process by which a tenant is evicted is called a (an):
   (a) Eviction action
   (b) Ejectment action
   (c) Possessory action
   (d) Unlawful detainer action

10. The professional designation CPM stands for:
    (a) Certificate of Public Management
    (b) Certified Practical Manager
    (c) Certificate of Practical Management
    (d) Certified Property Manager

Chapter 12
Land-Use Planning, Subdivisions, and Other Public Controls

Preview This chapter highlights the principles of government land-use planning, and stresses zoning and subdivision regulations. Condominiums, planned unit developments, and the selling of undivided interests are also discussed. The chapter concludes with an explanation of fair housing laws. When you finish this chapter you will be able to:

1. *Describe the main goals of a community general plan.*

2. *Explain the difference between government use of police power and eminent domain and give two examples of each.*

3. *List the major characteristics of the Subdivision Map Act and the Subdivided Lands Act.*

4. *Discuss the differences between a condominium development and a planned unit development.*

5. *List the major fair housing laws that prohibit discrimination in the selling or renting of real estate.*

12.1 GOVERNMENT LAND-USE PLANNING Government land-use controls are controversial. Some people feel that land is a commodity to be bought and sold like any other product. They consider any type of land-use control an infringement on free enterprise. At the other extreme are those who believe land is a resource that belongs to all the people, the use of which should be completely controlled by government. Somewhere in the middle is the view that land is both a commodity and a resource that should be privately owned, but used constructively to benefit society.

Private Deed Restrictions Most attention regarding land-use control has focused on government regulations. However, it should be noted that for many years covenants, conditions, and restrictions (CC&Rs) in deeds have been used by private individuals to regulate real estate usage.

California owners are allowed to limit the use of land by contract as long as the restrictions are not a violation of the law. Thus, land-use controls are not new, but in the last 30 years the bulk of the controls have shifted from private imposition to government imposition. Private deed restrictions were discussed in more detail in Chapter 3.

Public Land-Use Controls

Industrialization and urban crowding have created a need for public controls to maintain order and promote social harmony. One way to maintain order is to control the use of land. The two main powers which allow government to control land use are police power and the power of eminent domain.

Police power refers to the constitutional right of government to regulate private activity to promote the general health, welfare, and safety of society. Police power has often been used in the United States to direct land use. Major real estate examples of police power include zoning ordinances, building and health codes, set-back requirements, pollution abatement, and rent controls. Of the many police power enactments, zoning and subdivision regulations emerge as the most influential methods for controlling land use.

Police power allows government to regulate private land use without the payment of compensation. The power of *eminent domain* is different in that it allows the government to acquire title to private land for public use in exchange for the payment of just compensation. Eminent domain is used for a variety of government land-use projects such as highways, public housing, and urban renewal.

All levels of government may exercise the power of eminent domain regardless of how unwilling the property owner may be. The main issue in most eminent domain cases is the amount of compensation. The courts have ruled that the property's fair market value is the proper basis for determining compensation. In addition, most federal and some state agencies must also pay for moving and other miscellaneous expenses incurred by those being displaced.

Planning

The dictionary defines "planning" as "thinking out acts and purposes beforehand." When applied to cities and counties, planning can be defined as anticipating and achieving community goals in light of social, economic, and physical needs. Planning requires that a community analyze its assets and liabilities, establish its goals, and then attempt to achieve these goals using land-use control as a primary tool.

California law requires that every incorporated city and county must have a planning commission. A *planning commission* is comprised of citizens appointed by the members of the city council or board of supervisors. Planning commissioners advise the elected officials on land-use matters. The planning commission only makes recommendations—the final decision on planning rests with the city council or board of supervisors.

In addition to planning commissions, many cities and counties have planning departments. *Planning departments* are agencies within city and county government, staffed with professionally trained planners.

Planning department employees provide technical services for the planning commissions, elected officials, and citizens.

Every city and county must develop a *general plan,* which outlines the goals and objectives for the community. The general plan then lists the steps needed to achieve these goals.

General Plan

The establishment of a community general plan requires three major steps: (1) resource analysis, (2) formulation of community goals, and (3) implementation of the plan.

RESOURCE ANALYSIS

The first step is to recognize the individual character of the community. What are its strong points? What are its weaknesses? To accomplish this, several substudies will be required, including an economic base study, a population trend study, a survey of existing land use, a city facilities study, and an analysis of the community's financial resources. Once a resource inventory has been taken, the next step is to formulate community goals in light of its resources.

FORMULATION OF COMMUNITY GOALS

The formulation of community goals is the most difficult phase of urban planning because of the conflict between various special interest groups, each trying to secure and establish its own definition of the community goal. In spite of this problem, citizen input should be encouraged. A community plan must be based on the desires of community residents as a whole, not on the desires of staff planners alone.

Once the goals are established, a comprehensive plan to achieve these objectives must be formulated. The plan is frequently referred to as the general plan or the master plan, and it should encompass all social, economic, and physical aspects of the projected growth. The plan should be long-range but provide for short-range flexibility as the need for modification arises. Under no circumstances must the master plan be viewed as an inflexible, permanent fixture that will never require modification. A community's attitude and resources can change, and the master plan must be modified to comply with these changes.

IMPLEMENTATION OF THE PLAN

The final step in urban planning is to implement the general plan. The implementation phase requires local government to use police power, eminent domain, taxation, and control over government spending to enact the plan. As previously indicated, the two most powerful tools for implementing a community plan are zoning and subdivision regulations.

Zoning

Zoning refers to the division of land into designated land-use districts. In its simplest form, zoning districts are divided into residential use, commercial use, industrial use, and rural use. Each use in turn can have several subclasses. For example, residential can be broken down into single-family, multifamily, and mobile home zones. Commercial zones are usually divided into retail, office, and wholesale space. Industrial zones are divided into light industry and heavy industry, and rural zones into agricultural, resource, or recreational uses.

Zoning as a land-control tool was not common in the United States until the 1920s; prior to this time there was some doubt about the constitutionality of zoning, although early zoning laws can be traced to colonial times. However, in 1926 the U.S. Supreme Court held that zoning was a reasonable exercise of government police power. Since this decision, every state has passed legislation allowing individual cities and counties to enact zoning ordinances.

Early zoning ordinances were aimed at safety and nuisance control. The idea was to use zoning to protect individual property values by prohibiting offensive use of surrounding land. The use of zoning has gradually been expanded, and now it is used to "promote the general welfare" of the entire community.

CONTROVERSY

Local versus State Planning

Historically, planning has been a local matter. Each community developed its own plans within the confines of its own territorial limits. In the process, each community attempted to optimize its own social and economic well-being, frequently at the expense of surrounding areas. For example, the planning of a smelly industrial plant on the border of one city has a spillover effect on the neighboring community located downwind.

The growth of multicity metropolitan areas has led the state to mandate planning on a regional basis. Water and sewage systems, rapid transit, highway traffic patterns, airports, and pollution controls are some examples of regional planning. However, from a political point of view, there is a widescale resistance to the creation of another layer of government. Moreover, local government officials are reluctant to surrender some of their power to regional or state commissioners.

Opposition to state controls also comes from individuals who feel that the power of land regulation should be limited to local government. They fear that planning on a state level will be insensitive to local needs. Who is correct? Like most land-use controls, the correct answer depends on one's value judgment. However, the current trend is toward more regional and state control over land use. Examples include *The Coastline Conservation Act* creating controls of the 1,000 mile California coast; the *California Environmental Quality Act* which requires an environmental impact report on major real estate projects; and the *Subdivision Map Act* and *Subdivided Lands Act* which control the creation of subdivision in the state.

Source: From *The Essentials of Real Estate Economics,* 2nd ed., Dennis J. McKenzie and Richard M. Betts (New York: John Wiley & Sons, Inc., 1980, p. 190).

SUMMARY OF PLANNING TERMS

Planning commission. An appointed body of citizens charged with the responsibility of advising the elected board of supervisors or city council members in matters of land use.

Planning department. City or county staff employees who lend professional and technical assistance to elected officials and citizens.

Zone. An area defined on a map by a boundary line within which the land-use regulations are the same.

Rezoning. The process of changing land-use regulations on property from one zone to another.

Variance. A deviation from the zoning regulations for a particular parcel.

Subdivision. A division of property into five or more parcels.

Lot split. A division of property into two, three, or four parcels.

Appeal. The right to request review of a negative planning commission decision. The appellate process goes from the planning commission to the board of supervisors or city council to the courts.

12.2 SUBDIVISIONS

Another important use of police power is *subdivision regulation.* Poorly conceived subdivisions, with inadequate streets and facilities, can become a burden to taxpayers in later years when expensive redevelopment is needed to correct earlier oversights. Proponents of subdivision controls believe that the origin of slums and urban blight can be traced to inadequate regulations. Opponents disagree, noting that today's slums are the result of government ordinances that prevent land from rising to its economic highest and best use.

Today, subdivision regulations are used in all areas of California.

Real estate developers are frequently required to provide water, sewer, paved streets, sidewalks, street lights, and school and park sites as a condition of being allowed to subdivide. The idea is to plan for the future at the inception and to require the purchaser of the subdivided lot, not the community as a whole, to pay the expense of added community facilities. Like all public controls, subdivision regulations are controversial since they require the surrender of some individual rights in an attempt to promote the general welfare.

SUBDIVISION

Subdivision Laws There are two basic laws under which subdivisions are controlled in California—the Subdivision Map Act and the Subdivided Lands Act. The *Subdivision Map Act* defines a subdivision as the division of land into two or more lots for the purpose of sale, lease, or financing, whether now or in the future. The Subdivision Map Act is administered by local officials and is concerned with the physical aspects of the subdivision, such as design, streets, sewers, and so on. The Subdivision Map Act outlines the procedure for filing subdivision maps to legally create a subdivision (see Figure 12-1).

The *Subdivided Lands Act* defines a subdivision as the division of land into five or more lots for the purpose of sale, lease, or financing, whether now or in the future. The Subdivided Lands Act is administered by the California real estate commissioner and is primarily concerned with the marketing and financing aspects of the subdivision. The basic objective of the Subdivided Lands Act is to protect the purchasers of property in new subdivisions from fraud and misrepresentation when buying new subdivided land.

No new subdivision of five or more parcels can be offered for sale in California until the real estate commissioner issues a public report. This law requiring the issuance of a public report applies not only to subdivisions located in California, but also to out-of-state subdivisions which are marketed in California.

The public report is not issued until the commissioner is satisfied that the developer has met all statutory requirements, with particular emphasis on the establishment of financial arrangements to assure completion of any promised facilities. *The issuance of a public report does not mean that in the eyes of the commissioner the subdivision is a good investment.* It merely means that the subdivider has conformed to all laws and regulations.

Before each lot in a new subdivision can be sold, the subdivider must deliver a copy of the commissioner's public report to the prospective buyer. The prospective buyer must then sign a statement acknowledging that he or she has received and read the public report

BASIC OUTLINE OF SUBDIVISION MAP PREPARATION AND APPROVAL

Preliminary Planning

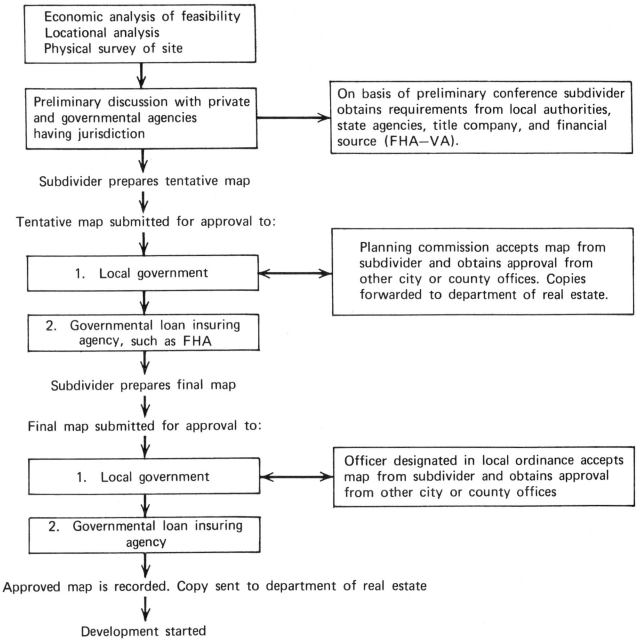

Economic analysis of feasibility
Locational analysis
Physical survey of site

Preliminary discussion with private and governmental agencies having jurisdiction

On basis of preliminary conference subdivider obtains requirements from local authorities, state agencies, title company, and financial source (FHA—VA).

Subdivider prepares tentative map

Tentative map submitted for approval to:

1. Local government

Planning commission accepts map from subdivider and obtains approval from other city or county offices. Copies forwarded to department of real estate.

2. Governmental loan insuring agency, such as FHA

Subdivider prepares final map

Final map submitted for approval to:

1. Local government

Officer designated in local ordinance accepts map from subdivider and obtains approval from other city or county offices

2. Governmental loan insuring agency

Approved map is recorded. Copy sent to department of real estate

Development started

Figure 12-1

Source: From *Reference Book,* California Department of Real Estate.

and this signed copy must be kept for three years. Only after these steps have taken place can the subdivider sell each lot.

The public report is good for five years; however, the law requires the commissioner to issue an amended public report when a material change occurs regarding the subdivision. Examples of material changes could include changes in contract forms, physical changes such as lot lines or street lines, or a sale of five or more lots to a single buyer.

Under certain circumstances, the commissioner can issue a *preliminary public report* which will allow the subdivider to take reservations for purchase pending the issuance of the final public report. The reservations are not binding upon the prospective buyer, who is allowed to back out and receive a full refund up until the final report is issued and a binding purchase agreement is signed.

It must be stressed that the public report process only applies on the first sale of each lot in a new subdivision. A subsequent resale of a lot by the original purchaser does not require that the second buyer receive a public report.

Subdivision Laws Summarized

Subdivided Lands Act	Subdivision Map Act
Five or more lots or parcels	Two or more lots or parcels
No contiguity requirement	Land must be contiguous units
160 acres and larger parcels designated as such by government survey are exempt	No exemption for 160 acres and larger
Administered by California Real Estate Commissioner	Administered by local officials
Requires a public report	No public report required

Red Tape

The actual processing of a subdivision is frequently a costly and time-consuming process. The data needed to complete the required forms are highly technical and beyond the skills of average property owners. The services of title officers, surveyors or engineers, contractors, and attorneys often are required. The average subdivision will take many months to process—a major development can take years. Delays are costly and, in the end, these costs are borne by the consumer.

Currently a debate is raging—increased regulations are designed to protect the consumer and the environment, but on the other hand, consumers must pay for these regulations via higher prices. Are the protections worth the price? This is a value judgment question that each person must answer.

LAND PROJECT RIGHT TO RESCIND SALE

A land project is defined as a speculative subdivision of 50 or more lots located in a sparsely populated area of the state. These types of subdivisions are frequently sold only after intensive promotion in urban areas, long distances away from the development.

A purchaser of a lot in the land project is allowed a limited time *after the sale* to "cool off" and rescind or cancel the purchase contract and receive a full refund with no further obligations. In 1990, the right to rescind extends for 14 days after the signing of the purchase agreement. But in the future, regulations might extend this period. (See time-sharing ownership regarding the right to rescind sale, page 237.)

INTERSTATE LAND SALES FULL-DISCLOSURE ACT

In 1969, Congress passed the Interstate Land Sales Full-Disclosure Act which regulates land sales between two or more states. If a developer of 50 or more lots located in one state wishes to market the lots in another state(s), the developer must conform to this law.

Basically the law requires the developer to obtain a public report issued by the Department of Housing and Urban Development (HUD) and to deliver a copy of the public report to each prospective buyer. This law is an attempt to reduce the number of fraudulent land sales that take place by mail or out-of-state advertising.

12.3 CONDOMINIUMS AND OTHER DEVELOPMENTS

An increase in population has caused an increase in urban land prices. As land becomes more scarce and prices begin to rise, there is a tendency to intensify development to obtain more living units per acre. Condominiums, planned unit developments (PUDs), stock cooperatives, and community apartments are examples of intensified owner-occupied developments that differ from the traditional single-family home type subdivision. All of these developments are considered subdivisions and are regulated by state law.

Condominiums

A *condominium* is a type of real estate ownership, not a type of structure. In a condominium a person owns his or her own apartment-type living unit. In a legal sense, a condominium owner acquires a fee title interest in the air space of the particular unit and an undivided interest (with other condominium owners) in the land plus all other common areas such as hallways, elevators, carports, and recreational facilities.

Each condominium owner has his or her own individual deed, real estate loan, and separate property tax assessment. A condominium interest is bought and sold like any other parcel of real estate.

All condominiums have owner associations which usually elect a governing board. The governing board is responsible for the management of the complex and they see that the building and common areas are maintained. The owners' association also sets the dues for each owner's share of the maintenance.

Condominium developments are expected to gradually gain an increasing share of the housing market. As the cost of new construction increases, there has been a tendency to convert existing renter-occupied apartments into owner-occupied condominiums. This has caused controversy because "condo conversion" reduces the supply of rental units, thereby making it more difficult for renters to find affordable housing. On the other hand, a "condo conversion" increases the supply of owner-occupied housing, thereby making it easier for owners to find affordable housing. Therefore, it is expected that the "condo conversion" controversy will rage on for years.

Planned Unit Development (PUD)

A planned unit development (PUD) is often confused with a condominium. They are not the same! In a *PUD* a person owns his or her own living unit and lot, plus an undivided interest in the common areas. A condominium owner owns his or her own living unit, but not his or her own lot. A PUD is often referred to as a "townhouse development," but this is incorrect, as a "townhouse" is a type of architecture and not a type of ownership. In a PUD there is no one living in the "airspace" above or below the owner, as is found in a condominium. PUDs are frequently located in the suburbs, while condominiums are usually located in urban areas. They are both found in resort areas such as Lake Tahoe and Hawaii.

PUDs are similar in operation to condominiums. An owners' association levies dues for upkeep and maintenance of the common areas. In addition, each property owner has covenants, conditions, and restrictions in his or her deed which dictate the do's and don't's of ownership.

Stock Cooperatives and Community Apartments

A *stock cooperative* is a corporation formed for the purpose of holding title to a building. Each shareholder of the entire corporation is given the right to occupy a living unit, but the entire building is owned by the corporation. A sale of a share in the corporation also passes the right of occupancy to a living unit within the stock cooperative.

A *community apartment* is created when a group of people jointly purchases an undivided interest in an entire apartment complex. Then each person is given the right to occupy a particular apartment unit. The undivided share can be sold and the new purchaser acquires the right to live in the particular apartment.

Under a stock cooperative and a community apartment, each person *does not* receive an individual deed, real estate loan, or property tax assessment. All of the shareholders and undivided interest owners must agree to pool their funds each month to make the mortgage payment, pay the property taxes, and pay for upkeep and maintenance.

Stock cooperatives and community apartments are not as popular as condominiums and PUDs. Most people prefer their own individual deed, real estate loan, and property tax assessment which are present in condominiums and PUDs, but not in stock cooperatives or community apartments.

Recreational Developments Selling Undivided Interests

Recreational land developments can be found throughout California. The developer usually begins with a large parcel of land, subdivides the land, and then sells parcels to individual owners. In some cases the parcels are fully developed, and in other cases just vacant lots are sold.

An alternative to subdividing recreational land into individual parcels is to keep the original large parcel intact and sell undivided interests or shares in the whole. An example might be a developer who has 1,000 acres of land and is considering subdividing the land into 1,000 one-acre lots to be sold to 1,000 recreational users. An alternative might be to sell a 1/1000 undivided interest to 1,000 recreational users. With selling 1,000 undivided interests, each owner has the right to use all 1,000 acres instead of just one acre as would be the case if a traditional subdivision were created.

A buyer of an undivided interest has 72 hours to recind the sale and receive a full refund. The marketing of undivided interest is controlled by the state subdivision laws and private deed restrictions similar to condominiums and PUDs.

Time-Sharing Ownership

Another interesting concept is one of time-sharing ownership. Under time sharing, a person buys an interest in a building—for example, a condominium in a resort area—where the right of occupancy is limited to a specified calendar time period. An example might be 12 people who pool their funds and each person purchases a 1/12 interest in a Lake Tahoe condominium. Each person's 1/12 interest gives that person the right to occupy the condominium for a month. The month or the time period is designated in the deed or by a separate instrument. This is a way to own your vacation home for the exact time period you desire, for an expense that covers just the pro rata time of occupancy.

There are other derivations of time-sharing ownership, such as purchasing the right of occupancy for a designated time period each year. But the purchaser does not acquire an interest in the land.

The time-sharing owners need covenants, conditions, and restrictions in deeds, as well as an owners' association to govern the use and maintenance of the unit. The buyer of a time share has 72 hours to rescind the purchase contract for any reason and receive a full refund.

HOUSING AND CONSTRUCTION LAWS

State housing laws. Establish minimum housing standards for the entire state. State housing laws are enforced by local inspectors. The state housing law is a uniform code that must be adopted by all cities and counties in California.

Local building codes. Until 1970, local codes were allowed to deviate from the state housing laws. However, with the passage of the uniform codes, local variances are permitted only if a study finds sufficient reason to deviate from the uniform code.

Contractor's license law. Requires every person who engages in the business of a contractor to be licensed. An owner doing his or her own work for his or her own use is exempt from the contractor license law. But if an owner builds with the intention to offer the finished real estate project for sale, a licensed contractor must do the work.

12.4 FAIR HOUSING

EQUAL HOUSING OPPORTUNITY

State Laws and Regulations

Over the years, several federal and state laws have been passed making it against public policy to discriminate in real estate based on race, color, religion, sex, marital status, national origin, ancestry, family status, or mental or physical handicap. The courts will not tolerate discrimination, and violators can expect to be fined and/or jailed.

Unruh Civil Rights Act. This law makes it unlawful for persons engaged in business in California, including real estate agents, to discriminate when providing business products and services.

Fair Housing Act (Rumford Act). This law forbids discrimination in the sale, rental, lease, or financing of practically all types of housing. This act creates the Fair Employment and Housing Commission whose staff investigates complaints from people who believe they have been discriminated against in housing.

Housing Financial Discrimination Act. This law prohibits financial institutions from engaging in discriminatory loan practices. This law attempts to prohibit "redlining." *Redlining* is a loan practice under which a lender refuses to grant a housing loan in certain geographic areas based on neighborhood trends, regardless of the worthiness of the borrower or of the individual home. (Renamed the *Holden Act* in 1982.)

Commissioner's Rules and Regulations. The California real estate commissioner has issued numerous regulations regarding housing discrimination. These regulations detail the types of discriminatory conduct which, if practiced by a real estate licensee, will be the basis for disciplinary action that can result in a suspension, fine, or even a prosecution by the local district attorney.

Federal Laws   *Civil Rights Act of 1968 and 1988 amendments.* This comprehensive law states that, within constitutional limits, fair housing should prevail throughout the United States. This act left it up to the courts to determine the constitutionality of this law.

Jones vs. *Mayer Case.* In this landmark case, the U.S. Supreme Court interpreted and applied an act of Congress, passed in 1866 right after the Civil War. The constitutionality rested on the Thirteenth Amendment, which prohibits slavery. Using the Act of 1866 and the Thirteenth Amendment, the U.S. Supreme Court upheld the provisions of the Civil Rights Act of 1968.

In short, what the *Jones* vs. *Mayer* case means is that the Unruh and Rumford Acts apply in California, and what discriminations they might not cover are now prohibited by federal law.

Many Other Laws   In addition to the laws listed above, there are numerous other laws and regulations that directly or indirectly attempt to prohibit discrimination in housing. The point to stress is that all real estate owners, agents, managers and lenders must give the public an equal opportunity to acquire real estate.

SUMMARY   Two powers that allow government to control land use are *police power* and the *power of eminent domain.* Major police power tools include zoning, building and health codes, and subdivision regulations.

Cities and counties in California must have a *planning commission.* In addition, most cities and counties also have *planning departments.* The planning commission and elected officials must adopt a *general plan* which outlines the goals and objectives for the community. The two most powerful tools for implementing the general plan are zoning and subdivision regulations.

The two major subdivision laws are the *Subdivision Map Act* and the *Subdivided Lands Act.* The Subdivision Map Act is administered by local officials and is mostly concerned with the physical aspects of the subdivision. The Subdivided Lands Act is administered by the California real estate commissioner and is primarily concerned with the marketing aspects of the subdivision. The key element of the Subdivided Lands Act is the required *public report* which must be delivered to each prospective buyer of a lot in a new subdivision.

Condominiums, planned unit developments (PUDs), stock cooperatives, and community apartments are examples of intensified owner-occupied developments that differ from the traditional single-family dwelling type subdivision.

Over the years laws have been passed making it against public policy to discriminate in the sale, lease, or renting of housing. The *Unruh Civil Rights Act* and the *Fair Housing Act* (Rumford Act) are two California antidiscrimination laws. The *Civil Rights Act of 1968* is a federal law that prohibits discrimination in housing.

Important Terms and Concepts

Civil Rights Act of 1968

Condominium

Eminent domain

Fair Housing (Rumford) Act

General plan

Planning commission

Planned unit development (PUD)

Police power

Public report

Selling undivided interests

Subdivided Lands Act

Subdivision Map Act

Unruh Civil Rights Act

Zoning

REVIEWING YOUR UNDERSTANDING

1. Which of the following is an example of government use of police power?
   (a) Rent controls
   (b) Building codes
   (c) Zoning ordinances
   (d) All of the above

2. The Subdivision Map Act is administered by:
   (a) California real estate commissioner
   (b) Local officials
   (c) California Department of Urban Planning
   (d) Department of Housing and Urban Development (HUD)

3. Before a developer can sell a lot in a new subdivision, the prospective buyer must receive a copy of the:
   (a) Preliminary title report
   (b) Builder's warranties
   (c) Public report
   (d) Zoning ordinances

4. A developer from Nevada wishes to sell 300 Las Vegas lots to California residents and opens sales offices in Los Angeles and San Francisco. The developer need *not* conform to the:
   (a) Subdivision Map Act
   (b) Subdivided Lands Act
   (c) Public report requirements
   (d) Interstate Land Sales Full-Disclosure Act

5. The right of the consumer, within a specified time, to rescind a land purchase contract and receive a full refund, applies to new:
   (a) Urban subdivisions of 50 lots or more
   (b) Suburban subdivisions of 50 lots or more
   (c) Farmland of 50 acres or more
   (d) Land projects of 50 lots or more

6. A development where a person individually owns his or her living unit, but has an undivided interest with the other owners in the land and common areas is a:
   (a) PUD
   (b) Townhouse
   (c) Condominium
   (d) Stock cooperative

7. The selling of a 1/2500 share in a Northern California recreational ranch is an example of:
   (a) An undivided interest
   (b) A condominium
   (c) A PUD
   (d) A time-sharing ownership

8. A person cannot refuse to sell a home based on the buyer's
   (a) Physical handicap
   (b) Marital status
   (c) Sex
   (d) Cannot refuse based on all of the above

9. The law that prevents agents from discriminating when providing real estate services is:
   (a) Fair Housing Act
   (b) Rumford Act
   (c) Unruh Civil Rights Act
   (d) Housing Financial Discrimination Act

10. The law which makes it illegal for real estate lenders to redline a neighborhood is:
    (a) Fair Housing Act
    (b) Rumford Act
    (c) Unruh Civil Rights Act
    (d) Housing Financial Discrimination Act

Chapter 13
Introduction to Taxation

Preview Government levies taxes to generate revenue to help pay for government expenditures. This chapter presents the principles of real property and income taxation, two forms of taxation that have a direct impact on real estate ownership. In addition, inheritance and gift taxes are briefly explained. When you have completed this chapter you will be able to:

1. *Describe the real property assessment procedure as required by Proposition 13.*

2. *List the rules regarding the date and manner of payment of real property taxes; describe the tax sale procedure in the event of nonpayment of property taxes.*

3. *Explain homeowner's, veteran's, and senior citizen's property tax exemptions.*

4. *List the income tax advantages of real estate ownership, including the changes due to recent changes in the law.*

13.1 REAL PROPERTY TAXES Property taxes are levied by cities and counties on an ad valorem basis. Ad valorem is a Latin phrase that means "according to value." Under the concept of *ad valorem*, owners of higher valued property pay more in property taxes than owners of lower valued property.

Property taxes can be divided into two categories:

1. Real property taxes levied on real estate such as land and buildings.

2. Personal property taxes levied on personal items used in a business such as trade fixtures, which include furniture and equipment.

In California, homeowners only pay real property taxes, while businesses may pay both real and personal property taxes.

Assessment Procedure On June 6, 1978, the voters of California passed Proposition 13, the Jarvis-Gann Initiative. Proposition 13 limits real property taxes to one percent of the full cash value of the real property.

No Change in Ownership since March 1, 1975

Under the terms of Proposition 13, if there has been no change in ownership since March 1, 1975, the 1975 value shall be the initial full cash value. To this figure the assessor is allowed to add an inflation factor of 2 percent per year *compounded* to arrive at full cash value for the present tax year. For example, assume that a person has owned his or her home since March 1, 1975. The 1975 value was $40,000. The 1976 full cash value would be $40,000 plus 2 percent or $40,800 ($40,000 × 2% = $800); 1977 would be $40,800 plus 2 percent or $41,616 ($40,800 × 2% = $816); 1978 would be $41,616 plus 2 percent or $42,448.32 ($41,616 × 2% = $832.32); and so on until the present tax year is reached. In this example, for the year 1988 the value for tax purposes will be $51,744.27. Therefore, the maximum real property tax for 1988-89 tax year will be one percent of $51,744.27 or $517.44 *plus* any amount needed to pay for voter approved bonds, *less* any exemptions, such as the California homeowner's exemption. *Again this applies only if there is no change in ownership since March 1, 1975.*

It must be stressed that the value for tax purposes in this example bears no relationship to the actual current market value of the property. A home worth $40,000 in 1975 may be worth $150,000 or more currently.

Change in Ownership since March 1, 1975

When there is a change in ownership, such as a sale, gift, or inheritance, *the new owner's full cash value for tax purposes shall be the sales price or value of the property as of the date of transfer.* To this figure the assessor is allowed to add the inflation factor of 2 percent per year to arrive at full cash value. A supplemental new tax bill is then mailed to the new owner.

Using the previous example, if a home worth $40,000 in 1975 is sold in 1991 for $150,000, the new owner's full cash value for 1991 will be $150,000, 2 percent of $153,000 (150,000 x 2% = $3,000). Therefore, the maximum real property tax for the 1991-92 tax year will be one percent of $153,000 or $1,530 *plus* any amount needed to pay for voter-approved bonds, *less* any exemptions, such as the California homeowner's exemption.

As you can see, whenever there is a change in ownership, the full cash value for tax purposes is adjusted to the current market value of the property. In many cases this can result in a dramatic increase in real property taxes.

Other Adjustments

On new construction since March 1, 1975, full cash value for tax purposes is the real estate value at the *time of completion* plus the inflation factor of 2 percent per year to the present tax year. If you add additional improvements to your existing home, such as a swimming pool or a new bathroom, does this affect your tax bill? Yes! Does it mean that the entire home is brought up to current market value for tax purposes? No! What happens is that your home keeps its present full cash value as shown on the tax records before your new improvements. Then the new improvements are valued separately as of the date of completion. Each of these figures are adjusted by the 2 percent yearly figure, and the sum of these two figures equals full cash value for tax purposes.

Transfers between spouses, such as changing title from joint tenancy to community property, or a deed of property from one spouse to the other spouse is not considered a transfer for property tax purposes. This means the county assessor *will not* reappraise the property and increase the property tax bill.

REAL PROPERTY TAX YEAR

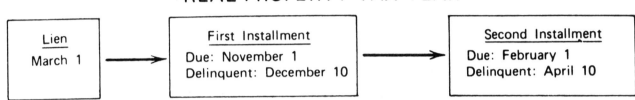

Real Property Tax Dates   Real property taxes cover a fiscal year that begins July 1 and runs through June 30 of the following year. For example, the fiscal tax year for 1988-89 would begin July 1, 1988, and end June 30, 1989.

The real property tax becomes a lien on March 1 preceding the fiscal tax year. Using our previous example, on March 1, 1988, a lien is placed on all taxable real estate for the 1988-89 tax year which begins July 1, 1988.

The real property tax can be paid in two equal installments. The first installment is due November 1 and is delinquent if not paid by 5:00 P.M. December 10. If December 10 falls on a weekend or holiday, the tax is due by 5:00 P.M. the next business day. The second installment is due on February 1, and is delinquent if not paid by 5:00 P.M. April 10. Again if April 10 falls on a weekend or holiday, the tax is due by 5:00 P.M. on the next business day.

If a taxpayer wishes, both installments can be paid when the first installment is due. *A 10 percent penalty is added to each installment that is not paid on time.* If both installments become delinquent, a small additional charge is added to the 10 percent penalty.

Tax Sale   If an owner fails to pay real property taxes when due, the tax collector, during the month of June, publishes a notice of "intent to sell" the property to the State of California because of unpaid taxes. This June "sale" is not a real sale, but rather what is known as a *book sale*. The property owner still owns the real estate, but the owner's name is entered into a delinquent account book and this begins a five-year redemption period.

During this five-year period an owner can redeem the property by paying back taxes, interests, and other penalties and costs. Delinquent taxes can be paid in five annual installments as long as the current taxes are kept current. For example, assume that a taxpayer owes three year's worth of back property taxes. If the owner pays the current year's taxes, the tax collector will allow the owner to pay partial payments on the back taxes, rather than demand full payment of all back taxes.

If after five years the property taxes are still unpaid, the delinquent property is deeded to the state and the former owner loses title. But as long as the state holds title, the former owner still has the right of redemption.

However, the state also has the right to sell tax deeded property to other public agencies or to private parties. Once the state sells the property, the former owner loses the right of redemption.

Public Auction

The sale of tax deeded property is conducted by the county tax collector who must first obtain the permission of the local board of supervisors and the state controller.

The actual sale is a public auction which begins with a minimum bid that varies with each parcel being sold. All tax sales are for cash—the state or county will not finance the sale. The successful bidder receives a *tax deed.* Under current title insurance practices, the holder of tax deeded property can acquire title insurance after a holding period of one year.

Real Property Tax Exemptions

Due to special laws, certain owners of real estate are partially or totally exempt from the payment of property taxes. For example, government-owned real estate such as public buildings, parks, and school sites are exempt from property taxation.

Major Property Tax Exemptions

CALIFORNIA HOMEOWNER'S EXEMPTION

Under current law, an owner-occupied residential dwelling is entitled to a $7,000 (as of 1990) deduction from full appraisal value. For example, if an owner-occupied condo is assigned an $80,000 full cash value by the assessor, from this figure a $7,000 homeowner's exemption is subtracted to obtain a $73,000 taxable value.

$80,000	Full cash value
− 7,000	Less homeowner's exemption
$73,000	Taxable value

Then according to Proposition 13, the actual tax will be 1 percent of taxable value ($730), plus any amount needed to pay for voter-approved bonds. In short, as of 1990, the California Homeowner's Exemption is worth $70 ($7,000 × 1%).

Sometimes the homeowner's exemption is expressed as $1,750 off assessed value. Assessed value is 25 percent of appraised value.

Example

$80,000 appraised value $\times$ 25% = $20,000 Assessed value
$$- 1,750 \text{ Homeowner's exemption}$$
$$\frac{\$18,250}{\$100} = \$182.5$$

$182.5 $\times$ $4 tax rate maximum per Proposition 13 = $730 property tax. Thus, the tax is the same if the appraised or the assessed value technique is used.

To claim the homeowner's exemption, a person must have been the owner and in residence on or before March 1, and must file for the exemption by April 15 with the assessor's office. Once filed, the exemption remains in effect until title is transferred or the exemption is terminated by actions of the owner. If a homeowner should miss the April 15 deadline, he or she can still file by December 1, but will only receive 80 percent ($5,600) of the $7,000 exemption.

VETERAN'S EXEMPTION

A California resident who has served in the military during time of war is entitled to a $4,000 exemption on the full value ($1,000 on assessed value) of property. However, a person may not have both a homeowner's exemption and a veteran's exemption on the same property. Therefore, a veteran who owns only one home is wiser taking the homeowner's exemption of $7,000, instead of the veteran's exemption of only $4,000. But if a veteran owns other real estate in addition to a personal residence, the veteran's exemption may be applied against the other property. *But* current rules prohibit a veteran whose net worth exceeds a designated sum from using the veteran's exemption. The designated net worth is subject to change, so a veteran should contact a veteran's official or tax consultant before applying for the veteran's exemption.

Upon the death of an eligible veteran, the exemption rights are extended to the unmarried surviving spouse or to a pensioned father or mother. *Special rules exist for disabled veterans* because of injuries incurred in military service. In some cases the disabled veteran may not be required to pay any property tax. The California Department of Veterans Affairs should be contacted regarding the special rules for disabled California veterans.

EXEMPTIONS FOR SENIOR CITIZENS

In recent years many laws have been enacted to help senior citizens, many of whom live on fixed incomes. A senior citizen is usually defined as a person 62 years of age or older.

In California there are special laws that may allow a partial or total refund of property taxes for senior citizens. In addition, the California legislature recently passed a law allowing certain senior citizens to defer the payment of property taxes due on their home. The way it works is that the state pays the property taxes due the county and city. Then the state places a lien against the senior citizen's home which accrues interest at 7 percent per annum. The postponed taxes and interest run for an indefinite period. The state can recover on the lien only when the senior citizen sells or no longer occupies the home.

The rules that determine the eligibility of senior citizens for special tax treatment are constantly changing; therefore, senior citizens should contact the local tax assessor or senior citizen's action council for the latest information. See the "Senior Citizen Special Treatment" Page 245 in this chapter as to what impact Proposition 60 and 90 has on property tax savings for senior citizens.

OTHER EXEMPTIONS Property tax exemptions of one sort or another also exist for a variety of other owners of real estate. Timber, growing crops, young orchard trees, grapevines less than three years old, churches, nonprofit organizations all qualify in some way for property tax exemptions. In addition, property tax incentives are used to keep agricultural land from being converted to urban use.

Special Assessments

Special assessments are different from real property taxes. Real property taxes help pay for the general operation of local government, whereas special assessments are levied to pay for a specific improvement such as streets and sewers. Special assessment liens usually are on a parity with property tax liens, and often they are collected at the same time.

A frequently used special assessment law is the Street Improvement Act of 1911. This law is used by cities and counties for street improvements. What usually occurs is local government or a specially formed district hires a contractor to install or improve streets. Each owner along the street is liable for a pro rata share of the cost. The owner can pay in full within 30 days after completion, or the local government can sell bonds to raise the revenue to pay the contractor. If the project goes to bond, the property owners can pay their prorated share in installments over a period of time. The lack of payment of a special assessment can result in a loss in the property owner's title, similar in nature to a tax sale.

Taxing Personal Property

As a general rule, only tangible personal property used in business is subject to taxes. Intangible property, such as shares of stock, loans due, as well as household furnishings and personal effects are not taxed. Personal property taxes are divided into secured and unsecured categories, depending upon whether the owner of the personal property also owns the real estate where the personal property is located. There are many rules that apply to personal property, but they are beyond the scope of this book. Local tax assessors have prepared numerous pamphlets to explain the personal property tax procedures. All business persons are encouraged to obtain these pamphlets.

Courthouse

PERSONS AND AGENCIES INVOLVED IN PROPERTY TAXES

Board of supervisors. Establish county budgets and set county property tax rates up to the maximum allowed by law.

City council members. Establish city budgets and set city property tax rates up to the maximum allowed by law.

City or county auditor. Maintains the tax rolls.

City or county assessor. Appraises property for tax purposes.

City or county tax collector. Responsible for actually collecting the taxes.

Local board of equalization. Composed of the members of the board of supervisors, which hears appeals from citizens who feel they have been taxed unfairly. In some areas this function is handled by an assessment appeals board which consists of citizens appointed by the board of supervisors.

State board of equalization. A state agency that audits and offers guidance to local taxing agencies.

13.2 INCOME TAXES

Income taxes are levied by both the federal government and the State of California. The income tax is a progressive tax. The federal and state rates increase as income levels being taxed increase.

The buying and selling of real estate has significant income tax consequences. Many times the income tax aspects are more important than the price of the property. Income tax aspects of a real estate transaction should be considered *before* the sale, not after. Once a sale takes place, it is too late to go back and restructure the sale to take advantage of any tax laws that were overlooked.

Income tax laws are complicated and constantly changing. Before entering into a complicated real estate transaction, a person should seek the advice of an income tax specialist, such as an attorney or accountant.

REAL ESTATE ASPECTS OF THE TAX REFORM ACT 1986 AND TAX REVENUE ACT 1987

This is a summary of the major changes that affect real estate.

New Rules for Homeowners

1. Beginning January 1,1988, mortgage interest deductions will be allowed for acquisition debt (purchase money loans) to a maximum of $1 million on all combined mortgages on a first and second residence. No deductions are allowed for three or more homes. This affects all home buyers who acquired their home after October 13, 1987. Existing loan balances on homes as of 10/13/87 are considered acquisition debt and are fully deductible with no $1 million limit.
2. For future refinances, the remaining loan balance on acquisitions loan(s) plus $100,000 will be the maximum interest deduction allowed as qualified residence loans.
3. The 60% exclusion as a capital gain has been abolished. Gain from the sale of a home will be reported as though it were ordinary income.
4. The 24-month-trade-up rule and the 55-year-old-once-in-a-lifetime exemption noted on page 251 are still valid.
5. Installment sale treatment is still allowed for homeowners.

New Rules for Income Property Owners

1. Depreciation on buildings and improvements will be 27 1/2 years for residential rental and 31 1/2 years for non-residential rental, all straight line.
2. The 60% exclusion as a capital gain has been abolished. Gain from the sale of income property will be reported as though it were ordinary income.
3. Rental property mortgage interest is fully deductible with no dollar limits such as the $1 million cap placed on certain homeowners. However, any paper tax loss created by interest and depreciation deductions will fall under the new passive tax loss rules.
4. All real estate rental activity will be considered "passive" . . . either passive income or passive loss, depending upon the property's cashflow. The general rule is that a passive real estate loss can only be used to offset other passive income NOT active or portfolio income such as salaries, commissions, profits, interest and dividends. Prior to this new tax law, real estate losses could be used to offset this type of active or portfolio income.
5. Special $25,000 exceptions if a person meets the following test:
    a. Be an individual owner of 10% or more interest in rental real estate.
    b. Be actively involved in the management (can use property managers but you must make the key decisions).
    c. Have an adjusted gross income of $100,000 or less.
    If the owner of rental real estate meets this test, he/she can use up to $25,000 in passive losses from real estate to offset active or portfolio income, such as salaries and interest, after first offsetting passive income.
6. If the rental property owner's adjusted gross income exceeds $100,000, then the $25,000 amount is reduced $1 for every $2 above the $100,000. At all times, the unused passive losses from rental real estate can be carried forward to reduce future passive income and gain upon sale of the property. The new passive loss rules do not eliminate the investor's right to use real estate losses. However, the new law in some cases will delay the right to use the loss until a later date, such as the date of resale. In addition, there are special phase in rules that will allow rental property owners who purchased before October 23, 1986 to continue to use some of the excess passive losses right away.
7. The right for a real estate investor to do a 1031 tax-deferred exchange remains the same; the new law did not affect this technique.
8. Installment sales treatment for real estate investors is still allowed as long as the seller does not carry more than $5 million in notes in any one year. Installment sale treatment for real estate dealers has been abolished.

There are many other new tax law changes, but these are the items that had a major impact on real estate. The above is listed for information purposes and should not be considered tax advice. For tax advice a person should seek competent tax advisors.

Major Income Tax Advantages for Homeowners

Income tax laws favor homeowners over renters by granting various income tax incentives for becoming a homeowner.

1. Interest paid on real estate loans is deductible against personal income to reduce tax liability, subject to the interest limitation noted on page 250.

2. Property taxes paid are also deductible against personal income.

3. No immediate taxable gain is recognized if a homeowner sells and purchases another residence within 24 months before or after the sale of the old residence, if the purchase price of the new residence is equal to or greater than the adjusted sales price of the old residence.

This last incentive only applies to owner-occupied residential property, *not* to investment property. A homeowner need not put all the profits from the sale of the old residence into the purchase of the new residence. The only factor is sales price versus purchase price. For example, a homeowner might sell his or her residence for $95,000 making a $50,000 profit. If the homeowner, within 24 months, purchases another residence for $100,000 using a no downpayment VA guaranteed loan, the $50,000 profit from the sale of the old residence will be tax deferred. *Note the phrase tax deferred!* Technically, the tax is only deferred, not eliminated. Under certain circumstances, the tax may be required if a person later sells and does not purchase another residence but instead rents.

If a homeowner trades down—that is, purchases another home that is less expensive than the former residence—gains from the sale of the former home are partially taxable using formula guidelines outlined by the Internal Revenue Service.

4. Income tax laws allow homeowners 55 years or older, who choose to sell their home, to be exempt from taxes on the gain or profit up to a $125,000 maximum. This option can be used only once, and if the gain is less than $125,000, the unused portion *cannot* be used later. If the homeowner is married, the once in a lifetime rule applies to both the husband and wife. Even if death or divorce results in a new marriage, the exemption, once used, cannot be used again by either spouse. To obtain this exemption there are special rules regarding length of ownership and occupancy, and these rules may change in the future.

5. Although not an advantage because it involves death, it should be noted that when a person dies and leaves real estate, the heirs acquire the property at fair market value at the date of death. Gain upon immediate resale by the heirs at fair market value would not trigger an income tax.

Major Income Advantages for Investment Property Owners

1. Interest on real estate loans and property taxes paid is deductible against the income earned by the property.

2. Repairs, maintenance, management, insurance, and other operating expenses are also deductible. Note: Repairs, maintenance, and other operating expenses *are not* deductible for homeowners on their own residences, only on investment real estate.

3. Depreciation deduction allowances can be used to shelter income. The depreciation deduction consists of a yearly allowance for wear, tear, and obsolescence which will permit the property owner to recover the original cost over the useful life of the property. Land is not depreciable, only the improvements such as buildings, fences, and so on. Depreciation cannot be taken on owner-occupied residential homes; it can only be taken on income real estate. Depreciation deductions reduce the taxable income, thereby giving the property owner more after-tax cashflow. However, recent tax law changes place restrictions on how real estate losses can be used to shelter other income (see page 250).

4. Under certain circumstances, an investment property owner can enter into a tax-deferred exchange. If properly structured, an investor can exchange one like property for another without paying immediate income taxes on any gain realized. The tax liability is not eliminated, but rather postponed until the investor disposes of the property in a taxable transaction—usually a sale. Some people incorrectly call this a "tax free" exchange, but technically it is only a tax-deferred exchange. To structure an Internal Revenue Code Section 1031 tax deferred exchange, an investor must not receive "boot". Boot is defined as unlike property receive in an exchange. Only like kind real estate qualifies as a tax deferred exchange. Examples of boot include: cash, notes, personal property and so on. There are technical rules regarding a tax-deferred exchange, and no one should proceed without the advice of tax counsel.

5. An installment sale is another way to reduce tax liability upon the sale of real estate. This method of selling allows the seller to spread the gain from the sale over a period of years. Rather than paying the entire tax in the year of sale, the investor pays income taxes only on that portion of the gain received in any one year. Recent tax law changes have reduced the attractiveness of installment sales. Once again it must be stressed that advice of tax counsel should be sought to make sure the sale qualifies as an installment sale.

State Income Tax   In some ways, California income tax law is patterned after the federal income tax laws. However, there are some notable differences in the area of computing gain upon resale and computing depreciation. Also the range of tax brackets for individuals and corporations is different from the federal law. There are special rules regarding new residents and their need to file a California income tax statement. All of these tax laws, plus many others, are administered by the California franchise tax board.

For most real estate transactions, the impact of federal income taxes is more important than the impact of state income taxes. But careful tax planning should attempt to capitalize on both federal and state laws.

13.3 OTHER TAXES

Documentary Transfer Tax   Upon the transfer of real estate, a documentary transfer tax of $.55 per $500 of consideration or fraction thereof ($1.10 per $1,000) is levied. If the property being transferred is in an unincorporated area, all of the tax goes to the county where the property is located. If the property is located in an incorporated city, the city and county divide the tax proceeds.

The tax is levied on the full price of the property if there is an all cash sale or if the buyer obtains a new loan which cashes the seller out. If the buyer assumes the seller's existing loan, the transfer tax is levied only on the equity being transferred. See Chapter 6, Real Estate Mathematics, for detailed examples of the documentary transfer tax.

Estate and Inheritance Tax   Both the federal government and the State of California have attempted to tax the estate of deceased persons. The federal government calls its tax an *estate tax*. The state calls its tax an *inheritance tax*. Recent laws have greatly reduced estate taxes on both the state and federal level. The trend is toward a phasing out of taxes levied on the estate of a deceased person.

There are several ways to reduce, or in some cases, avoid the payment of estate and inheritance taxes. However, the methods are technical and complicated and frequently require the use of *inter vivos* or testamentary trusts. For a good discussion of basic concepts a pamphlet entitled "A Guide to Federal Estate and Gift Taxation" (publication No. 448) can be obtained by writing the Superintendent of Documents, U.S. Government Printing Office, Washington, D.C. 20402 (price $.25).

Gift Taxes   Both the federal government and the State of California have tax laws that apply to gifts of real and personal property. A *gift* is a voluntary transfer of property from the owner called the *donor* to the receiver called the *donee.* The transfer must be free of charge or at least less than full consideration to be classified as a gift.

Both federal and state law allow a tax free gift of $10,000 of value per donee per year. The use of gift tax exclusions during the life of the donor can often be used to save estate and inheritance taxes upon death. Gift tax laws are complicated, and professional tax advice should be sought when planning an estate to minimize taxes by use of gifts.

Miscellaneous Taxes   Sales and use taxes occasionally arise in certain broker transactions—for example, the sale of a business opportunity, or a mobile home. In circumstances where sales tax is involved, it is the responsibility of the real estate agent to see that escrow instructions are correctly drafted to account for the tax liability.

Unemployment insurance fees, workperson's compensation fees, and Social Security taxes may need to be collected when a real estate salesperson is hired by a broker and acts as an employee, instead of an independent contractor.

SUMMARY   Property taxes are levied on an ad valorem basis. Two classifications of property taxes are: (1) real property taxes and (2) personal property taxes. With passage of the Jarvis-Gann Initiative (Proposition 13) the maximum real property tax allowed is 1 percent of full cash value, plus 2 percent annual inflationary factor, plus an additional sum to pay for voter approved bonds that affect the property.

If there has been no change in ownership since March 1, 1975, the tax year 1975–1976 is the base year for computing full cash value. A change in ownership after March 1, 1975, will cause the full cash value for tax purposes to be increased to the sales price, or value of, as of the date of transfer. There are special rules for the handling of remodeling and additions that will cause the taxable value to rise.

Real property taxes are paid over a fiscal year beginning July 1 and ending June 30. The first installment is due November 1 and delinquent if not paid by December 10. The second installment is due February 1 and delinquent if not paid by April 10. Real property taxes become a lien March 1 preceding the fiscal tax year. If the required taxes are not paid, the owner's title will eventually revert to the State of California for delinquent taxes.

Real property tax exemptions include $7,000 on appraised value for homeowners ($1,750 on assessed value), $4,000 for qualified veterans ($1,000 on assessed value), and special exemptions for senior citizens. There are several other property tax exemptions for certain classes of property such as timber, growing crops, and so on.

Income taxes are levied by both federal and state government. Income taxes are progressive—that is, the tax rate increases as income levels increase. The buying and selling of real estate has significant income tax consequences. Many times the income tax aspects are more important than price. Income tax laws are complicated and constantly changing. Before entering into a real estate transaction, a person should seek the advice of a tax expert.

Other taxes that have an impact on real estate are estate and inheritance taxes, gift taxes, transfer taxes, and use and sales taxes.

Important Terms and Concepts

Ad valorem

California homeowner's exemption

Depreciation deduction

Estate and inheritance taxes

Fiscal property tax year

Installment sale

Proposition 13

Senior citizen exemption

Special assessments

Tax-deferred exchange

Tax sale

1. Under Proposition 13, the maximum real property tax cannot exceed what percent of full cash value, after adjustments for inflation and voter approved bonds?
   (a) 1 percent
   (b) 2 percent
   (c) 5 percent
   (d) 10 percent

2. Real property taxes become a lien on:
   (a) February 1
   (b) March 1
   (c) December 1
   (d) November 1

3. Real property is deeded to the state if property taxes are delinquent for:
   (a) One year
   (b) Three years
   (c) Five years
   (d) Seven years

4. If full cash value of a home is $90,000, what will be the taxable value after a subtraction for a homeowner's exemption?
   (a) $80,000
   (b) $90,000
   (c) $86,000
   (d) $83,000

5. The second installment of real property taxes are due:
   (a) November 1
   (b) December 10
   (c) February 1
   (d) April 10

6. Which of the following is incorrect?
   (a) To obtain the full homeowner's exemption, a person must file by April 15.
   (b) The California veterans exemption is $4,000.
   (c) Property taxes are collected by the assessor.
   (d) Special assessments are liens on real property.

7. A homeowner can defer the taxable gains from the sale of a home by purchasing another existing residence of equal or greater adjusted sales price within:
   (a) 12 months
   (b) 15 months
   (c) 24 months
   (d) 30 months

8. The 55 year old once in a lifetime exemption is:
   (a) $50,000
   (b) $75,000
   (c) $100,000
   (d) $125,000

9. Income real estate is entitled to use:
   (a) Tax-deferred exchanges
   (b) Installment sale provisions
   (c) Depreciation deductions on improvements
   (d) All of the above

10. The passive loss rules apply to:
    (a) principal residence
    (b) vacant land
    (c) rental real estate
    (d) personal automobiles

Chapter 14
Single-Family Homes and Mobile Homes

Preview

In this chapter you will explore the characteristics of a house, including construction details, roof styles, and architectural designs. Mobile homes, condominiums, and vacation or second homes, will also be presented. At the conclusion of this chapter, you will be able to:

1. *Identify some construction terms associated with home building.*

2. *Differentiate among various architectural styles.*

3. *List the advantages and disadvantages of buying or renting a home.*

4. *Discuss the advantages and disadvantages of owning a mobile home, condominium, or vacation home.*

14.1 HOME CONSTRUCTION STYLES

There are many varieties of home construction styles, but the three most common types are the one-story, split level, and two-story homes.

Obviously the *one-story* home is the most simple to build and the easiest to maintain, but it occupies more land per square foot of living space than the others.

The *split-level* home is popular in California because of the better utilization of land of varying topography as well as the pleasing cosmetic effect. However, it is usually more expensive to build.

The *two-story* home has a lower cost per square foot because a single foundation and roof supports two floors of living area. But the principal disadvantage is the stairs to climb to reach the second floor. Also, the difficulty of reaching exterior portions for repair and maintenance presents some problems.

Roof Styles   There are numerous roof styles, but the major ones are as follows:

The *gable* roof is a pitched roof with sloping two sides—the sides meeting at the top.

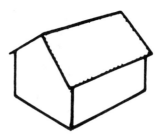

A *gambrel* roof has a steeper lower slope with a flatter upper slope above—usually found on barns. This is also called a Dutch barn roof.

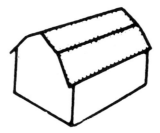

A *hip* roof is a pitched roof with sloping sides and ends—all sides slope to the eaves.

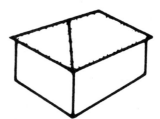

A *mansard* roof is a French style with sloping lower part on all sides, flat on top.

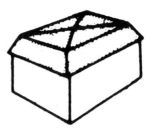

Architectural Styles
It would be an impossible task to become familiar with all architectural designs. However, a description of the most common are:

A *colonial* style is usually referred to as early American. Usually it is two stories, gable roof style, and has shutters on the windows.

Colonial

The *California cape cod* style has a high pitched roof, large chimney, wood siding and shutters, and is usually two stories high.

California Cape Cod

Source: From *Reference Book,* California Department of Real Estate.

Monterey (Spanish) style is a large two-story building, white stucco, red tile roof, with the second-story balcony having decorative iron railings.

Monterey

Modern or *contemporary* style is one story, ultra modern, with plenty of glass, and open walls.

Modern or Contemporary

California bungalow or *ranch* style is a one-story structure, with a low pitch roof and sliding-glass windows and a ground hugging (sprawling) floor plan.

California Bungalow/Ranch

Source: California Department of Real Estate.

CONSTRUCTION DETAILS

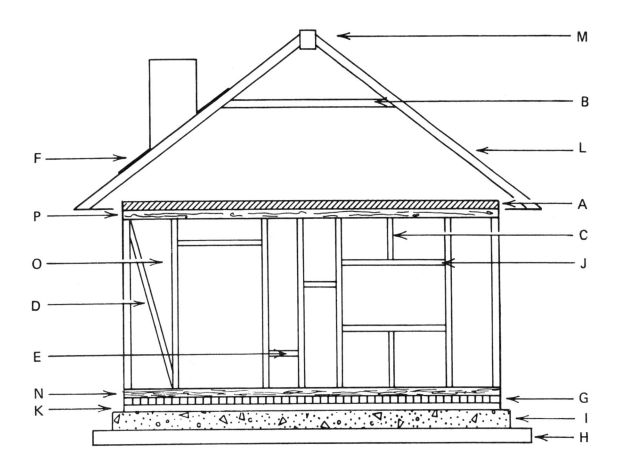

A CEILING JOIST. Horizontal beams supporting ceiling
B COLLAR BEAM. A beam that connects opposite rafters above the floor
C CRIPPLES. Short vertical piece 2 x 4 above or below an opening
D DIAGONAL BRACE. A brace across corner of structure to prevent swaying
E FIRE STOP. Short board or wall between studs to prevent fire spreading
F FLASHING. Metal sheet usually aroung chimeny to prevent water seapage
G FLOOR JOIST. Horizontal beams supporting floor
H FOOTING. Base or bottom of a foundation wall
I FOUNDATION. The supporting portion of structure resting on footing
J LINTEL. A horizontal board over a door or window also called header
K MUDSILL. Perimer meter board anchored directly to foundation
L RAFTERS. Boards designed to support roof loads
M RIDGE BOARD. Highest board in the house supporting upper ends
N SOLE PLATE. Usually 2 x 4 on which wall and studs rest
O STUDS. Vertical boards 2 x 4 suporting the walls every 16'' (on center)
P TOP PLATE. A horizontal board fastened to upper end of studs
Other Construction Terms
R — VALUE = ranking of insulation materials
EER   = Energy Efficiency Rating

Figure 14-1

14.2 MOBILE HOMES

Since building codes, zoning laws, and other practices as well as inflation make it difficult to build low-cost conventional houses, many families have turned to mobile homes as a solution.

A mobile home is defined by the California health and safety code as "a vehicle designed and equipped to contain not more than two dwelling units, to be used without permanent foundation."

To give some idea of the importance of this type of property, mobile homes accounted for about 80 percent of all new homes under $30,000 produced in the United States during the last several years.

Mobile homes in the past were confused with trailers. The major difference is that trailers usually provide temporary housing only, while a mobile home is a permanent living unit. The word "mobile" may be confusing; actually, studies show that once in place, mobile homes are seldom moved. They are usually located in mobile home parks, although in many rural areas they can be found on individual lots.

The Mobile Home Parks Act defines a mobile home park as "any area or tract of land where one or more mobile home lots are rented or leased." The rental operation of a mobile home park is within the jurisdiction of the State Department of Housing and Community Development. If a mobile home park has five or more lots for sale or lease, it is considered a subdivision and consequently subject to subdivision laws.

Under certain circumstances, mobile homes purchased after July 1, 1980 can be taxed as real property if they are attached to a permanent foundation.

Types of Mobile Homes

The four basic types of mobile homes are illustrated below.

Single, 8 foot and 10 foot wide units.

Single, 12 foot wide units.

Multiple wide, double wide, or triple wide units.

Quads—four units together.

Legal Requirements Related to Mobile Homes

In order to list or sell a mobile home, a real estate licensee must comply with special aspects of the real estate law.

1. *New mobile homes cannot be sold by real estate licensees*, but only through mobile home dealers licensed by the Department of Motor Vehicles.

2. *A real estate licensee can sell used mobile homes* provided they have been licensed for at least one year and are at least 8 feet wide and 32 feet long.

3. The mobile home must be capable of being transported over a road. The hitch must be attached to the unit or stored underneath, and the axles must still be attached to the frame.

4. The licensee is responsible for the proper completion and delivery of the title to the buyer.

5. Notification of transfer of ownership must be made within five days of the date of the sale.

6. All fees must be paid to the Department of Motor Vehicles within 20 days of the sale date.

7. No concealment of a material fact or any other fraudulent act may be committed.

8. The buyer must be assured that the purchased mobile home may occupy a private lot for at least one year.

9. If the mobile home was manufactured after June 15, 1976, it must have a Department of Housing and Urban Development (HUD) tag, guaranteeing its proper construction.

Violations of Business and Professions Code

Under this code, real estate licensees may have their licenses suspended or revoked if they are found guilty of any of the following:

1. Failure to provide for delivery of proper certificate of ownership of the mobile home.

2. Have knowingly participated in the purchase or sale of a stolen mobile home.

3. Submitted a check, draft, or money order to the Department of Motor Vehicles for payment of fees and the draft is dishonored upon presentation to the bank.

Financing Mobile Homes

Because mobile homes are considered to be personal property, the method of encumbering the ownership is through the certificate of ownership (pink slip).

Mobile homes can be financed through FHA, VA, and Cal-Vet loans. In addition, loans are obtainable from banks, savings and loan associations, and other real estate lenders. Most mobile home loans are amortized over a 15 to 20 year period. Interest rates on mobile home loans are usually higher than on conventional home loans.

Termination of Tenancy in a Mobile Home Park

The Civil Code provides for the termination of tenancy by the landlord of a mobile home park tenant, when any of these occur:

1. Failure of the tenant to comply with local ordinances and state laws and regulations related to mobile homes.

2. Conduct of the tenant upon park premises which constitutes a substantial annoyance to other tenants.

3. Failure of the tenant to comply with reasonable rules and regulations of the mobile home park.

4. The nonpayment of rent, utility charges, or incidental service charges.

5. Failure to maintain the mobile home in a state of repair acceptable to park management.

6. If single-width units are over 17 years of age, when they are sold, the park owner can request they be removed from the park.

7. If double-width units are over 20 years of age and sold, the park owner can ask that the home be removed from the park. However, for all mobile homes manufactured after September, 1971, a park owner cannot ask that the tenant remove the home for age, until the mobile home is 25 years old.

Advantages in Mobile Home Ownership

1. The price of traditional homes has risen so rapidly that low-income families, young adults, and senior citizens are purchasing mobile homes because of their lower prices as compared to conventional homes.

2. Mobile home parks are relatively quiet places to live.

3. There is a definite feeling of security, because there is usually only one entrance or exit and most residents know who lives in the mobile home park.

4. Mobile homes are transportable.

5. Existing mobile homes are taxed as personal property; therefore, taxes are usually lower. New mobile homes are taxed as real property.

6. Better financing terms are now available for mobile home purchasers. VA, FHA, and Cal-Vet financing are available.

7. Minimal yard maintenance or none at all.

Disadvantages to Mobile Home Ownership

1. Mobile homes can depreciate rapidly.

2. Mobile homes have a lower resale value than conventional houses.

3. Financing is considered to be a distinct disadvantage. The terms of loans offered by banks and savings and loan associations are not as favorable as conventional homes.

4. When your mobile home is located in a mobile home park, you may be required to buy extras, such as steps with handrails or skirting to conceal wheels.

5. Many cities and counties have severe restrictions regarding the placement of mobile homes; therefore, sites are often difficult to obtain.

Purchasing a Mobile Home

If you are ready to purchase a mobile home, here are a few instructions and bits of information:

1. The site should be well drained and free from excessive slopes, rocky ground, swampy, or marshy areas.

2. Try to avoid a park in close proximity to a noisy industrial area.

3. The best parks group their homes around open spaces that contain recreational facilities or stagger the homes so that windows and doors do not face each other.

4. Over 400 firms produce mobile homes, and there are many styles to choose from—make sure you choose the right one.

14.3 CONDOMINIUMS

A *condominium* is a system of individual fee ownership of units in a multifamily structure, combined with joint ownership of common areas of the structure and the land.

Advantages in Condominium Ownership

1. You can sell your own unit as you would a residential home.

2. Insurance companies offer special packages for condominium owners.

3. Combines the benefits of owning a house with the advantages of apartment living.

4. Receive the same tax benefits as a home owner.

5. You build an equity with each payment as you do in a home.

6. There is little or no yardwork to perform.

7. Common areas included in your ownership can include game rooms, swimming pools, tennis courts, and putting greens.

8. The law offers some protection to the owner, in that he or she cannot be made to leave because of infractions of by-laws and regulations of the governing association.

Disadvantages in Condominium Ownership

1. You are responsible for all building maintenance problems in your unit.

2. You are required to pay your share of the fee to cover maintenance costs in common areas.

3. Sometimes the developer controls parking and recreation areas, the use for which he or she may charge.

4. You will find yourself living rather compactly in close proximity to neighbors. Noises emanating from swimming pool and game areas may prove distracting.

Cautions in Buying a Condominium

If you decide to purchase a condominium, first check on these items:

1. Check on the reputation of the builder.

2. Know and understand what you are doing and what your responsibilities as an owner are.

3. Read all legal documents carefully (consult an attorney if necessary).

4. Make sure management fees cover all contingencies.

5. Ask yourself these specific questions:
   a. Is exterior and/or interior maintenance included in the established fees?
   b. Are there any restrictions on the sale or lease?
   c. Are there any warranties on equipment? If so, for how long?
   d. Does the developer have reserve funds in case of an emergency?
   e. Are you required to pay maintenance costs for unsold units?

14.4 VACATION HOMES

It is estimated that over two million people own second homes, and the projection is that increasing amounts of money will be spent on second homes.

Second homes can include: (1) a cabin in the mountains, (2) a cottage by the lake, (3) a house near the beach, (4) a chalet near a skiing slope, (5) a hunting shack in the wilderness, and (6) investment property.

Where You Buy Is Important

You should ask yourself these questions before you make your final decision regarding ownership of a second home:

1. Can I tolerate close neighbors, or do I want complete privacy?

2. Do I want a place close to conveniences or one that is "out of sight and sound?"

3. Depending upon the area chosen, can I afford it? If not, can I interest someone in a joint venture?

A Second Home as an Investment

There are usually four internal factors that influence investments. They are: risk, liquidity, management, and increment.

Risk is the chance that you take that you may lose all or part of your initial investment. The risk involved in a second home as an investment will vary, depending upon the quality and the market conditions at the time of purchase. Generally speaking, if you purchase carefully, your property may appreciate 10 percent or more per year.

Liquidity is being able to convert your investment to cash. Real estate is not as liquid as other investments. However, if the home is priced right, it can be sold in a reasonable length of time.

Management is a must in all investments. On smaller real estate investments such as a second home, you may choose to manage the property yourself and take advantage of any possible tax writeoffs.

Increment is the hope of selling your investment later for more than you paid for it. Real estate as an investment has statistically tended to increase significantly in value over the years.

However, recent tax changes do not make the second home as attractive for investment purposes as in past years. Check with an accountant or tax attorney before buying a second home as an investment.

14.5 SHOULD YOU BUY OR RENT?

The question of whether to buy or to rent is best studied by examining the pros and cons as they relate to buying or renting. Keep in mind that the advantages in renting will closely parallel the disadvantages of buying, and the disadvantages in renting will closely relate to the advantages of buying.

Advantages of Renting and Disadvantages of Buying

1. Only a comparatively *small initial outlay* of money is required to rent, while in purchasing, you are required to pay a sizable downpayment as well as closing costs and possible prorations.

2. The *risk is less* in renting since your initial outlay is limited. You don't stand to lose much even if you decide to move earlier than you had planned. While in purchasing, whenever you invest money there is a greater risk that you might lose some or all of it if property values decline.

3. In renting, in the short run your *costs are fixed.* You know pretty well how much your rent will be each month, so you can usually budget accordingly. In buying, the mortgage payment may remain constant, but property taxes and above all maintenance costs will increase as the property ages.

4. In renting, if the neighborhood should decline, you can move without suffering a personal loss because of a decline in real estate values.

5. Instead of involving your money in property where it is fairly rigid, while renting you can take that same money and deposit it in the bank, giving your money greater liquidity. When you purchase property, your money is usually tied up, even though you may be able to borrow on your equity.

6. Suppose you have to move. If you're on a month-to-month tenancy, you only need to give a 30-day notice, which gives you greater *mobility*. To a degree, you're less mobile when you purchase a home, because it usually takes a while to sell a home.

7. When you rent, you don't have the same *responsibility* for maintenance as you do when you own your own property. If you are renting, you can take a vacation trip without worrying about the maintenance and upkeep of the property. If the property is yours, the responsibility is yours.

Advantages of Buying and Disadvantages of Renting

1. If you buy a home, it is an investment for the future. Well located properties usually increase in value. If recent experience is any guide, the house that costs $150,000 now could be worth more than $200,000 in the next few years. When you rent, you have only rent receipts to show for your investment at the end of each month.

2. As a homeowner, you may deduct your property taxes and interest payments on the income tax statement.

3. As a buyer many costs are fixed. It is true your maintenance costs fluctuate, but good repairs last for a long time and may increase the value of your investment. On a month-to-month tenancy, can you reasonably expect your rent to remain the same? Not really; it is subject to too many variables, for example property taxes and spiraling maintenance costs.

4. You will feel secure and permanent in your own home. You will cement that security by becoming involved in community affairs, putter around the yard, and make minor repairs. On the other hand, it is difficult to establish permanence in a rented home. At the whim of the landlord you may be asked to leave.

5. A home is usually larger than an apartment, allowing plenty of room for activities. Few apartments provide the same freedom of movement as a home. In addition, you can build on to your home if you need more space.

6. Pride of ownership. The pride of being an owner often exceeds the pride of being a tenant.

7. There are few restrictions placed on you in your own home. You can have pets if you wish. You can have children if you wish. You can even play the stereo after 10:00 P.M if you wish.

8. Homeowners are frequently viewed as better credit risks than renters.

These items are just a few of the restrictions that might accompany the rental of an apartment.

Most Costs Have Increased—Buy Now! In recent years, studies show that the typical family income has increased less than the price of homes.

Thus, most experts have urged people to buy their homes now, rather than wait for prices or interest rates to drop.

SUMMARY This chapter discussed the characteristics of one-story, two-story, and split-level homes. The chapter presented various architectural designs and types of roof styles. The principles of mobile home, condominium, and vacation home ownership were discussed.

The chapter ended with an explanation of the pros and cons of buying versus renting property.

Important Terms and Concepts

Condominiums	Mobile home
Double-wide mobile homes	Single story
Gable roof	Single-wide mobile homes
Hip roof	Split-level home
Mansard roof	Two-story home

REVIEWING YOUR UNDERSTANDING

1. The ownership of a mobile home is transferred by means of a:
   (a) Deed
   (b) Certificate of ownership
   (c) Bill of sale
   (d) Sales agreement

2. All fees relating to licensing or transferring of title to mobile homes must be paid to the:
   (a) Department of Motor Vehicles
   (b) Mobile home owners' association
   (c) Department of real estate
   (d) Division of mobile homes

3. Which of the following is considered an advantage for buying a home?
   (a) Security or permanence
   (b) Future investment
   (c) Privacy
   (d) All of the above

4. An advantage to renting that means you can move quickly without inconvenience is known as:
   (a) Liquidity
   (b) Convenience
   (c) Mobility
   (d) Permanence

5. There are numerous roof styles. Which of the following fits this description: "a pitched roof with sloping two sides—the sides meeting at the top."
   (a) Gambrel
   (b) Hip
   (c) Mansard
   (d) None of the above

6. What style of house fits this description: "A large two-story building with red tile roof and decorative iron railings?"
   (a) Modern or contemporary
   (b) California bungalow
   (c) Monterey (Spanish)
   (d) Colonial

7. A real estate license can sell used mobile homes if the mobile home has been registered for:
   (a) 12 months
   (b) 9 months
   (c) 6 months
   (d) 3 months

8. The foundation of a standard built home sits upon the:
   (a) mudsill
   (b) collar beam
   (c) footing
   (d) stud

9. Recent changes in the income tax law have made the ownership of a vacation home:
    (a) more advantageous
    (b) less advantageous

10. The advantage of owning over renting a home includes:
    (a) equity appreciation
    (b) income tax deductions
    (c) hedge against inflation
    (d) all of the above

Chapter 15
A Career in Real Estate

Preview   A career in real estate can be an exciting opportunity for certain people. The various types of job opportunities within the real estate industry may offer a greater potential for movement and advancement than many other areas of employment. The real estate business is a people-oriented industry. Real estate professionals help or assist clients to achieve their financial and investment goals. Thus a career in real estate can lead to a wide range of employment activities from the entry level of sales agent to the sophisticated role of the real estate counselor. However, there are pitfalls to consider! Not everyone can succeed in real estate. It is definitely not to be viewed as a get-rich-quick industry. Success takes dedication and hard work. When you have finished this chapter, you will be able to:

1. *Describe all aspects of the real estate industry, both private and public.*

2. *Examine the potential for a successful career in real estate.*

3. *Compare the pros and cons of various career opportunities within the total range of the real estate industry.*

In addition, in Appendix A of this chapter you will find suggested guidelines for an interview with a real estate broker when you are seeking a sales position. Appendix B duplicates the Code of Ethics issued by the California Real Estate Commissioner which must be adhered to by all real estate licensees in California.

4. *List the requirements to obtain a California real estate license.*

15.1 STRUCTURE OF THE REAL ESTATE INDUSTRY

Anyone interested in a real estate career must recognize from the outset that the real estate field encompasses more than acting as an agent for the buying and selling of properties. The real estate field includes construction, financing, escrow, appraising, management, land development, and other related occupational specializations. Each of these areas offers opportunities for well-trained, qualified specialists who earn educational credentials and designations and who may wish to work with any one defined area of the industry or may interweave several specializations.

Real Estate Agents

The potential as a real estate sales agent is unlimited. A variety of opportunities exist as a result of the growth in America's population and the continued expansion of our nation's economy. As a consequence, real estate agents are needed to assist home buyers, to direct those seeking new business opportunities, and to assist those who wish to expand land and subdivision developments.

A real estate salesperson's license qualifies one to work for a real estate broker as a selling agent. But as newcomers enter the industry, they soon realize that more specialized and advanced training is not only advantageous but also is usually required to perform at a professional level. A new licensee may be considered an expert in the eyes of the public and the law, but most newcomers soon realize that additional training and education are necessary in order to live up to the public's expectations. Although a number of the real estate firms which employ large sales staffs do offer some form of training, the majority of these educational sessions are geared toward sales techniques.

As a salesperson develops and becomes more involved with specialized training and educational course work, it is possible for that individual to become a real estate broker. Brokers are allowed to own and operate their own business, while a real estate salesperson cannot own nor solely operate a real estate firm. Within the range of real estate brokerage, there are the recognized *sales specializations* in the areas of residential, commercial, industrial, farm, and land brokerage. For those brokers interested in the *developmental aspects* of real estate, opportunities exist in land development, urban planning, as well as the promotion of real estate securities and syndication. Some real estate brokers may wish to become consultants and work on a professional fee basis rather than get a commission, and for these individuals a *real estate counselor* designation is available. Personal interests may be followed in a wide and varying direction. These opportunities might include the additional opportunities to earn the *professional designations* available in the areas of property management, syndication, investment, and land development (see Figure 15-1).

Although the field of real estate is complex, there are boundless opportunities for personal satisfaction as well as the potential for above-average income. One who prepares for entry into the real estate field must remember that the combinations of experience and education, coupled with integrity and resourcefulness, create the professional image that the public wishes to see in real estate agents.

However, there are pitfalls! Real estate is a competitive business, and the failure and turnover rate are very high. Later in this chapter the reasons for failure will be discussed in detail.

Real Estate Trade Associations

People who select real estate as an occupation quickly become aware of the established real estate trade associations. The largest is the

National Association of Realtors (NAR) which is identified by the symbol ⌐R⌐. The National Association of Realtors has two recognized agency designations, the realtor and the realtor-associate. A *realtor* is a broker member, while the *realtor-associate* is usually a salesperson who is affiliated with a realtor.

NAR's organizational network extends to affiliated state associations each of which controls a respective roster of memberships. In California, NAR's State Association is the California Association of Realtors (CAR).

The objects and purposes of the California Association of Realtors (CAR) are set forth in its constitution:

1. To unite its members.

2. To promote high standards.

3. To safeguard the land-buying public.

4. To foster legislation for the benefit and protection of real estate.

5. To cooperate in the economic growth and development of the state.

The national association unites and unifies the organized real estate interests of the nation and presents a common cause and program in behalf of national legislation affecting real property.

The California Association of Realtors is an organization composed of the members of local real estate boards throughout the state. When no board exists in the community, brokers and salespersons who wish to belong to CAR may join an adjacent board or the association directly as an individual member.

At the local level there is the structured network of individual real estate boards located within counties and cities. The California Association of Realtors has nearly 200 boards of realtors. The main thrust of trade associations is to promote information and education for their members. This is accomplished by various means, such as seminars, state-national-international conferences, textbooks, films and cassettes, and training sessions. Another advantage of association membership is the substantial savings on insurance and other health benefits by virtue of group rates.

Another national real estate organization is the National Association of Real Estate Brokers. This trade association was formed in 1947 and consists of predominantly black real estate brokers whose members are called "Realtist." The organization has local boards in the principal cities of 40 states.

A realtist must be a member of a local board as well as a member of the national organization. Both nationally and locally, realtists are working for better housing for the communities they serve. In many cases, individuals are both realtors and realtists by virtue of voluntary dual membership.

The California Association of Real Estate Brokers is affiliated with Consolidated Real Estate Brokers, Sacramento; Consolidated Realty Board, Los Angeles; and San Diego Board of Realtists. The national office of this association is located in Washington, D.C.

Professional Designations

If one wishes to aspire to an advanced certified designation in fields such as appraiser, professional counselor, or property manager, the education necessary to qualify is provided by the National Association of Realtors and their affiliate organizations. Once earned, the professional designations enjoy a national recognition and career mobility

---

PROFESSIONAL DESIGNATIONS ISSUED BY THE NATIONAL ASSOCIATION OF REALTORS AND THEIR AFFILIATES

Alphabetical List by Affiliate

ASREC American Society of Real Estate Counselors
    CRE   Counselor in Real Estate

FLI Farm and Land Institute
    AFLM   Accredited Farm and Land Member

IREF International Real Estate Federation (American Chapter)

IREM Institute of Real Estate Management
    CPM   Certified Property Manager
    AMO   Accredited Management Organization
    ARM   Accredited Resident Manager

RESSI Real Estate Securities and Syndication Institute
    CRSM   Certified Real Estate Securities Marketer
    CRSS   Certified Real Estate Securities Sponsor

RNMI Realtors National Marketing Institute
    CCIM   Certified Commercial-Investment Member
    CRB   Certified Residential Broker
    CRS   Certified Residential Specialist

SIR Society of Industrial Realtors

WCR Women's Council of Realtors

In addition to the above, many other real estate trade associations issue their own professional designations.

Figure 15-1

is further enhanced. Virtually all trade associations have a code of ethics for their members. Several professional designations are shown in Figure 15-1.

Other Real Estate Employment

In addition to commission jobs, salaried positions are available as loan officers or appraisers for financial institutions, escrow and title officers for title companies, escrow companies, and financial institutions. Real estate developers and contractors frequently hire salaried personnel.

Additional opportunities for real estate students can exist in local, state, and federal governments. These may include a variety of occupational levels such as right-of-way agents, appraisers, leasing negotiators, planners, and HUD housing program staff.

15.2 LICENSE REQUIREMENTS AND COMPETITION

Real Estate Salespersons

The current requirements (1990) to become a real estate salesperson are:

1. Must be at least 18 years of age.

2. Effective Jan. 1986, a college-level course in real estate principles must be taken before sitting for the salesperson examination.

3. Must be able to pass the state examination consisting of 150 multiple-choice questions within a three and one-quarter hour time period. A passing score is 105 or more correct answers representing 70 percent and up.

    The salesperson's examination is given every week at designated locations in California, usually San Francisco, Los Angeles, San Diego, and Sacramento. The examination is difficult, and a failure rate of 50 percent or more is common.

4. After passing the examination, the required license fee must be submitted and the application must be signed by the employing real estate broker.

5. License is granted for 18 months, during which time two broker-level courses must be completed. Then the remaining term of a four-year license is issued.

Real Estate Brokers

Current requirements to become a real estate broker are:

1. Must be at least 18 years of age.

2. Must complete the educational requirements of eight approved real estate courses consisting of the following:
    a. Real estate practice
    b. Legal aspects of real estate
    c. Real estate finance
    d. Real estate appraisal
    e. Real estate economics or accounting

State Examination

For a detailed explanation of the state real estate examination see Appendix D of this chapter.

f. Three of the following courses: real estate principles, business law, property management, real estate office administration, escrow, or another approved advanced real estate course. The courses must be taken through an accredited college or at a private vocational school approved by the Real Estate Commissioner.

3. Must complete the experience requirements which consist of two years' full-time experience as a real estate salesperson, or its equivalent. "Equivalent" is experience in an allied field such as title, escrow, or finance. Equivalence can in some cases include education in lieu of experience, although this may be subject to change.

4. Must pass the state examination consisting of 200 multiple-choice questions within five hours with a score of 150 or more correct answers, representing a score of 75 percent or better. The test for the broker's license is more difficult than the salesperson's examination and the failure rate is frequently high, averaging approximately 50 percent.

5. Must complete the license application and pay the proper fee.

6. The broker's examination is given monthly or more often depending upon demand.

> Real estate licensees are allowed to sell business opportunities and some types of mobile homes. See Appendix C of this chapter for details.

Continuing Education Requirements

Effective January 1, 1981, all licensees must show proof of completion of 45 clock hours of real estate commissioner approved continuing education before a real estate license will be renewed. The rule *is not* 45 hours per year, but rather 45 hours within the four-year licensing period. The 45 hours must include a 3 hour course in ethics and a 3 hour course in agency. A 70% passing test score is required on all continuing education classes.

If a real estate salesperson obtains a broker's license before the time to renew the salesperson license, the new broker will not need to meet the continuing education requirement until the renewal date of the broker's license.

Real estate commissioner approved continuing education courses are offered throughout the state by private enterprises, as well as real estate trade associations and California colleges.

The California Department of Real Estate — A Summary

The Department of Real Estate is a public agency that has responsibility over certain real estate activities in California. Here are some key points:

1. The California Real Estate Commissioner is appointed by the Governor and serves as the chief executive of the Department of Real Estate.

2. The Commissioner enforces the Real Estate Law and issues regulations that have the force of law and become a part of the California Administrative Code.

3. The Commissioner and the Department screen applicants for licenses and investigate complaints against licensees. After a proper hearing, if a licensee has violated a law or regulation, the Commissioner can restrict, suspend, or revoke a real estate license.

> Restricted License: allows licensee to continue to work, but under limited conditions.
> Suspended License: a temporary loss of license
> Revoked License: a loss of license

4. A real estate license is required when a person performs a real estate act for another for compensation. The compensation may be in the form of a commission, fee, salary, or anything of value. The following exceptions do *not* need a real estate license:
   a. Principal handling his or her own affairs
   b. Attorney in Fact acting under a power of attorney
   c. Appraiser
   d. Attorney at Law (Lawyer) while performing duties as an attorney. If the attorney charges a fee as a broker, then a real estate license is required.
   e. Trustee selling under a deed of trust
   f. Residential property manager. A full-service, off-site property manager must have a real estate license.

5. The fine for an unlicensed person who receives an illegal commission is $10,000 for an individual and $50,000 for a corporation. The fine for paying a commission to an unlicensed person is $100.

6. *Fictitious Business Name.* A licensed broker, corporation, or partnership may operate under a fictitious name (DBA, Doing Business As) if the name is approved by the Commissioner.

7. A corporate real estate license requires an officer to be licensed as a broker. A partnership real estate license requires one partner to be licensed as a broker. A real estate salesperson and a broker can form a real estate brokerage partnership.

8. *Mineral, Oil, and Gas License.* When the principal items sold or leased are mineral, oil, and gas rights, a separate Mineral, Oil, and Gas License is required. For a $50 special permit, a regular real estate broker can handle up to 10 mineral, oil, and gas transactions without such a license.

9. *Prepaid Rental Listing License.* A special license that allows licensee to collect a fee for supplying a prospective tenant with a list of available rentals. This does not allow licensee to negotiate rental contracts or perform any other real estate activity. Real estate

brokers can collect a prepaid fee without a special license if done at their regular place of business.

10. *Real Estate Advisory Commission.* Consists of the Commissioner and ten other members appointed by the Commissioner. Six members are real estate brokers, four are public members. The purpose of the Real Estate Advisory Commission is to advise the Commissioner on real estate matters important to the industry and the public.

Real Estate Licensees in California

Statistics provided by the Department of Real Estate indicate that the total number of real estate licenses has escalated.

In a basic description of career and educational opportunities, the State of California's Department of Real Estate indicates to potential job seekers that general real estate brokerage — particularly involving the sale and leasing of residential properties—offers the largest volume of opportunity. Compensation, on the other hand, is largely based on earnings from commissions. As a consequence, anyone contemplating a real estate sales career should be aware that they are in direct competition with a large number of licensees whose numbers are continuously expanding.

How About a Part-Time Real Estate Job?

Many potential licensees hope to work part-time until their sales volume will support full-time employment. However, many brokers will not hire part-time salespeople. The reason relates to the time and financial cost to train part-time salespersons, the distractions from the assignment, and the requirement for fully employed staff to follow or cover the part-timer's assignment and client contacts. Unless skillfully maneuvered and covered in a suitable manner, part-time salespeople can create management and personnel frictions for brokers and their staff. This does not mean that part-time real estate salespeople are unwanted, but rather that part-timers usually are not as successful as fully committed salespeople.

Working Hours and Fringe Benefits

The individual who makes the decision to enter real estate on a full-employment basis must face the prospect of long hours that may include evenings and weekends. In addition, many times the package of fringe benefits which has been incorporated in past employment earnings may not exist or may cost the real estate employee a portion of his or her gross earnings—for example, vacation allowances, insurance benefits, or retirement funds are not common in the real estate business. Some firms do offer these benefits, but in order to do so, their brokers must be affiliated with the local, state, and national associations. However, some firms are too small to justify fringe benefits for their sales staff. If fringe benefits are of overriding concern, each prospective salesperson should explore these areas of question prior to joining a particular firm. Additional inquiry should be made regarding job orientation, sales training, and requirements for basic costs (telephone, professional dues, advertising, etc.). Many real estate assignments also require working on the weekend days when clients are available to inspect properties, and this may be another serious consideration for a job applicant.

Realistic Picture   Real estate sales and related activities can offer unlimited opportunities for motivated individuals. Perseverance and hard work, coupled with good training and additional educational course work, can help a person become financially independent and provide a valuable service for the public. Real estate is not a get-rich-quick business—it takes work and a willingness to be helpful and understanding.

15.3 PERSONAL PREPARATION TO ENTER INTO THE REAL ESTATE INDUSTRY   Too frequently individuals who envision a career in real estate are motivated by what appears to be an open entry into an occupation that provides unlimited earnings. Frequently, there are unrealistic expectations for earnings which do not materialize, and this results in a negative employment experience. If possible, a prospective licensee should meet with a career counselor and an experienced real estate broker in order to extensively explore the qualifications for entry into real estate. Inasmuch as the recommended counseling may not be readily available to those interested in a real estate career, the following checklist and self-analysis may help a prospective licensee decide whether or not to enter the field.

Personal Checklist   1. If at all possible an interest inventory, such as the Strong Inventory Test, should be taken. This test is available at most local community colleges and the Registrar's Office generally knows when the tests are given and what they entail.

2. If the local college has a career center, check with a counselor to verify which courses are required for entry and how they may be taken. This discussion might also indicate the cost for textbooks, registration fees, matriculation requirements, class hours, as well as the total scope of course offerings. In addition, private real estate schools are available throughout the state. For a fee, these schools offer license preparatory courses.

3. Once the arrangements for a course of study have been established, it is a good idea to check the local real estate employment market. This would include a check of the local real estate boards, the territorial radius serviced by each board, the numbers of brokers and sales affiliates listed on the membership rosters, and so forth.

    The executive officers of local real estate boards can give excellent indications of the sales activities in the local area. These indicators might include a list of the number of new licensees, new listings and sales activities, and average dollar volumes.

4. Select a location where you might like to work and survey the real estate offices situated within this territory. It is further recommended that a visual examination of the exterior appearance of various real estate offices be made. Although an exterior screening does not indicate the success of an operation—a large, attractive

office may not necessarily be more efficient than the smaller office—it does give one some important first impressions.

5. Check local newspaper real estate advertisements to determine which real estate offices are working what neighborhoods.

6. Narrow the real estate office choices to perhaps one to five offices, and then attempt to identify the personnel within these offices. If possible, make an appointment with an employed salesperson to discuss the activities within each office. This can provide valuable facts concerning management, number of employees, rapport, and so on. Many times the decision to affiliate with a firm is made at this time.

7. Once the selection process is narrowed, an appointment should be made for an interview with either the owner-broker or the personnel manager. Prior to doing so, however, an application form should be requested (for many small offices, application forms are not used). The form should be completed in advance of the appointment and accompanied by a personal resume. To assure a more informative interview pre-list specific questions such as the number of employees hired by the firm, support personnel, training programs, ratio of commission adjustments, fringe benefits, vacation arrangements, advertising and listing policies, employee-independent contractor arrangements, commission ratios once certain sales quotas have been reached, personal costs for office expenses (telephone), etc. This suggested range of questions does not intend to imply that the applicant is to *interview* management—to the contrary. However, many pertinent facts should be cleared at this time and not later. Not asking enough questions has led to regret on the part of many unsuccessful real estate salespeople. A well-conducted interview usually brings out important information for both the applicant and the employer.

Questions to Ask Yourself before You Enter the Real Estate Business

1. Why am I leaving my current employment? Are my reasons valid and logical, or are they emotional?

2. How many sales and commission dollars will I have to earn to equal my present salary? (This projection should include present and future potential earnings.)

3. What arrangements will be made for my annual vacation and holiday arrangements? (Will these be on my own time or at the expense of the firm?)

4. What about the fringe benefits—health, life, dental packages? Will these be provided by the employing broker or at my expense?

5. Will I have to work on weekends and during evening hours? If so, will this be a continuing activity and for what time periods? (A number of real estate firms staff their personnel so that clientele services may be extended throughout the maximum number of day and evening hours.)

6. What about my current status? Is it possible for me to leave my prestige and personal recognition behind (if one does exist because of education, training, and years of experience) and be willing to start at the bottom of the training ladder with other entry personnel?

7. How do my personal health and age relate to the continuing pace of sales activities?

8. Are my personality traits such that I will be continually charged and challenged—or will I find the real estate business discouraging if sales do not materialize on a regular basis? Can I take the peaks and valleys?

9. Am I financially prepared for a sales position? This should include the ability to carry yourself and family for a period of time before sales start to materialize. In addition, each prospective salesperson should recognize the fact that there are continuing out-of-pocket expenses such as:
    a. Local board, state, and national professional fees.
    b. The cost to drive and maintain a suitable automobile for use in escorting clients to and from properties. (This would include repair costs, additional gasoline mileage, and comprehensive insurance coverage.)
    c. Incidental daily costs that arise in connection with food services for clients, such as, coffee, luncheons, or dinners.
    d. Monthly office costs—telephone, listing materials, keys for properties.
    e. Personal appearance which requires a businesslike wardrobe, personal grooming, or the uniform wardrobe required by certain franchise offices.

10. How will my family cope with the change? Are they supporting my decision?

The above listing of self-analysis questions is not intended to be presented as a negative overview of real estate sales, but rather as a serious review of what must be considered for a successful and professional entrance into the real estate field. Once the qualified applicant is aware of these aspects, then each entrance step and subsequent progress can be logically planned and anticipated. Continuing professional training is necessary, and a professional image is created only by a professional attitude.

Ending Note The real estate business provides an opportunity for a personally challenging and a financially rewarding career, but it is not "easy for the taking." With dedication and hard work, you can become a successful real estate person, and earn a substantial income and open up opportunities for personal investments.

SUMMARY Real estate offers many opportunities for employment. Entrance into the industry requires serious forethought and adequate preparation. For those persons who choose the academic route of preparation, training can start with a real estate certificate (which embodies the vocational portion of the education). Any college or postgraduate courses or degrees can help to provide the necessary information and education to prepare for advanced industry-level certifications and designations. An academic degree helps you to prepare for state licensing and the educational training is credited toward experience requirements.

For those individuals who do not wish formal academic training, there are several other avenues. These include courses given by the local real estate boards, trade associations, and private real estate schools.

To uphold the standards of professionalism, as well as to offer a direction for ethical performance, the National Association of Realtors and the National Association of Real Estate Brokers have developed a Code of Ethics for their membership. The enforcement and adherence to the by-laws is through the network of state and local board affiliations.

Board affiliates must adhere to the code for a standard of professional performance. Local boards have organized ethics committees to hear and deliberate the outcome of abuses to the code. For serious violations or potentially criminal ones, the ethics hearing may solicit additional assistance from the State Association or refer the matter to the State department of real estate for further disciplinary action. A criminal implication requires the hearing review to refer the issue to the local district attorney's office.

The State department of real estate adheres rigidly to its licensing laws which are well publicized so that the licensed population may be aware of the specific areas of violation. Infractions may result in serious damages to the public sector. The State department's review of violation complaints may result in a restriction or revocation of an individual's license. Disciplinary activities are publicized in the state bulletins which are mailed to all licensees for public notice as to which sections of the code have been violated. State bulletins also provide very helpful information in that they provide a continuing source of updated information regarding new licensing regulations resulting from legislative and statutory changes.

In conclusion, each individual who contemplates real estate as an occupational field must make a serious self-appraisal of personal abilities and the financial implications, as well as thoroughly investigate the potential of office associations available at the time of entry into the field.

Important Terms and Concepts

National Association of Real Estate Brokers (NAREB)

National Association of Realtors (NAR)

Real estate broker

Real estate salesperson

Realtist

Realtor

Realtor-associate

REVIEWING YOUR UNDERSTANDING

1. Entry into the real estate industry offers an agent an opportunity to:
   (a) Earn unlimited sums of money
   (b) Help people obtain housing
   (c) Become a recognized professional
   (d) All of the above

2. The requirements for a salesperson's license are:
   (a) Be at least 18 years of age
   (b) Have the ability to pass a state examination
   (c) Find an employing broker
   (d) All of the above

3. The designation MAI which stands for "Member Appraisal Institute" is a:
   (a) Local designation
   (b) State designation
   (c) National designation
   (d) None of the above

4. Which of the following is the major reason some individuals do not succeed in real estate?
   (a) They do not enjoy working with people.
   (b) They do not possess a license—nor do they have to acquire one.
   (c) They have not successfully appraised their personal qualifications for entrance into the industry.
   (d) Properties are difficult to sell.

5. The requirements for a broker's license are:
   (a) Be at least 18 years of age
   (b) Have at least two years' experience as a salesperson
   (c) Complete certain course requirements as prescribed by law
   (d) All of the above

6. The designation CPM stands for:
   (a) Certified property manager
   (b) Certified professional member
   (c) Certified property member
   (d) Certified professional marketing

7. The initials AIREA stand for:
   (a) Associated Institute of Real Estate Appraisers
   (b) American Institute of Real Estate Appraisers
   (c) Amalgamated Institute of Real Estate Appraisers
   (d) Associated Individual Real Estate Appraisers

8. The career cluster, or allied real estate fields, may include such occupations as:
   (a) Governmental agencies
   (b) Escrow and title
   (c) Banking and savings and loan associations
   (d) All of the above

9. Compensation in the real estate industry may be earned through:
   (a) Commission from affiliation with a broker
   (b) Commission if self-employed
   (c) Salary and commission
   (d) All of the above

10. Those individuals who are contemplating a serious career in real estate should do which of the following?
    (a) Take an interest inventory test at a local community college or high school
    (b) Talk with friends and neighbors about the potential entry
    (c) Make a snap decision based on personal appraisal of personality traits
    (d) Enter the sales field and then appraise personal qualifications

Appendix A

SUGGESTED GUIDELINES FOR AN INTERVIEW WITH A REAL ESTATE BROKER FOR EMPLOYMENT

1. Phone the broker for a copy of the application form.

2. Does the broker provide a sales manual?

3. Details of training program should include (a) duration of program, (b) management cooperation or follow up, and (c) frequency of sales meetings.

4. Commissions—how are they split, and when are they paid. Are there any motivating plans to stimulate sales?

5. Expenses—what items are charged to a salesperson?

6. Floor time—what are the involvements and how are outside interferences handled?

7. Open house policy? How are clients referred by the office's salespeople handled?

8. Telephone—is its use charged to salesperson or to the broker?

9. What are hours and days of duty?

10. Amount of vacation time and any fringe benefits?

Appendix B

Revised Code of Ethics and Suggestions for Professional Conduct - Commissioner's Regulations effective June 10, 1990 and applicable to all licensees

**CODE OF ETHICS AND
PROFESSIONAL CONDUCT**

2785. Professional Conduct. In order to enhance the professionalism of the California real estate industry, and maximize protection for members of the public dealing with real estate licensees, whatever their area of practice, the following standards of professional conduct and business practices are adopted.

(a) Unlawful Conduct in Sale, Lease, and Exchange Transactions. Licensees when performing acts within the meaning of Section 10131(a) of the Business and Professions Code shall not engage in conduct which would subject the licensee to adverse action, penalty or discipline under Sections 10176 and 10177 of the Business and Professions Code including, but not limited to, the following acts and omissions:

(1) Knowingly making a substantial misrepresentation of the likely value of real property to:
(A) Its owner either for the purpose of securing a listing or for the purpose of acquiring an interest in the property for the licensee's own account.
(B) A prospective buyer for the purpose of inducing the buyer to make an offer to purchase the real property.

(2) Representing to an owner of real property when seeking a listing that the licensee has obtained a bona fide written offer to purchase the property, unless at the time of the representation the licensee has possession of a bona fide written offer to purchase.

(3) Stating or implying to an owner of real property during listing negotiations that the licensee is precluded by law , by regulation, or by the rules of any organization, other than the broker firm seeking the listing, from charging less than the commission or fee quoted to the owner by the licensee.

(4) Knowingly making substantial misrepresentations regarding the licensee's relationship with an individual broker, corporate broker, or franchised brokerage company or that entity's/person's responsibility for the licensee's activities.

(5) Knowingly underestimating the probable closing costs in a communication to the prospective buyer or seller of real property in order to induce that person to make or to accept an offer to purchase the property.

(6) Knowingly making a false or misleading representation to the seller of real property as to the form, amount and/or treatment of a deposit toward the purchase of the property made by an offeror.

(7) Knowingly making a false or misleading representation to a seller of real property, who has agreed to finance all or part of a purchase price by carrying back a loan, about a buyer's ability to repay the loan in accordance with its terms and conditions.

(8) Making an addition to or modification of the terms of an instrument previously signed or initialed by a party to a transaction without the knowledge and consent of the party.

(9) A representation made as a principal or agent to a prospective purchaser of a promissory note secured by real property about the market value of the securing property without a reasonable basis for believing the truth and accuracy of the representation.

(10) Knowingly making a false or misleading representation or representing, without a reasonable basis for believing its truth, the nature and/or condition of the interior or exterior features of a property when soliciting an offer.

(11) Knowingly making a false or misleading representation or representing, without reasonable basis for believing its truth, the size of parcel, square footage of improvements or the location of the boundary lines of real property being offered for sale, lease or exchange.

(12) Knowingly making a false or misleading representation or representing to a prospective buyer or lessee of real property, without reasonable basis to believe its truth, that the property can be used for certain purposes with the intent of inducing the prospective buyer or lessee to acquire an interest in the real property.

(13) When acting in the capacity of an agent in a transaction for the sale, lease or exchange of real property, failing to disclose to a prospective purchaser or lessee facts known to the licensee materially affecting the value or desirability of the property, when the licensee has reason to believe that such facts are not known to nor readily observable by a prospective purchaser or lessee.

(14) Willfully failing, when acting as a listing agent, to present or cause to be presented to the owner of the property any written offer to purchase received prior to the closing of a sale, unless expressly instructed by the owner not to present such an offer, or unless the offer is patently frivolous.

(15) When acting as the listing agent, presenting competing written offers to purchase real property to the owner in such a manner as to induce the owner to accept the offer which will provide the greatest compensation to the listing broker without regard to the benefits, advantages and/or disadvantages to the owner.

(16) Failing to explain to the parties or prospective parties to a real estate transaction for whom the licensee is acting as an agent the meaning and probable significance of a contingency in an offer or contract that the licensee knows or reasonably believes may affect the closing date of the transaction, or the timing of the vacating of the property by the seller or its occupancy by the buyer.

(17) Failing to disclose to the seller of real property in a transaction in which the licensee is an agent for the seller the nature and extent of any direct or indirect interest that the licensee expects to acquire as result of the sale. The prospective purchase of the property by a person related to the licensee by blood or marriage, purchase by an entity in which the licensee has an ownership interest, or purchase by any other person with whom the licensee occupies a special relationship where there is a reasonable probability that the licensee could be indirectly acquiring an interest in the property shall be disclosed to the seller.

(18) Failing to disclose to the buyer of real property in a transaction in which the licensee is an agent for the buyer the nature and extent of a licensee's direct or indirect ownership interest in such real property. The direct or indirect ownership interest in the property by a person related to the licensee by blood or marriage, by an entity in which the licensee has an ownership interest, or by any other person with whom the licensee occupies a special relationship shall be disclosed to the buyer.

(19) Failing to disclose to a principal for whom the licensee is acting as an agent any significant interest the licensee has in a particular entity when the licensee recommends the use of services or products of such entity.

(20) The refunding by a licensee, when acting as an agent for the seller, all or part of an offeror's purchase money deposit in a real estate transaction after the seller has accepted the offer to purchase, unless the licensee has the express permission of the seller to make the refund.

(b) Unlawful Conduct When Soliciting, Negotiating, or Arranging a Loan Secured by Real Property or the Sale of a Promissory Note Secured by Real Property. Licensees when performing acts within the meaning of subdivision (d) or (e) of Section 10131 of the Business and Professions Code shall not violate any of the applicable provisions of subdivision (a), or act in a manner which would subject the licensee to adverse action, penalty or discipline under Section 10176 and 10177 of the Business and Professions Code including, but not limited to, the following acts or omissions:

(1) Knowingly misrepresenting to a prospective borrower of a loan to be secured by real property to to an assignor/endorser of a promissory note secured by real property that there is an existing lender willing to make the loan or that there is a purchaser for the note, for the purpose of inducing the borrower or assignor/endorser to utilize the services of the licensee.

(2) (a) Knowingly making a false or misleading representation to a prospective lender or purchaser of a loan secured directly or collaterally by real property about a borrower's ability to repay the loan in accordance with its terms and conditions:
(b) Failing to disclose to a prospective lender or note purchaser information about the prospective borrower's identity, occupation, employment, income and credit data as represented to the broker by the prospective borrower;
(c) Failing to disclose information known to the broker relative to the ability of the borrower to meet his or her potential or existing contractual obligations under the note or contract including information known about the borrower' s payment history on an existing note, whether the note is in default or the borrower in bankruptcy.

(3) Knowingly underestimating the probable closing costs in a communication to a prospective borrower or lender of a loan to be secured by a lien on real property for the purpose of inducing the borrower or lender to enter into the loan transaction.

(4) When soliciting a prospective lender to make a loan to be secured by real property, falsely representing or representing without reasonable basis to believe its truth, the priority of the security, as a lien against the real property securing the loan, i.e., a first, second or third deed of trust.

(5) Knowingly misrepresenting in any transaction that a specific service is free when the licensee knows or has a reasonable basis to know that it is covered by a fee to be charged as part of the transaction.

(6) Knowingly making a false or misleading representation to a lender or assignee/endorsee of a lender of a loan secured directly or collaterally by a lien on real property about the amount and treatment of loan payments, including loan payoffs, and the failure to account to the lender or assignee/endorsee of a lender as to the disposition of such payments.

(7) When acting as a licensee in a transaction for the purpose of obtaining a loan, and in receipt of an "advance fee" from the borrower for this purpose, the failure to account to the borrower for the disposition of the "advance fee."

(8) Knowingly making false or misleading representation about the terms and conditions of a loan to be secured by a lien on real property when soliciting a borrower or negotiating the loan.

(9) Knowingly making a false or misleading representation or representing, without reasonable basis for believing its truth, when soliciting a lender for negotiating a loan to be secured by a lien on real property about the market value of the securing real property, the nature and /or condition of the interior or exterior features of the securing real property, its size or the square footage of any improvements on the securing real property.

Suggestions of professional conduct
As part of the effort to promote ethical business practices of real estate licensees, the Real Estate Commissioner has issued the following Suggestions for Professional Conduct as a companion to the Code of Professional Conduct (Section 2785, Title 10, California Code of Regulations):

(a) **Suggestions for Professional Conduct in Sale, Lease and Exchange Transactions.** In order to maintain a high level of ethics and professionalism in their business practices, real estate licensees are encouraged to adhere to the following suggestions in conducting their business activities.

(1) Aspire to give a high level of competent, ethical and quality service to buyers and sellers in real estate transactions.

(2) Stay in close communication with clients or customers to ensure that questions are promptly answered and all significant events or problems in a transaction are conveyed in a timely manner.

(3) Cooperate with the California Department of Real Estate's enforcement of , and report to that department evident violations of, the Real Estate Law.

(4) Use care in the preparation of any advertisement to present an accurate picture or message to the reader, viewer or listener.

(5) Submit all written offers in a prompt and timely manner.

(6) Keep oneself informed and current on factors affecting the real estate market in which the licensee operates as an agent.

(7) Make a full, open and sincere effort to cooperate with other licensees, unless the principal has instructed the licensee to the contrary.

(8) Attempt to settle disputes with other licensees through mediation or arbitration.

(9) Advertise or claim to be an expert in an area of specialization in real estate brokerage activity, e.g., appraisal, property management, industrial siting, mortgage loan, etc., only if the licensee has had special training, preparation or experience in such area.

(10) Strive to provide equal opportunity for quality housing and a high level of service to all persons regardless of race, color, sex, religion, ancestry, physical handicap, martial status or national origin.

(11) Base opinions of value, whether for the purpose of advertising or promoting real estate brokerage business, upon documented objective data.

(12) Make every attempt to comply with these Guidelines for Professional Conduct and the Code of Ethics of any organized real estate industry group of which the licensee is a member.

(b)   Suggestions for Professional Conduct When Negotiating or Arranging Loans Secured by Real Property or Sale of a Promissory Note Secured by Real Property. In order to maintain a high level of ethics and professionalism in their business practices when performing acts within the meaning of subdivisions (d) and (e) of Section 10131 and Sections 10131.1 and 10131.2 of the Business and Professions Code, real estate licensees are encouraged to adhere to the following suggestions, in addition to any applicable provisions of subdivision (a), in conducting their business activities:

(1) Aspire to give a high level of competent, ethical and quality service to borrowers and lenders in loan transactions secured by real estate.

(2) Stay in close communication with borrowers and lenders to ensure that reasonable questions are promptly answered and all significant events or problems in a loan transaction are conveyed in a timely manner.

(3) Keep oneself informed and current on factors affecting the real estate loan market in which the licensee acts as an agent.

(4) Advertise or claim to be an expert in an area of real estate loan transactions only if the licensee has had special training, preparation or experience in such area.

(5) Strive to provide equal opportunity for quality mortgage loan services and a high level of service to all borrowers or lenders regardless of race, color, sex, religion, ancestry, physical handicap, martial status or national origin.

(6) Base opinions of value in a loan transaction, whether for the purpose of advertising or promoting real estate mortgage loan brokerage business, on documented objective data.

(7) Respond to reasonable inquires of a principal as to the status or extent of efforts to negotiate the sale of an existing loan.

(8) Respond to reasonable inquires of a borrower regarding the net proceeds available from a loan arranged by the licensee.

(9) Make every attempt to comply with the standards of professional conduct and the code of ethics of any organized mortgage loan industry group of which the licensee is a member.

The conduct suggestions set forth in subsections (a) and (b) are not intended as statements of duties imposed by law nor as grounds for disciplinary action by the Department of Real Estate, but as guidelines for elevating the professionalism of real estate licensees.

Appendix C

**BUSINESS
OPPORTUNITIES**
A real estate license allows an agent to sell business opportunities. A business opportunity is defined as the sale or lease of a business, including stock, trade fixtures, trade name, and good will. This involves the sale of personal property and all the rules of personal property apply.

The essential elements of the sale of a business opportunity include:

1. A bill of sale is the written instrument which passes title to personal property.

2. The financial statements needed when a business is sold are:
   a. Balance Sheet — Shows the financial position of the business as of a given date.

      Assets. Things of value owned by the business.
      Liabilities. Unpaid debts and expenses of the business.
      Net Worth. Owners' equity, the difference between the assets and liabilities.

   b. Profit and Loss Statement — Shows the profit and loss of the business during a specific time period.

      Gross Income (revenue from sales)
      $\underline{- \text{Expenses}}$ (cost of goods and expenses)
      Net Income (profit)

3. Bulk Sales Rules apply when a business is sold that involves inventory. A bulk transfer is defined as the transfer of a major portion of inventory other than a sale to customers. Transferee (buyer) must give public notice 12 business days before transfer takes place. The notice requires recording a Notice of Intent to Sell Bulk and publishing it in a newspaper of general circulation. Purpose is to let creditors of the seller file a claim if trade credit is still owed on the inventory.

   If the buyer and seller do not comply with the bulk sale law, the sale is valid between them, *but* is void against the creditors who can then attach the inventory.

4. Other terms and definitions are:
   a. *Goodwill.* Expectation of continued public patronage.
   b. *Turnover.* Number of times the inventory is sold per year.
   c. *Sales and Use Tax.* A tax on the sale of personal property.
   d. *Alcoholic Beverage Control Act (ABC).* Rules involving the sale of a liquor license. One of these rules states that the person must be of good moral character. If a new license is issued by the state, the fees are $4,500 for a seasonal license and $6,000 for a general license. Because the number of liquor licenses is limited by population, a free market develops and the price for a liquor license can skyrocket.

MOBILE HOMES   A real estate agent can handle the sale of *used* mobile homes. Used is defined as a mobile home more than one year old. If a new mobile home is affixed to foundation and certified as real property, a real estate licensee may sell this home. The mobile home must be at least 8 feet wide and 40 feet long. To sell other mobil homes, a special mobil home dealer's license is required.

TRUST FUNDS   A broker is required to keep an official record of all trust fund deposits which pass through his or her real estate business. This account must be kept using acceptable accounting procedures and is subject to audit by the California Real Estate Commissioner.

Although not required by law, most real estate brokers also open a trust fund account at a financial institution where all monies received on behalf of clients and customers can be deposited for safekeeping. Withdrawals can only be made by the broker or other authorized persons. The broker cannot put his or her personal funds in this trust fund account, with the exception of up to $100 to cover bank service fees.

If a broker receives a deposit from a prospective buyer who does not ask that the deposit be held uncashed, the broker must act within one business day either to:
1. give the deposit to the seller
2. put the deposit in escrow
3. put the deposit in a trust fund account

2 The Real Estate License Examinations

The Commissioner is required by law to ascertain by written examination the competency qualifications of applicants for a real estate license. (Section 10153 of the Business and Professions Code.) Examination requirements cannot be waived. (Sections 10153 and 10158 of the Business and Professions Code and Commissioner's Regulation 2761).

An application to take the examination may be obtained by calling or writing any of the Department of Real Estate district offices. A pamphlet entitled "Instructions to License Applicants" that gives detailed instructions on license application and qualification procedures is furnished with each application.

This chapter is devoted to the license examination process itself, giving some idea of the extent and scope of the examinations for real estate broker and salesperson licenses.

EXAMINATION PURPOSE

Real estate license examinations are designed to test the candidate's practical knowledge of real estate, appraisal techniques, and the handling of real estate transactions in the best interest of the principals. It must be emphasized that a few personal experiences with real estate transactions will not usually give the exam candidate knowledge of sufficient scope and depth to enable the candidate to pass the examination.

Every effort is made to construct the examinations in such a way as to give the candidate for a license an opportunity to demonstrate his or her knowledge of the fundamentals of real estate and the ability to handle transactions properly without endangering the interests of the public.

EXAMINATION SCOPE

Business and Professions Code Section 10153 requires that the Commissioner structure an examination as follows:

Section 10153. In addition to the proof of honesty and truthfulness required of any applicant for a real estate license, the Commissioner shall ascertain by written examination that the applicant, and in case of a corporation applicant for a real estate broker's license, that each officer, or agent thereof through whom it proposes to act as a real estate licensee, has all of the following:

(a) An appropriate knowledge of the English language, including reading, writing and spelling and arithmetical computations common to real estate and business opportunity practices.

(b) An understanding of the principles of real estate and business opportunity conveyancing, the general purposes and general legal effect of agency contracts, deposit receipts, deeds, mortgages, deeds of trust, chattel mortgages, bills of sale, land contracts of sale, leases, and of the principles of business and land economics and appraisals.

(c) A general and fair understanding of the obligations between principal and agent, the principles of real estate and business opportunity practice and the canons of business ethics pertaining thereto, and the provisions of Part I (commencing with Section 10000) and, of Chapter 1 (commencing with Section 11000) of Part 2, and the regulations of the Real Estate Commissioner as contained in Title 10 of the California Code of Regulations.

Exam Preparation

Unless the applicant for a real estate broker or salesperson license has had experience with the various instruments used in real estate transactions, has good general knowledge of real estate fundamentals, and of the obligations of an agent as well as familiarity with the laws and regulations governing an agent's activities, it is suggested that serious study be undertaken prior to taking the examination. Even those persons well grounded in these areas will find a review extremely valuable. It is well to remember that a substantial number of those who take the real estate license examination fail to pass it.

Real estate practice in the last two decades has become much more professional in its outlook. As transactions become more and more complex, the licensee is expected to have a broader knowledge of the field of real estate. This knowledge must be acquired through a combination of academic channels and experience. Therefore, it is important that the person striving for real estate licensure be adequately prepared before appearing for the examination. The *Reference Book* and the *Real Estate Law* book published by the Department touch on most of those subjects covered in the examinations.

In addition, there are a number of excellent textbooks on California real estate law, practice, finance, economics and appraising available at public libraries and bookstores. Resident courses of study in the above-mentioned subjects and others are offered by universities, state universities, community colleges, the University of California Extension and private vocational schools.

For those who prefer independent study (correspondence instruction), the University of California (Berkeley) and some private vocational schools offer basic real estate courses for home study.

EXAMINATION CONSTRUCTION

The Department of Real Estate's testing program primarily follows guidelines and techniques set by the State Personnel Board and other test authorities. The format and outline of all real estate license examinations as we know them today were originally created through a research grant to the University of California in 1956. Since that time several research studies have been conducted to update the test specifications. The most recent study was conducted in 1986 by Educational Testing Service. The study researched the tasks performed by brokers and salespersons and the knowledge areas necessary to competently perform these tasks. They found differences in the level and amount of knowledge required of salespersons and brokers in performing their work. These differences account for the variation in weighting in the test outlines presented below. Because knowledge requirements for entry-level salespersons and brokers have changed, new salesperson and broker licensing examinations are constantly being developed to conform with the findings and recommendations of the most recent validation study.

Examination Weighting

The subject matter covered in the examinations is based on laws and procedures applicable within the State of California. As new broker and salesperson licensing examinations are developed, each of the content areas is weighted as indicated on the test outlines presented below. The subject matter outlines are presented to assist applicants for licensure in preparing for the licensing examination.

REAL ESTATE SALESPERSON LICENSING EXAMINATION
TEST OUTLINE AND CONTENT WEIGHTINGS

General Topics	Overall Weightings
REAL PROPERTY AND LAWS RELATING TO OWNERSHIP	11%
Ownership of property	
Encumbrances	
Public power over property	
TAX IMPLICATIONS OF REAL ESTATE OWNERSHIP	8%
Knowledge of current tax laws affecting real estate ownership	
VALUATION/APPRAISAL OF REAL PROPERTY	15%
Methods of appraising and valuing property	
Factors which may influence value estimate	
FINANCING REAL ESTATE	17%
Sources of financing	
Common clauses in mortgage instruments	
Types of loans	
Terms and conditions	
TRANSFER OF PROPERTY	10%
Titles	
Escrow reports	
REAL ESTATE PRACTICE	22%
Listing of real property	
Sales contracts	
Marketing	
BROKERAGE: RESPONSIBILITIES AND FUNCTIONS OF SALESPERSONS	17%
State real estate laws and regulations	
Laws relating to fair practices	
Knowledge of trends and developments	
Knowledge of forms and calculations	

REAL ESTATE BROKER LICENSING EXAMINATION
TEST OUTLINE AND CONTENT WEIGHTINGS

REAL PROPERTY AND LAWS RELATING TO OWNERSHIP	9%
Ownership of property	
Encumbrances	
Public power over property	

TAX IMPLICATIONS OF REAL ESTATE
    OWNERSHIP 8%
      Knowledge of current tax laws
        affecting real estate ownership
VALUATION/APPRAISAL OF REAL PROPERTY 15%
      Methods of appraising and valuing property
      Factors which may influence value estimate
FINANCING REAL ESTATE 16%
      Sources of financing
      Common clauses in mortgage instruments
      Types of loans
      Terms and conditions
TRANSFER OF PROPERTY 9%
      Title
      Escrow reports
REAL ESTATE PRACTICE 21%
      Listing of real property
      Sales contracts
      Marketing
BROKER'S RESPONSIBILITY FOR OFFICE
    MANAGEMENT 22%
      State real estate laws and regulations
      Laws relating to fair practices
      Knowledge of trends and developments
      Knowledge of forms and calculations

Question Writing

The license examination is similar to an achievement test, in that it is a mastery test of a specific knowledge. Since the examination is not competitive, its nature becomes qualifying and no set quota or rank of applicants is required. The examination process is not designed to predict future success in the business of real estate. It is meant to select the better qualified or competent over the less competent or less knowledgeable applicants.

To construct a good measuring device, it is essential that the component parts be consistent with relevancy to the subject matter and the knowledge being evaluated. Accordingly, each question or item is a test in itself and must meet the technical characteristics demanded of the test as a whole.

EXAMINATION RULES AND GRADING

The time allowed to complete an examination is subject to change as examination content and construction may dictate. Currently applicants for a broker license are allowed a maximum of five hours to complete the test—$2\frac{1}{2}$ hours in the morning and $2\frac{1}{2}$ hours in the afternoon. A candidate for a real estate salesperson license is allowed $3\frac{1}{4}$ hours to complete the test. To pass an examination, a broker candidate must answer at least 75 percent of the questions correctly out of a total of 200 and the candidate for a salesperson license must correctly answer 70 percent of the questions out of 150. Tests are objective, consisting of multiple-choice items, and they are impersonally graded by mechanical means.

Experience shows that an applicant for either a broker or a salesperson license who has earnestly applied himself or herself in preparing for the test has no difficulty finishing within the prescribed time limits. Naturally, the examination for broker license is more comprehensive in nature than the test for a real estate salesperson license.

Applicants are urged to arrive at the designated place for the examination promptly, and preferably 15 minutes prior to the scheduled time for the start of the test. Anxiety about being late and missing part of the time allotted to complete the test is detrimental to the candidate's chances of passing the examination. Also late examinees are required to waive the normal allotted time.

The usual rules for examinations apply—conversation is not permitted, the use of notes or references to texts is strictly forbidden, dishonest practice of any kind will result in a non-passing grade, and may be grounds for denying future examinations. (Business and Professions Code Section 10153.1 and Regulation 2763.) Pursuant to legislation which became effective January 1, 1984, the Department and other testing agencies are affected by the provisions of law relating to test security. This legislation added Sections 496 and 497 to the Business and Professions Code. These sections provide that the Department may deny, suspend, revoke or restrict the license of an applicant or licensee who subverts or attempts to subvert a licensing examination. Conduct which constitutes subversion includes but is not limited to the following:

1. Removing exam material from a test site.
2. Reproducing exam material without authorization.
3. Using paid test takers for the purpose of reconstructing an examination.
4. Using improperly obtained test questions to prepare persons for examination.
5. Selling, distributing, or buying exam material.
6. Cheating during an exam.
7. Possessing unauthorized equipment or information during an examination.
8. Impersonating an examinee or having an impersonator take an examination.

Examination Sessions

In administering examinations, the same procedure is followed in both morning and afternoon sessions. The applicant receives prepared instructions, scratch paper, an examination booklet, answer sheet and a special pencil. Answers must be recorded on the answer sheet and care must be exercised in marking the space provided for the examinee's selection of what examinee considers to be the correct alternative. Following is an example:

EXAMINATION BOOKLET	ANSWER SHEET
22. When examinees and licensees refer to the Reference Book, as published by the Department of Real Estate, they should use: (a) the first edition (b) any edition available (c) the 1960 edition (d) the latest edition published	22 A B C D ○○○○ 23 A B C D ○○○○ 24 A B C D ○○○○ 25 A B C D ○○○○

It is most important that the number on the answer sheet coincide with the number of the question in the examination booklet since misplaced answers become wrong answers. If more than one answer is marked on a question, no credit is given for that question. An answer may be changed by erasing and marking another.

No question is meant to be a trick or catch question. Interpret the words according to their commonly accepted meanings. Look over the entire test before beginning to work and apportion your time to the best advantage. It is wise to read all questions completely and attempt to answer every question.

Check carefully to be sure you have not skipped any pages and that you have matched the numbers on the answer sheet to the numbers in the examination booklet, as *there may be more numbers on the answer sheet than there are questions in the examination booklet.*

Nothing but the examination booklet, the answer sheet, a special pencil, and slide rule or silent, battery-operated, pocket-size, electronic calculator without a print-out capability or an alphabetic keyboard, are allowed on your desk, other than the single page of scratch paper for arithmetical calculations with which you will be supplied and which you MUST turn in with your answer sheet and examination booklet on completing the test.

QUESTION CONSTRUCTION

New test items must be prepared periodically and new examinations constructed to reflect the changing conditions in the field of real estate. This is also necessary to maintain the validity and reliability of the license testing process in California, where such a large number real estate license exams are given during the course of each year.

One of the most difficult tasks in the preparation of an effective exam is the preparation of test items phrased in such a manner that they truly probe the applicant's knowledge without making him or her wonder about their meaning. The questions must not be too difficult, too easy, unimportant or inappropriate for any reason.

Multiple Choice Exam

All test items in the real estate exams are multiple-choice. Each multiple-choice item is constructed to provide several answers which *seem* to be correct. While the examinee may feel that more than one answer has some element of correctness, the examinee must be able to eliminate the incorrect responses and choose the *best* answer.

Question Analyses

The following analyses of multiple-choice questions should be helpful to the examinee preparing for a license exam.

1. Under no circumstances may a broker:
   - (a) receive a commission from both buyer and seller
   - (b) appoint a subagent
   - (c) misrepresent material facts
   - (d) sell the principal's property to a relative.
     - (a) *is incorrect.* A broker may receive a commission from both parties provided both buyer and seller have knowledge of the arrangement.

(b) *is incorrect.* A broker may get prior consent from the principal to appoint other brokers as subagents to cooperate in selling the property.

(c) **is correct.** A material misrepresentation of fact is fraud. Acts of fraud are violations of law.

(d) *is incorrect.* The broker may sell to any purchaser provided the principal has full knowledge.

2. A valid bill of sale must contain:
   (a) a date
   (b) an acknowledgment
   (c) the seller's signature
   (d) a verification.

   (a) *is incorrect.* Although a date is advisable it is not required.

   (b) *is incorrect.* The law does not require an acknowledgment.

   (c) **is correct.** A bill of sale is an instrument which has been executed (signed) and delivered to convey title to personal property.

   (d) *is incorrect.* Verification means to confirm the correctness of an instrument by an affidavit or oath. Verification may be desirable but not required.

Be alert for questions which call for a response such as: "All of the following statements are correct, *except;*" or "which of the following are *not* liens?". In the following sample question, for example, three of the responses would be correct. The answer called for, however, is the *incorrect* statement.

3. A valid deed must contain all of the following, *except:*
   (a) the signature of the grantor
   (b) a granting clause
   (c) an adequate description of the property
   (d) an acknowledgment of the grantor's signature.

A deed is a written instrument used to convey title to real property.

   (a) *is a correct statement.* The grantor is the person who passes title to another and without grantor's signature title will not pass.

   (b) *is a correct statement.* The granting clause is necessary to evidence the intent of the grantor.

   (c) *is a correct statement.* The property being transferred must be described so the grantor knows exactly what property is being conveyed to the grantee.

   (d) **is the incorrect statement.** An acknowledgment is only necessary to enable the deed to be recorded but is not required to make the deed valid.

Sample Multiple Choice Items

The following multiple choice items are examples of the types of questions that may appear in the examination. No answers are provided because it is felt the student may more effectively use these examples to test retention of material studied by answering them and checking answers against appropriate sources.

1. Real estate taxes become a lien on the property:
   (a) on July 1st of the applicable tax year
   (b) the first Monday of November of the fiscal tax year
   (c) if not paid by December 10 of the tax year
   (d) on March 1st of each year.

1.   A B C D
        ○ ○ ○ ○

2. Tax delinquent real property not redeemed by the owner during the 5 year statutory redemption period is deeded to:
   (a) the city
   (b) the county
   (c) the state
   (d) the school district.

2.   A B C D
        ○ ○ ○ ○

3. Crowell bought the contents of a store for $9,300. Crowell sold the goods for 33⅓% more than they cost, but lost 15% of the selling price in bad debts. His profit on the venture was:
   (a) 18⅓%
   (b) $1,240
   (c) $1,860
   (d) $3,100.

3.   A B C D
        ○ ○ ○ ○

4. In a typical percentage lease, rent is calculated as a percentage of:
   (a) assets of the lessee's business
   (b) net sales of the lessee's business
   (c) gross sales of the lessee's business
   (d) net taxable income of the lessee's business.

4.   A B C D
        ○ ○ ○ ○

5. The position of trust assumed by the broker as an agent for a principal is described most accurately as:
   (a) a gratuitous relationship
   (b) a trustor relationship
   (c) a fiduciary relationship
   (d) an employment relationship.

5.   A B C D
        ○ ○ ○ ○

6. The Federal Housing Administration's role in financing the purchase of real property is to:
   (a) act as the lender of funds
   (b) insure loans made by approved lenders
   (c) purchase specific trust deeds
   (d) do all of the above.

6.   A B C D
        ○ ○ ○ ○

7. The instrument used to remove the lien of a trust deed from record is called a:
   (a) satisfaction
   (b) release
   (c) deed of reconveyance
   (d) certificate of redemption.

7.   A B C D
        ○ ○ ○ ○

8. Which item would be used by an appraiser in arriving at a net income for capitalization purposes?
   (a) cost of loans against the property
   (b) allowance for rent loss and vacancies
   (c) federal income tax
   (d) reserve for appreciation of buildings.

8.   A B C D
        ○ ○ ○ ○

9. The type of mortgage loan which permits borrowing additional funds at a later date is called:
(a) an equitable mortgage
(b) a junior mortgage
(c) an open-end mortgage
(d) an extendible mortgage.

9.   A B C D
      ○ ○ ○ ○

10. Private restrictions on the use of land may be created by:
(a) private land use controls
(b) written agreement
(c) general plan restrictions in subdivisions
(d) all of the above.

10.   A B C D
      ○ ○ ○ ○

11. Which approach to value would be given most consideration in an appraisal of a shopping center?
(a) market data
(b) cost
(c) summation
(d) income.

11.   A B C D
      ○ ○ ○ ○

12. A quitclaim deed conveys only the present right, title and interest of the:
(a) grantor
(b) servient tenement
(c) grantee
(d) property.

12.   A B C D
      ○ ○ ○ ○

13. Broker Carter negotiated a lease for 3,000 square feet of warehouse storage space at a monthly rental of $2.00 per sq. ft. Carter's commission is 8% of the first year's gross rent. Carter will receive:
(a) $4720
(b) $5360
(c) $5760
(d) none of the above.

13.   A B C D
      ○ ○ ○ ○

14. You are a California real estate broker. A prospect is referred to you by an out-of-state broker and a sale is consummated by you. You want to split your commission with the cooperating broker. Under the California Real Estate Law:
(a) You may pay a commission to a broker of another state
(b) You cannot divide a commission with a broker of another state
(c) You can pay a commission to a broker of another state only if he is also licensed in California
(d) None of the above.

14.   A B C D
      ○ ○ ○ ○

15. A loan to be completely repaid, principal and interest, by a series of regular equal installment payments is a:
(a) straight loan
(b) balloon payment loan
(c) fully amortized loan
(d) variable rate mortgage loan.

15.   A B C D
      ○ ○ ○ ○

16. The age of a house can be determined most accurately by inspecting which of the following:
(a) physical condition of the house
(b) architectural style of the house
(c) tax assessor's records
(d) recorded subdivision map.

16.   A B C D
      ○ ○ ○ ○

17. In a legal sales contract, the seller is often referred to as the:
    (a) trustor
    (b) divisor
    (c) donor
    (d) vendor.

17.   A B C D
      ○ ○ ○ ○

18. The instrument used to secure a loan on personal property is called a:
    (a) bill of sale
    (b) trust deed
    (c) security agreement
    (d) bill of exchange.

18.   A B C D
      ○ ○ ○ ○

19. Community property is property owned by:
    (a) churches
    (b) husband and wife
    (c) the municipality
    (d) the community.

19.   A B C D
      ○ ○ ○ ○

20. An apartment complex cost $450,000. It brings in a net income of $3,000 per month. The owner is making what percentage of return on the investment?
    (a) 7%
    (b) 8%
    (c) 11%
    (d) none of the above.

20.   A B C D
      ○ ○ ○ ○

21. A person holding title to real property in severalty would most likely have:
    (a) a life estate
    (b) an estate for years
    (c) ownership in common with others
    (d) sole ownership.

21.   A B C D
      ○ ○ ○ ○

22. Under the Federal Truth-in-Lending Law, two of the most critical facts which must be disclosed to buyers or borrowers are:
    (a) duration of the contract and discount rate
    (b) finance charge and annual percentage rate
    (c) carrying charge and advertising expense
    (d) installment payments and cancellation rights.

22.   A B C D
      ○ ○ ○ ○

23. Appraisals of single-family dwellings are usually based on:
    (a) capitalization of rental value
    (b) asking prices of comparable houses
    (c) sales prices of comparable properties
    (d) the assessed valuations.

23.   A B C D
      ○ ○ ○ ○

24. A contract based on an illegal consideration is:
    (a) valid
    (b) void
    (c) legal
    (d) enforceable.

24.   A B C D
      ○ ○ ○ ○

25. The California "standard form" policy of title insurance on real property insures against loss occasioned by:
    (a) a forgery in the chain of recorded title
    (b) liens or encumbrances not disclosed by official records
    (c) rights of parties in possession of the property
    (d) actions of governmental agencies regulating the use or occupancy of the property.

25.   A B C D
      ○ ○ ○ ○

26. A house sold for $113,900, which was 11% more than the cost of the house. The cost of the house was most nearly:
   (a) $99,960
   (b) $100,400
   (c) $101,370
   (d) $102,610.

26. A B C D
   ○ ○ ○ ○

27. A secured real property loan usually consists of:
   (a) financing statement and trust deed
   (b) the debt (note) and the lien (deed of trust)
   (c) FHA or PMI insurance
   (d) security agreement and financing statement.

27. A B C D
   ○ ○ ○ ○

28. During escrow, if an unresolved dispute should arise between the seller and buyer preventing the close of escrow, the escrow holder may legally:
   (a) arbitrate the dispute as a neutral party
   (b) rescind the escrow and return all documents and monies to the respective parties
   (c) file an interpleader action in court
   (d) do any of the above.

28. A B C D
   ○ ○ ○ ○

29. Copies of all listings, deposit receipts, cancelled checks, and trust records must be retained by a licensed real estate broker for:
   (a) one year
   (b) two years
   (c) three years
   (d) five years.

29. A B C D
   ○ ○ ○ ○

30. Parallel wooden members used to support floor and ceiling loads are called:
   (a) rafters
   (b) joists
   (c) headers
   (d) studs.

30. A B C D
   ○ ○ ○ ○

31. When a loan is fully amortized by equal monthly payments of principal and interest the amount applied to principal:
   (a) and interest remains constant
   (b) decreases while the interest payment increases
   (c) increases while the interest payment decreases
   (d) increases by a constant amount.

31. A B C D
   ○ ○ ○ ○

32. Joint ownership of real property by two or more persons each of whom has an undivided interest (not necessarily equal) without right of survivorship is a:
   (a) tenancy in partnership
   (b) tenancy by the entireties
   (c) tenancy in common
   (d) leasehold tenancy.

32. A B C D
   ○ ○ ○ ○

33. A "loss in value from any cause" is a common definition of:
   (a) Economic Obsolescence
   (b) Depreciation
   (c) Principle of Contribution
   (d) Adverse Leverage.

33. A B C D
   ○ ○ ○ ○

34. Which of the following is a lien?
    (a) an easement
    (b) a zoning restriction
    (c) an attachment
    (d) all of the above are liens.

34. A B C D
    ○ ○ ○ ○

35. An owner sold a lot with a front footage of 120 feet and a depth of 300 feet for $3.50 a square foot. What was the selling price?
    (a) $12,600
    (b) $16,200
    (c) $54,500
    (d) $126,000.

35. A B C D
    ○ ○ ○ ○

36. If an appraiser finds that the fair rent for a vacant parcel of land is $700 per month and the interest rate is 11%, what is the approximate indicated land value?
    (a) $54,545
    (b) $69,280
    (c) $76,360
    (d) $105,000.

36. A B C D
    ○ ○ ○ ○

37. Economic obsolescence could result from each of the following, *except*:
    (a) new zoning laws
    (b) a city's leading industry moving out
    (c) misplacement of improvements
    (d) an outdated kitchen.

37. A B C D
    ○ ○ ○ ○

38. Which of the following is an appraiser's primary concern in the analysis of residential property?
    (a) Marketability and acceptability
    (b) Square foot area
    (c) Functional utility
    (d) Fixed and operating expenses.

38. A B C D
    ○ ○ ○ ○

39. A subordination clause in a trust deed may:
    (a) permit the obligation to be paid off ahead of schedule
    (b) prohibit the trustor from making an additional loan against the property before the trust deed is paid off
    (c) allow for periodic renegotiation and adjustment in the terms of the obligation
    (d) give priority to liens subsequently recorded against the property.

39. A B C D
    ○ ○ ○ ○

40. In order to evaluate a vacant commercial site, an appraiser decides to use the land residual technique. Here is the information the appraiser gathered:
Cost new of a proper building—$250,000;
Estimated net income before recapture $32,800 per year; interest rate—8.5%;
Estimated remaining economic life of building—40 years.
What is the approximate estimated value of the land using this technique?
    (a) $31,000
    (b) $47,000
    (c) $48,182
    (d) $62,353.

40. A B C D
    ○ ○ ○ ○

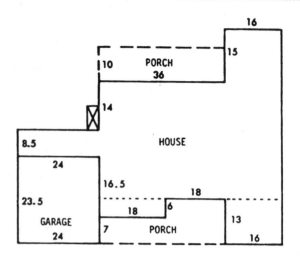

41. In the diagram above how many square feet are contained in the living area of the dwelling only?
    (a) 2236
    (b) 2272
    (c) 2476
    (d) Cannot be computed from information given.

    41. A B C D
         ○ ○ ○ ○

42. A contractor obtained a construction loan, and the loan funds are to be released in a series of progress payments. Most lenders disburse the last payment when the:
    (a) building is completed
    (b) notice of completion is filed
    (c) buyer approves the construction
    (d) period to file a lien has expired.

    42. A B C D
         ○ ○ ○ ○

43. To estimate the value of a parcel of real property, an appraiser concentrated only upon the cost to the buyer of acquiring a comparable, substitute parcel. This estimate approach is most similar to which of the following appraisal methods?
    (a) Cost
    (b) Income
    (c) Market
    (d) None of the above.

    43. A B C D
         ○ ○ ○ ○

44. Brown purchased a $1,400 note secured by a second mortgage for investment purposes. The seller allowed a 15% discount. The note provided for monthly payments of $122 including interest at 9% per annum over a one-year term. Brown received full payment on the above terms. The yield on Brown's investment expressed as a percentage is:
    (a) 23%
    (b) 31%
    (c) 34%
    (d) 40%.

    44. A B C D
         ○ ○ ○ ○

45. The covenant of quiet enjoyment most directly relates to:
    (a) nuisances maintained on adjoining property
    (b) possession of real property
    (c) title to real property
    (d) all of the above.

45.   A B C D
      ○ ○ ○ ○

46. An interest in real property may be acquired by either prescription or by adverse possession. The interest resulting from prescription is:
    (a) the right to use another's land
    (b) a possessory title
    (c) an equitable interest
    (d) a private grant.

46.   A B C D
      ○ ○ ○ ○

47. Generally the taking of private land by governmental bodies for public use is governed by due process of law and is accomplished through:
    (a) exercise of the police power
    (b) eminent domain
    (c) reverter
    (d) escheat.

47.   A B C D
      ○ ○ ○ ○

48. Governmental land use planning and zoning are important examples of:
    (a) exercise of eminent domain
    (b) use of police power
    (c) deed restrictions
    (d) encumbrances.

48.   A B C D
      ○ ○ ○ ○

49. Capitalization is a process whereby an appraiser:
    (a) converts income into capital value
    (b) determines depreciation reserves
    (c) establishes cost of capital investment
    (d) finds gross income of equity capital.

49.   A B C D
      ○ ○ ○ ○

50. In arriving at an effective gross income figure, an appraiser of rental property makes a deduction for:
    (a) real property taxes
    (b) repairs
    (c) vacancy
    (d) depreciation.

50.   A B C D
      ○ ○ ○ ○

AUTHOR'S NOTE

As mentioned on Page 302 under the section entitled "**Sample Multiple Choice Items**", the Department of Real Estate Reference Book does not give the answers to the 50 questions presented in this textbook on pages 303-309. The authors feel the correct answers are as follows:

1. (D) 2. (C) 3. (B) 4. (C) 5. (C) 6. (B) 7. (C) 8. (B) 9. (C) 10. (D)

11. (D) 12. (A) 13. (C) 14. (A) 15. (C) 16. (C) 17. (D) 18. (C)

19. (B) 20. (B) 21. (D) 22. (B) 23. (C) 24. (B) 25. (A) 26. (D)

27. (B) 28. (C) 29. (C) 30. (D) 31. (C) 32. (C) 33. (B) 34. (C)

35. (D) 36. (C) 37. (D) 38. (A) 39. (D) 40. (D) 41. (C) 42. (D)

43. (C) 44. (D) 45. (B) 46. (A) 47. (B) 48. (B) 49. (A) 50. (C)

A complete 150 question practice examination can be found with answers in your textbook beginning on page 365.

Answers to Reviewing Your Understanding Questions

Glossary

ALTA Owner's Policy (Standard Form B-1962, as amended 1969)	An owner's extended coverage policy that provides buyers or owners the same protection the ALTA policy gives to lenders.
ALTA Title Policy (American Land Title Association)	A type of title insurance policy issued by title insurance companies that expands the risks normally insured against under the standard type policy to include unrecorded mechanic's liens; unrecorded physical easements; facts a physical survey would show; water and mineral rights; and rights of parties in possession, such as tenants and buyers under unrecorded instruments.
Abatement of Nuisance	Extinction or termination of a nuisance.
Absolute Fee-Simple Title	Absolute or fee-simple title is one that is absolute and unqualified. It is the best title one can have.
Abstract of Judgment	A condensation of the essential provisions of a court judgment.
Abstract of Title	A summary or digest of the conveyances, transfers, and any other facts relied on as evidence of title, together with any other elements of record that may impair the title.
Abstraction	A method of valuing land. The indicated value of the improvement is deducted from the sale price.
Acceleration Clause	Clause in trust deed or mortgage giving lender right to call all sums owed to the lender to be immediately due and payable upon the happening of a certain event.
Acceptance	When the seller or agent's principal agrees to the terms of the agreement of sale and approves the negotiation on the part of the agent and acknowledges receipt of the deposit in subscribing to the agreement of sale, that act is termed an acceptance.
Access Right	The right of an owner to have ingress and egress to and from his property, also called right of way.
Accretion	An addition to land from natural causes as, for example, from gradual action of the ocean or river waters.
Accrued Depreciation	The difference between the cost of replacement new as of the date of the appraisal and the present appraised value.

This glossary is reprinted from *Student Study Guide for Real Estate Principles*, Dennis J. McKenzie, by permission of California Department of Real Estate.

Accrued Items of Expense	Those incurred expenses which are not yet payable. The seller's accrued expenses are credited to the purchaser in a closing statement.
Acknowledgment	A formal declaration before a duly authorized officer by a person who has executed an instrument that such execution is his or her act and deed.
Acoustical Tile	Blocks of fiber, mineral or metal, with small holes or rough-textured surface to absorb sound, used as covering for interior walls and ceilings.
Acquisition	The act or process by which a person procures property.
Acre	A measure of land equalling 160 square rods, or 4,840 square yards, or 43,560 square feet, or a tract about 208.71 feet square.
Adjustments	A means by which characteristics of a residential property are regulated by dollar amount or percentage to conform to similar characteristics of another residential property.
Administrator	A person appointed by the probate court to administer the estate of a person deceased.
Ad Valorem	A Latin phrase meaning, "according to value." Usually used in connection with real estate taxation.
Advance	Transfer of funds from a lender to a borrower in advance on a loan.
Advance Commitment	The institutional investor's prior agreement to provide long-term financing upon completion of construction.
Advance Fee	A fee paid in advance of any services rendered. Specifically that unethical practice of obtaining a fee in advance for the advertising of property or businesses for sale, with no obligation to obtain a buyer, by persons representing themselves as real estate licensees, or representatives of licensed real estate firms.
Adverse Possession	The open and notorious possession and occupancy under an evident claim or right, in denial or opposition to the title of another claimant.
Affiant	A person who has made an affidavit.
Affidavit	A statement or declaration reduced to writing sworn to or affirmed before some officer who has authority to administer an oath or affirmation.
Affidavit of Title	A statement, in writing, made under oath by seller or grantor, acknowledged before a notary public in which the affiant provides identification certifying that since the examination of title on the contract date there are no judgments, bankruptcies, or divorces, no unrecorded deeds, contracts, unpaid repairs or improvements or defects of title known and that the seller is in possession of the property.

Affirm	To confirm, to aver, to ratify, to verify.
AFLB	Accredited Farm and Land Broker.
Agency	The relationship between principal and agent which arises out of a contract, either expressed or implied, written or oral, wherein the agent is employed by the principal to do certain acts dealing with a third party.
Agent	One who represents another from whom he or she has derived authority.
Agreement of Sale	A written agreement or contract between seller and purchaser in which they reach a meeting of minds on the terms and conditions of the sale.
Air Rights	The rights in real property to use the air space above the surface of the land.
Alienation	The transferring of property to another; the transfer of property and possession of lands, or other things, from one person to another.
Allodial Tenure	A real property ownership system where ownership may be complete except for those rights held by government. Allodial is in contrast to feudal tenure.
Alluvion	(Alluvium) Soil deposited by accretion. Increase of earth on a shore or bank of a river.
Amenities	Satisfaction of enjoyable living to be derived from a home; conditions of agreeable living or a beneficial influence arising from the location or improvements.
American Institute of Real Estate Appraisers	A trade association of real estate appraisers.
AMO	Accredited Management Organization.
Amortization	The liquidation of a financial obligation on an installment basis; also, recovery over a period, of cost or value.
Amortized Loan	A loan that is completely paid off, interest and principal, by a series of regular payments that are equal or nearly equal. Also called a level payments loan.
Annuity	A series of assured equal or nearly equal payments to be made over a period of time or it may be a lump-sum payment to be made in the future. The installment payments due to the landlord under a lease is an annuity. So are the installment payments due to a lender. In real estate finance we are most concerned with the first definition.
Anticipation, Principle of	Affirms that value is created by anticipated benefits to be derived in the future.

Appraisal	An estimate and opinion of value; a conclusion resulting from the analysis of facts.
Appraiser	One qualified by education, training and experience who is hired to estimate the value of real and personal property based on experience, judgment, facts, and use of formal appraisal processes.
Appropriation of	A legal term including the act or acts involved in the taking and reducing to personal possession of water occurring in a stream or other body of water, and if applying such water to beneficial uses or purposes.
Appurtenance	Something annexed to another thing which may be transferred incident to it. That which belongs to another thing, as a barn, dwelling, garage, or orchard is incident to the land to which it is attached.
Architectural Style	Generally the appearance and character of a building's design and construction.
ASA	American Society of Appraisers.
Assessed Valuation	A valuation placed upon property by a public officer or board, as a basis for taxation.
Assessed Value	Value placed on property as a basis for taxation.
Assessment	The valuation of property for the purpose of levying a tax or the amount of the tax levied.
Assessor	The official who has the responsibility of determining assessed values.
Assignment	A transfer or making over to another of the whole of any property, real or personal, in possession or in action, or of any estate or right therein.
Assignor	One who assigns or transfers property.
Assigns; Assignees	Those to whom property shall have been transferred.
Assumption Agreement	An undertaking or adoption of a debt or obligation primarily resting upon another person.
Assumption Fee	A lender's charge for changing over and processing new records for a new owner who is assuming an existing loan.
Assumption of Mortgage	The taking of title to property by a grantee, wherein he assumes liability for payment of an existing note secured by a mortgage or deed of trust against the property; becoming a co-guarantor for the payment of a mortgage or deed of trust note.
Attachment	Seizure of property by court order, usually done to have it available in event a judgment is obtained in a pending suit.
Attest	To affirm to be true or genuine; an official act establishing authenticity.

Attorney in Fact	One who is authorized to perform certain acts for another under a power of attorney; power of attorney may be limited to a specific act or acts, or be general.
Avulsion	The sudden tearing away or removal of land by action of water flowing over or through it.
Axial Growth	City growth which occurs along main transportation routes. Usually takes the form of star-shaped extensions outward from the center.
Backfill	The replacement of excavated earth into a hole or against a structure.
Balloon Payment	Where the final installment payment on a note is greater than the preceding installment payments and it pays the note in full, such final installment is termed a balloon payment.
Bargain and Sale Deed	Any deed that recites a consideration and purports to convey the real estate; a bargain and sale deed with a covenant against the grantor's acts is one in which the grantor warrants that nothing has been done to harm or cloud the title.
Baseboard	A board placed against the wall around a room next to the floor.
Base and Meridian	Imaginary lines used by surveyors to find and describe the location of private or public lands.
Base Molding	Molding used at top of baseboard.
Base Shoe	Molding used at junction of baseboard and floor. Commonly called a carpet strip.
Batten	Narrow strips of wood or metal used to cover joints, interiorly or exteriorly; also used for decorative effect.
Beam	A structural member transversely supporting a load.
Bearing Wall or Partition	A wall or partition supporting any vertical load in addition to its own weight.
Bench Marks	A location indicated on a durable marker by surveyors.
Beneficiary	(1) One entitled to the benefit of a trust; (2) one who receives profit from an estate, the title of which is vested in a trustee; (3) the lender on the security of a note and deed of trust.
Bequeath	To give or hand down by will; to leave by will.
Bequest	That which is given by the terms of a will.
Betterment	An improvement upon property which increases the property value and is considered as a capital asset as distinguished from repairs or replacements where the original character or cost is unchanged.
Bill of Sale	A written instrument given to pass title of personal property from vendor to the vendee.

Binder	An agreement to consider a downpayment for the purchase of real estate as evidence of good faith on the part of the purchaser. Also, a notation of coverage on an insurance policy, issued by an agent, and given to the insured prior to issuing of the policy.
Blacktop	Asphalt paving used in streets and driveways.
Blanket Mortgage	A single mortgage that covers more than one piece of real estate.
Blighted Area	A declining area in which real property values are seriously affected by destructive economic forces, such as encroaching inharmonious property usages, infiltration of lower social and economic classes of inhabitants, and/or rapidly depreciating buildings.
Board Foot	A unit of measurement of lumber; one foot wide, one foot long, one inch thick; 144 cubic inches.
Bona Fide	In good faith, without fraud.
Boot	Unlike property received in an exchange that creates an income tax liability. Examples: Cash, notes, personal property.
Bracing	Framing lumber nailed at an angle in order to provide rigidity.
Breach	The breaking of a law, or failure of duty, either by omission or commission.
Breezeway	A covered porch or passage, open on two sides, connecting house and garage or two parts of the house.
Bridging	Small wood or metal pieces used to brace floor joists.
Broker	A person employed by another, to carry on any of the activities listed in the license law definition of a broker, for a fee.
B.T.U.	British thermal unit. The quantity of heat required to raise the temperature of one pound of water one degree Fahrenheit.
Building Code	A systematic regulation of construction of buildings within a municipality established by ordinance or law.
Building Line	A line set by law a certain distance from a street line in front of which an owner cannot build on his or her lot (a setback line).
Building, Market Value of	The sum of money which the presence of that structure adds to or subtracts from the value of the land it occupies. Land valued on the basis of highest and best use.
Building Paper	A heavy waterproofed paper used as sheathing in wall or roof construction as a protection against air passage and moisture.
Built-in	Cabinets or similar features built as part of the house.
Bundle of Rights	Beneficial interests or rights.
CBD	Central Business District.
CCIM	Certified Commercial Investment Member.

CC and Rs	Abbreviation for covenants, conditions and restrictions.
CPM	Certified property manager, a designation of the Institute of Real Estate Management.
Capital Assets	Assets of a permanent nature used in the production of an income, such as: land, buildings, machinery, and equipment. Under income tax law, it is usually distinguishable from "inventory" which comprises assets held for sale to customers in ordinary course of the taxpayers' trade or business.
Capital Gain	Income from a sale of an asset rather than from the general business activity. Capital gains are generally taxed at a lower rate than ordinary income.
Capitalization	In appraising, determining value of property by considering net income and percentage of reasonable return on the investment. Thus, the value of an income property is determined by dividing annual net income by the capitalization rate.
Capitalization Rate	The rate of interest which is considered a reasonable return on the investment, and used in the process of determining value based upon net income. It may also be described as the yield rate that is necessary to attract the money of the average investor to a particular kind of investment. This amortization factor can be determined in various ways—for example, by the straight-line depreciation method. (To explore this subject in greater depth, the student should refer to current real estate appraisal texts.)
Casement Window	Frames of wood or metal, which swing outward.
Cash Flow	The net income generated by a property before depreciation and other noncash expenses.
Caveat Emptor	Let the buyer beware. The buyer must examine the goods or property and buy at his or her own risk.
Center of Influence	One, who, by nature of his relationships is in a position to sway others.
Certificate of Reasonable Value (CRV)	The Veterans Administration appraisal commitment of property value.
Certificate of Taxes Due	A written statement or guaranty of the condition of the taxes on a certain property, made by the county treasurer of the county wherein the property is located. Any loss resulting to any person from an error in a tax certificate shall be paid by the county which such treasurer represents.
Chain	A unit of measurement used by surveyors. A chain consists of 100 links equal to 66 feet.

Chain of Title	A history of conveyances and encumbrances affecting the title from the time the original patent was granted, or as far back as records are available.
Change, Principle of	Holds that it is the future, not the past, which is of prime importance in estimating value.
Characteristics	Distinguishing features of a (residential) property.
Chattel Mortgage	A claim on personal property (instead of real property) used to secure or guarantee a promissory note. (See definitions of *Security Agreement* and *Security Interest*.)
Chattel Real	An estate related to real estate, such as a lease on real property.
Chattels	Goods or every species of property movable or immovable which are not real property.
Circuit Breaker	An electrical device which automatically interrupts an electric circuit when an overload occurs; may be used instead of a fuse to protect each circuit and can be reset.
Clapboard	Boards usually thicker at one edge used for siding.
Closing Statement	An accounting of funds made to the buyer and seller separately. Required by law to be made at the completion of every real estate transaction.
Cloud on the Title	Any conditions revealed by a title search that affect the title to property; usually relatively unimportant items but which cannot· be removed without a quitclaim deed or court action.
Collar Beam	A beam that connects the pairs of opposite roof rafters above the attic floor.
Collateral	This is the property subject to the security interest. (See definition of *Security Interest*.)
Collateral Security	A separate obligation attached to contract to guarantee its performance; the transfer of property or of other contracts, or valuables, to insure the performance of a principal agreement.
Collusion	An agreement between two or more persons to defraud another's rights by the forms of law, or to obtain an object forbidden by law.
Color of Title	That which appears to be good title but which is not title in fact.
Combed Plywood	A grooved building material used primarily for interior finish.
Commercial Acre	A term applied to the remainder of an acre of newly subdivided land after the area devoted to streets, sidewalks and curbs, and so on, has been deducted from the acre.
Commercial Paper	Bills of exchange used in commercial trade.
Commission	An agent's compensation for performing agency duties; in real estate practice, a percentage of the selling price of property, percentage of rentals, and·so forth.

Commitment	A pledge or a promise or firm agreement.
Common Law	The body of law that grew from customs and practices developed and used in England "since the memory of man runneth not to the contrary."
Community	A part of a metropolitan area that has a number of neighborhoods that have a tendency toward common interests and problems.
Community Property	Property accumulated through joint efforts of a couple living together.
Compaction	Whenever extra soil is added to a lot to fill in low places or to raise the level of the lot, the added soil is often too loose and soft to sustain the weight of the buildings. Therefore, it is necessary to compact the added soil so that it will carry the weight of buildings without the danger of their tilting, settling or cracking.
Comparable Sales	Sales which have similar characteristics as the subject property and are used for analysis in the appraisal process.
Competent	Legally qualified.
Competition, Principle of	Holds that profits tend to breed competition and excess profits tend to breed ruinous competition.
Component	One of the features making up the whole property.
Compound Interest	Interest paid on original principal and also on the accrued and unpaid interest that has accumulated.
Conclusion	The final estimate of value, realized from facts, data, experience and judgment.
Condemnation	The act of taking private property for public use by a political subdivision; declaration that a structure is unfit for use.
Condition	A qualification of an estate granted which can be imposed only in conveyances. They are classified as *conditions precedent* and *conditions subsequent*.
Condition Precedent	A condition that requires certain action or the happening of a specified event before the estate granted can take effect. An example would be most installment real estate sale contracts state all payments shall be made at the time specified before the buyer may demand transfer of title.
Condition Subsequent	When there is a condition subsequent in a deed, the title vests immediately in the grantee, but upon breach of the condition the grantor has the power to terminate the estate—for example, a condition in the deed prohibiting the grantee from using the premises as a liquor store.
Conditional Commitment	A commitment of a definite loan amount for some future unknown purchaser of satisfactory credit standing.
Conditional Sale Contract	A contract for the sale of property stating that delivery is to be made

to the buyer, title to remain vested in the seller until the conditions of the contract have been fulfilled. (See definition of *Security Interest.*)

Condominium A system of individual fee ownership of units in a multifamily structure, combined with joint ownership of common areas of the structure and the land. (Sometimes referred to as a vertical subdivision.)

Conduit Usually a metal pipe in which electrical wiring is installed.

Confession of Judgment An entry of judgment upon the debtor's voluntary admission or confession.

Confirmation of Sale A court approval of the sale of property by an executor, administrator, guardian or conservator.

Confiscation The seizing of property without compensation.

Conformity, Principle of Holds that the maximum of value is realized when a reasonable degree of homogeneity of improvements is present.

Conservation The process of utilizing resources in such a manner which minimizes their depletion.

Consideration Anything of value given to induce entering into a contract; it may be money, personal services, or even love and affection.

Constant The percentage which, when applied directly to the face value of a debt, develops the annual amount of money necessary to pay a specified net rate of interest on the reducing balance and to liquidate the debt in a specified time period. For example, a 6% loan with a 20 year amortization has a constant of approximately 8½%. Thus, a $10,000 loan amortized over 20 years requires an annual payment of approximately $850.00.

Construction Loans Loans made for the construction of homes or commercial buildings. Usually funds are disbursed to the contractor-builder during construction and after periodic inspections. Disbursements are based on an agreement between borrower and lender.

Constructive Eviction Breach of a covenant of warranty or quiet enjoyment, e.g., the inability of a lessee to obtain possession because of a paramount defect in title, or a condition making occupancy hazardous.

Constructive Notice Notice given by the public records.

Consumer Goods These are goods used or bought for use primarily for personal, family or household purposes.

Consummate Dower A widow's dower interest which, after the death of her husband, is complete or may be completed and become an interest in real estate.

Contour The surface configuration of land.

Contract An agreement, either written or oral, to do or not to do certain things.

Contribution, Principle of	Holds that maximum real property values are achieved when the improvements on the site produce the highest (net) return, commensurate with the investment.
Conventional Mortgage	A mortgage securing a loan made by investors without governmental underwriting—that is, not FHA-insured or VA-guaranteed.
Conversion	Change from one character or use to another.
Conveyance	This has two meanings. One meaning refers to the process of transferring title to property from one person to another. In this sense it is used as a verb. The other meaning refers to the document used to effect the transfer of title (usually some kind of deed). In this last sense, it is used as a noun.
Cooperative Ownership	A form of apartment ownership. Ownership of shares in a cooperative venture which entitles the owner to use, rent, or sell a specific apartment unit. The corporation usually reserves the right to approve certain actions such as a sale or improvement.
Corner Influence Table	A statistical table that may be used to estimate the added value of a corner lot.
Corporation	A group or body of persons established and treated by law as an individual or unit with rights and liabilities or both, distinct and apart from those of the persons composing it.
	A corporation is a creature of law having certain powers and duties of a natural person. Being created by law it may continue for any length of time the law prescribes.
Corporeal Rights	Possessory rights in real property.
Correction Lines	A system for compensating inaccuracies in the government rectangular survey system due to the curvature of the earth. Every fourth township line, 24 mile intervals, is used as a correction line on which the intervals between the north and south range lines are remeasured and corrected to a full 6 miles.
Correlate the Findings	Interpret the data and value estimates to bring them together to a final conclusion of value.
Correlation	To bring the indicated values developed by the three approaches into mutual relationship with each other.
Cost	A historical record of past expenditures, or an amount which would be given in exchange for other things.
Cost Approach	One of three methods in the appraisal process. An analysis in which a value estimate of a property is derived by estimating the replacement cost of the improvements, deducting therefrom the estimated accrued depreciation, then adding the market value of the land.

Counterflashing	Flashing used on chimneys at roofline to cover shingle flashing and to prevent moisture entry.
Covenant	Agreements written into deeds and other instruments promising performance or nonperformance of certain acts or stipulating certain uses or nonuses of the property.
Crawl Hole	Exterior or interior opening permitting access underneath building, as required by building codes.
CRB	Certified residential broker.
CRE	Counselor of real estate; member of American Society of Real Estate Counselors.
Cubage	The number or product resulting by multiplying the width of a thing by its height and by its depth or length.
Curable Depreciation	Items of physical deterioration and functional obsolescence which are customarily repaired or replaced by a prudent property owner.
Curtail Schedule	A listing of the amounts by which the principal sum of an obligation is to be reduced by partial payments and of the dates when each payment will become payable.
Curtesy	The right which a husband has in a wife's estate at her death.
Damages	The indemnity recoverable by a person who has sustained an injury, either in his person, property, or relative rights, through the act or default of another.
Data Plant	An appraiser's file of information on real estate.
Debenture	Bonds issued without security.
Debtor	This is the party who "owns" the property which is subject to the security interest—previously known as the *mortgagor* or the *pledgor*.
Deciduous Trees	Lose their leaves in the autumn and winter.
Deck	Usually an open porch on the roof of a ground or lower floor, porch or wing.
Decree of Foreclosure	Decree by a court in the completion of foreclosure of a mortgage, contract, or lien.
Dedication	An appropriation of land by its owner for some public use accepted for such use by authorized public officials on behalf of the public.
Deed	Written instrument which, when properly executed and delivered, conveys title.
Deed Restrictions	This is a limitation in the deed to a property that dictates certain uses that may or may not be made of the property.
Default	Failure to fulfill a duty or promise or to discharge an obligation; omission or failure to perform any act.

Defeasance Clause	The clause in a mortgage that gives the mortgagor the right to redeem his or her property upon the payment of obligations to the mortgagee.
Defeasible Fee	Sometimes called a base fee or qualified fee; a fee-simple absolute interest in land that is capable of being defeated or terminated upon the happening of a specified event.
Deferred Maintenance	Existing but unfulfilled requirements for repairs and rehabilitation.
Deferred Payment Options	The privilege of deferring income payments to take advantage of the tax statutes.
Deficiency Judgment	A judgment given when the security pledge for a loan does not satisfy the debt upon its default.
Depreciation	Loss of value in real property brought about by age, physical deterioration or functional or economic obsolescence. Broadly, a loss in value from any cause.
Depth Table	A statistical table that may be used to estimate the value of the added depth of a lot.
Desist and Refrain Order	An order directing a person to desist and refrain from committing an act in violation of the real estate law.
Deterioration	Impairment of condition. One of the causes of depreciation and reflecting the loss in value brought about by wear and tear, disintegration, use in service, and the action of the elements.
Devisee	One who receives a bequest made by will.
Devisor	One who bequeaths by will.
Directional Growth	The location or direction toward which the residential sections of a city are destined or determined to grow.
Discount	An amount deducted in advance from the principal before the borrower is given the use of the principal (see *Point(s)*).
Disintermediation	The relatively sudden withdrawal of substantial sums of money savers have deposited with savings and loan associations, commercial banks, and mutual savings banks. This term can also be considered to include life insurance policy purchasers borrowing against the value of their policies. The essence of this phenomenon is financial intermediaries losing within a short period of time billions of dollars as owners of funds held by those institutional lenders exercise their prerogative of taking them out of the hands of these financial institutions.
Disposable Income	The after-tax income a household receives to spend on personal consumption.
Dispossess	To deprive one of the use of real estate.
Documentary Transfer Tax	A state enabling act allowing a county to adopt a documentary transfer tax to apply on all transfer of real property located in the county. Notice

of payment is entered on face of the deed or on a separate paper filed with the deed.

Donee A person to whom a gift is made.

Donor A person who makes a gift.

Dower The right which a wife has in her husband's estate at his death.

Duress Unlawful constraint exercised upon a person whereby the person is forced to do some act unwillingly.

Earnest Money Downpayment made by a purchaser of real estate as evidence of good faith.

Easement Created by grant or agreement for a specific purpose, an easement is the right, privilege or interest which one party has in the land of another—for example, right of way.

Eaves The lower part of a roof projecting over the wall.

Ecology The relationship between organisms and their environment.

Economic Life The period over which a property will yield a return on the investment, over and above the economic or ground rent due to land.

Economic Obsolescence A loss in value due to factors away from the subject property but adversely affecting the value of the subject property.

Economic Rent The reasonable rental expectancy if the property were available for renting at the time of its valuation.

Effective Age of Improvement The number of years of age that is indicated by the condition of the structure.

Effective Date of Value The specific day the conclusion of value applies.

Effective Interest Rate The percentage of interest that is actually being paid by the borrower for the use of the money.

Eminent Domain The right of the government to acquire property for necessary public or quasi-public use by condemnation; the owner must be fairly compensated. The right of the government to do this and the right of the private citizen to get paid is spelled out in the Fifth Amendment to the United States Constitution.

Encroachment Trespass, the building of a structure or construction of any improvements, partly or wholly on the property of another.

Encumbrance Anything which affects or limits the fee-simple title to property, such as mortgages, easements or restrictions of any kind. Liens are special encumbrances which make the property security for the payment of a debt or obligation, such as mortgages and taxes.

Endorsement The act of signing one's name on the back of a check or note, with or without further qualification.

Equity	The interest or value which an owner has in real estate over and above the liens against it; branch of remedial justice by and through which relief is afforded to suitors in courts of equity.
Equity of Redemption	The right to redeem property during the foreclosure period, such as a mortgagor's right to redeem within a year after foreclosure sale.
Erosion	The wearing away of land by the action of water, wind or glacial ice.
Escalation	The right reserved by the lender to increase the amount of the payments and/or interest upon the happening of a certain event.
Escalator Clause	A clause in a contract providing for the upward or downward adjustment of certain items to cover specified contingencies.
Escheat	The reverting of property to the state when heirs capable of inheriting are lacking.
Escrow	The deposit of instruments and funds with instructions to a third neutral party to carry out the provisions of an agreement or contract; when everything is deposited to enable carrying out the instructions, it is called a complete or perfect escrow.
Estate	As applied to the real estate practice, the term signifies the quantity of interest, share, right, equity, of which riches or fortune may consist, in real property. The degree, quantity, nature, and extent of interest which a person has in real property.
Estate of Inheritance	An estate which may descend to heirs. All freehold estates are estates of inheritance, except estates for life.
Estate for Life	A freehold estate, not of inheritance, but which is held by the tenant for his or her own life or the life or lives of one or more other persons, or for an indefinite period which may endure for the life or lives of persons in being and beyond the period of life.
Estate from Period to Period	An interest in land where there is no definite termination date but the rental period is fixed at a certain sum per week, month, or year. Also called a periodic tenancy.
Estate at Sufferance	An estate arising when the tenant wrongfully holds over after the expiration of his term. The landlord has the choice of evicting the tenant as a trespasser or accepting such tenant for a similar term and under the conditions of the tenant's previous holding. Also called a tenancy at sufferance.
Estate of Will	The occupation of lands and tenements by a tenant for an indefinite period, terminable by one or both parties.
Estate for Years	An interest in lands by virtue of a contract for the possession of them for a definite and limited period of time. A lease may be said to be an estate for years.
Estimate	To form a preliminary opinion of value.

Estimated Remaining Life	The period of time (years) it takes for the improvements to become valueless.
Estoppel	A doctrine which bars one from asserting rights which are inconsistent with a previous position or representation.
Ethics	That branch of moral science, idealism, justness, and fairness, which treats of the duties which a member of a profession or craft owes to the public, to clients or patrons, and to other professional members.
Eviction	Dispossession by process of law. The act of depriving a person of the possession of lands, in pursuance of the judgment of a court.
Exclusive Agency Listing	A written instrument giving one agent the right to sell property for a specified time but reserving the right of the owner to sell the property without the payment of a commission.
Exclusive Right to Sell Listing	A written agreement between owner and agent giving agent the right to collect a commission if the property is sold by anyone during the term of his agreement.
Execute	To complete, to make, to perform, to do, to follow out; to execute a deed, to make a deed, including especially signing, sealing, and delivery; to execute a contract is to perform the contract, to follow out to the end, to complete.
Executor	A person named in a will to carry out its provisions as to the disposition of the estate of a person deceased.
Expansible House	Home designed for further expansion and additions in the future.
Expansion Joint	A bituminous fiber strip used to separate units of concrete to prevent cracking due to expansion as a result of temperature changes.
Expenses	Certain items that may appear on a closing statement in connection with a real estate sale.
Facade	Front of a building.
Fair Market Value	This is the amount of money that would be paid for a property offered on the open market for a reasonable period of time with both buyer and seller knowing all the uses to which the property could be put and with neither party being under pressure to buy or sell.
Farmers Home Administration	An agency of the Department of Agriculture. Primary responsibility is to provide financial assistance for farmers and others living in rural areas where financing is not available on reasonable terms from private sources.
Federal Deposit Insurance Corporation	(FDIC) Agency of the federal government which insures deposits at commercial banks and savings banks.
Federal Home Loan Bank	(FHLB) A district bank of the Federal Home Loan Bank system that lends only to member savings and loan associations.

Federal Home Loan Bank Board	(FHLBB) The administrative agency that charters federal savings and loan associations and exercises regulatory authority over the FHLB system.
Federal Housing Administration	(FHA) An agency of the federal government that insures mortgage loans.
Federal National Mortgage Association	(FNMA) "Fanny Mae" a quasi-public agency being converted into a private corporation whose primary function is to buy and sell FHA and VA mortgages in the secondary market.
Federal Savings and Loan Association	An association chartered by the FHLBB in contrast to a state-chartered savings and loan association.
Federal Savings and Loan Insurance Corporation	(FSLIC) An agency of the federal government that insures savers' accounts at savings and loan associations.
Fee	An estate of inheritance in real property.
Fee Simple	In modern estates, the terms "fee" and "fee simple" are substantially synonymous. The term "fee" is of Old English derivation. "Fee-Simple Absolute" is an estate in real property, by which the owner has the greatest power over the title which it is possible to have, being an absolute estate. In modern use, it expressly establishes the title of real property in the owner, without limitation or end. The owner may dispose of it by sale, or trade or will.
Feudal Tenure	A real property ownership system where ownership rests with a sovereign who, in turn, may grant lesser interests in return for service or loyalty. In contrast to allodial tenure.
Feuds	Grants of land.
Fidelity Bond	A security posted for the discharge of an obligation of personal services.
Fiduciary	A person in a position of trust and confidence, as between principal and broker; broker as fiduciary owes certain loyalty which cannot be breached under the rules of agency.
Filtering Down	The process of making housing available to successively lower income groups.
Financial Intermediary	Financial institutions such as commercial banks, savings and loan associations, mutual savings banks and life insurance companies which receive relatively small sums of money from the public and invest them in the form of large sums. A considerable portion of these funds are loaned on real estate.
Financing Statement	An instrument filed in order to give public notice of the security interest and thereby protect the interest of the secured parties in the collateral. See definitions of *Security Interest* and *Secured Party*.
Finish Floor	Finish floor strips are applied over wood joists, deadening felt and

diagonal subflooring before finish floor is installed; finish floor is the final covering on the floor: wood, linoleum, cork, tile or carpet.

Fire Stop	A solid, tight closure of a concealed space, placed to prevent the spread of fire and smoke through such a space.
First Mortgage	A legal document pledging collateral for a loan (see "mortgage") that has first priority over all other claims against the property except taxes and bonded indebtedness.
First Trust Deed	A legal document pledging collateral for a loan (see definition of *Trust Deed)* that has first priority over all other claims against the property except taxes and bonded indebtedness.
Fiscal Controls	Federal tax revenue and expenditure policies used to control the level of economic activity.
Fixity of Location	The physical characteristic of real estate that subjects it to the influence of its surroundings.
Fixtures	Appurtenances attached to the land or improvements, which usually cannot be removed without agreement as they become real property—for example, plumbing fixtures, or store fixtures built into the property.
Flashing	Sheet metal or other material used to protect a building from seepage of water.
Footing	The base or bottom of a foundation wall, pier, or column.
Foreclosure	Procedure whereby property pledged as security for a debt is sold to pay the debt in event of default in payments or terms.
Forfeiture	Loss of money or anything of value, due to failure to perform.
Foundation	The supporting portion of a structure below the first floor construction, or below grade, including the footings.
Franchise	A specified privilege awarded by a government or business firm which awards an exclusive dealership.
Fraud	The intentional and successful employment of any cunning, deception, collusion, or artifice, used to circumvent, cheat or deceive another person, whereby that person acts upon it to the loss of his property and to his legal injury.
Freehold	An estate of indeterminable duration, such as fee simple or life estate.
Frontage	Land bordering a street.
Front Foot	Property measurement for sale or valuation purposes; the property measures by the front foot on its street line—each front foot extending the depth of the lot.
Front Money	The minimum amount of money necessary to initiate a real estate venture.

Frostline	The depth of frost penetration in the soil. Varies in different parts of the country. Footings should be placed below this depth to prevent movement.
Functional Obsolescence	A loss of value due to adverse factors from within the structure which affect the utility of the structure.
Furring	Strips of wood or metal applied to a wall or other surface to even it, to form an air space, or to give the wall an appearance of greater thickness.
Future Benefits	The anticipated benefits the present owner will receive from property in the future.
Gable Roof	A pitched roof with sloping sides.
Gambrel Roof	A curb roof, having a steep lower slope with a flatter upper slope above.
General Lien	A lien on all the property of a debtor.
Gift Deed	A deed for which the consideration is love and affection and where there is not material consideration.
Girder	A large beam used to support beams, joists and partitions.
Grade	Ground level at the foundation.
Graduated Lease	Lease which provides for a varying rental rate, often based upon future determination; sometimes rent is based upon result of periodical appraisals; used largely in long-term leases.
Grant	A technical term made use of in deeds of conveyance of lands to import a transfer.
Grant Deed	A deed in which "grant" is used as the word of conveyance. The grantor impliedly warrants that he or she has not already conveyed to any other person, and that the estate conveyed is free from encumbrances done, made or suffered by the grantor or any person claiming under him or her, including taxes, assessments, and other liens.
Grantee	The purchaser; a person to whom a grant is made.
Grantor	Seller of property; one who signs a deed.
GRI	Graduate, Realtors Institute.
Grid	A chart used in rating the borrower risk, property, and the neighborhood.
Gross Income	Total income from property before any expenses are deducted.
Gross National Product	(GNP) The total value of all goods and services produced in an economy during a given period of time.

Gross Rate	A method of collecting interest by adding total interest to the principal of the loan at the outset of the term.
Gross Rent Multiplier	A figure which, times the gross income of a property, produces an estimate of value of the property.
Ground Lease	An agreement for the use of the land only, sometimes secured by improvements placed on the land by the user.
Ground Rent	Earnings of improved property credited to earnings of the ground itself after allowance is made for earnings of improvements; often termed *economic rent.*
Habendum Clause	The "to have and to hold" clause in a deed.
Header	A beam placed perpendicular to joists and to which joists are nailed in framing for chimney, stairway, or other opening.
Highest and Best Use	An appraisal phrase meaning that use which at the time of an appraisal is most likely to produce the greatest net return to the land and/or buildings over a given period of time; that use which will produce the greatest amount of amenities or profit. This is the starting point for appraisal.
Hip Roof	A pitched roof with sloping sides and ends.
Holder in Due Course	One who has taken a note, check or bill of exchange in due course: (1) before it was overdue, (2) in good faith and for value, (3) without knowledge that it has been previously dishonored without notice of any defect at the time it was negotiated to him.
Holdover Tenant	Tenant who remains in possession of leased property after the expiration of the lease term.
Homestead	A home upon which the owner or owners have recorded a Declaration of Homestead, as provided by statutes in some states; protects home against judgments up to specified amounts.
Hundred Percent Location	A city retail business location which is considered the best available for attracting business.
Hypothecate	To give a thing as security without the necessity of giving up possession of it.
Impounds	A trust-type account established by lenders for the accumulation of funds to meet taxes, FHA mortgage insurance premiums, and/or future insurance policy premiums required to protect their security. Impounds are usually collected with the note payment.
Inchoate Right of Dower	A wife's interest in the real estate of her husband during his life which upon his death may become a dower interest.
Income Approach	One of the three methods in the appraisal process; an analysis in which the estimated gross income from the subject residence is used as a basis for estimating value along with gross rent multipliers derived.

Incompetent	One who is mentally incompetent, incapable; any person who, though not insane, is, by reason of old age, disease, weakness of mind, or any other cause, unable, unassisted, to properly manage and take care of him- or herself or property and by reason thereof would be likely to be deceived or imposed upon by artful or designing persons.
Incorporeal Rights	Nonpossessory rights in real estate.
Increment	An increase. Most frequently used to refer to the increase of value of land that accompanies population growth and increasing wealth in the community. The term unearned increment is used in this connection since values are supposed to have increased without effort on the part of the owner.
Indenture	A formal written instrument made between two or more persons in different interests.
Indirect Lighting	The light is reflected from the ceiling or other object external to the fixture.
Injunction	A writ or order issued under the seal of a court to restrain one or more parties to a suit or proceeding from doing an act which is deemed to be inequitable or unjust in regard to the rights of some other party or parties in the suit or proceeding.
Input	Data, information, and so on, that is fed into a computer or other system.
Installment Contract	Purchase of real estate wherein the purchase price is paid in installments over a long period of time, title is retained by seller, upon default the payments are forfeited. Also known as a land contract.
Installment Note	A note that provides that payments of a certain sum or amount be paid on the dates specified in the instrument.
Installment Reporting	A method of reporting capital gains by installments for successive tax years to minimize the impact of the totality of the capital gains tax in the year of the sale.
Instrument	A written legal document; created to effect the rights of the parties.
Interest	The charge in dollars for the use of money for a period of time. In a sense, the "rent" paid for the use of money.
Interest Rate	The percentage of a sum of money charged for its use.
Interim Loan	A short-term loan until long-term financing is available.
Intestate	A person who dies having made no will, or one which is defective in form in which case the estate descends to the heirs at law or next of kin.
Involuntary Lien	A lien imposed against property without consent of an owner;—for example, taxes, special assessments, federal income tax liens.

Irrevocable	Incapable of being recalled or revoked; unchangeable.
Irrigation Districts	Quasi-political districts created under special laws to provide for water services to property owners in the district; an operation governed to a great extent by law.
Jalousie	A slatted blind or shutter, like a venetian blind but used on the exterior to protect against rain as well as to control sunlight.
Jamb	The side post or lining of a doorway, window or other opening.
Joint	The space between the adjacent surfaces of two components joined and held together by nails, glue, cement, or mortar.
Joint Note	A note signed by two or more persons who have equal liability for payment.
Joint Tenancy	Joint ownership by two or more persons with right of survivorship; all joint tenants own equal interest and have equal rights in the property.
Joint Venture	Two or more individuals or firms joining together on a single project as partners.
Joist	One of a series of parallel beams to which the boards of a floor and ceiling laths are nailed, and supported in turn by larger beams, girders, or bearing walls.
Judgment	The final determination of a court of competent jurisdiction of a matter presented to it; money judgments provide for the payment of claims presented to the court, or are awarded as damages.
Judgment Lien	A legal claim on all of the property of a judgment debtor which enables the judgment creditor to have the property sold for payment of the amount of the judgment.
Junior Mortgage	A mortgage second in lien to a previous mortgage.
Jurisdiction	The authority by which judicial officers take cognizance of and decide causes; the power to hear and determine a cause; the right and power which a judicial officer has to enter upon the inquiry.
Laches	Delay or negligence in asserting one's legal rights.
Land Contract	A contract ordinarily used in connection with the sale of property in cases where the seller does not wish to convey title until all or a certain part of the purchase price is paid by the buyer; often used when property is sold on small down payment.
Land and Improvement Loan	A loan obtained by the builder-developer for the purchase of land and to cover expenses for subdividing.
Landlord	One who rents property to another.
Later Date Order	The commitment for an owner's title insurance policy issued by a title insurance company which covers the seller's title as of the date of the contract. When the sale closes the purchaser orders the title

company to record the deed to purchaser and bring down their examination to cover this later date so as to show purchaser as owner of the property.

Lateral Support The support which the soil of an adjoining owner gives to a neighbor's land.

Lath A building material of wood, metal, gypsum, or insulating board fastened to the frame of a building to act as a plaster base.

Lease A contract between owner and tenant, setting forth conditions upon which tenant may occupy and use the property, and the term of the occupancy.

Leasehold Estate A tenant's right to occupy real estate during the term of the lease. This is a personal property interest.

Legal Description A description recognized by law; a description by which property can be definitely located by reference to government surveys or approved recorded maps.

Lessee One who contracts to rent property under a lease contract.

Lessor An owner who enters into a lease with a tenant.

Level-Payment Mortgage A loan on real estate that is paid off by making a series of equal (or nearly equal) regular payments. Part of the payment is usually interest on the loan and part of it reduces the amount of the unpaid balance of the loan. Also sometimes called an amortized mortgage.

Lien A form of encumbrance which usually makes property security for the payment of a debt or discharge of an obligation. Example: judgments, taxes, mortgages, deeds of trust, etc.

Life Estate An estate or interest in real property which is held for the duration of the life of some certain person.

Limited Partnership A partnership composed of some partners whose contribution and liability are limited.

Lintel A horizontal board that supports the load over an opening such as a door or window.

Liquidated Damages A sum agreed upon by the parties to be full damages if a certain event occurs.

Lis Pendens Suit pending, usually recorded so as to give constructive notice of pending litigation.

Listing An employment contract between principal and agent authorizing the agent to perform services for the principal involving the latter's property; listing contracts are entered into for the purpose of securing persons to buy, lease, or rent property. Employment of an agent by a prospective purchaser or lessee to locate property for purchase or lease may be considered a listing.

Loan Administration	Mortgage bankers not only originate loans, but also "service" them from origination to maturity of the loan. Also called loan servicing.
Loan Application	The loan application is a source of information on which the lender decides whether to make the loan, defines the terms of the loan contract; gives the name of the borrower, place of employment, salary, bank accounts, and credit references; and, describes the real estate that is to be mortgaged. It also stipulates the amount of loan being applied for and repayment terms.
Loan Closing	When all conditions have been met, the loan officer authorizes the recording of the trust deed or mortgage. The disbursal procedure of funds is similar to the closing of a real estate sales escrow. The borrower can expect to receive less than the amount of the loan, as title, recording, service, and other fees may be withheld, or he can expect to deposit the cost of these items into the loan escrow. This process is sometimes called "funding" the loan.
Loan Commitment	Lender's contractual commitment to a loan based on the appraisal and underwriting.
Loan-Value Ratio	The percentage of a property's value that a lender can or may loan to a borrower. For example, if the ratio is 80 percent this means that a lender may loan 80 percent of the property's appraised value to a borrower.
Louver	An opening with a series of horizontal slats set at an angle to permit ventilation without admitting rain, sunlight, or vision.
MAI	Member of the Appraisal Institute. Designates a person who is a member of the American Institute of Real Estate Appraisers of the National Association of Realtors.
Margin of Security	The difference between the amount of the mortgage loan(s) and the appraised value of the property.
Marginal Land	Land which barely pays the cost of working or using.
Market Data Approach	One of the three methods in the appraisal process. A means of comparing similar type residential properties, which have recently sold, to the subject property.
Market Price	The price paid regardless of pressures, motives, or intelligence.
Market Value	(1) The price at which a willing seller would sell and a willing buyer would buy, neither being under abnormal pressure; (2) as defined by the courts, is the highest price estimated in terms of money which a property will bring if exposed for sale in the open market allowing a reasonable time to find a purchaser with knowledge of property's use and capabilities for use.
Marketable Title	Merchantable title; title free and clear of objectionable liens or encumbrances.

Material Fact	A fact is material if it is one which the agent should realize would be likely to affect the judgment of the principal in giving consent to the agent to enter into the particular transaction on the specified terms.
Mechanics' Lien	A lien created by statute which exists against real property in favor of persons who have performed work or furnished materials for the improvement of the real estate.
Memory Bank	Data and information held in storage in the computer.
Meridians	Imaginary north-south lines that intersect base lines to form a starting point for the measurement of land.
Metes and Bounds	A term used in describing the boundary lines of land, setting forth all the boundary lines together with their terminal points and angles.
Minor	All persons under 18 years of age.
Misplaced Improvements	Improvements on land which do not conform to the most profitable use of the site.
Modular	A building composed of modules constructed on an assembly line in a factory. Usually, the modules are self-contained.
Moldings	Usually patterned strips used to provide ornamental variation of outline or contour, such as cornices, bases, window and door jambs.
Monetary Controls	Federal Reserve tools for regulating the availability of money and credit to influence the level of economic activity.
Monument	A fixed object and point established by surveyors to establish land locations.
Moratorium	The temporary suspension, usually by statute, of the enforcement of liability for debt.
Mortgage	An instrument recognized by law by which property is hypothecated to secure the payment of a debt or obligation; procedure for foreclosure in event of default is established by statute.
Mortgage Contracts with Warrants	Warrants make the mortgage more attractive to the lender by providing both the greater security that goes with a mortgage, and the opportunity of a greater return through the right to buy either stock in the borrower's company or a portion of the income property itself.
Mortgage Guaranty Insurance	Insurance against financial loss available to mortgage lenders from Mortgage Guaranty Insurance Corporation, a private company organized in 1956.
Mortgagee	One to whom a mortgagor gives a mortgage to secure a loan or performance of an obligation, a lender. (See definition of *Secured Party.*)
Mortgagor	One who gives a mortgage on his or her property to secure a loan

or assure performance of an obligation; a borrower. (See definition of *Debtor*.)

Multiple Listing A listing, usually an exclusive right to sell, taken by a member of an organization composed of real estate brokers, with the provisions that all members will have the opportunity to find an interested client; a cooperative listing.

Mutual Water Company A water company organized by or for water users in a given district with the object of securing an ample water supply at a reasonable rate; stock is issued to users.

NAR National Association of Realtors.

NAREB National Association of Real Estate Brokers.

Narrative Appraisal A summary of all factual materials, techniques, and appraisal methods used by the appraiser to determine the value conclusion.

Negotiable Capable of being negotiated; assignable or transferable in the ordinary course of business.

Net Listing A listing which provides that the agent may retain as compensation for his services all sums received over and above a net price to the owner.

Nominal Interest Rates The percentage of interest stated in loan documents.

Notary Public An appointed officer with authority to take the acknowledgment of persons executing documents, to sign the certificate, and affix a seal.

Note A signed written instrument acknowledging a debt and promising payment.

Notice Actual knowledge acquired by being present at the occurrence.

Notice of Nonresponsibility A notice provided by law designed to relieve a property owner from responsibility for the cost of work done on the property or materials furnished therefor; notice must be verified, recorded and posted.

Notice to Quit A notice to a tenant to vacate rented property.

Obsolescence Loss in value due to reduced desirability and usefulness of a structure because its design and construction become obsolete; loss because of becoming old-fashioned and not in keeping with modern needs, with consequent loss in income.

Offset Statement Statement by owner of property or owner of lien against property, setting forth the present status of liens against said property.

Open-End Mortgage A mortgage containing a clause that permits the mortgagor to borrow additional money after the loan has been reduced, without rewriting the mortgage.

Open Housing Law Congress passed a law in April 1968 that prohibits discrimination in the sale of real estate because of race, color, or religion of buyers.

Open Listing	An authorization given by a property owner to a real estate agent wherein said agent is given the nonexclusive right to secure a purchaser; open listings may be given to any number of agents without liability to compensate any except the one who first secures a buyer ready, willing and able to meet the terms of the listing, or secures the acceptance by the seller of a satisfactory offer.
Opinion of Title	An attorney's evaluation of the condition of the title to a parcel of land after examination of the abstract of title to the land.
Option	A right given for a consideration to purchase or lease a property upon specified terms within a specified time.
Oral Contract	A verbal agreement; one which is not reduced to writing.
Orientation	Placing a house on its lot with regard to its exposure to the rays of the sun, prevailing winds, privacy from the street and protection from outside noises.
Overhang	The part of the roof extending beyond the walls, to shade buildings and cover walks.
Over Improvement	An improvement which is not the highest and best use for the site on which it is placed by reason of excess size or cost.
Participation	In addition to base interest on mortgage loans on income properties, a small percentage of gross income is required, sometimes predicated on certain conditions being fulfilled, such as minimum occupancy or a percentage of net income after expenses, debt service, and taxes.
Partition Action	Court proceedings by which co-owners seek to sever their joint ownership.
Partnership	A decision of the California Supreme Court has defined a partnership in the following terms: "A partnership as between partners themselves may be defined to be a contract of two or more persons to unite their property, labor or skill, or some of them, in prosecution of some joint or lawful business, and to share the profits in certain proportions."
Party Wall	A wall erected on the line between two adjoining properties, which are under different ownership, for the use of both properties.
Par Value	Market value, nominal value.
Patent	Conveyance of title to government land.
Penalty	An extra payment or charge required of the borrower for deviating from the terms of the original loan agreement. Usually levied for being late in making regular payment or for paying off the loan before it is due.
Penny	The term, as applied to nails, serves as a measure of nail length and is abbreviated by the letter "d."
Percentage Lease	Lease on the property, the rental for which is determined by amount

of business done by the lessee; usually a percentage of gross receipts from the business with provision for a minimum rental.

Perimeter Heating Baseboard heating, or any system in which the heat registers are located along the outside walls of a room, especially under the windows.

Personal Property Any property that is not real property.

Physical Deterioration Impairment of condition. Loss in value brought about by wear and tear, disintegration, use, and actions of the elements.

Pier A column of masonry, usually rectangular in horizontal cross section, used to support other structural members.

Pitch The incline or rise of a roof.

Planned Unit Development (PUD) A land-use design that provides intensive utilization of the land through a combination of private and common areas with prearranged sharing of responsibilities for the common areas.

Plate A horizontal board placed on a wall or supported on posts or studs to carry the trusses of a roof or rafters directly; a shoe, or base member as of a partition or other frame; a small flat board placed on or in a wall to support girders, rafters, and so on.

Pledge The depositing of personal property by a debtor with a creditor as security for a debt or engagement.

Pledgee One who is given a pledge or a security. (See definition of *Secured Party*.)

Pledgor One who offers a pledge or gives security. (See definition of *Debtor*.)

Plottage Increment The appreciation in unit value created by joining smaller ownerships into one large single ownership.

Plywood Laminated wood made up in panels; several thicknesses of wood glued together with grain at different angles for strength.

Points Under FHA-insured or VA-guaranteed loans, discounts or points paid to lenders are, in effect, prepaid interest, and are used by lenders to adjust the effective interest rate so that it is equal to or nearly equal to the prevailing market rate (the rate charged on conventional loans). The discounts are absorbed by the sellers, and a point is one percent of the loan amount. On FHA-insured and VA-guaranteed loans, buyers may be charged only one percent ("service charge"). This restriction does not apply to conventional loans. Under conventional loans the charge for making a loan at most institutions is usually called a loan fee, service charge, commitment fee, or may be referred to as points to the buyer.

Police Power The right of the state to enact laws and enforce them for the order, safety, health, morals, and general welfare of the public.

Power of Attorney	An instrument authorizing a person to act as the agent of the person granting it, and a general power authorizing the agent to act generally in behalf of the principal. A special power limits the agent to a particular or specific act as: a landowner may grant an agent special power of attorney to convey a single and specific parcel of property. Under the provisions of a general power of attorney, the agent having the power may convey any or all property of the principal granting the general power of attorney.
Prefabricated House	A house manufactured and sometimes partly assembled before delivery to building site.
Prepaid Items of Expense	Prorations of prepaid items of expense that are credited to the seller in the closing statement.
Prepayment	Provision made for loan payments to be larger than those specified in the note.
Prepayment Penalty	Penalty for the payment of a mortgage or trust deed note before it actually becomes due if the note does not provide for prepayment.
Prescription	The securing of title to property by adverse possession; by occupying it for the period determined by law barring action for recovery.
Present Value	The lump-sum value today of an annuity. A $100 bill to be paid to someone in *one year* is worth *less* than if it were a $100 bill to be paid to someone *today*. This is due to several things, one of which is that the money has *time value*. How much the $100 bill to be paid in one year is worth today will depend on the interest rate that seems proper for the particular circumstances. For example, if 6 percent is the appropriate rate, the $100 to be paid one year from now would be worth $94.34 today.
Presumption	A rule of law that courts and judges shall draw a particular inference from a particular fact, or from particular evidence, unless and until the truth of such inference is disproved.
Prima Facie	Presumptive on its face.
Principal	This term is used to mean either the employer of an agent or the amount of money borrowed or the amount of the loan.
Principal Note	The promissory note that is secured by the mortgage or trust deed.
Privity	Mutual relationship to the same rights of property, contractual relationship.
Procuring Cause	That cause originating from series of events that, without break in continuity, results in the prime object of an agent's employment producing a final buyer.
Progression, Principle of	The worth of a lesser valued residence tends to be enhanced by association with many higher valued residences in the same area.
Promissory Note	Following a loan commitment from the lender, the borrower signs a

note, promising to repay the loan under stipulated terms. The promissory note establishes personal liability for its repayment.

Property The rights of ownership. The right to use, possess, enjoy, and dispose of a thing in every legal way and to exclude everyone else from interfering with these rights. Property is generally classified into two groups, personal property and real property.

Proration Adjustments of interest, taxes, and insurance, on a prorata basis as of the closing date. Fire insurance is normally paid for three years in advance. If a property is sold during this time, the seller wants a refund on that portion of the advance payment that has not been used at the time the title to the property is transferred. For example, if the property is sold two years later, the original buyer will want to receive one-third of the advance premium that was paid.

Proration of Taxes To divide or prorate the taxes equally or proportionately to time of use.

Proximate Cause That cause of an event which, in a natural and continuous sequence unbroken by any new cause, produced that event, and without which the event would not have happened. Also, the procuring cause.

Public Trustee The county public official whose office has been created by statute, to whom title to real property, in certain states—such as Colorado— is conveyed by trust deed for the use and benefit of the beneficiary, who usually is the lender.

Purchase and Installment Saleback Involves purchase of the property upon completion of construction and immediate saleback on a long-term installment contract.

Purchase of Land, Leaseback, and Leasehold Mortgages An arrangement whereby land is purchased by the lender and leased back to the developer with a mortgage negotiated on the resulting leasehold of the income property constructed. The lender receives an annual ground rent, plus a percentage of income from the property.

Purchase and Leaseback Involves the purchase of property subject to an existing mortgage and immediate leaseback.

Purchase Money Mortgage or Trust Deed A trust deed or mortgage given as part or all of the purchase consideration for property. In some states the purchase money mortgage or trust deed loan can be made by a seller who extends credit to the buyer of property or by a third-party lender (typically a financial institution) that makes a loan to the buyer of real property for a portion of the purchase price to be paid for the property. (In many states there are legal limitations upon mortgagees and trust deed beneficiaries collecting deficiency judgments against the purchase money borrower after the collateral hypothecated under such security instruments has been sold through the foreclosure process. Generally no deficiency judgment is allowed if the collateral property under the mortgage or trust deed is residential property of four units or less with the debtor occupying the property as a place of residence.)

Quantity Survey	A highly technical process in arriving at cost estimate of new construction, and sometimes referred to in the building trade as the *price take-off* method. It involves a detailed estimate of the quantities of raw material (lumber, plaster, brick, cement) used, as well as the current price of the material and installation costs. These factors are all added together to arrive at the cost of a structure. It is usually used by contractors and experienced estimators.
Quarter Round	A molding that presents a profile of a quarter circle.
Quiet Enjoyment	Right of an owner to the use of the property without interference of possession.
Quiet Title	A court action brought to establish title; to remove a cloud on the title.
Quitclaim Deed	A deed to relinquish any interest in property which the grantor may have.
Radiant Heating	A method of heating, usually consisting of coils or pipes placed in the floor, wall, or ceiling.
Rafter	One of a series of boards of a roof designed to support roof loads. The rafters of a flat roof are sometimes called *roof joists.*
Range	A strip of land six miles wide determined by a government survey, running in a north to south direction.
Ratification	The adoption or approval of an act performed on behalf of a person without previous authorization.
Real Estate Board	An organization whose members consist primarily of real estate brokers and salespersons.
Real Estate Settlement Procedures Act	A federal disclosure law effective June 20, 1975, requiring new procedures and forms for settlements (closing costs) involving federally related loans.
Real Estate Trust	A special arrangement under federal and state law whereby investors may pool funds for investments in real estate and mortgages and yet escape corporation taxes.
Realtist	A real estate broker holding active membership in a real estate board affiliated with the National Association of Real Estate Brokers.
Realtor	A real estate broker holding active membership in a real estate board affiliated with the National Association of Realtors.
Recapture	The rate of interest necessary to provide for the return of an investment. Not to be confused with interest rate, which is a rate of interest on an investment.
Reconveyance	The transfer of the title of land from one person to the immediate

preceding owner. This particular instrument of transfer is commonly used when the performance or debt is satisfied under the terms of a deed of trust, when the trustee conveys the title that was being held on condition back to the owner.

Recording

The process of placing a document on file with a designated public official for everyone to see. This public official is usually a county officer known as the *county recorder.* The recorder designates the fact that a document has been given to him or her by stamping it and indicating the time of day and the date when it was officially placed on file. Documents filed with the recorder are considered to be placed on open notice to the general public of that county. Claims against property usually are given a priority on the basis of the time and the date they are recorded with the most preferred claim status going to the earliest one recorded and the next claim going to the next earliest one recorded, and so on. This type of notice is called "constructive notice" or "legal notice."

Redemption

Buying back one's property after a judicial sale.

Refinancing

The paying off of an existing obligation and assuming a new obligation in its place.

Reformation

An action to correct a mistake in a deed or other document.

Rehabilitation

The restoration of a property to satisfactory condition without drastically changing the plan, form, or style of architecture.

Release Clause

This is a stipulation that upon the payment of a specific sum of money to the holder of a trust deed or mortgage, the lien of the instrument as to a specific described lot or area shall be removed from the blanket lien on the whole area involved.

Release Deed

An instrument executed by the mortgagee or the trustee reconveying to the mortgagor the real estate which secured the mortgage loan after the debt has been paid in full. Upon recording it cancels the mortgage lien created when the mortgage or trust deed was recorded.

Remainder

An estate that takes effect after the termination of the prior estate, such as a life estate.

Remainder Depreciation

The possible loss in value of an improvement that will occur in the future.

Replacement Cost

The cost to replace the structure with one having utility equivalent to that being appraised, but constructed with modern materials, and according to current standards, design and layout.

Reproduction Costs

The cost of replacing the subject improvement with one that is the exact replica, having the same quality of workmanship, design, and layout.

Rescission of Contract	The abrogation or annulling of contract; the revocation or repealing of contract by mutual consent by parties to the contract, or for cause by either party to the contract.
Reservation	A right retained by a grantor in conveying property.
RESPA	Real Estate Settlement Procedures Act.
Restriction	The term as used relating to real property means the owner of real property is restricted or prohibited from doing certain things relating to the property, or using the property for certain purposes. Property restrictions fall into two general classifications—public and private. Zoning ordinances are examples of the former type. Restrictions may be created by private owners, typically by appropriate clauses in deeds, or in agreements, or in general plans of entire subdivisions. Usually they assume the form of a convenant, or promise to do or not do a certain thing. They cover a multitude of matters including use for residential or business purposes—for example, houses in tract must cost more than $25,000, etc.
Retrospective Value	The value of the property as of a previous date.
Reversion	The right to future possession or enjoyment by the person, or heirs, creating the preceding estate.
Reversionary Interest	The interest which a person has in lands or other property, upon the termination of the preceding estate.
Ridge	The horizontal line at the junction of the top edges of two sloping roof surfaces. The rafters at both slopes are nailed at the ridge.
Ridge Board	The board placed on edge at the ridge of the roof to support the upper ends of the rafters; also called roof tree, ridge piece, ridge plate, or ridgepole.
Right of Survivorship	Right to acquire the interest of a deceased joint owner; distinguishing feature of a joint tenancy.
Right of Way	A privilege operating as an easement upon land, whereby the owner does by grant, or by agreement, give to another the right to pass over his land, to construct a roadway, or use as a roadway; a specific part of his or her land; or the right to construct through and over the land telephone, telegraph, or electric power lines; or the right to place underground water mains, gas mains, or sewer mains.
Riparian Rights	The right of a landowner to water on, under, or adjacent to his land.
Riser	The upright board at the back of each step of a stairway. In heating, a riser is a duct slanted upward to carry hot air from the furnace to the room above.
Risk Analysis	A study made, usually by a lender, of the various factors that might affect the repayment of a loan.

Risk Rating	A process used by the lender to decide on the soundness (syn) of making a loan and to reduce all the various factors affecting the repayment of the loan to a qualified rating of some kind.
Roman Brick	Thin brick of slimmer proportions than standard building brick.
Sale-Leaseback	A situation where the owner of a piece of property wishes to sell the property and retain occupancy by leasing it from the buyer.
Sales Contract	A contract by which buyer and seller agree to terms of a sale.
Sandwich Lease	A leasehold interest which lies between the primary lease and the operating lease.
Sash	Wood or metal frames containing one or more window panes.
Satisfaction	Discharge of mortgage or trust deed lien from the records upon payment of the evidenced debt.
Satisfaction Piece	An instrument for recording and acknowledging payment of an indebtedness secured by a mortgage.
Scribing	Fitting woodwork to an irregular surface.
Seal	An impression made to attest the execution of an instrument—for example, a notary public's seal.
Secondary Financing	A loan secured by a second mortgage or trust deed on real property. These can be third, fourth, fifth, sixth—on and on ad infinitum.
Section	Section of land is established by government survey and contains 640 acres.
Secured Party	This is the party having the security interest. Thus the *mortgagee*, the *conditional seller*, the *pledgee*, and so on, are all now referred to as the secured party.
Security Agreement	An agreement between the secured party and the debtor which creates the security interest.
Security Interest	A term designating the interest of the creditor in the property of the debtor in all types of credit transactions. It thus replaces such terms as the following: *chattel mortgage, pledge, trust receipt, chattel trust, equipment trust, conditional sale,* and *inventory lien.*
Seizin	Possession of real estate by one entitled thereto.
Separate Property	Property owned by a husband or wife which is not community property; property acquired by either spouse prior to marriage or by gift or devise after marriage.
Septic Tank	An underground tank in which sewage from the house is reduced to liquid by bacterial action and drained off.
Servicing	Supervising and administering a loan after it has been made. This involves such things as collecting the payments, keeping accounting

records, computing the interest and principal, foreclosure of defaulted loans, and so on.

Set-Back Ordinance An ordinance prohibiting the erection of a building or structure between the curb and the set-back line.

Severalty Ownership Owned by one person only; sole ownership.

Shake A hand-split shingle, usually edge grained.

Sheathing Structural covering usually boards, plywood, or wallboards, placed over exterior studding or rafters of a house.

Sheriff's Deed Deed given by court order in connection with sale of property to satisfy a judgment.

Shopping Center, Regional A large shopping center with 250,000 to 1,000,000 square feet of store area, serving 200,000 or more people.

Sill The lowest part of the frame of a house, resting on the foundation and supporting the uprights of the frame. The board or metal forming the lower side of an opening, as a door sill or window sill.

Sinking Fund Fund set aside from the income from property which, with accrued interest, will eventually pay for replacement of the improvements.

SIR Society of Industrial Realtors.

Soil Pipe Pipe carrying waste out from the house to the main sewer line.

Sole or Sole Plate A member, usually a 2 by 4, on which wall and partition studs rest.

Span The distance between structural supports such as walls, columns, piers, beams, girders, and trusses.

Special Assessment Legal charge against real estate by a public authority to pay cost of public improvements such as street lights, sidewalks, or street improvements.

Special Warranty Deed A deed in which the grantor warrants or guarantees the title only against defects arising during his or her ownership of the property and not against defects existing before the time of his or her ownership.

Specific Liens Liens that attach to only a certain specific parcel of land or piece of property.

Specific Performance An action to compel performance of an agreement—for example, sale of land.

SRA Designates a person who is a member of the Society of Real Estate Appraisers.

SREA Society of Real Estate Appraisers.

Standard Depth Generally the most typical lot depth in the neighborhood.

Standby Commitment	The mortgage banker frequently protects a builder by a "standby" agreement, under which the banker agrees to make mortgage loans at an agreed price for many months in the future. The builder deposits a "standby fee" with the mortgage banker for this service. Frequently, the mortgage banker secures a "standby" from a long-term investor for the same period of time, paying a fee for this privilege.
Statute of Frauds	State law which provides that certain contracts must be in writing in order to be enforceable at law. Examples would be real property lease for more than one year or agent's authorization to sell real estate.
Statutory Warranty Deed	A short form warranty deed which warrants by inference that the seller is the undisputed owner and has the right to convey the property and that the owner will defend the title if necessary. This type of deed protects the purchaser in that the conveyor covenants to defend all claims against the property. If the seller fails to do so, the new owner can defend said claims and sue the former owner.
Straight Line Depreciation	Definite sum set aside annually from income to pay cost of replacing improvements, without reference to interest it earns.
String, Stringer	A timber or other support for cross members. In stairs, the support on which the stair treads rest.
Studs or Studding	Vertical supporting timbers in the walls and partitions.
Subject to Mortgage	When a grantee takes a title to real property subject to mortgage, he or she is not responsible to the holder of the promissory note for the payment of any portion of the amount due. The most that the grantee can lose in the event of a foreclosure is equity in the property. (See definition of *Assumption of Mortgage*.) In neither case is the original maker of the note released from his or her responsibility.
Sublease	A lease given by a lessee.
Subordinate	To make subject to, or junior to.
Subordination Clause	Clause in a junior or a second lien permitting retention of priority for prior liens. A subordination clause may also be used in a first deed of trust permitting it to be subordinated to subsequent liens as, for example, the liens of construction loans.
Subpoena	A process to cause a witness to appear and give testimony.
Subrogation	The substitution of another person in place of the creditor, to whose rights the former succeeds in relation to the debt. The doctrine is used very often where one person agrees to stand surety for the performance of a contract by another person.
Substitution, Principle of	Affirms that the maximum value of a property tends to be set by the cost of acquiring an equally desirable and valuable substitute property, assuming no costly delay is encountered in making the substitution.
Sum of the Years Digits	An accelerated depreciation method.

Supply and Demand, Principle of	Affirms that price or value varies directly, but not necessarily proportionally with demand, and inversely, but not necessarily proportionately with supply.
Surety	One who guarantees the performance of another—a guarantor.
Surplus Productivity, Principle of	Affirms the net income that remains after the proper costs of labor, organization and capital have been paid, which surplus is imputable to the land and tends to fix the value thereof.
Survey	The process by which a parcel of land is measured and its area is ascertained.
Syndicate	A partnership organized for participation in a real estate venture. Partners may be limited or unlimited in their liability.
Take-Out Loan	The loan arranged by the owner or builder-developer for a buyer. The construction loan made for construction of the improvements is usually paid from the proceeds of this loan.
Tax-Free Exchange	Income property exchanged on an even basis for other income property which does not require a capital gain tax at the time.
Tax Sale	Sale of property after a period of nonpayment of taxes.
Tenancy in Common	Ownership by two or more persons who hold undivided interest, without right of survivorship; interests need not be equal.
Tenants by the Entireties	Under certain state laws, ownership of property acquired by a husband and wife during marriage which is jointly owned. Upon death of one spouse, it becomes the property of the survivor.
Tentative Map	The Subdivision Map Act requires subdividers to submit initially a tentative map of their tract to the local planning commission for study. The approval or disapproval of the planning commission is noted on the map. Thereafter a final map of the tract embodying any changes requested by the planning commission is required to be filed with the planning commission.
Tenure in Land	The mode or manner by which an estate in lands is held.
Termites	Ant-like insects that feed on wood.
Termite Shield	A shield, usually of noncorrodible metal, placed on top of the foundation wall or around pipes to prevent passage of termites.
Testator	One who leaves a will in force upon death.
Threshold	A strip of wood or metal beveled on each edge and used above the finished floor under outside doors.
Time Is the Essence	One of the essential requirements to forming of a binding contract; contemplates a punctual performance.
Title	Evidence that owner of land is in lawful possession thereof, an instrument evidencing such ownership.

Title Insurance	Insurance written by a title company to protect property owner against loss if title is imperfect.
Title Report	A report that discloses condition of the title, made by a title company preliminary to issuance of title insurance.
Title Theory	Mortgage arrangement whereby title to mortgaged real property vests in the lender.
Topography	Nature of the surface of land; topography may be level, rolling, or mountainous.
Torrens Title	System of title records provided by state law (no longer used in California).
Tort	A wrongful act; wrong, injury; violation of a legal right.
Township	A territorial subdivision six miles long, six miles wide and containing 36 sections, each one mile square.
Trade Fixtures	Articles of personal property annexed to real property, but which are necessary to the carrying on of a trade and are removable by the owner.
Trade-In	An increasingly popular method of guaranteeing an owner a minimum amount of cash upon sale of present property to permit the purchase of another. If the property is not sold within a specified time at the listed price, the broker agrees to arrange financing to purchase the property at an agreed-upon discount.
Treads	Horizontal boards of a stairway.
Trim	The finish materials in a building, such as moldings, applied around openings (window trim, door trim) or at the floor and ceiling (baseboard, cornice, picture molding).
Trust Account	An account separate and apart and physically segregated from broker's own funds, in which broker is required by law to deposit all funds collected for clients.
Trust Deed	Just as with a mortgage, this is a legal document by which a borrower pledges certain real property or collateral as guarantee for the repayment of a loan. However, it differs from the mortgage in a number of important respects. For example, instead of there being two parties to the transaction, there are three. There is the borrower who gives the trust deed and who is called the trustor. There is the third, neutral party (just as there is with an escrow) who receives the trust deed and who is called the trustee. And, finally, there is the lender who is called the beneficiary since the lender benefits from the pledge arrangement in that in the event of a default the trustee can sell the property and transfer the money obtained at the sale to the lender as payment of the debt.

Trustee	One who holds property in trust for another to secure the performance of an obligation.
Trustor	One who deeds property to a trustee to be held as security until the trustor has performed any obligations to a lender under terms of a deed of trust.
Under Improvement	An improvement which, because of its deficiency in size or cost, is not the highest and best use of the site.
Underwriting	The technical analysis by a lender to determine the borrower's ability to repay a contemplated loan.
Undue Influence	Taking any fraudulent or unfair advantage of another's weakness of mind, or distress or necessity.
Unearned Increment	An increase in value of real estate due to no effort on the part of the owner; often due to increase in population.
Uniform Commercial Code	Establishes a unified and comprehensive scheme for regulation of security transactions in personal property, superseding the existing statutes on chattel mortgages, conditional sales, trust receipts, assignment of accounts receivable, and others in this field.
Unit-in-Place Method	The cost of erecting a building by estimating the cost of each component part, that is, foundations, floors, walls, windows, ceilings, roofs (including labor and overhead).
Urban Property	City property; closely settled property.
Usury	On a loan, claiming a rate of interest greater than that permitted by law.
Utilities	Refers to services rendered by public utility companies, such as: water, gas, electricity, or telephone.
Utility	The ability to give satisfaction and/or excite desire for possession.
Valid	Having force, or binding force; legally sufficient and authorized by law.
Valley	The internal angle formed by the junction of two sloping sides of a roof.
Valuation	Estimated worth or price; estimation; the act of valuing by appraisal.
Vendee	A purchaser; buyer.
Vendor	A seller; one who disposes of a thing in consideration of money.
Veneer	Thin sheets of wood.
Vent	A pipe installed to provide a flow of air to or from a drainage system or to provide a circulation of air within such system to protect trap seals from siphonage and back pressure.

Verification	Sworn statement before a duly qualified officer to correctness of contents of an instrument.
Vested	Bestowed upon someone; secured by someone, such as a title to property.
Void	To have no force or effect; that which is unenforceable.
Voidable	That which is capable of being adjudged void, but is not void unless action is taken to make it so.
Voluntary Lien	Any lien placed on property with consent of, or as a result of, the voluntary act of the owner.
Wainscoting	Wood lining of an interior wall; lower section of a wall when finished differently from the upper part.
Waive	To relinquish, or abandon; to forego a right to enforce or require anything.
Warranty Deed	A deed used to convey real property which contains warranties of title and quiet possession, and the grantor thus agrees to defend the premises against the lawful claims of third persons. It is commonly used in many states but in others the grant deed has supplanted it due to the modern practice of securing title insurance policies which have reduced the importance of express and implied warranty in deeds.
Waste	The destruction, or material alteration of, or injury to premises by a tenant for life or years.
Water Table	Distance from surface of ground to a depth at which natural ground-water is found.
Wraparound Mortgage	Involves the borrower entering into a second mortgage. This arrangement represents the means by which the borrower can add to development without refinancing the first mortgage at substantially higher current rates.
Yield	The interest earned by an investor on his investment (or bank on the money it has lent). Also, called return.
Yield Rate	The yield expressed as a percentage of the total investment. Also, called rate of return.
Zone	The area set off by the proper authorities for specific use; subject to certain restrictions or restraints.
Zoning	Act of city or county authorities specifying type of use to which property may be put in specific areas.

EXCLUSIVE AUTHORIZATION AND RIGHT TO SELL
MULTIPLE LISTING AUTHORIZATION
THIS IS INTENDED TO BE A LEGALLY BINDING AGREEMENT — READ IT CAREFULLY.
CALIFORNIA ASSOCIATION OF REALTORS® (CAR) STANDARD FORM

1. **EXCLUSIVE RIGHT TO SELL:** I hereby employ and grant _____ hereinafter called "Broker," the exclusive and irrevocable right commencing on _____ , 19_____ , and expiring at midnight on _____ , 19_____ , to sell or exchange the real property situated in the City of _____ , County of _____ , California described as follows: _____

2. **TERMS OF SALE:** The purchase price shall be _____ ($_____), to be paid as follows _____

   The following items of personal property are included in the above stated price: _____

3. **MULTIPLE LISTING SERVICE (MLS):** Broker is a Participant of _____ ASSOCIATION/BOARD OF REALTORS® Multiple Listing Service (MLS) and this listing information will be provided to the MLS to be published and disseminated to its Participants in accordance with its Rules and Regulations. Broker is authorized to cooperate with other real estate brokers, to appoint subagents and to report the sale, its price, terms and financing for the publication, dissemination, information and use by authorized Association/Board members, MLS Participants and Subscribers.

4. **TITLE INSURANCE:** Evidence of title shall be a California Land Title Association policy of title insurance in the amount of the selling price.

   Notice: The amount or rate of real estate commissions is not fixed by law. They are set by each Broker individually and may be negotiable between the Seller and Broker.

5. **COMPENSATION TO BROKER:** I hereby agree to compensate Broker, irrespective of agency relationship(s), as follows:
   (a) _____ percent of the selling price, or $_____ , if the property is sold during the term hereof, or any extension thereof, by Broker or through any other person, or by me on the terms herein set forth, or any other price and terms I may accept, or _____ percent of the price shown in 2, or $_____ , if said property is withdrawn from sale, transferred, conveyed, leased, or rented without the consent of Broker, or made unmarketable by my voluntary act during the term hereof or any extension thereof.
   (b) The compensation provided for in subparagraph (a) above if property is sold, conveyed or otherwise transferred within _____ calendar days after the termination of this authority or any extension thereof to anyone with whom Broker has had negotiations prior to final termination, provided I have received notice in writing, including the names of the prospective purchasers, before or upon termination of this agreement or any extension hereof. However, I shall not be obligated to pay the compensation provided for in subparagraph (a) if a valid listing agreement is entered into during the term of said protection period with another licensed real estate broker and a sale, lease or exchange of the property is made during the term of said valid listing agreement.
   (c) I authorize Broker to cooperate with other brokers, to appoint subagents, and to divide with other brokers such compensation in any manner acceptable to brokers.
   (d) In the event of an exchange, permission is hereby given Broker to represent all parties and collect compensation or commissions from them, provided there is full disclosure to all principals of such agency. Broker is authorized to divide with other brokers such compensation or commissions in any manner acceptable to brokers.
   (e) Seller shall execute and deliver an escrow instruction irrevocably assigning Broker's compensation in an amount equal to the compensation provided in subparagraph (a) (above) from the Seller's proceeds.

6. **DEPOSIT:** Broker is authorized to accept and hold on Seller's behalf a deposit to be applied toward purchase price.

7. **HOME PROTECTION PLAN:** Seller is informed that home protection plans are available. Such plans may provide additional protection and benefit to a Seller and Buyer. Cost and coverage may vary.

* 8. **KEYBOX:** I authorize Broker to install a KEYBOX:
   Refer to reverse side for important keybox information. (Initial) YES (____/____) NO (____/____)

9. **SIGN:** Authorization to install a FOR SALE/SOLD sign on the property: (Initial) YES (____/____) NO (____/____)

10. **PEST CONTROL:** Seller shall furnish a current Structural Pest Control Report of the main building and all structures of the property, except _____ . (Initial) YES (____/____) NO (____/____)

11. **DISCLOSURE:** Unless exempt, Seller shall provide a Real Estate Transfer Disclosure Statement concerning the condition of the property. I agree to save and hold Broker harmless from all claims, disputes, litigation, and/or judgments arising from any incorrect information supplied by me, or from any material fact known by me which I fail to disclose. (Initial) (____/____)

* 12. **TAX WITHHOLDING:** Seller agrees to perform any act reasonably necessary to carry out the provisions of FIRPTA (Internal Revenue Code §1445) and California Revenue and Taxation Code §§18805 and 26131, and regulations promulgated thereunder. Refer to the reverse side for withholding provisions and exemptions.

13. **EQUAL HOUSING OPPORTUNITY:** This property is offered in compliance with federal, state, and local anti-discrimination laws.

* 14. **ARBITRATION OF DISPUTES:** Any dispute or claim in law or equity arising out of this contract or any resulting transaction shall be decided by neutral binding arbitration in accordance with the rules of the American Arbitration Association, and not by court action except as provided by California law for judicial review of arbitration proceedings. Judgment upon the award rendered by the arbitrator(s) may be entered in any court having jurisdiction thereof. The parties shall have the right to discovery in accordance with Code of Civil Procedure §1283.05. The following matters are excluded from arbitration hereunder: (a) a judicial or non-judicial foreclosure or other action or proceeding to enforce a deed of trust, mortgage, or real property sales contract as defined in Civil Code §2985, (b) an unlawful detainer action, (c) the filing or enforcement of a mechanic's lien, (d) any matter which is within the jurisdiction of a probate court, or (e) an action for bodily injury or wrongful death, or for latent or patent defects to which Code of Civil Procedure §337.1 or §337.15 applies. The filing of a judicial action to enable the recording of a notice of pending action, for order of attachment, receivership, injunction, or other provisional remedies, shall not constitute a waiver of the right to arbitrate under this provision.
   "NOTICE: BY INITIALLING IN THE SPACE BELOW YOU ARE AGREEING TO HAVE ANY DISPUTE ARISING OUT OF THE MATTERS INCLUDED IN THE 'ARBITRATION OF DISPUTES' PROVISION DECIDED BY NEUTRAL ARBITRATION AS PROVIDED BY CALIFORNIA LAW AND YOU ARE GIVING UP ANY RIGHTS YOU MIGHT POSSESS TO HAVE THE DISPUTE LITIGATED IN A COURT OR JURY TRIAL. BY INITIALLING IN THE SPACE BELOW YOU ARE GIVING UP YOUR JUDICIAL RIGHTS TO DISCOVERY AND APPEAL, UNLESS THOSE RIGHTS ARE SPECIFICALLY INCLUDED IN THE 'ARBITRATION OF DISPUTES' PROVISION. IF YOU REFUSE TO SUBMIT TO ARBITRATION AFTER AGREEING TO THIS PROVISION, YOU MAY BE COMPELLED TO ARBITRATE UNDER THE AUTHORITY OF THE CALIFORNIA CODE OF CIVIL PROCEDURE. YOUR AGREEMENT TO THIS ARBITRATION PROVISION IS VOLUNTARY."
   "WE HAVE READ AND UNDERSTAND THE FOREGOING AND AGREE TO SUBMIT DISPUTES ARISING OUT OF THE MATTERS INCLUDED IN THE 'ARBITRATION OF DISPUTES' PROVISION TO NEUTRAL ARBITRATION."
   (Initial) BROKER (_____) SELLER (____/____)

15. **ATTORNEY'S FEES:** In any action, proceeding or arbitration arising out of this agreement, the prevailing party shall be entitled to reasonable attorney's fees and costs.

16. **ADDITIONAL TERMS:** _____

17. **ENTIRE AGREEMENT:** I, the Seller, warrant that I am the owner of the property or have the authority to execute this agreement. The Seller and Broker further intend that this agreement constitutes the complete and exclusive statement of its terms and that no extrinsic evidence whatsoever may be introduced in any judicial or arbitration proceeding, if any, involving this agreement.

   I acknowledge that I have read and understand this agreement, including the information on the reverse side, and have received a copy.

Date _____ , 19 _____ _____ , California

Seller _____ Address _____

Seller _____ City _____ State _____ Zip _____

In consideration of the above, Broker agrees to use diligence in procuring a purchaser. Phone _____

Real Estate Broker _____ By _____

Address _____ City _____ Date _____

FORM A-14

— OFFICE USE ONLY —
Reviewed by Broker or Designee _____
Date _____

SF-Oct-89

REAL ESTATE PURCHASE CONTRACT AND RECEIPT FOR DEPOSIT

THIS IS MORE THAN A RECEIPT FOR MONEY. IT IS INTENDED TO BE A LEGALLY BINDING CONTRACT. READ IT CAREFULLY.
CALIFORNIA ASSOCIATION OF REALTORS® (CAR) STANDARD FORM

_____ , California, _____ , 19_____

Received from _____

herein called Buyer, the sum of _____ Dollars $_____

evidenced by ☐ cash, ☐ cashier's check, ☐ personal check or ☐ _____ , payable to _____

_____ , to be held uncashed until acceptance of this offer as deposit on account of purchase price of

_____ Dollars $_____

for the purchase of property, situated in _____ , County of _____ California,

described as follows: _____.

1. **FINANCING:** The obtaining of Buyer's financing is a contingency of this agreement.

   A. DEPOSIT upon acceptance, to be deposited into _____ $ _____

   B. INCREASED DEPOSIT within _____ days of acceptance to be deposited into _____ $ _____

   C. BALANCE OF DOWN PAYMENT to be deposited into _____ on or before _____ $ _____

   D. Buyer to apply, qualify for and obtain a NEW FIRST LOAN in the amount of _____ $ _____

     payable monthly at approximately $_____ including interest at origination not to exceed _____%,

     ☐ fixed rate, ☐ other _____ all due _____ years from date of origination. Loan fee not to

     exceed _____ . Seller agrees to pay a maximum of _____ FHA/VA discount points.

     Additional terms _____

     _____

   E. Buyer ☐ to assume, ☐ to take title subject to an EXISTING FIRST LOAN with an approximate balance of .... $ _____

     in favor of _____ payable monthly at $_____ including interest at _____% ☐ fixed rate,

     ☐ other _____ . Fees not to exceed _____ .

     Disposition of impound account _____

     Additional terms _____

   F. Buyer to execute a NOTE SECURED BY a ☐ first, ☐ second, ☐ third DEED OF TRUST in the amount of .... $ _____

     IN FAVOR OF SELLER payable monthly at $_____ ☐ or more, including interest at _____% all due

     _____ years from date of origination, ☐ or upon sale or transfer of subject property. A late charge of _____

     _____ shall be due on any installment not paid within _____ days of the due date.

     ☐ Deed of Trust to contain a request for notice of default or sale for the benefit of Seller. Buyer ☐ will, ☐ will not execute a request

     for notice of delinquency. Additional terms _____

     _____

   G. Buyer ☐ to assume, ☐ to take title subject to an EXISTING SECOND LOAN with an approximate balance of .... $ _____

     in favor of _____ payable monthly at $_____ including interest at _____%

     ☐ fixed rate, ☐ other _____ . Buyer fees not to exceed _____ .

     Additional terms _____

   H. Buyer to apply, qualify for and obtain a NEW SECOND LOAN in the amount of .... $ _____

     payable monthly at approximately $_____ including interest at origination not to exceed _____% ☐ fixed rate,

     ☐ other _____ , all due _____ years from date of origination.

     Buyer's loan fee not to exceed _____ . Additional terms _____

   I. In the event Buyer assumes or takes title subject to an existing loan, Seller shall provide Buyer with copies of applicable notes and Deeds

     of Trust. A loan may contain a number of features which affect the loan, such as interest rate changes, monthly payment changes, balloon

     payments, etc. Buyer shall be allowed _____ calendar days after receipt of such copies to notify Seller in writing of disapproval.

     FAILURE TO NOTIFY SELLER IN WRITING SHALL CONCLUSIVELY BE CONSIDERED APPROVAL. Buyer's approval shall not be

     unreasonably withheld. Difference in existing loan balances shall be adjusted in ☐ Cash, ☐ Other _____

     _____

   J. Buyer agrees to act diligently and in good faith to obtain all applicable financing. _____

     _____

     _____

   K. ADDITIONAL FINANCING TERMS: _____

     _____

     _____

     _____

   L. TOTAL PURCHASE PRICE .... $ _____

2. **OCCUPANCY:** Buyer ☐ does, ☐ does not intend to occupy subject property as Buyer's primary residence.

3. **SUPPLEMENTS:** The ATTACHED supplements are incorporated herein:

   ☐ Interim Occupancy Agreement (CAR FORM IOA-11)   ☐ _____

   ☐ Residential Lease Agreement after Sale (CAR FORM RLAS-11)   ☐ _____

   ☐ VA and FHA Amendments (CAR FORM VA/FHA-11)   ☐ _____

4. **ESCROW:** Buyer and Seller shall deliver signed instructions to _____ the escrow holder, within _____ calendar days

   of acceptance of the offer which shall provide for closing within _____ calendar days of acceptance. Escrow fees to be paid as follows: _____

   _____

   _____

Buyer and Seller acknowledge receipt of copy of this page, which constitutes Page 1 of _____ Pages.

Buyer's Initials (_____) (_____)   Seller's Initials (_____) (_____)

┌─────────── OFFICE USE ONLY ───────────┐
Reviewed by Broker or Designee _____
Date _____
└───────────────────────────────────────┘

BROKER'S COPY

M-MB-Aug-89

Subject Property Address: _____

5. TITLE: Title is to be free of liens, encumbrances, easements, restrictions, rights and conditions of record or known to Seller, other than the following: (a) Current property taxes, (b) covenants, conditions, restrictions, and public utility easements of record, if any, provided the same do not adversely affect the continued use of the property for the purposes for which it is presently being used, unless reasonably disapproved by Buyer in writing within _____ calendar days of receipt of a current preliminary report furnished at _____ expense, and (c) _____
_____
Seller shall furnish Buyer at _____ expense a California Land Title Association policy issued by _____
_____ Company, showing title vested in Buyer subject only to the above. If Seller is unwilling or unable to eliminate any title matter disapproved by Buyer as above, Buyer may terminate this agreement. If Seller fails to deliver title as above, Buyer may terminate this agreement; in either case, the deposit shall be returned to Buyer.

6. VESTING: Unless otherwise designated in the escrow instructions of Buyer, title shall vest as follows: _____
_____
(The manner of taking title may have significant legal and tax consequences. Therefore, give this matter serious consideration.)

7. PRORATIONS: Property taxes, payments on bonds and assessments assumed by Buyer, interest, rents, association dues, premiums on insurance acceptable to Buyer, and _____ shall be paid current and prorated as of ☐ the day of recordation of the deed; or ☐ _____ . Bonds or assessments now a lien shall be ☐ paid current by Seller, payments not yet due to be assumed by Buyer; or ☐ paid in full by Seller, including payments not yet due; or ☐ _____ . County Transfer tax shall be paid by _____ . The _____ transfer tax or transfer fee shall be paid by _____ . **PROPERTY WILL BE REASSESSED UPON CHANGE OF OWNERSHIP. THIS WILL AFFECT THE TAXES TO BE PAID.** A Supplemental tax bill will be issued, which shall be paid as follows: (a) for periods after close of escrow, by Buyer (or by final acquiring party if part of an exchange), and (b) for periods prior to close of escrow, by Seller. TAX BILLS ISSUED AFTER CLOSE OF ESCROW SHALL BE HANDLED DIRECTLY BETWEEN BUYER AND SELLER.

8. POSSESSION: Possession and occupancy shall be delivered to Buyer, ☐ on close of escrow, or ☐ not later than _____ days after close of escrow, or ☐ _____

9. KEYS: Seller shall, when possession is available to Buyer, provide keys and/or means to operate all property locks, and alarms, if any.

10. PERSONAL PROPERTY: The following items of personal property, free of liens and without warranty of condition, are included: _____
_____

11. FIXTURES: All permanently installed fixtures and fittings that are attached to the property or for which special openings have been made are included in the purchase price, including electrical, light, plumbing and heating fixtures, built-in appliances, screens, awnings, shutters, all window coverings, attached floor coverings, TV antennas, air cooler or conditioner, garage door openers and controls, attached fireplace equipment, mailbox, trees and shrubs, and _____ except _____ .

12. SMOKE DETECTOR(S): State law requires that residences be equipped with an operable smoke detector(s). Local law may have additional requirements. Seller shall deliver to Buyer a written statement of compliance in accordance with applicable state and local law prior to close of escrow.

13. TRANSFER DISCLOSURE: Unless exempt, Transferor (Seller), shall comply with Civil Code §§1102 et seq., by providing Transferee (Buyer) with a Real Estate Transfer Disclosure Statement: (a) ☐ Buyer has received and read a Real Estate Transfer Disclosure Statement; or (b) ☐ Seller shall provide Buyer with a Real Estate Transfer Disclosure Statement within _____ calendar days of acceptance of the offer after which Buyer shall have three (3) days after delivery to Buyer, in person, or five (5) days after delivery by deposit in the mail, to terminate this agreement by delivery of a written notice of termination to Seller or Seller's Agent.

14. TAX WITHHOLDING: Under the Foreign Investment in Real Property Tax Act (FIRPTA), IRC §1445, *every* Buyer of U.S. real property *must*, unless an exemption applies, deduct and withhold from Seller's proceeds 10% of the gross sales price. Under California Revenue and Taxation Code §§18805 and 26131, the Buyer must deduct and withhold an additional one-third of the amount required to be withheld under federal law. The primary FIRPTA exemptions are: No withholding is required if (a) Seller provides Buyer with an affidavit under penalty of perjury, that Seller is not a "foreign person," or (b) Seller provides Buyer with a "qualifying statement" issued by the Internal Revenue Service, or (c) Buyer purchases real property for use as a residence and the purchase price is $300,000 or less and Buyer or a member of Buyer's family has definite plans to reside at the property for at least 50% of the number of days it is in use during each of the first two twelve-month periods after transfer. Seller and Buyer agree to execute and deliver as directed any instrument, affidavit, or statement reasonably necessary to carry out those statutes and regulations promulgated thereunder.

15. MULTIPLE LISTING SERVICE: If Broker is a Participant of an Association/Board multiple listing service ("MLS"), the Broker is authorized to report the sale, its price, terms, and financing for the publication, dissemination, information, and use of the authorized Board members, MLS Participants and Subscribers.

16. ADDITIONAL TERMS AND CONDITIONS:
ONLY THE FOLLOWING PARAGRAPHS 'A' THROUGH 'K' *WHEN INITIALLED BY BOTH BUYER AND SELLER* ARE INCORPORATED IN THIS AGREEMENT.
Buyer's Initials   Seller's Initials

_____/_____   _____/_____   **A. PHYSICAL AND GEOLOGICAL INSPECTION:** Buyer shall have the right, at Buyer's expense, to select a licensed contractor and/or other qualified professional(s), to make "Inspections" (including tests, surveys, other studies, inspections, and investigations) of the subject property, including but not limited to structural, plumbing, sewer/septic system, well, heating, electrical, built-in appliances, roof, soils, foundation, mechanical systems, pool, pool heater, pool filter, air conditioner, if any, possible environmental hazards such as asbestos, formaldehyde, radon gas and other substances/products, and geologic conditions. Buyer shall keep the subject property free and clear of any liens, indemnify and hold Seller harmless from all liability, claims, demands, damages, or costs, and repair all damages to the property arising from the "Inspections." All claimed defects concerning the condition of the property that adversely affect the continued use of the property for the purposes for which it is presently being used (☐ or as _____) shall be in writing, supported by written reports, if any, and delivered to Seller within _____ calendar days FOR "INSPECTIONS" OTHER THAN GEOLOGICAL, and/or within _____ calendar days FOR GEOLOGICAL "INSPECTIONS," **of acceptance of the offer.** Buyer shall furnish Seller copies, at no cost, of all reports concerning the property obtained by Buyer. When such reports disclose conditions or information unsatisfactory to the Buyer, which the Seller is unwilling or unable to correct, Buyer may cancel this agreement. Seller shall make the premises available for all Inspections. BUYER'S FAILURE TO NOTIFY SELLER IN WRITING SHALL CONCLUSIVELY BE CONSIDERED APPROVAL.
Buyer's Initials   Seller's Initials

_____/_____   _____/_____   **B. CONDITION OF PROPERTY:** Seller warrants, through the date possession is made available to Buyer: (1) property and improvements, including landscaping, grounds and pool/spa, if any, shall be maintained in the same condition as upon the date of acceptance of the offer, and (2) the roof is free of all known leaks, and (3) built-in appliances, and water, sewer/septic, plumbing, heating, electrical, air conditioning, pool/spa systems, if any, are operative, and (4) Seller shall replace all broken and/or cracked glass; (5) _____

Buyer's Initials   Seller's Initials

_____/_____   _____/_____   **C. SELLER REPRESENTATION:** Seller warrants that Seller has no knowledge of any notice of violations of City, County, State, Federal, Building, Zoning, Fire, Health Codes or ordinances, or other governmental regulation filed or issued against the property. This warranty shall be effective until the date of close of escrow.

Buyer and Seller acknowledge receipt of copy of this page, which constitutes Page 2 of _____ Pages.
Buyer's Initials (_____·_____) (_____)   Seller's Initials (_____) (_____)

┌─ OFFICE USE ONLY ─────────────┐
│ Reviewed by Broker or Designee _____ │
│ Date _____ │
└───────────────────────────────┘

M-MB-Aug-89

356

Buyer's Initials   **Seller's Initials**

_____ / _____   _____ / _____   **D. PEST CONTROL:** (1) Within _____ calendar days of acceptance of the offer, Seller shall furnish Buyer at the expense of ☐ Buyer, ☐ Seller, a current written report of an inspection by _____ , a licensed Structural Pest Control Operator, of the main building, ☐ detached garage(s) or carport(s), if any, and ☐ the following other structures on the property:

_____

(2) If requested by either Buyer or Seller, the report shall separately identify each recommendation for corrective measures as follows:

    "Section 1": Infestation or infection which is evident.

    "Section 2": Conditions that are present which are deemed likely to lead to infestation or infection.

(3) If no infestation or infection by wood destroying pests or organisms is found, the report shall include a written Certification as provided in Business and Professions Code § 8519(a) that on the date of inspection "no evidence of active infestation or infection was found."

(4) All work recommended to correct conditions described in "Section 1" shall be at the expense of ☐ Buyer, ☐ Seller.

(5) All work recommended to correct conditions described in "Section 2," if requested by Buyer, shall be at the expense of ☐ Buyer, ☐ Seller.

(6) The repairs shall be performed with good workmanship and materials of comparable quality and shall include repairs of leaking showers, replacement of tiles and other materials removed for repairs. It is understood that exact restoration of appearance or cosmetic items following all such repairs is not included.

(7) Funds for work agreed to be performed after close of escrow, shall be held in escrow and disbursed upon receipt of a written Certification as provided in Business and Professions Code § 8519(b) that the inspected property "is now free of evidence of active infestation or infection."

(8) Work to be performed at Seller's expense may be performed by Seller or through others, provided that (a) all required permits and final inspections are obtained, and (b) upon completion of repairs a written Certification is issued by a licensed Structural Pest Control Operator showing that the inspected property "is now free of evidence of active infestation or infection."

(9) If inspection of inaccessible areas is recommended by the report, Buyer has the option to accept and approve the report, or within _____ calendar days from receipt of the report to request in writing further inspection be made. BUYER'S FAILURE TO NOTIFY SELLER IN WRITING OF SUCH REQUEST SHALL CONCLUSIVELY BE CONSIDERED APPROVAL OF THE REPORT. If further inspection recommends "Section 1" and/or "Section 2" corrective measures, such work shall be at the expense of the party designated in subparagraph (4) and/or (5), respectively. If no infestation or infection is found, the cost of inspection, entry and closing of the inaccessible areas shall be at the expense of the Buyer.

(10) Other _____

_____

_____ .

Buyer's Initials   **Seller's Initials**

_____ / _____   _____ / _____   **E. FLOOD HAZARD AREA DISCLOSURE:** Buyer is informed that subject property is situated in a "Special Flood Hazard Area" as set forth on a Federal Emergency Management Agency (FEMA) "Flood Insurance Rate Map" (FIRM), or "Flood Hazard Boundary Map" (FHBM). The law provides that, as a condition of obtaining financing on most structures located in a "Special Flood Hazard Area," lenders require flood insurance where the property or its attachments are security for a loan.

    The extent of coverage and the cost may vary. For further information consult the lender or insurance carrier. No representation or recommendation is made by the Seller and the Broker(s) in this transaction as to the legal effect or economic consequences of the National Flood Insurance Program and related legislation.

Buyer's Initials   **Seller's Initials**

_____ / _____   _____ / _____   **F. SPECIAL STUDIES ZONE DISCLOSURE:** Buyer is informed that subject property is situated in a Special Studies Zone as designated under §§ 2621-2625, inclusive, of the California Public Resources Code; and, as such, the construction or development on this property of any structure for human occupancy may be subject to the findings of a geologic report prepared by a geologist registered in the State of California, unless such a report is waived by the City or County under the terms of that act.

    Buyer is allowed _____ calendar days from acceptance of the offer to make further inquiries at appropriate governmental agencies concerning the use of the subject property under the terms of the Special Studies Zone Act and local building, zoning, fire, health, and safety codes. When such inquiries disclose conditions or information unsatisfactory to the Buyer, which the Seller is unwilling or unable to correct, Buyer may cancel this agreement. BUYER'S FAILURE TO NOTIFY SELLER IN WRITING SHALL CONCLUSIVELY BE CONSIDERED APPROVAL.

Buyer's Initials   **Seller's Initials**

_____ / _____   _____ / _____   **G. ENERGY CONSERVATION RETROFIT:** If local ordinance requires that the property be brought in compliance with minimum energy Conservation Standards as a condition of sale or transfer, ☐ Buyer, ☐ Seller shall comply with and pay for these requirements. Where permitted by law, Seller may, if obligated hereunder, satisfy the obligation by authorizing escrow to credit Buyer with sufficient funds to cover the cost of such retrofit.

Buyer's Initials   **Seller's Initials**

_____ / _____   _____ / _____   **H. HOME PROTECTION PLAN:** Buyer and Seller have been informed that Home Protection Plans are available. Such plans may provide additional protection and benefit to a Seller or Buyer. The CALIFORNIA ASSOCIATION OF REALTORS® and the Broker(s) in this transaction do not endorse or approve any particular company or program:

a) ☐ A Buyer's coverage Home Protection Plan to be issued by _____

    Company, at a cost not to exceed $_____ , to be paid by ☐ Buyer, ☐ Seller; or

b) ☐ Buyer and Seller elect not to purchase a Home Protection Plan.

Buyer's Initials   **Seller's Initials**

_____ / _____   _____ / _____   **I. CONDOMINIUM/P.U.D.:** The subject of this transaction is a condominium/planned unit development (P.U.D.) designated as unit _____ and _____ parking space(s) and an undivided interest in community areas, and _____

_____ . The current monthly assessment charge by the homeowner's association or other governing body(s) is

$_____ . As soon as practicable, Seller shall provide Buyer with copies of covenants, conditions and restrictions, articles of incorporation, by-laws, current rules and regulations, most current financial statements, and any other documents as required by law. Seller shall disclose in writing any known pending special assessment, claims, or litigation to Buyer. Buyer shall be allowed _____ calendar days from receipt to review these documents. If such documents disclose conditions or information unsatisfactory to Buyer, Buyer may cancel this agreement. BUYER'S FAILURE TO NOTIFY SELLER IN WRITING SHALL CONCLUSIVELY BE CONSIDERED APPROVAL.

Buyer's Initials   **Seller's Initials**

_____ / _____   _____ / _____   **J. LIQUIDATED DAMAGES: If Buyer fails to complete said purchase as herein provided by reason of any default of Buyer, Seller shall be released from obligation to sell the property to Buyer and may proceed against Buyer upon any claim or remedy which he/she may have in law or equity; provided, however, that by initialling this paragraph Buyer and Seller agree that Seller shall retain the deposit as liquidated damages. If the described property is a dwelling with no more than four units, one of which the Buyer intends to occupy as his/her residence, Seller shall retain as liquidated damages the deposit actually paid, or an amount therefrom, not more than 3% of the purchase price and promptly return any excess to Buyer. Buyer and Seller agree to execute a similar liquidated damages provision, such as CALIFORNIA ASSOCIATION OF REALTORS® Receipt for Increased Deposit (RID-11), for any increased deposits. (Funds deposited in trust accounts or in escrow are not released automatically in the event of a dispute. Release of funds requires written agreement of the parties, judicial decision or arbitration.)**

Buyer and Seller acknowledge receipt of copy of this page, which constitutes Page 3 of _____ Pages.

Buyer's Initials (_____) (_____)   Seller's Initials (_____) (_____)

┌─────── OFFICE USE ONLY ───────┐
Reviewed by Broker or Designee _____
Date _____
└────────────────────────────────┘

EQUAL HOUSING OPPORTUNITY

M-MB-Aug-89

Subject Property Address _____

K. ARBITRATION OF DISPUTES: Any dispute or claim in law or equity arising out of this contract or any resulting transaction shall be decided by neutral binding arbitration in accordance with the rules of the American Arbitration Association, and not by court action except as provided by California law for judicial review of arbitration proceedings. Judgment upon the award rendered by the arbitrator(s) may be entered in any court having jurisdiction thereof. The parties shall have the right to discovery in accordance with Code of Civil Procedure § 1283.05. The following matters are excluded from arbitration hereunder: (a) a judicial or non-judicial foreclosure or other action or proceeding to enforce a deed of trust, mortgage, or real property sales contract as defined in Civil Code § 2985, (b) an unlawful detainer action, (c) the filing or enforcement of a mechanic's lien, (d) any matter which is within the jurisdiction of a probate court, or (e) an action for bodily injury or wrongful death, or for latent or patent defects to which Code of Civil Procedure § 337.1 or § 337.15 applies. The filing of a judicial action to enable the recording of a notice of pending action, for order of attachment, receivership, injunction, or other provisional remedies, shall not constitute a waiver of the right to arbitrate under this provision.

Any dispute or claim by or against broker(s) and/or associate licensee(s) participating in this transaction shall be submitted to arbitration consistent with the provision above only if the broker(s) and/or associate licensee(s) making the claim or against whom the claim is made shall have agreed to submit it to arbitration consistent with this provision.

"NOTICE: BY INITIALLING IN THE SPACE BELOW YOU ARE AGREEING TO HAVE ANY DISPUTE ARISING OUT OF THE MATTERS INCLUDED IN THE 'ARBITRATION OF DISPUTES' PROVISION DECIDED BY NEUTRAL ARBITRATION AS PROVIDED BY CALIFORNIA LAW AND YOU ARE GIVING UP ANY RIGHTS YOU MIGHT POSSESS TO HAVE THE DISPUTE LITIGATED IN A COURT OR JURY TRIAL. BY INITIALLING IN THE SPACE BELOW YOU ARE GIVING UP YOUR JUDICIAL RIGHTS TO DISCOVERY AND APPEAL, UNLESS THOSE RIGHTS ARE SPECIFICALLY INCLUDED IN THE 'ARBITRATION OF DISPUTES' PROVISION. IF YOU REFUSE TO SUBMIT TO ARBITRATION AFTER AGREEING TO THIS PROVISION, YOU MAY BE COMPELLED TO ARBITRATE UNDER THE AUTHORITY OF THE CALIFORNIA CODE OF CIVIL PROCEDURE. YOUR AGREEMENT TO THIS ARBITRATION PROVISION IS VOLUNTARY."

"WE HAVE READ AND UNDERSTAND THE FOREGOING AND AGREE TO SUBMIT DISPUTES ARISING OUT OF THE MATTERS INCLUDED IN THE 'ARBITRATION OF DISPUTES' PROVISION TO NEUTRAL ARBITRATION."

Buyer's Initials   Seller's Initials
____ / ____   ____ / ____

17. OTHER TERMS AND CONDITIONS: _____
_____
_____
_____
_____

18. ATTORNEY'S FEES: In any action, proceeding or arbitration arising out of this agreement, the prevailing party shall be entitled to reasonable attorney's fees and costs. .

19. ENTIRE CONTRACT: Time is of the essence. All prior agreements between the parties are incorporated in this agreement which constitutes the entire contract. Its terms are intended by the parties as a final expression of their agreement with respect to such terms as are included herein and may not be contradicted by evidence of any prior agreement or contemporaneous oral agreement. The parties further intend that this agreement constitutes the complete and exclusive statement of its terms and that no extrinsic evidence whatsoever may be introduced in any judicial or arbitration proceeding, if any, involving this agreement.

20. CAPTIONS: The captions in this agreement are for convenience of reference only and are not intended as part of this agreement.

21. AGENCY CONFIRMATION: The following agency relationship(s) are hereby confirmed for this transaction:
LISTING AGENT: _____ is the agent of (check one):
                                (Print Firm Name)
      ☐ the Seller exclusively; or ☐ both the Buyer and Seller

SELLING AGENT: _____ (if not the same as Listing Agent) is the agent of (check one):
                                (Print Firm Name)
      ☐ the Buyer exclusively; or ☐ the Seller exclusively; or ☐ both the Buyer and Seller.

22. AMENDMENTS: This agreement may not be amended, modified, altered or changed in any respect whatsoever except by a further agreement in writing executed by Buyer and Seller.

23. OFFER: This constitutes an offer to purchase the described property. Unless acceptance is signed by Seller and a signed copy delivered in person, by mail, or facsimile, and received by Buyer at the address below, or by _____ who is authorized to receive it, on behalf of Buyer, within _____ calendar days of the date hereof, this offer shall be deemed revoked and the deposit shall be returned. Buyer has read and acknowledges receipt of a copy of this offer. This agreement and any supplement, addendum or modification relating hereto, including any photocopy or facsimile thereof, may be executed in two or more counterparts, all of which shall constitute one and the same writing.

REAL ESTATE BROKER _____   BUYER _____
By _____   BUYER _____
Address _____   Address _____

Telephone _____   Telephone _____

ACCEPTANCE

The undersigned Seller accepts and agrees to sell the property on the above terms and conditions and agrees to the above confirmation of agency relationships
(☐ subject to attached counter offer).
Seller agrees to pay to Broker(s) _____
compensation for services as follows: _____ .
Payable: (a) On recordation of the deed or other evidence of title, or (b) if completion of sale is prevented by default of Seller, upon Seller's default, or (c) if completion of sale is prevented by default of Buyer, only if and when Seller collects damages from Buyer, by suit or otherwise, and then in an amount not less than one-half of the damages recovered, but not to exceed the above fee, after first deducting title and escrow expenses and the expenses of collection, if any. Seller shall execute and deliver an escrow instruction irrevocably assigning the compensation for service in an amount equal to the compensation agreed to above. In any action, proceeding, or arbitration between Broker(s) and Seller arising out of this agreement, the prevailing party shall be entitled to reasonable attorney's fees and costs. The undersigned has read and acknowledges receipt of a copy of this agreement and authorizes Broker(s) to deliver a signed copy to Buyer.

Date _____   Telephone _____   SELLER _____
Address _____
_____   SELLER _____
Real Estate Broker(s) agree to the foregoing.
Broker _____ By _____ Date _____
Broker _____ By _____ Date _____

┌─ OFFICE USE ONLY ─────────┐
Reviewed by Broker or Designee _____
Date _____
└───────────────────────────┘

Page 4 of _____ Pages.

M-MB-Aug-89

BROKER'S COPY

REAL ESTATE TRANSFER DISCLOSURE STATEMENT
(CALIFORNIA CIVIL CODE 1102, ET SEQ.)
CALIFORNIA ASSOCIATION OF REALTORS® (CAR) STANDARD FORM

THIS DISCLOSURE STATEMENT CONCERNS THE REAL PROPERTY SITUATED IN THE CITY OF_____
_____, COUNTY OF_____, STATE OF CALIFORNIA,
DESCRIBED AS_____.
THIS STATEMENT IS A DISCLOSURE OF THE CONDITION OF THE ABOVE DESCRIBED PROPERTY IN COMPLIANCE
WITH SECTION 1102 OF THE CIVIL CODE AS OF _____, 19____. IT IS NOT A WARRANTY
OF ANY KIND BY THE SELLER(S) OR ANY AGENT(S) REPRESENTING ANY PRINCIPAL(S) IN THIS TRANSACTION,
AND IS NOT A SUBSTITUTE FOR ANY INSPECTIONS OR WARRANTIES THE PRINCIPAL(S) MAY WISH TO OBTAIN.

I
COORDINATION WITH OTHER DISCLOSURE FORMS

This Real Estate Transfer Disclosure Statement is made pursuant to Section 1102 of the Civil Code. Other statutes require disclosures, depending upon the details of the particular real estate transaction (for example: special study zone and purchase-money liens on residential property).

Substituted Disclosures: The following disclosures have or will be in connection with this real estate transfer, and are intended to satisfy the disclosure obligations on this form, where the subject matter is the same:_____
_____
_____
_____
(LIST ALL SUBSTITUTED DISCLOSURE FORMS TO BE USED IN CONNECTION WITH THIS TRANSACTION)

II
SELLER'S INFORMATION

The Seller discloses the following information with the knowledge that even though this is not a warranty, prospective Buyers may rely on this information in deciding whether and on what terms to purchase the subject property. Seller hereby authorizes any agent(s) representing any principal(s) in this transaction to provide a copy of this statement to any person or entity in connection with any actual or anticipated sale of the property.

THE FOLLOWING ARE REPRESENTATIONS MADE BY THE SELLER(S) AND ARE NOT THE REPRESENTATIONS OF THE AGENT(S), IF ANY. THIS INFORMATION IS A DISCLOSURE AND IS NOT INTENDED TO BE PART OF ANY CONTRACT BETWEEN THE BUYER AND SELLER.

Seller ☐ is ☐ is not occupying the property.

A. The subject property has the items checked below (read across):

☐ Range	☐ Oven	☐ Microwave
☐ Dishwasher	☐ Trash Compactor	☐ Garbage Disposal
☐ Washer/Dryer Hookups	☐ Window Screens	☐ Rain Gutters
☐ Burglar Alarms	☐ Smoke Detector(s)	☐ Fire Alarm
☐ T.V. Antenna	☐ Satellite Dish	☐ Intercom
☐ Central Heating	☐ Central Air Conditioning	☐ Evaporator Cooler(s)
☐ Wall/Window Air Conditioning	☐ Sprinklers	☐ Public Sewer System
☐ Septic Tank	☐ Sump Pump	☐ Water Softener
☐ Patio/Decking	☐ Built-in Barbeque	☐ Gazebo
☐ Sauna	☐ Pool	☐ Spa ☐ Hot Tub
☐ Security Gate(s)	☐ Garage Door Opener(s)	☐ Number of Remote Controls_____
Garage: ☐ Attached	☐ Not Attached	☐ Carport
Pool/Spa Heater: ☐ Gas	☐ Solar	☐ Electric
Water Heater: ☐ Gas	☐ Solar	☐ Electric
Water Supply: ☐ City	☐ Well	☐ Private Utility ☐ Other_____
Gas Supply: ☐ Utility	☐ Bottled	

Exhaust Fan(s) in_____220 Volt Wiring in_____
Fireplace(s) in_____ ☐ Gas Starter
☐ Roof(s): Type:_____Age:_____(approx.)
☐ Other:_____
Are there, to the best of your (Seller's) knowledge, any of the above that are not in operating condition? ☐ Yes ☐ No If yes, then
describe. (Attach additional sheets if necessary.):_____
_____
_____

B. Are you (Seller) aware of any significant defects/malfunctions in any of the following? ☐ Yes ☐ No If yes, check
appropriate space(s) below.
☐ Interior Walls ☐ Ceilings ☐ Floors ☐ Exterior Walls ☐ Insulation ☐ Roof(s) ☐ Windows ☐ Doors ☐ Foundation ☐ Slab(s)
☐ Driveways ☐ Sidewalks ☐ Walls/Fences ☐ Electrical Systems ☐ Plumbing/Sewers/Septics ☐ Other Structural Components
(Describe:_____
_____
_____)
If any of the above is checked, explain. (Attach additional sheets if necessary):_____
_____
_____
_____

Buyer and Seller acknowledge receipt of copy of this page, which constitutes Page 1 of 2 Pages.
Buyer's Initials (_____) (_____) Seller's Initials (_____) (_____)

BROKER'S COPY

┌─ OFFICE USE ONLY ─┐
Reviewed by Broker or Designee_____
Date_____

EQUAL HOUSING
OPPORTUNITY
SF-Oct-89

C. Are you (Seller) aware of any of the following:

1. Substances, materials, or products which may be an environmental hazard such as, but not limited to, asbestos, formaldehyde, radon gas, lead-based paint, fuel or chemical storage tanks, and contaminated soil or water on the subject property. . . . . □ Yes □ No
2. Features of the property shared in common with adjoining landowners, such as walls, fences, and driveways, whose use or responsibility for maintenance may have an effect on the subject property. . . . . □ Yes □ No
3. Any encroachments, easements or similar matters that may affect your interest in the subject property. . . . . □ Yes □ No
4. Room additions, structural modifications, or other alterations or repairs made without necessary permits. . . . . . . □ Yes □ No
5. Room additions, structural modifications, or other alterations or repairs not in compliance with building codes. . . . □ Yes □ No
6. Landfill (compacted or otherwise) on the property or any portion thereof. . . . . □ Yes □ No
7. Any settling from any cause, or slippage, sliding, or other soil problems. . . . . □ Yes □ No
8. Flooding, drainage or grading problems. . . . . □ Yes □ No
9. Major damage to the property or any of the structures from fire, earthquake, floods, or landslides. . . . . □ Yes □ No
10. Any zoning violations, nonconforming uses, violations of "setback" requirements. . . . . □ Yes □ No
11. Neighborhood noise problems or other nuisances. . . . . □ Yes □ No
12. CC&R's or other deed restrictions or obligations. . . . . □ Yes □ No
13. Homeowners' Association which has any authority over the subject property. . . . . □ Yes □ No
14. Any "common area" (facilities such as pools, tennis courts, walkways, or other areas co-owned in undivided interest with others). . . . . □ Yes □ No
15. Any notices of abatement or citations against the property. . . . . □ Yes □ No
16. Any lawsuits against the seller threatening to or affecting this real property. . . . . □ Yes □ No

If the answer to any of these is yes, explain. (Attach additional sheets if necessary.): _____

_____

_____

Seller certifies that the information herein is true and correct to the best of the Seller's knowledge as of the date signed by the Seller.

Seller_____ Date_____

Seller_____ Date_____

III
AGENT'S INSPECTION DISCLOSURE
(To be completed only if the seller is represented by an agent in this transaction.)
THE UNDERSIGNED, BASED ON THE ABOVE INQUIRY OF THE SELLER(S) AS TO THE CONDITION OF THE PROPERTY AND BASED ON A REASONABLY COMPETENT AND DILIGENT VISUAL INSPECTION OF THE ACCESSIBLE AREAS OF THE PROPERTY IN CONJUNCTION WITH THAT INQUIRY, STATES THE FOLLOWING:

_____

_____

Agent (Broker
Representing Seller) _____ By _____ Date_____
                         (PLEASE PRINT)   (ASSOCIATE LICENSEE OR BROKER-SIGNATURE)

IV
AGENT'S INSPECTION DISCLOSURE
(To be completed only if the agent who has obtained the offer is other than the agent above.)
THE UNDERSIGNED, BASED ON A REASONABLY COMPETENT AND DILIGENT VISUAL INSPECTION OF THE ACCESSIBLE AREAS OF THE PROPERTY, STATES THE FOLLOWING:

_____

_____

Agent (Broker
obtaining the Offer) _____ By _____ Date_____
                         (PLEASE PRINT)   (ASSOCIATE LICENSEE OR BROKER-SIGNATURE)

V
BUYER(S) AND SELLER(S) MAY WISH TO OBTAIN PROFESSIONAL ADVICE AND/OR INSPECTIONS OF THE PROPERTY AND TO PROVIDE FOR APPROPRIATE PROVISIONS IN A CONTRACT BETWEEN BUYER AND SELLER(S) WITH RESPECT TO ANY ADVICE/INSPECTIONS/DEFECTS.

I/WE ACKNOWLEDGE RECEIPT OF A COPY OF THIS STATEMENT.

Seller_____ Date_____   Buyer_____ Date_____

Seller_____ Date_____   Buyer_____ Date_____

Agent (Broker
Representing Seller) _____ By _____ Date_____
                         (PLEASE PRINT)   (ASSOCIATE LICENSEE OR BROKER-SIGNATURE)

Agent (Broker
obtaining the Offer) _____ By _____ Date_____
                         (PLEASE PRINT)   (ASSOCIATE LICENSEE OR BROKER-SIGNATURE)

A REAL ESTATE BROKER IS QUALIFIED TO ADVISE ON REAL ESTATE. IF YOU DESIRE LEGAL ADVICE, CONSULT YOUR ATTORNEY.

BROKER'S COPY

Page 2 of _____ Pages.

OFFICE USE ONLY
Reviewed by Broker or Designee _____
Date _____

EQUAL HOUSING OPPORTUNITY
SF-Oct-89

DISCLOSURE REGARDING
REAL ESTATE AGENCY RELATIONSHIPS
(As required by the Civil Code)
CALIFORNIA ASSOCIATION OF REALTORS® (CAR) STANDARD FORM

When you enter into a discussion with a real estate agent regarding a real estate transaction, you should from the outset understand what type of agency relationship or representation you wish to have with the agent in the transaction.

SELLER'S AGENT
A Seller's agent under a listing agreement with Seller acts as the agent for the Seller only. A Seller's agent or a subagent of that agent has the following affirmative obligations:
To the Seller:
    (a) A Fiduciary duty of utmost care, integrity, honesty, and loyalty in dealings with the Seller.
To the Buyer & the Seller:
    (a) Diligent exercise of reasonable skill and care in performance of the agent's duties.
    (b) A duty of honest and fair dealing and good faith.
    (c) A duty to disclose all facts known to the agent materially affecting the value or desirability of property that are not known to, or within the diligent attention and observation of, the parties.

An agent is not obligated to reveal to either party any confidential information obtained from the other party which does not involve the affirmative duties set forth above.

BUYER'S AGENT
A selling agent can, with a Buyer's consent, agree to act as agent for the Buyer only. In these situations, the agent is not the Seller's agent, even if by agreement the agent may receive compensation for services rendered, either in full or in part from the Seller. An agent acting only for a Buyer has the following affirmative obligations:
To the Buyer:
    (a) A fiduciary duty of utmost care, integrity, honesty, and loyalty in dealings with the Buyer.
To the Buyer & Seller:
    (a) Diligent exercise of reasonable skill and care in performance of the agent's duties.
    (b) A duty of honest and fair dealing and good faith.
    (c) A duty to disclose all facts known to the agent materially affecting the value or desirability of the property that are not known to, or within the diligent attention and observation of, the parties.

An agent is not obligated to reveal to either party any confidential information obtained from the other party which does not involve the affirmative duties set forth above.

AGENT REPRESENTING BOTH SELLER & BUYER
A real estate agent, either acting directly or through one or more associate licensees, can legally be the agent of both the Seller and the Buyer in a transaction, but only with the knowledge and consent of both the Seller and the Buyer.

In a dual agency situation, the agent has the following affirmative obligations to both the Seller and the Buyer:
    (a) A fiduciary duty of utmost care, integrity, honesty and loyalty in the dealings with either Seller or the Buyer.
    (b) Other duties to the Seller and the Buyer as stated above in their respective sections.

In representing both Seller and Buyer, the agent may not, without the express permission of the respective party, disclose to the other party that the Seller will accept a price less than the listing price or that the Buyer will pay a price greater than the price offered.

The above duties of the agent in a real estate transaction do not relieve a Seller or a Buyer from the responsibility to protect their own interests. You should carefully read all agreements to assure that they adequately express your understanding of the transaction. A real estate agent is a person qualified to advise about real estate. If legal or tax advice is desired, consult a competent professional.

Throughout your real property transaction you may receive more than one disclosure form, depending upon the number of agents assisting in the transaction. The law requires each agent with whom you have more than a casual relationship to present you with this disclosure form. You should read its contents each time it is presented to you, considering the relationship between you and the real estate agent in your specific transaction.

This disclosure form includes the provisions of article 2.5 (commencing with Section 2373) of Chapter 2 of Title 9 of Part 4 of Division 3 of the Civil Code set forth on the reverse hereof. Read it carefully.

I/WE ACKNOWLEDGE RECEIPT OF A COPY OF THIS DISCLOSURE.

BUYER/SELLER._____ Date_____ TIME_____ AM/PM

BUYER/SELLER._____ Date_____ TIME_____ AM/PM

AGENT _____ By _____ Date_____
      (Please Print)   (Associate Licensee or Broker-Signature)

CONFIRMATION
REAL ESTATE AGENCY RELATIONSHIPS

Subject Property Address_____.

The following agency relationship(s) is/are hereby confirmed for this transaction:

LISTING AGENT: _____   **SELLING AGENT:** _____
    is the agent of (check one):   (if not the same as Listing Agent)
    ☐ the Seller exclusively; or   is the agent of (check one):
    ☐ both the Buyer and Seller   ☐ the Buyer exclusively; or
                                           ☐ the Seller exclusively; or
                                         ☐ both the Buyer and Seller

I/WE ACKNOWLEDGE RECEIPT OF A COPY OF THIS CONFIRMATION.

Seller_____ Date_____   Buyer _____ Date_____

Seller_____ Date_____   Buyer _____ Date_____

Listing Agent_____ By _____ Date_____
        (Please Print)   (Associate Licensee or Broker-Signature)

Selling Agent_____ By _____ Date_____
        (Please Print)   (Associate Licensee or Broker-Signature)

A REAL ESTATE BROKER IS QUALIFIED TO ADVISE ON REAL ESTATE. IF YOU DESIRE LEGAL ADVICE, CONSULT YOUR ATTORNEY.

This form is available for use by the entire real estate industry. The use of this form is not intended to identify the user as a REALTOR®. REALTOR® is a registered collective membership mark which may be used only by real estate licensees who are members of the NATIONAL ASSOCIATION OF REALTORS® and who subscribe to its Code of Ethics.

Copyright© 1987, CALIFORNIA ASSOCIATION OF REALTORS®
525 South Virgil Avenue, Los Angeles, California 90020   **FORM AD-11/AC-6**
                                                  (combined)

┌─ OFFICE USE ONLY ─┐
Reviewed by Broker or Designee _____
Date _____

SF-Sep-89

CHAPTER 2 OF TITLE 9 OF PART 4 OF DIVISION 3 OF THE CIVIL CODE

Article 2.5. Agency Relationships in Residential Real Property Transactions

2373. As used in this article, the following terms have the following meanings:

(a) "Agent" means a person acting under provisions of this title in a real property transaction, and includes a person who is licensed as a real estate broker under Chapter 3 (commencing with Section 10130) of Part 1 of Division 4 of the Business & Professions Code, and under whose license a listing is executed or an offer to purchase is obtained.

(b) "Associate licensee" means a person who is licensed as a real estate broker or salesperson under Chapter 3 (commencing with Section 10130) of Part 1 of Division 4 of the Business & Professions Code and who is either licensed under a broker or has entered into a written contract with a broker to act as the broker's agent in connection with acts requiring a real estate license and to function under the broker's supervision in the capacity of an associate licensee.

The agent in the real property transaction bears responsibility for his or her associate licensees who perform as agents of the agent. When an associate licensee owes a duty to any principal, or to any buyer or seller who is not a principal, in a real property transaction, that duty is equivalent to the duty owed to that party by the broker for whom the associate licensee functions.

(c) "Buyer" means a transferee in a real property transaction, and includes a person who executes an offer to purchase real property from a seller through an agent, or who seeks the services of an agent in more than a casual, transitory, or preliminary manner, with the object of entering into a real property transaction. "Buyer" includes vendee or lessee.

(d) "Dual agent" means an agent acting, either directly or through an associate licensee, as agent for both the seller and the buyer in a real property transaction.

(e) "Listing agreement" means a contract between an owner of real property and an agent, by which the agent has been authorized to sell the real property or to find or obtain a buyer.

(f) "Listing agent" means a person who has obtained a listing of real property to act as an agent for compensation.

(g) "Listing price" is the amount expressed in dollars specified in the listing for which the seller is willing to sell the real property through the listing agent.

(h) "Offering price" is the amount expressed in dollars specified in an offer to purchase for which the buyer is willing to buy the real property.

(i) "Offer to purchase" means a written contract executed by a buyer acting through a selling agent which becomes the contract for the sale of the real property upon acceptance by the seller.

(j) "Real property" means any estate specified by subdivision (1) or (2) of Section 761 in property which constitutes or is improved with one to four dwelling units, any leasehold in this type of property exceeding one year's duration, and mobilehomes, when offered for sale or sold through an agent pursuant to the authority contained in Section 10131.6 of the Business & Professions Code.

(k) "Real property transaction" means a transaction for the sale of real property in which an agent is employed by one or more of the principals to act in that transaction, and includes a listing or an offer to purchase.

(l) "Sell," "sale," or "sold" refers to a transaction for the transfer of real property from the seller to the buyer, and includes exchanges of real property between the seller and buyer, transactions for the creation of a real property sales contract within the meaning of Section 2985, and transactions for the creation of a leasehold exceeding one year's duration.

(m) "Seller" means the transferor in a real property transaction, and includes an owner who lists real property with an agent, whether or not a transfer results, or who receives an offer to purchase real property of which he or she is the owner from an agent on behalf of another. "Seller" includes both a vendor and a lessor.

(n) "Selling agent" means a listing agent who acts alone, or an agent who acts in cooperation with a listing agent, and who sells or finds and obtains a buyer for the real property, or an agent who locates property for a buyer for the property for which no listing exists and presents an offer to purchase to the seller.

(o) "Subagent" means a person to whom an agent delegates agency powers as provided in Article 5 (commencing with Section 2349) of Chapter I. However, "subagent" does not include an associate licensee who is acting under the supervision of an agent in a real property transaction.

2374. Listing agents and selling agents shall provide the seller and buyer in a real property transaction with a copy of the disclosure form specified in Section 2375, and, except as provided in subdivision (c), shall obtain a signed acknowledgement of receipt from that seller or buyer, except as provided in this section of Section 2374.5, as follows:

(a) The listing agent, if any, shall provide the disclosure form to the seller prior to entering into the listing agreement.

(b) The selling agent shall provide the disclosure form to the seller as soon as practicable prior to presenting the seller with an offer to purchase, unless the selling agent previously provided the seller with a copy of the disclosure form pursuant to subdivision (a).

(c) Where the selling agent does not deal on a face-to-face basis with the seller, the disclosure form prepared by the selling agent may be furnished to the seller (and acknowledgement of receipt obtained for the selling agent from the seller) by the listing agent, or the selling agent may deliver the disclosure form by certified mail addressed to the seller at his or her last known address, in which case no signed acknowledgement of receipt is required.

(d) The selling agent shall provide the disclosure form to the buyer as soon as practicable prior to execution of the buyer's offer to purchase, except that if the offer to purchase is not prepared by the selling agent, the selling agent shall present the disclosure form to the buyer not later than the next business day after the selling agent receives the offer to purchase from the buyer.

2374.5 In any circumstance in which the seller or buyer refuses to sign an acknowledgement of receipt pursuant to Section 2374, the agent, or an associate licensee acting for an agent, shall set forth, sign and date a written declaration of the facts of the refusal.

2375.5 (a) As soon as practicable, the selling agent shall disclose to the buyer and seller whether the selling agent is acting in the real property transaction exclusively as the buyer's agent, exclusively as the seller's agent, or as a dual agent representing both the buyer and the seller and this relationship shall be confirmed in the contract to purchase and sell real property or in a separate writing executed or acknowledged by the seller, the buyer, and the selling agent prior to or coincident with execution of that contract by the buyer and the seller, respectively.

(b) As soon as practicable, the listing agent shall disclose to the seller whether the listing agent is acting in the real property transaction exclusively as the seller's agent, or as a dual agent representing both the buyer and seller and this relationship shall be confirmed in the contract to purchase and sell real property or in a separate writing executed or acknowledged by the seller and the listing agent prior to or coincident with the execution of that contract by the seller.

(c) The confirmation required by subdivisions (a) and (b) shall be in the following form.

_____ is the agent of (check one):   _____ is the agent of (check one):
(Name of Listing Agent)   (Name of Selling Agent if not the same as the Listing Agent)

[ ] the seller exclusively; or   [ ] the buyer exclusively; or
[ ] both the buyer and seller.   [ ] the seller exclusively; or
                                                                              [ ] both the buyer and seller.

(d) The disclosures and confirmation required by this section shall be in addition to the disclosure required by Section 2374.

2376. No selling agent in a real property transaction may act as an agent for the buyer only, when the selling agent is also acting as the listing agent in the transaction.

2377. The payment of compensation or the obligation to pay compensation to an agent by the seller or buyer is not necessarily determinative of a particular agency relationship between an agent and the seller or buyer. A listing agent and a selling agent may agree to share any compensation or commission paid, or any right to any compensation or commission for which an obligation arises as the result of a real estate transaction, and the terms of any such agreement shall not necessarily be determinative of a particular relationship.

2378. Nothing in this article prevents an agent from selecting, as a condition of the agent's employment, a specific form of agency relationship not specifically prohibited by this article if the requirements of Section 2374 and Section 2375.5 are complied with.

2379. A dual agent shall not disclose to the buyer that the seller is willing to sell the property at a price less than the listing price, without the express written consent of the seller. A dual agent shall not disclose to the seller that the buyer is willing to pay a price greater than the offering price, without the express written consent of the buyer.

This section does not alter in any way the duty or responsibility of a dual agent to any principal with respect to confidential information other than price.

2380. Nothing in this article precludes a listing agent from also being a selling agent, and the combination of these functions in one agent does not, of itself, make that agent a dual agent.

2381. A contract between the principal and agent may be modified or altered to change the agency relationship at any time before the performance of the act which is the object of the agency with the written consent of the parties to the agency relationship.

2382. Nothing in this article shall be construed to either diminish the duty of disclosure owed buyers and sellers by agents and their associate licensees, subagents, and employees or to relieve agents and their associate licensees, subagents, and employees from liability for their conduct in connection with acts governed by this article or for any breach of a fiduciary duty or a duty of disclosure.

INDEX

Practice Examination

There is an old education adage that says the best way to learn is to "read, recite, and review." To help with your review, you will find a 150-question practice examination. As noted in Chapter 15, Appendix D, the California Department of Real Estate provides that the State Salesperson Examination is segmented along certain lines.

The enclosed examination has been segmented along the same lines and should form a comprehensive review. Real estate principles cover such a vast amount of material that every single topic cannot be tested. But the questions that follow are a representative sample of the types of questions that frequently appear in examinations.

TEST-TAKING TIPS

1. Take three passes through the examination. The first time through answer only the questions you know for sure, skipping everything else. This will give you a sense of success and allow you to get a feel for the examination. The second time through answer those questions you think you know, skipping those that are completely unfamiliar to you. The third time through, guess. **Remember to go back and answer all the questions.**

2. Reading pitfalls: Make sure you read all the answer choices. Sometimes an answer may appear correct, but another reading reveals the actual correct answer. Watch out for questions that say *"except for," "which is not,"* and so on. The wording is confusing and you may select the wrong answer if you are not careful.

3. Here are some guessing suggestions:
   (a) Take the longest answer.
   (b) Do not take "all of the above" unless you can identify two answers as being right.
   (c) Two answers will be close and two answers are obviously wrong. Eliminate the obviously wrong two and select the most logical of the remaining two.

4. Math phobia: If math is not your strong point, leave the math until last. If you have done well on the rest of the examination, missing every math question will not usually cause you to fail. If you cannot do a math question, just take a wild guess.

5. Take the entire exam in one sitting in quiet surroundings. Upon completion, check your answers and look up the textbook discussion regarding the questions you missed.
   DO NOT WRITE ON THE EXAMINATION. USE A SEPARATE PAPER FOR YOUR ANSWERS SO YOU CAN RETAKE THE EXAMINATION SEVERAL TIMES FOR PRACTICE.

1. A "loss in value from any cause" is a definition of:
   - (a) economic obsolescence
   - (b) depreciation
   - (c) leverage
   - (d) goodwill

2. A couple recently married and each had children from a previous marriage. They wish to take title to property so that they each could pass their share to their own children by will. The best form of title would be:
   - (a) joint tenancy
   - (b) severalty
   - (c) tenancy in common
   - (d) tenancy in whole

3. A valid deed passes title when it is:
   - (a) signed
   - (b) recorded
   - (c) delivered
   - (d) acknowledged

4. When a governmental body takes private real estate for public use, the process is called:
   - (a) eminent domain
   - (b) police power
   - (c) zoning
   - (d) adverse possession

5. The main purpose of the Truth-in-Lending Act is to:
   - (a) prevent usury
   - (b) require disclosure of credit terms
   - (c) reduce the cost of credit
   - (d) regulate annual percentage rates

6. The difference between judgment liens and mechanic's liens is:
   - (a) mechanic's liens are general liens
   - (b) mechanic's liens can take priority before they are recorded
   - (c) mechanic's liens are voluntary liens
   - (d) judgment liens are involuntary liens

7. Private restrictions (CC&Rs) cannot be conveyed by:
   - (a) deed
   - (b) written agreement
   - (c) easement
   - (d) general plan restrictions in a subdivision

8. On September 1, 1988, Garcia agreed to purchase Chan's home. Both parties agreed that possession would take place October 30, 1988, and that property taxes would be prorated as of date of possession. On December 1, 1988, Chan paid the property taxes for the year 1988-89. According to the escrow closing statement, which of the following is true?
   - (a) Garcia paid Chan for 8 months' taxes
   - (b) Garcia paid Chan for 4 months' taxes
   - (c) Chan paid Garcia for 8 months' taxes
   - (d) Chan paid Garcia for 4 months' taxes

9. A quitclaim deed conveys only the present rights of:
   (a) the grantor
   (b) the servient tenant
   (c) the grantee
   (d) the trustee

10. To have a valid homestead, certain elements are essential. Which of the following is not essential:
    (a) a description of the property
    (b) a statement of residence
    (c) to be a married person
    (d) to be recorded

11. A licensed loan broker arranged for a loan and has the borrower sign the required statement. The broker then discovers that there is a lien that the borrower did not disclose. If the loan cannot be arranged due to the lien, the borrower would be liable for:
    (a) cost and expenses incurred to date
    (b) no cost and expenses
    (c) all cost and expenses and half the commission
    (d) none of the above

12. A person purchased a property for $200,000, which was equal to $4.75 per square foot. The rectangular lot was 300 feet deep. The cost per front foot was:
    (a) $1,425
    (b) $950
    (c) $827
    (d) $793

13. Which of the following is not essential to form an agency:
    (a) a fiduciary relationship
    (b) agreement of the parties
    (c) consideration
    (d) competent parties

14. An owner sells a property for cash and receives $67,100 from escrow. The only expenses were a 6% commission and $517 in other expenses. The property sold for:
    (a) $71,643
    (b) $71,933
    (c) $72,591
    (d) $73,137

15. A real estate agent must disclose all material facts to a seller principal. Which of the following is considered a material fact:
    (a) the buyer's racial background
    (b) the agent's knowledge of a pending better offer
    (c) the lender's requirement that a buyer pay a loan fee
    (d) that the buyer has a medical problem

16. In appraising improved property, the least important factor is:
    (a) sales price
    (b) highest and best use
    (c) prices of comparables
    (d) assessed value

17. Community apartments and condominium projects fall within the sub-division laws of the California Real Estate Law when they contain:
    (a) one or more units
    (b) two or more units
    (c) three or more units
    (d) five or more units

18. Studs are attached to rest upon:
    (a) the mud sill
    (b) the subfloor
    (c) the header
    (d) the sole plate

19. A person borrowed 80% of the value of a condo. The loan interest rate was 9%. The first-year interest was $5,050. The value of the condo was:
    (a) $63,313
    (b) $65,459
    (c) $70,139
    (d) none of the above

20. Adams, Brown, and Chow are owners of commercial land as joint tenants. Adams dies and is survived by Brown and Chow. Which is correct:
    (a) Brown and Chow receive title by succession
    (b) the joint tenancy is terminated
    (c) Adams's interest terminates
    (d) Brown and Chow are now tenants in common

21. To completely fence the NW quarter of the SE quarter of Section 3 would take how much fencing:
    (a) 2 miles
    (b) 1 mile
    (c) 1/2 mile
    (d) 1/4 mile

22. When both the landlord and tenant mutually agree to cancel a lease, their action is called:
    (a) a termination
    (b) a rescission
    (c) a release
    (d) an abandonment

23. An amortized loan has equal monthly installments consisting of:
    (a) interest alone
    (b) principal alone
    (c) principal and interest
    (d) principal, interest, taxes, and insurance

24. Which of the following is an operating expense to be subtracted from gross income when appraising a property using the income approach:
    (a) interest payments
    (b) principal payments
    (c) property taxes
    (d) all of the above

25. The word "emblements" refers to:
    (a) attachments to a contract
    (b) growing crops
    (c) machinery
    (d) fixtures on a building

26. A salesperson working for a broker had been wrongfully selling information to a loan company. When the broker, who had been using reasonable supervision, discovered this, the salesperson was fired. Based upon the information given:
    (a) the broker is probably not liable if he had no knowledge of the wrongdoing
    (b) both the salesperson and the broker are liable
    (c) there is no liability
    (d) the salesperson is licensed to sell loan information in his name only

27. Which of the following is worded incorrectly:
    (a) Federal National Mortgage Association (Fannie Mae)
    (b) Government National Mortgage Association (Ginnie Mae)
    (c) Federal Housing Association (FHA)
    (d) Veterans Administration (VA)

28. Williams entered into a 9-month oral lease on July 1 to start on September 1 at a rate of $1,000 per month. On August 15, Williams backs out of the lease. The lease is:
    (a) unenforceable
    (b) enforceable
    (c) void
    (d) restricted by the Statute of Frauds

29. Title insurance does not protect a buyer against:
    (a) forgery in the chain of title
    (b) lack of capacity of the grantor
    (c) recorded easements
    (d) zoning restrictions

30. If state housing codes conflict with local codes, usually:
    (a) state codes prevail
    (b) local codes prevail
    (c) the stricter of the two prevail
    (d) the more lenient of the two prevail

31. A broker received deposits from principals and placed the funds in a safe for several days before putting the funds in the broker's trust fund account at the bank. The broker is guilty of:
    (a) conversion
    (b) commingling
    (c) misrepresentation
    (d) fraud

32. A husband dies intestate. His separate property is distributed to his wife and two children as follows:
    (a) all to the wife
    (b) half to the wife and half to the children
    (c) all to the children
    (d) one third to the wife, the rest to the children

33. Under the Subdivided Lands Act, the Real Estate Commissioner is primarily concerned with:
    (a) physical design and layout
    (b) health facilities
    (c) financing and marketing arrangements
    (d) none of the above

34. Jones leases a home from Santos under a 3-month written lease. Upon expiration of the lease, Jones retains possession. Santos has not decided upon the next step. Jones has an estate at:
    (a) will
    (b) sufferance
    (c) years
    (d) tenancy

35. An investor has an apartment building with no vacancies in which each unit rents for $600. The investor raises the rent 15% and suffers a 15% vacancy factor. Rental income:
    (a) increases
    (b) decreases
    (c) remains the same
    (d) the question cannot be answered with the information given

36. A valid homestead is filed by a head of a household. The residence is later sold to a buyer giving a grant deed. The sale is:
    (a) invalid unless an abandonment of homestead is recorded
    (b) valid
    (c) unenforceable if the grantee wishes to back out
    (d) void because of lack of implied warranties

37. The maximum amount of personal funds a broker may have in a trust fund account to cover charges and not be guilty of commingling is:
    (a) $50
    (b) $100
    (c) $500
    (d) $1,000

38. Property is being sold where the buyer is going to take over the seller's existing loan. To avoid legal conflict immediately after closing, the real estate agent should check to be sure the loan does not include:
    (a) a release clause
    (b) a prepayment penalty
    (c) an acceleration clause
    (d) a subordination clause

39. The stated policy of the Real Estate Commissioner is to create a "color blind" industry. This means agents should:
    (a) maintain an attitude free from bias
    (b) realize that race, creed, and color are not material facts
    (c) do unto others as you would have them do unto you
    (d) all of the above

40. A subdivider sold five lots to one buyer and optioned five other lots to another buyer. The subdivider must:
    (a) notify the Department of Real Estate of a material change
    (b) close the option sales within 3 business days
    (c) record the sales within 5 business days
    (d) not sell five lots to a single purchaser

41. Under the Federal Truth-in-Lending Law (Regulation Z), certain borrowers have ___ days to rescind the loan:
    (a) 30
    (b) 10
    (c) 5
    (d) 3

42. A seller employed a broker under an open listing. The seller indicated to the broker that the roof leaked. While showing the home to a buyer, the broker stated that the roof was in good condition. After the sale the buyer discovered that the roof leaked. The buyer would logically sue:
    (a) only the broker
    (b) both the seller and broker for specific performance
    (c) both the seller and broker for damages
    (d) only the seller

43. Under Division 6 of the Uniform Commercial Code (Bulk Sale Rules), a public notice must be given 12 days before transfer by:
    (a) the seller
    (b) the buyer
    (c) the creditors
    (d) all of the above

44. The value of the subject property as set by the price of comparable properties is based on the principle of:
    (a) change
    (b) regression
    (c) substitution
    (d) highest and best use

45. A California real estate broker sold a ranch in Montana to a California resident. A Montana broker assisted in the sale. To show her appreciation, the California broker gave part of the commission to the Montana broker. This action was:
    (a) unlawful, because the California broker was not licensed in Montana
    (b) unlawful, because the Montana broker was not licensed in California
    (c) lawful
    (d) none of the above

46. Income tax benefits for homeowners include deductions for:
    (a) interest on home loans
    (b) depreciation on buildings
    (c) expenses and repairs
    (d) all of the above

47. All real estate licensees in California are bound by which Code of Ethics:
    (a) Realtors
    (b) Realtist
    (c) Real Estate Commissioners
    (d) all of the above

48. In issuing a policy of title insurance, the title company is least likely to make an on-site inspection if the policy is:
    (a) a CLTA standard owners policy
    (b) an ALTA extended policy
    (c) a construction loan policy
    (d) a lender's policy

49. A real estate broker must retain copies of all listings and deposit receipts for how many years:
   (a) 1
   (b) 3
   (c) 4
   (d) 5

50. The first half of real property taxes are due and payable on November 1. They become delinquent after December 10, at which time a penalty is added to the amount. The penalty is:
   (a) 10%
   (b) 8%
   (c) 6%
   (d) 3%

51. A Notice of Non-Responsibility is usually posted and recorded by an owner when:
   (a) a bulk sale takes place
   (b) a tenant makes repairs
   (c) a transfer of title takes place
   (d) a mechanic's lien is filed

52. Covenants and conditions are frequently placed in deeds. If a covenant or condition is breached, the enforcement is:
   (a) more severe for a condition
   (b) more severe for a covenant
   (c) equal for both a condition and a covenant
   (d) under current law neither can be enforced

53. Which of the following is not a fiduciary relationship:
   (a) broker to seller
   (b) trustor to beneficiary
   (c) attorney to client
   (d) attorney-in-fact to principal

54. An appraiser determines that the market rent for a parcel of land is $700 per month and that interest (capitalization) rates should be 11%. The approximate value is:
   (a) $54,545
   (b) $69,280
   (c) $76,360
   (d) $105,000

55. A parcel of land is planned to be divided into 9 parcels, with the intention of selling 3 parcels per year for each of the next 3 years. The owner:
   (a) must satisfy the Subdivision Map Act
   (b) must report to the Real Estate Commissioner, but need not conform to the Subdivision Map Act
   (c) must comply with the Subdivision Map Act and the Subdivided Lands Act
   (d) need not comply with any special law, as fewer than 5 lots are being sold in any one year

56. Which of the following is a less-than-freehold estate:
   (a) fee simple defeasible
   (b) fee simple absolute
   (c) leasehold estate
   (d) life estate

57. A lease that lies between the primary lease and the sublessee is:
    (a) a sandwich lease
    (b) a percentage lease
    (c) a ground lease
    (d) a wedge lease

58. An easement acquired by prescription can be lost by nonuse for a period of:
    (a) 5 years
    (b) 3 years
    (c) 2 years
    (d) 1 year

59. A corporation built a large tract of homes and hired a handyman to take care of the maintenance. He was given extra compensation for showing the homes on weekends to prospective buyers.
    (a) the corporation is not in violation of real estate regulations
    (b) the handyman could be fined for showing homes without a license
    (c) as an employee, the handyman does not need a license to show homes
    (d) all corporate employees and officers selling the homes must be licensed

60. After a Trustee's Sale, any money remaining after paying lienholders and costs is remitted to:
    (a) the trustor
    (b) the trustee
    (c) the beneficiary
    (d) the mortgagor

61. The person who acquires title to real property under the terms of a will is known as:
    (a) the devisee
    (b) the administrator
    (c) the testator
    (d) the executrix

62. A "commercial acre" is:
    (a) 43,560 sq. ft.
    (b) a normal acre, less deductions for streets and setbacks
    (c) an acre zoned for commercial use
    (d) 42,513 sq. ft.

63. Legal seizure of property to be held for payment of money, pending the outcome of a lawsuit, is called:
    (a) a writ of execution
    (b) an attachment
    (c) an abstract of judgment
    (d) a lis pendens

64. Shay gives a quitclaim deed to Wilson for a parcel of real estate. Wilson does not record the deed. Which of the following is true:
    (a) the deed is invalid as between Shay and Wilson
    (b) the deed is invalid as between Shay and Wilson but valid to subsequent recorded interest
    (c) the deed is valid as between Shay and Wilson but invalid as to subsequent recorded interest without notice
    (d) the deed is valid as between Shay and Wilson and valid as to subsequent recorded interest without notice

65. When public records are used to establish a chain of title, a written summary of the results is known as:
    (a) a guarantee of title
    (b) an abstract of title
    (c) an opinion of title
    (d) an affidavit of title

66. After a mortgage is executed and recorded, title:
    (a) remains with the mortgagor
    (b) transfers to the mortgagee
    (c) is given to the trustee
    (d) remains with the trustor

67. A real estate contract by a married couple under the age of 18 is:
    (a) void
    (b) voidable
    (c) unenforceable
    (d) valid

68. An exclusive agency listing differs from an exclusive right to sell listing in that:
    (a) only the exclusive right to sell listing must have a definite termination date
    (b) the broker is entitled to a commission if the owner sells the property under the exclusive agency listing
    (c) only the exclusive right to sell listing must be in writing to be enforceable
    (d) under the exclusive right to sell listing the broker is entitled to a commission no matter who sells the property during the term of the listing

69. A buyer in a land project can rescind the purchase for any reason and obtain a refund within:
    (a) 3 days
    (b) 5 days
    (c) 10 days
    (d) 14 days

70. Which of the following represents the four essentials of value:
    (a) scarcity, cost, demand, utility
    (b) utility, transferability, cost, demand
    (c) transferability, utility, demand, scarcity
    (d) demand, cost, utility, price

71. All of the following are contracts, except:
    (a) escrow instructions
    (b) a listing agreement
    (c) a deed
    (d) a deposit receipt

72. The cost approach to value has limited use when appraising:
   - (a) a new building
   - (b) tract homes
   - (c) museum buildings
   - (d) special-purpose properties

73. When an agent violates antidiscrimination regulations, the Real Estate Commissioner can:
   - (a) sue for damages
   - (b) file a criminal action
   - (c) revoke a license
   - (d) all of the above

74. Mr. Zowski holds a life estate measured by his own life. He leased the property to Anderson for 5 years, but died 2 months later. The lease is:
   - (a) still valid
   - (b) no longer valid
   - (c) invalid from the inception
   - (d) binding on the heirs of Zowski

75. An owner sold a lot for $70,400, realizing a 20% profit over what was originally paid for the lot. The profit is:
   - (a) $11,733
   - (b) $14,080
   - (c) $13,714
   - (d) $12,509

76. Which of the following is not essential to a general contract:
   - (a) that it be in writing
   - (b) mutual consent
   - (c) capable parties
   - (d) lawful object

77. An example of a lender who frequently uses loan correspondents and funds large commercial loans is:
   - (a) a savings and loan association
   - (b) a commercial bank
   - (c) a credit union
   - (d) a life insurance company

78. RESPA (Real Estate Settlement Procedures Act) requires that certain lenders and/or closers must deliver a Uniform Settlement Statement to the borrower and seller within:
   - (a) 10 days after the loan commitment
   - (b) 3 days prior to closing
   - (c) 5 days after closing
   - (d) on or before date of close

79. A deeds a title to B with the condition that B never sell alcoholic beverages on the property. B has:
   - (a) a less than freehold estate
   - (b) a fee simple absolute
   - (c) a fee simple defeasible
   - (d) a periodic tenancy

80. An abstract of judgment can be recorded:
    (a) in any county
    (b) only in the county where the judgment is to be placed
    (c) only in the county where the debtor has real property
    (d) only in the county where the creditor resides

81. The amount of real estate sales commission is:
    (a) regulated by the Real Estate Commissioner
    (b) subject to negotiation
    (c) fixed by trade groups
    (d) governed by state law

82. A roof that is pitched with two sloping sides is called:
    (a) a hip
    (b) a gable
    (c) a mansard
    (d) a gambrel

83. A contract that is executory:
    (a) has not been performed
    (b) has been signed
    (c) is completed
    (d) has been notarized

84. How much money would have to be invested at a 7% return to give an investor $200 per month:
    (a) $34,286
    (b) $48,000
    (c) $43,705
    (d) $39,325

85. A person who feels he or she has been discriminated against in seeking housing can file a complaint with:
    (a) the Federal Trade Commission
    (b) the Rumford Commission
    (c) the Unruh Commission
    (d) the Fair Employment Practices Commission

86. If a borrower fails to make a loan payment, which financing instrument would be to the borrower's advantage:
    (a) deed of trust
    (b) mortgage
    (c) contract of sale
    (d) lease

87. Rapid inflation would most benefit:
    (a) a borrower with an ARM loan
    (b) a fixed-interest rate beneficiary
    (c) a trustor with fixed interest rate
    (d) a trustee

88. The most difficult depreciation to correct is:
    (a) physical
    (b) economic
    (c) functional
    (d) accrued

89. Properties A and B each have a value of $200,000. Property A was appraised using a capitalization rate of 9%, whereas Property B was appraised using a capitalization rate of 10%.
    (a) Property B has more income than Property A
    (b) Property B has less income than Property A
    (c) Property A and Property B have the same income
    (d) none of the above

90. Which of the following is not appurtenant or incidental to the land:
    (a) stock in mutual water company
    (b) an easement
    (c) reasonable airspace
    (d) a picked crop

91. Recording of an instrument gives:
    (a) actual notice
    (b) constructive notice
    (c) preliminary notice
    (d) recorded notice

92. A rate of interest that exceeds the legal rate is:
    (a) the nominal rate
    (b) the going rate
    (c) the stated rate
    (d) none of the above

93. The Federal National Mortgage Association (Fannie Mae) was primarily created to:
    (a) insure low-income housing loans
    (b) increase the amount of money available to finance housing
    (c) insure savings and loan association depositors for up to $100,000 per account
    (d) lengthen the term for real estate loans

94. Broker Smith and Broker Roberts both have an open listing on a home. Broker Smith showed the home to a buyer who decided not to make an offer. A month later, Broker Roberts showed the same home to the same buyer who then decided to buy. The seller owes a commission to:
    (a) Broker Smith only
    (b) Broker Smith and Broker Roberts
    (c) Broker Roberts only
    (d) Broker Smith, who will need to split it with Broker Roberts

95. Both the buyer and the seller initial the liquidated damages clause in a deposit receipt.
    Later the buyer backs out. The seller is entitled to:
    (a) actual damages
    (b) no damages
    (c) punitive damages
    (d) liquidated damages

96. A person borrowed $2,500 on a straight note. In 8 months $150 in interest was paid. The interest rate is:
    (a) 8.4%
    (b) 9%
    (c) 10.1%
    (d) 10.6%

97. If a dispute arises during escrow and the buyer and seller cannot agree, the escrow holder may legally:
   (a) file an interpleader action
   (b) return all funds to the respective parties
   (c) cancel the escrow
   (d) do all of the above

98. The SW quarter of the NW quarter of the SE quarter of the SE quarter of the NW quarter of a section contains:
   (a) 1 1/4 acres
   (b) 2 1/2 acres
   (c) 5 acres
   (d) none of the above

99. A couple on a deed that reads "husband and wife" without indicating how the title is to be held will be presumed to:
   (a) be joint tenants
   (b) hold community property
   (c) be tenants in common
   (d) hold severalty ownership

100. An owner hired a broker to act as property manager and collect rent from tenants. Rents are due on the first of the month. On June 1, the broker collected rents from all but one of the tenants. The next day the owner died. On June 2, the broker asked the remaining tenant for the rent. The tenant refused to give the rent money to the broker. The tenant:
   (a) must give the rent to the broker
   (b) should not give the rent to anyone but the heirs or the court
   (c) is in default by not giving the rent to the broker
   (d) need not pay the rent

101. Which of the following employment situations is primarily concerned with results, not direction of work:
   (a) employer-employee
   (b) jobber
   (c) independent contractor
   (d) agent

102. If there is no notice of completion, a subcontractor must file a mechanic's lien in:
   (a) 10 days
   (b) 30 days
   (c) 60 days
   (d) 90 days

103. Which of the following is not issued by the Department of Real Estate:
   (a) mineral, oil, gas broker license
   (b) prepaid rental listing license
   (c) real estate sales license
   (d) escrow license

104. The fine for an unlicensed person who receives a real estate commission is:
   (a) $10,000
   (b) $1,000
   (c) $100
   (d) none of the above

105. Probate hearings are handled in:
    (a) Superior Court
    (b) Municipal Court
    (c) Small Claims Court
    (d) Inheritance Court

106. An out-of-state developer wishes to sell lots to Californians. All of the following apply, except:
    (a) a California Public Report is required
    (b) advertising will need to be approved by the California Real Estate Commissioner
    (c) the Subdivision Map Act will be enforced
    (d) all of the above apply

107. The once-in-a-lifetime exemption on the profits from the sale of a qualified principal residence for homeowners 55 years or older is:
    (a) $150,000
    (b) $125,000
    (c) $100,000
    (d) $75,000

108. Equity in real property is:
    (a) the cash-flow value
    (b) the total of all mortgages
    (c) the difference between mortgage balance and value
    (d) the appraised value

109. The maximum time urban real estate can be leased is:
    (a) 99 years
    (b) 51 years
    (c) 30 years
    (d) 15 years

110. Which of the following is not required to acquire title to unimproved land by adverse possession:
    (a) minimum of 5 years
    (b) open and notorious use
    (c) color of title or claim of right
    (d) that the acquiring party live on the property

111. Certain unities are required to maintain a joint tenancy relationship. They are:
    (a) grantee, unity, possession, claim
    (b) time, title, interest, unity
    (c) interest, time, title, possession
    (d) ownership, time, title, interest

112. The Health and Safety Code specifies minimum standards for water and sewer facilities in a new subdivision. Approval and control for local water and sewer rest with:
    (a) the Health Officer
    (b) the Real Estate Commissioner
    (c) the Building Inspector
    (d) the Planning Commissioner

113. Most real estate syndicates in California use which form of ownership:
   (a) corporation
   (b) limited partnership
   (c) real estate investment trust
   (d) joint venture

114. The words "procuring cause" would have the most important meaning under which circumstance:
   (a) a lawsuit by the buyer
   (b) a dispute between brokers over a commission
   (c) a disagreement between buyer and seller
   (d) a dispute over loan proceeds

115. Which of the following would violate the advertising provisions of the Truth-in-Lending Law? Ads that state:
   (a) no money down
   (b) $100,000 all-cash sale
   (c) $200,000 price, easy terms
   (d) qualification for FHA financing

116. In the event that a seller backs out of a valid purchase contract, all of the following are true, except:
   (a) the buyer could sue for damages
   (b) the buyer could sue for specific performance
   (c) the broker could sue for damages
   (d) the broker could sue for specific performance

117. A federal law regarding the sale of subdivided lots is:
   (a) the Subdivision Map Act
   (b) the Interstate Land Sales Full Disclosure Act
   (c) the Land Project Act
   (d) the Subdivided Lands Act

118. The instrument used to transfer title to personal property is:
   (a) the deed
   (b) the bill of lading
   (c) the lease
   (d) the bill of sale

119. An example of functional obsolescence is:
   (a) a one-car garage
   (b) a cracked foundation
   (c) a truck route in front of a home
   (d) a detrimental change in zoning

120. When the Real Estate Commissioner receives a valid complaint against a licensee, the Commissioner institutes action against the licensee under:
   (a) the Business and Professional Code
   (b) the Administrative Procedures Code
   (c) the Real Estate Code
   (d) the Rules and Regulations Code

121. When a business opportunity is sold, frequently a price is paid for continued patronage. This continued patronage is called:
    (a) goodwill
    (b) blue sky
    (c) turnover
    (d) future sales

122. A cloud on the title could be created by:
    (a) a recorded homestead
    (b) a deed of trust paid, but never reconveyed
    (c) an easement for utility poles
    (d) recorded covenants and conditions

123. A written agency betwen a real estate broker and a principal would not be:
    (a) executed
    (b) implied
    (c) expressed
    (d) a contract

124. The lowest interest rates and costs would probably be found with:
    (a) CAL-Vet loans
    (b) FHA loans
    (c) conventional loans
    (d) VA loans

125. The process by which land builds up due to the action of water is called:
    (a) erosion
    (b) avulsion
    (c) reliction
    (d) accretion

126. The most important factor in estimating the value of residential homes is:
    (a) square footage
    (b) demand by ready, willing, and able buyers
    (c) floor plan
    (d) rent

127. Which of the following is correct regarding net listings:
    (a) they are not allowed in California
    (b) the broker has the exclusive right to sell the property
    (c) the broker is required to disclosed the full commission prior to close of sale
    (d) the seller's net cannot exceed the difference between the sales price and the appraised value

128. Once an abstract of judgment is recorded it remains in force for:
    (a) 1 year
    (b) 3 years
    (c) 5 years
    (d) 10 years

129. The "secondary mortgage market" refers to:
    (a) the resale of existing loans
    (b) the granting of second loans
    (c) mortgage brokers who arrange loans
    (d) none of the above

130. Real estate loans that are pegged to some index and in which the interest rate may change during the term of the loan are called:
(a) conventional loans
(b) FHA loans
(c) ARM loans
(d) seller carry loans

131. The unauthorized use of the term "Realtor" is:
(a) a criminal offense
(b) a violation of California Real Estate Law
(c) not a problem if the person is a licensed broker
(d) not punishable in California

132. If a tenant is late on the rent, an owner should serve:
(a) a 30-day notice
(b) a 3-day notice
(c) an unlawful detainer warrant
(d) an eviction notice

133. Once a real estate broker's license has been revoked or suspended, his or her sales associates can:
(a) be paid commissions earned prior to the suspension
(b) collect rents as property managers
(c) continue to work on existing listings
(d) take new listings with a post date on the contract

134. A woman died and left an estate. Thirty-seven percent went to her husband, 18% went to each of the two sons and one daughter. The rest went to a college foundation. The college foundation received $37,000. The daughter's share was:
(a) $74,000
(b) $84,000
(c) $96,000
(d) $124,000

135. Adams sells Blackacre to Baker. Baker places the deed to Blackacre in his safety deposit box without recording same. Baker lets Adams retain possession of Blackacre. Some time later, Adams sells Blackacre to Collins. Collins records her deed and takes possession of Blackacre from Adams. When Baker gains knowledge of the transfer from Adams to Collins, he could do which of the following:
(a) record his prior deed and charge Collins rent
(b) take possession away from Collins and let Collins collect the money paid she paid to Adams
(c) sue Collins
(d) nothing regarding Collins if she had no prior knowledge of the transfer to Baker

136. Personal property attached to a building in such a way that it becomes part of the building is known as:
(a) an appurtenance
(b) a fixture
(c) an attachment
(d) a dedication

137. The situation by which property reverts to the state for lack of heirs is called:
    (a) escheat
    (b) eminent domain
    (c) condemnation
    (d) intestate succession

138. When work is done per the Street Improvement Act of 1911, property owners are allowed to pay their pro-rata share within how many day before it goes to bond:
    (a) 30
    (b) 60
    (c) 90
    (d) 180

139. The real property tax year runs:
    (a) January 1 to December 31
    (b) March 1 to February 28
    (c) July 1 to June 30
    (d) December 10 to December 9

140. Ingress and egress apply to:
    (a) fee simple
    (b) lease
    (c) encumbrance
    (d) less than freehold

141. In qualifying a buyer for a loan, the least important is:
    (a) regular income
    (b) spouse's income
    (c) monthly debts
    (d) overtime pay

142. Rates for title insurance are established by:
    (a) title insurance companies
    (b) the Department of Real Estate
    (c) the Department of Insurance
    (d) the Corporation Commissioner

143. A duly licensed real estate salesperson may lawfully receive a commission from:
    (a) the seller
    (b) the escrow holder
    (c) the broker
    (d) all of the above

144. A real estate broker would not be disciplined by the Real Estate Commissioner for:
    (a) making a secret profit
    (b) making a false promise
    (c) making a misrepresentation
    (d) acting as a dual agent with full knowledge and approval of all parties

145. "Time is of the essence" would most likely be found in which contract:
    (a) a deposit receipt
    (b) a listing agreement
    (c) an option
    (d) a lease

146. The important case of the U.S. Supreme Court that prohibits discrimination in housing is:
    (a) Wellenkamp vs. Wilson
    (b) Jones vs. Mayer
    (c) Unruh vs. Smith
    (d) Rumford vs. Brown

147. The maximum commission allowed on a $5,000 second trust deed loan due in 7 years is:
    (a) $250
    (b) $500
    (c) $750
    (d) $1,000

148. The maximum amount allowed from the Real Estate Recovery Fund for all parties in a single judgment case against a broker is:
    (a) $10,000
    (b) $25,000
    (c) $50,000
    (d) $100,000

149. A corporation is prohibited from holding title as:
    (a) joint tenants
    (b) tenancy in partnership
    (c) tenants in common
    (d) severalty

150. In a 1031 real estate exchange, taxable unlike property is called:

    (a) like for like
    (b) basis
    (c) foreign property
    (d) boot

Answers to Practice Examination

As you grade your practice examination, keep track of each question missed. A passing score is 105 questions correct (70%).

After you compute your score, go back and reread each question missed, then look up the explanation in the textbook. Wait a day or two, review the glossary in the textbook, and then take the examination again.

1. (b) Chapter 9
2. (c) Chapter 2
3. (c) Chapter 2
4. (a) Chapter 12
5. (b) Chapter 7
6. (b) Chapter 3
7. (c) Chapter 3
8. (a) Chapter 6
9. (a) Chapter 2
10. (c) Chapter 3
11. (c) Chapter 7
12. (a) $200,000/$4.75 = 42,105.26 sq. ft./300 ft. = 140.35 front ft., then $200,000/140.35 = $1,425
13. (a) Chapter 5 (fiduciary is result of agency, not needed to form an agency)
14. (b) $67,100 + 517 = (94% of total) $67,617/0.94 = $71,933
15. (b) Chapter 5
16. (d) Chapter 9
17. (b) Chapter 12 (Subdivision Map Act 2 or more units)
18. (d) Chapter 14
19. (c) $5,050/0.09 = 56,111/0.80 = $70,139 value
20. (c) Chapter 2
21. (b) Chapter 2
22. (a) Chapter 11
23. (c) Chapter 7
24. (c) Chapter 9
25. (b) Chapter 1
26. (b) Chapter 4
27. (c) Chapter 8
28. (b) Chapter 11
29. (d) Chapter 10
30. (c) Chapter 12

31. (b) Chapter 4
32. (d) Chapter 2
33. (c) Chapter 12
34. (b) Chapter 11
35. (b) Chapter 9 (15% rent increase will not cover 15% vacancy)
36. (b) Chapter 3
37. (b) Chapter 15
38. (c) Chapter 7
39. (d) Chapter 12
40. (a) Chapter 12
41. (d) Chapter 7
42. (c) Chapter 4 (by inference, not stated)
43. (b) Chapter 15
44. (c) Chapter 9
45. (c) Chapter 4
46. (a) Chapter 13
47. (c) Chapter 15
48. (a) Chapter 10
49. (b) Chapter 5
50. (a) Chapter 13
51. (b) Chapter 3
52. (a) Chapter 3
53. (b) Chapter 7
54. (c) $700 × 12 mo. = 8,400/0.11 = $76,364
55. (c) Chapter 12
56. (c) Chapter 11
57. (a) Chapter 11
58. (a) Chapter 3
59. (b) Chapter 15
60. (a) Chapter 7
61. (a) Chapter 2
62. (b) Chapter 2
63. (b) Chapter 3
64. (c) Chapter 2
65. (b) Chapter 11
66. (a) Chapter 7
67. (d) Chapter 5
68. (d) Chapter 5
69. (d) Chapter 12
70. (c) Chapter 9
71. (c) Chapter 5
72. (b) Chapter 9
73. (c) Chapter 15
74. (b) Chapter 3
75. (a) $70,400/1.20 = 58,667, then 70,400 less 58,667 = $11,733

76. (a) Chapter 5 (only contracts under Statute of Frauds need be in writing, not a general contract)
77. (d) Chapter 8
78. (d) Chapter 10
79. (c) Chapter 2
80. (a) Chapter 3
81. (b) Chapter 5
82. (b) Chapter 14
83. (a) Chapter 5
84. (a) $200 mo. × 12 mo. = $2,400/0.07 = $34,286
85. (d) Chapter 12
86. (b) Chapter 7
87. (c) Chapter 7
88. (b) Chapter 9
89. (a) Chapter 6
90. (d) Chapter 1
91. (b) Chapter 2
92. (d) Chapter 7
93. (b) Chapter 8
94. (c) Chapter 5
95. (d) Chapter 5
96. (b) $150/8 = 18.75 mo. × 12 mo. = $225 int. yr./$2,500 loan = 9%
97. (a) Chapter 10
98. (d) Chapter 2
99. (b) Chapter 2
100. (b) Chapter 4
101. (c) Chapter 4
102. (d) Chapter 3
103. (d) Chapter 15
104. (a) Chapter 15
105. (a) Chapter 2
106. (c) Chapter 12
107. (b) Chapter 13
108. (c) Glossary
109. (a) Chapter 11
110. (d) Chapter 2
111. (c) Chapter 2
112. (a) Chapter 12 (not stated in text, but by inference)
113. (b) Chapter 2
114. (b) Glossary
115. (a) Chapter 7
116. (d) Chapter 5
117. (b) Chapter 12
118. (d) Chapter 15
119. (a) Chapter 9

120. (b) Chapter 15
121. (a) Chapter 15
122. (b) Chapter 7
123. (b) Chapter 5
124. (a) Chapter 8
125. (d) Chapter 2
126. (b) Chapter 9
127. (c) Chapter 5
128. (d) Chapter 3
129. (a) Chapter 8
130. (c) Chapter 7
131. (b) Chapter 15
132. (b) Chapter 11
133. (a) Chapter 15 (not stated in text, but true)
134. (a) 18% × 3 = 54% children's share, then 54% + 37% = 91% husband and children combined, then 100% — 91% = 9% college share, then daughter has twice as much as college, $37,000 × 2 = $74,000
135. (d) Chapter 2
136. (b) Chapter 1
137. (a) Chapter 2
138. (a) Chapter 13
139. (c) Chapter 13
140. (c) Chapter 3
141. (d) Chapter 8 (not stated in text, but true)
142. (a) Chapter 10
143. (c) Chapter 4
144. (d) Chapter 4
145. (a) Chapter 5
146. (b) Chapter 12
147. (c) Chapter 7
148. (d) Chapter 4
149. (a) Chapter 2
150. (d) Chapter 13